MILES FROM NOWHERE

A ROUND-THE-WORLD BICYCLE ADVENTURE

BARBARA SAVAGE

THE
MOUNTAINEERS

THE MOUNTAINEERS: Organized 1906
"...to encourage a spirit of good fellowship
among all lovers of outdoor life.

First printing 1984, second printing 1985, third printing 1985, fourth printing
1986, fifth printing 1987, sixth printing 1988, seventh printing 1990, eighth
printing 1992, ninth printing 1995, tenth printing 1998

Published by The Mountaineers
1001 S.W. Klickitat Way, Suite 201, Seattle, WA 98134
First cloth edition: October 1983
First paper edition: December 1984

Published in New Zealand by Hutchinson Group (N.Z.) Ltd.
32-34 View Road, P.O. Box 40-086, Glenfield, Auckland, 10.

Book design by Elizabeth Watson
Cover design by Jennifer Shontz
Cover: Barbara Savage at the entrance to the
Valley of the Kings in Luxor, Egypt. Photo by Larry Savage.
Edited by Diane Hammond
Photographs by Barbara and Larry Savage
Map by Larry Savage

Manufactured in the United States of America

Library of Congress Cataloging in Publication Data
Savage, Barbara.
    Miles from nowhere.

    1. Bicycle touring.   I. Title.
GV1044.S28   1983   796.6   83-13484
ISBN 0-89886-084-9
ISBN 0-89886-109-8 Pbk.

To my husband, Larry

CONTENTS

BEWARE

◆ CHAPTER ONE ◆

NEW DELHI (AP)—*An American woman cyclist was eaten alive yesterday some 200 miles southeast of this Indian capital city by a giant, wild ape.*

News of my death would surely make the headlines in all the big newspapers back home in the U.S. of A. Larry, I hoped, would tell the story right, giving it a sensational and tragic ring, conjuring up a horrifying death race between an innocent woman bicycler and an ape with jaws large enough to inhale an entire human being. If he told it right, there I'd be, pedaling through the starving masses of a primitive country filled with cobras, tigers, and bands of cutthroat thieves, when suddenly a wild, semierect primate lunges from its treetop sanctuary and chases me down, killing me with the brutal force of its jaws and limbs.

As I watched the ape swing toward me, I prayed that Larry would tell a good story; that he would be kind enough not to tell the truth about the way I was to die.

In late November of 1979, there were three of us bicycling through India together. Larry and I had met Geoff Thorpe, a blond-haired, blue-eyed New Zealander in his early twenties, at the campground in New Delhi a few days after we arrived in India. Geoff too was headed toward Nepal, and we agreed to travel as a threesome. We were all a bit nervous

5

about bicycling through such a strange and exotic country.

The day we set out from New Delhi I suggested that we take back roads so that we could visit the small Indian villages and farms and avoid the heavy truck traffic on the highways. It took us five days to meander our way to the town of Mainpuri, one hundred eighty-three miles southeast of New Delhi, and everywhere during that time crowds gathered to stare at us. In Mainpuri we drew more crowds than anywhere else, probably because we were farther away from the main highways.

When we rolled into town, it became immediately evident that Mainpuri was not like the other Indian towns we had stayed in. Its streets were so narrow that only one car could pass through at a time; yet there were no cars—only people, bicycles, rickshaws, motorscooters, and a few sacred cows milling about. Tiny wooden kiosks large enough to seat one or two adults lined the alleys. The kiosks were shops that sold everything from food to textiles to jewelry. No one in the shops spoke English, and the people in the town stared at us more in disbelief than curiosity. Eventually, we scouted out the town doctor, who understood our language, and led us to the only boardinghouse in Mainpuri. I waited with Geoff in the dusty, manure-strewn street while Larry went upstairs with the doctor to get a room.

By then, after two weeks in this overflowing country of dark-skinned people with their contrasting ivory teeth and penetrating eyes that continually searched our faces for answers to their silent questions (Who were we? Why were we here? Where were we going? Where had we come from?), Geoff and I expected the crowds. But we did not expect what was to happen next.

Word of our arrival spread instantaneously, and mobs of Indians rushed toward us through the narrow alleyways, oblivious of any obstacles in their paths. Given our foreign appearance and our space-age fifteen-speed bicycles and equipment, we probably drew as much attention as would a flying saucer. Geoff and I, crushed and jostled by the force of the bodies around us, held onto our bikes and leaned our backs together in an effort to keep ourselves and bikes upright. The Indians on the outside of the crowd clawed and shoved their way forward in an effort to attain a ringside position, but those nearest us ran a tough defense, frantically protecting their prized positions. Some men attempted to climb up the side of the nearby kiosks for an aerial view, but the shopkeepers poked them with the long bamboo poles normally used for swatting at any sacred cows that tried to steal food from the shops.

Five minutes after the mob had begun to swell, a scream, pleading and helpless, slashed through the frenzy of the crowd like the cry of a drowning child over the pounding surf. Geoff and I glanced about nervously; because of the force of the bodies pressing against us from all sides, we were unable to move any part of our bodies except our heads. I swung my head around and spotted a rickshaw taxi that had been overturned and trampled by the walls of humanity pouring in from the side streets. The two riders, a man and a woman, were caught underneath, but the mob swarmed over the toppled carriage in total disregard of its buried and shrieking occupants. The man who had been pulling the rickshaw behind his bicycle had fallen free. He too ignored the trapped couple and abandoned his work to join in the madness.

While I surveyed the collage of staring faces jiggling around me and listened to the explosions of shouts and squeals echo through the passageways, I heard Geoff say something behind me.

"Ah, B-Barb," he stammered. "I've got to go."

Both of us were near suffocation and about ready to bolt over the top of our spectators, but Geoff was referring to something else.

"Barb, I can't hold it any longer," he whispered.

After picking up dysentery in Iran or Pakistan, Geoff was no longer very polished at controlling himself, and the picture that flashed in my mind of him losing control of his bowels right there in the midst of a few hundred unsuspecting Indian onlookers started me laughing hysterically.

The more I laughed the quieter the crowd became, and the men squeezed in even closer to get a better look at the strange phenomenon before them—a woman laughing. To set eyes on a foreign woman on a bicycle was probably in itself a once-in-a-lifetime experience for the men of Mainpuri, but to hear such a woman laugh seemed to fascinate them even more. It was as if the Indians hadn't really expected me to be human, to be capable of speech or laughter.

"OK, you two, we've got a room!" Larry hollered from one of the windows on the second floor of the boardinghouse. His words brought a quick halt to my giggling and Geoff's worries, and the two of us began fighting our way through the sea of human forms between us and the boardinghouse. We pushed aside scores of men dressed in long white tunics and baggy cotton pants who had taken root to the ground. It took a hard shove to break their trances.

Once I'd gotten myself and my bike into the boardinghouse and upstairs, I closed the shutters on the windows in our room to block out the roar of the crowds below. The floors, walls, and the five cots in our room were dirty—filthy by American standards. A rat scurried about the floor, periodically disappearing then reappearing through the gap between the floor and the bottom of the door. After one of its exits I stuffed the gap full of dirty socks. There was a functioning ceiling fan in the room, and we turned it on full force and collapsed on the cots. We wanted to take advantage of the fan, because within a few hours all electricity in the town would be transferred for the night to the countryside, to run the irrigation pumps on the farms. India was experiencing a severe drought this year.

After a few moments I asked Larry where the toilets were. He frowned, rolled his eyes, then pointed upstairs. Two floors up, on the roof, I found the only toilet in the boardinghouse—a bucket. At first I could not bring my feet to approach it, but after arguing with myself for a while I situated my body atop the open-air throne and stared over the surrounding rooftops. The bucket was half full and reeked.

When I first spied the animal, I wanted to believe that it was either stuffed or on a leash. I wanted to refuse to accept what I was seeing while I squatted over the pail, but my mind would not allow that. I was forced to acknowledge the terrible fact that only a few rooftops away from me and my bucket was a live, unfettered, four-foot-tall ape, which at that very moment was swinging over the alleys and leaping along cement roofs straight for me.

So this is how I'm to die, I thought to myself. Ever since the day Larry and I first came up with the idea of bicycling around the world, deep down inside I'd always known I wouldn't make it. The ape was so close now that I was sure it would grab me before I had time to get off the roof. All I could do was to hope that neither Larry nor Geoff would ever tell the truth of what was about to happen: that I was attacked and killed by an ape while I was relieving myself in a bucket on a rooftop in India.

I opened my mouth to scream but heard myself shout, "Downstairs! Get back downstairs!" My rational thought processes had finally kicked in, and by reflex reaction I was on my feet and outdistancing the ape, no doubt setting India's all-time record for the fifty-yard dash on the flat and down steps. I sprang into our room and slammed the door behind me.

"You know," I muttered to Larry and Geoff after I'd calmed my heartbeat, "this is turning out to be one hell of a first-time bicycle trip!"

⚬⚬⚬

Now had all this happened to me at the very beginning of our trip, I am positive I would have called it quits and headed for home that very evening. But by then, after eighteen months on the road, Larry and I had come to accept, and at times to thrive on, the bizarre and demanding situations of our journey. While I sat on my cot that evening in Mainpuri I thought about how, although the going was often mentally and physically draining, the longer Larry and I bicycled the more we craved challenges to our newfound stamina, strength, and self-reliance. As exhausted and shaken as I felt that evening in India, I was still very glad we had set out on our journey.

BEFORE IT'S TOO LATE

CHAPTER TWO

Bicycle around the world? Because it was such a spur-of-the-moment idea, and because we refused to dwell too long upon the dangers, it had a good chance for survival. It began in early 1977 while Larry and I were eating dinner in our tiny apartment in Santa Barbara.

"Ever notice how often people say, 'I wish I'd done something really exciting and challenging when I was younger, because now I'm too old and don't have much to look back on'?" Larry mumbled through a mouthful of potatoes.

I nodded my head.

"Well, pretty soon we're going to have enough money to make a down payment on a house. But once we do that we'll be tied down to the monthly payments. And then again, if we don't buy but instead spend our money on something else, like traveling, we might find ourselves priced out of the market by the time we return."

I nodded again and Larry went on.

"But on the other hand, we're both in good physical shape right now, and who knows what'll happen in the next ten years. One of us might get injured, and then we wouldn't be able to bicycle across America like you've been talking about lately. And as for seeing the rest of the world, the way things are going, who knows how much of it will still be around years from now."

A thoughtful silence followed. We both knew the conclusion to Larry's ramblings. It had been building up within us for months now. We were tired of our monotonous, dull security, and we were ready to plan our break.

After graduating from the University of California at Santa Barbara in 1973, getting married, working in Spain for a year, and traveling through Europe for a summer, Larry and I had returned to Santa Barbara to settle down, begin our careers, and save money for our own home. We quickly fell into the eight-to-five workweek: Larry as a mechanical engineer and I as a Spanish-English bilingual welfare worker. And soon that warm, secure sensation that accompanies a steady job, company benefits, and regular paychecks enveloped our souls. We bicycled to and from work each day. On weekends we played beach volleyball and backpacked; and every few months we traveled to San Diego to visit my parents or to San Jose to visit Larry's.

But by 1977 both of us had grown restless. I'd developed the traditional welfare worker burn-out syndrome, losing my ability to cope with or care about the mountains of paperwork, reams of ever-changing government regulations and forms, forms, and more forms, and a caseload of one hundred thirty demanding clients. Larry felt walled in, sitting at a desk every day designing and redesigning computers. Were we to spend the bulk of our lives toiling at unfulfilling jobs inside sterile office buildings? we wondered. Society kept answering yes, keep working, buy a house, start a family, save for retirement, and along the way be sure to pick up a color television, microwave oven, stereo, new car, and an electric knife sharpener.

But what about adventure and the outside world? I'd recently attended a slide presentation by a Santa Barbara couple who had pedaled across the United States. Before I'd seen the presentation, if someone had asked me how long it might take to pedal across the continent I would have figured years. But now I knew it could be done in three months or less and that hundreds of people were doing it each year.

I wanted to bicycle across the United States, then fly to Spain and bicycle. Larry was all for that, and more. He wanted to visit Egypt.

"Well, then why stop there?" I answered. "I've always wanted to go to Nepal and have a good look at the Himalayas. Maybe we could fly up there after our jaunt through the Nile Valley."

We were picking up momentum now. We both agreed that if we went all the way to Nepal, we might just as well continue on around to New Zealand. We had heard a lot of good things about New Zealand and had occasionally thought of moving there. And then there was Tahiti, the mystical lure of a South Sea island paradise. Travel around the world? Why not? If we were going to quit our jobs, give up our apartment, and pack away our worldly belongings, we might just as well take full advantage of our freedom and continue traveling after Spain. If we saved our money for one more year, through the rest of 1977 and into the first part of 1978, we could afford a two-year journey on the cheap.

"OK, so it's decided. We'll quit work in a year and travel around the world," I proclaimed at the end of our discussion. "And since we're going to start out bicycling, why don't we just keep right on pedaling and do the whole trip on bicycles. Now *that* ought to be a real adventure!"

I was shocked to hear such words spring from my vocal cords. What the hell was I saying? Me, a five-foot, four-inch, one-hundred-and-fifteen-pound human being, bicycle around the world for two years? I chuckled out loud as I swallowed the last of my meal. It was a thoroughly stupid idea.

Larry, however, was not laughing, and I looked up to see a pleasant, self-confident grin form on his lips. The smile sent a chill through my body. Oh my God! I thought, he's taken a liking to the idea.

"Sure we can do it!" Larry burst out. "If we can make it across the United States, then we can make it the rest of the way. It's a great idea! It has everything: challenge, adventure, accomplishment—you name it. Forget flying from place to place or sitting comfortably in some super-duper deluxe tour bus that stops at all the catchy tourist spots. We'll hit the world on bicycles and camp out everywhere. We'll struggle and sweat and meet the people and experience the world as it really is. And we'll learn to be self-sufficient and tough. It'll be an experience to treasure for the rest of our lives!"

Wrong, I muttered to myself, we'll die. Pure and simple death. The whole idea was too overwhelming—absurd, to be exact.

But Larry's enthusiasm began to grab hold of me. He honestly believed that we could make it, and the more he talked about it, the more I was caught up by his emotion. He cleared the dishes off the table and spread out our world atlas. We were like two small children sharing a new Christmas toy. Each of us tried to edge our way in closer for a better view. The United States, Canada, and Europe looked familiar enough, but as we headed east the questions started to pop. Could a woman bicycle in the Muslim countries? Would I have to wear layers of clothing and a veil while I pumped through the hot desert sands of the Middle East?

Larry worried most about India, about the starving masses. He wondered if crowds of begging Indians would follow us everywhere, and if so, how we would react. With his gargantuan appetite, he fretted about a possible food shortage. We had heard about the road from the Indian border into Kathmandu, Nepal, a two-hundred-mile stretch of unpaved switchbacks with no food or water available anywhere along the way. Impossible to cycle, I figured. But Larry was optimistic.

"We'll make arrangements with the bus drivers at the border and have 'em drop off food and water when they pass us each day. We'll figure out something. By the time we reach Nepal we ought to be pros at solving

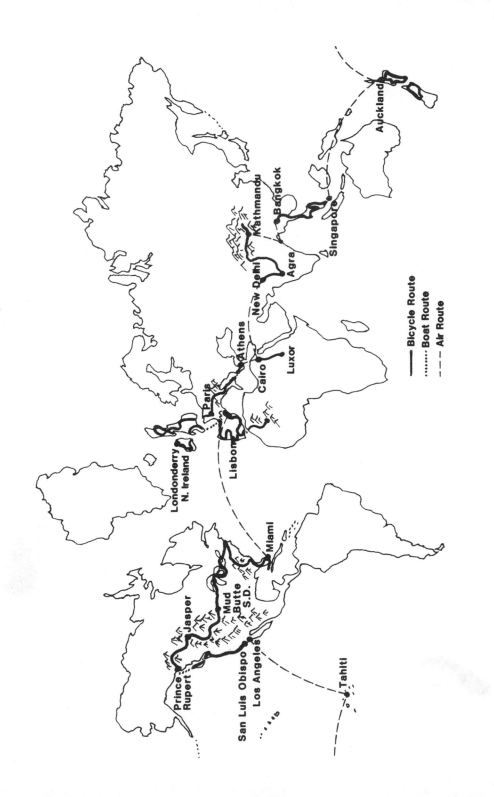

Prince Rupert

Jasper

Mud
Butte
S.D.

San Luis Obispo
Los Angeles

Tahiti

Miami

Londonderry
N. Ireland

Lisbon

Paris

Athens

Cairo

Luxor

New Dehli

Agra

Kathmandu

Bangkok

Singapore

Auckland

——— Bicycle Route
.... Boat Route
– – – Air Route

cycling problems," he reasoned.

I drew a blank when we came to Southeast Asia. We knew almost nothing about Thailand, Malaysia, and Indonesia. My notion was that they were primitive countries. What if we got there and found nothing but snake- and tiger-infested jungles? I wondered. I'd never been real keen on snakes.

There were heaps of unanswered questions to worry about, but Larry and I chose to ignore them. If we started thinking now about all the things that might go wrong, the trip would vanish beneath the weight of our hesitations. Instead, we talked about snorkeling over beds of coral in Tahiti, climbing through King Tut's tomb, and conquering the Rockies, the Alps, and the Himalaya. In the back of my mind I continued to believe that the trip would kill me, but it sounded like a great way to go.

Months after our momentous decision was made, I decided it might be prudent to give long-distance bicycling a try. After all, I'd never done it before. I based my enthusiasm for cycle touring on one slide presentation and Larry's not-too-reassuring claim that his one and only bicycle tour, a three-hundred-fifty-mile, four-day pedal between Eureka and San Jose, California, was "overall, one hell of a lot of fun, even though my body experienced excruciating pain those first two days." The farthest I'd ever bicycled in one day was twenty-five miles; yet Larry expected us to cover over three times that distance a day across the barren stretches in the United States. So one Saturday in the spring of 1977 I decided to jump on my bike and pump eighty miles just to see what it was like. Larry and I rode southeast from Santa Barbara over some mountains into Ojai, turned south to Ventura, then north back home along the coast.

The ride went smoothly until Larry got a flat tire halfway between Ojai and Ventura. His tire wouldn't seat properly unless it was pumped up to one hundred ten pounds, and our hand pump couldn't do the job. He bounced into Ventura. None of the gas stations in town had air pumps, but one attendant advised us to check the Harley-Davidson motorcycle dealership at the edge of town.

We took the attendant's advice and wheeled our bicycles into the back room of the dealership. There, we were confronted by seven men, each of whom had the distinct appearance of a genuine, membership-card-totin' Hell's Angel. Nude women, heavy chains, and MOM were tattooed on arms and chests. Who looked more concerned when Larry and I rolled in was anyone's guess: the seven men at the sight of us two pencilnecks with our featherweight wheels entering their den of chrome and steel hogs, or us at the sight of seven big mothers glaring us down. The expressions on the faces of these burly, beer-bellied motorcycle men as they watched us creep into their sacred domain were like those one might expect on the faces of the proud French circuit officials had a racer shown up at the starting line of the Tour de France with playing cards clipped to his spokes, an air horn, and colored streamers dangling from the ends of his handlebars.

Larry was the first to speak. I knew that nonchalant tone, meant to disguise his nervous embarrassment.

"Howdy. How's it going? Lotta nice-looking machinery here."

His words were met by silent, cold stares.

"Say, my wife and I couldn't find an air pump in town, so we were wondering if we could use yours to put some air in my tire so it'll seat better?"

Someone spit a wad of tobacco at the floor, and I began edging toward the door. But before I got there, the biggest fellow in the group broke the silence by indicating that we should follow him. Larry and I tiptoed our skinny bike frames past rows of mean machines to the center of the room.

"Here's the pump, man. Now you take it real slow and keep eyein' that gauge," the man growled. "Shit, that tire ain't gonna hold no more'n thirty pounds, so you pay lots attention 'cause I don't like no loud explosions, and that's what you'll likely be gettin' usin' this here big pump on that no good strip of rubber."

The rest of the men were laughing and shaking their heads. They knew that tire would blow apart, and most of them put their bets on thirty pounds or under. One fellow said thirty-five. Larry attached the pump to his tire, then pushed the valve, and the big man watched the gauge and called out the pounds.

"Fifteen—twenty—twenty-five—thirty—thirty-five." The broad, knowing smiles began to fade.

"Forty—forty-five—fifty."

Knitted brows indicated outright concern.

"Fifty-five—sixty—sixty-five—seventy."

The announcer jammed his fingers into his ears and squinted. A few of the men moved to the far end of the room.

"Seventy-five—eighty."

I looked up at the big man. His eyes were so wide now they took up a third of his face.

"Shit man, you're gonna blast me with them tire pieces!" he yelled as he ran for cover. Larry carried on the announcing himself, and there was a tinge of malicious delight in his voice.

"Ninety—ninety-five—one hundred—hundred-five—hundred-ten. There, that should do it."

Larry and I looked around the room. Beady eyes glazed in disbelief could be seen peering from behind fat chrome spokes. Larry disconnected the pump and yelled to no one in particular, "Thanks! That did the trick just fine. I'll put more air in when I get home. Don't want to take up any more of your time."

Not a single biker moved from his position of cover as we rolled out of the room. The bumper sticker on the front door read GOD RIDES A HARLEY.

Grinding out the thirty miles between Ventura and Santa Barbara against a brutal, coastal head wind proved to be the first truly religious experience of my life. The pain set in almost immediately. Within an hour, my knees, legs, feet, hands, and shoulder muscles were in piercing agony. Ten miles before Santa Barbara tears began to blur my vision. A creeping fog dropped the temperature, and I began shivering. My whole body hurt, and I felt delirious.

One-half mile from home, at the foot of the hill we lived on, I quit. It was not a quiet surrender. My wailing sobs brought the occupants of the nearby houses to their windows and front porches.

"Oh Lord, I'm gonna *die!*" I screamed. The worst thing imaginable had happened. When I finally admitted defeat, I consoled myself by thinking that my misery would ease once I got off my wretched, pain-inflicting bicycle. But instead of experiencing a rush of relief when I slid off my bike, things got worse. My muscles tightened up as they cooled down, and I soon found that I couldn't move. I stood in the middle of the road balancing myself against my bike, slightly bent at the waist and neck, drooling. I was gasping for air.

"Get me home! I'm dying! Oh help me! Help me! I am dy-ing n-o-w!" I wailed.

"Wait right here. I'll go home and get the van. I'll be right back to drive you and your bike home," said Larry.

"The bike? Forget the bike! I don't care if I ever lay eyes on this damned instrument of torture ever again. Just get ME home. Oh please, *help!*"

Fortunately, no one called the ambulance or those little men with white jackets and butterfly nets while I stooped in the street uttering a frenzied mixture of curses and pleas. Larry was back in an instant. I was too stiff to climb up into the van, so he picked me up and placed me on the front seat. The short but bumpy ride home about did me in. I kept shrieking, "Oh please don't let me die!"; but as comical as my fear of death seemed to him, Larry knew enough not to laugh.

I'll take a hot shower and everything will be all right, I thought as I shuffled into our apartment. We didn't have a bathtub, so it had to be a shower. But the force of the water felt like a sledgehammer smashing against my aching muscles.

"This can't be. Just can't be," I breathed. "It even hurts to shower!"

Shivering and streaked with ribbons of foul-smelling mud, I headed for the bedroom. Larry toweled me off as I hobbled across our apartment, then I moved onto the bed and curled up into a ball as if to guard myself against any further blows.

By then it was seven-thirty. We hadn't eaten a thing since noon, and there was no food in the refrigerator.

"Don't worry about a thing. I'll go get a pizza," Larry shouted as he raced out the door.

While he was gone, I prayed for a swift return to normal life. I hurt all over. How long would it be before I could sit and stand upright again? I wondered. Weeks? Months? Years?

The aroma of the pizza when it came through the door helped ease my worries. Larry had to feed me because I couldn't straighten out my arm to pick up the food; but even so, I never tasted anything so delicious in all my life.

By morning I felt fine. However, I now harbored some real doubts about those eighty-mile days. I had barely survived the previous day, and that was without the forty or fifty pounds of gear that would be strapped to my bike throughout the trip. I decided that I'd better start cycling for an hour or more each evening after work to get into shape. Larry, who worked in the outskirts of Santa Barbara, was already pedaling thirty miles each day to and from work. Yet both of us knew that the real training and conditioning would occur during the first few painful weeks at the start of our journey.

When 1977 drew to an end, we began to research equipment, study maps, and set up a vague itinerary. We wrote to the embassies of those countries we knew the least about, explaining our plans and requesting information. What we received back from the Thai and Malaysian embassies alleviated some of our fears: the pamphlets had pictures of modern roads and buildings. We still wondered about Nepal though. The Nepali embassy sent us nothing.

We spent months studying and comparing equipment before we started to buy what we needed. Larry picked out a lightweight backpacking tent high enough for me to stand up in and large enough to hold the two of us and all our gear except our bikes. The cookstove we bought ran on white gas but could also tolerate regular gasoline, preferably unleaded or premium, if we cleaned the jets regularly; and it fit inside a lightweight cookset, which consisted of two bowls and a lid that doubled as a fry pan.

Both of us already had our down jackets and sleeping bags, and we each bought a sleeping pad (which, because of its closed-cell construction, would not absorb water), and a waterproof nylon rain jacket. Next, we looked into panniers, the bike bags that would carry our minimum of clothing for all four seasons, the stove and cookset, fuel cannisters, food, spare water bottle, tools, spare parts, towel, toiletries, maps, candle lantern, books, and camera—the tent, sleeping bags, and sleeping pads would be strapped to our aluminum rear racks. We decided on the largest capacity Kirtland rear panniers and handlebar bags.

We also took a couple of weeks to outfit our touring bike frames— Larry had an American-made Eisentraut and mine was a French Follis—with Campagnolo and Suntour parts, Avocet touring saddles, Super Champion twenty-seven-inch clincher rims, heavy-gauge spokes, and fenders for the rain. Larry was designated the trip photographer, while I would keep a journal and send installments home to my parents for safekeeping.

As the last few months before our departure crept up on us there were passports to renew, money to be deposited in a bank account in our names and my parents' names (so they could wire us funds throughout the trip), travelers' checks to buy, and shots to flinch under. When we explained our plans to the nurse at the immunization center in Santa Barbara, she pulled out handfuls of tiny bottles of liquid for typhoid, typhus, tetanus, diphtheria, and smallpox shots. Since they only lasted a year, our cholera immunizations would come later in our journey.

By then, our friends and acquaintances had come to realize that we were, in fact, perfectly serious about our strange undertaking, and they all hurried to voice their reactions.

"There's no way I'd survive without a shower every night. I couldn't sleep with my smelly body all covered with dirt and sweat," said Mrs. Hazard, the owner of a local bike shop.

"Hey you can't do that!" said a good friend. "You'll never make it. There are too many unknowns. I mean, how do you know you won't be killed by restless natives somewhere? Besides, it's got to be physically impossible to bicycle that far."

"Great idea. Do it. I envy you your courage."

"You're both crazy."

"Now that sounds like a typical idea for a college-educated punk. Can't you two settle down, take on responsibilities, and spend your lives making an honest living? You should be starting a family and saving for your kids' education. You're just spoiled!" There was a disdainful tone in this man's voice. He worked at the same company as Larry, and to him Larry was an overpaid, know-nothing, cocky engineer about to throw away his easy money and waste two years of his life indulging in world travel. The man saw no adventure, no challenge, no conquest, no sweat, and no sense of accomplishment in what we were about to do—only stupidity. There was no way to explain to him our need to explore, to find out about the rest of the world, and to discover and develop ingenuity, endurance, and self-reliance—that pioneer spirit that had been buried under the comforts of modern society.

"Don't you hate it when your husband comes up with such unladylike things for you to do?" an elderly woman friend whispered to me when she found out about our plans. "Imagine bicycling around the world. It just ain't natural for a woman to want to do a thing like that."

The reaction we heard more than any other, however, especially after we started our journey and rode through the western United States, was, "I've always wanted to do something like what you're doing, to travel the world and see all those far-off places and peoples. But I never did. Just got caught up in the routine of work and buying things, I guess. And now it's too late. I really feel bad about that. So what you're doing is real important. Don't ever lose sight of that." During the rough times on the trip these words helped us to keep going.

When May of 1978 rolled around, and we decided that the fourteenth would be the day to leave, there remained one haunting doubt, which continued to shadow us both. It had nothing to do with pedaling twenty thousand miles, or being filthy, or being robbed or murdered or stricken by some exotic disease. Rather, we wondered what effect our constant togetherness would have on our marriage (which during the past three years had been shaky at times, as Larry and I were both very independent). After all, being with one's spouse for two years, day in and day out, oftentimes under physically and mentally trying situations, might sound like the perfect path to murder or divorce.

As it turned out, there were moments throughout the two years we were bicycling around the world when we nearly molded our bike frames around each other's necks. The most horrendous statements we ever made and most probably ever will make about one another were ragingly proclaimed—and accompanied by some choice threats of desertion and eternal damnation—along the blacktop, and dirt and cobblestone roads of our journey. But partway through our adventure, in a ditch in Spain, after one of those screaming matches that so often flared when physical and emotional exhaustion or a gnawing homesickness got the better of us, we discovered that our constant companionship had changed our feelings toward each other in a way we hadn't expected.

ACHING MUSCLES

◆ CHAPTER THREE ◆

Neither Larry nor I slept much the night before we set out on our journey. We were too nervous. Our stomachs were bundles of twitching, raw, nerve endings, and both of us had a royal case of the runs. My hands and feet were damp with sweat. No matter how hard or how often I swallowed, I couldn't dislodge the huge lump in my throat.

Lying on our living room floor in my sleeping bag, I stared at the darkness. Our apartment was completely bare except for our bikes and the two piles of gear that would accompany and sustain us through the next two years of our lives. The emptiness made me feel uneasy and insecure. My mind whispered, no jobs, no earnings, no home, over and over. In the morning we would leave behind everything that was familiar to us and step off an invisible ledge into a way of life we knew almost nothing about. Now that the day we had so anxiously planned and waited for for over a year was almost here, I was frightened. I wondered if maybe we shouldn't leave after all.

The next morning at six o'clock, on May 14, 1978, Larry and I dragged ourselves out of bed and began packing our panniers. We didn't say much to each other while we packed. We were too jittery to carry on a decent conversation. As is the case with most inexperienced bicyclers, both of us had too much gear, and we could barely cram everything into our packs. It wouldn't be long though before we'd begin tossing out or mailing home a good portion of our clothing to reduce the weight and bulk of our panniers. After two months on the road, we would each have scaled ourselves down to a couple of pairs of shorts, a few T-shirts, one pair of long pants, a sweat shirt, rain jacket, down jacket, some socks and underwear.

Once our panniers were packed and attached to our bikes along with our sleeping bags, mats, and tent, we pedaled—wobbled is a more appropriate description—into town to catch the train to San Luis Obispo, a city one hundred miles north of Santa Barbara, where our journey would officially begin. A young friend of ours, John Warren, had convinced us that San Luis would be a good place to start out from.

"I want to ride with you your first day out," he had told us at the beginning of the month. "And I've always wanted to take that ride from San Luis out to the coast and north a ways; so let's combine the two. Besides, we've all done a lot of cycling around Santa Barbara already. Let's start out from someplace new."

The short ride from our apartment to the station was our first attempt ever at riding our bikes with the full weight of our gear. A few days earlier Larry and I had strapped part of our gear onto our bikes and ridden to Carpinteria and back, twenty miles round trip, as a trial run. "No sweat!" Larry had quipped along the way. "Carp today, tomorrow the world!" But now that his bike weighed ninety pounds and mine seventy we discovered it took all our concentration and strength just to keep ourselves wobbling along in a somewhat forward direction. As we struggled to inch our way toward the station, the awful thought occurred to me that at the rate we were moving we could easily spend the entire next two years pedaling to the Oregon border.

A group of our friends was waiting at the station to see us off. Cary Holst, a friend who would later join us in Scotland, broke out a bottle of champagne after we rolled up, and everyone laughed and joked and snapped pictures. And then it was time to leave, and I was immediately homesick. I could barely see through my tears while my friends hugged and kissed me good-bye. I started to step up into the train, but then I stepped back and grabbed a friend's hand.

"I'm scared, Ann," I blurted. "I feel so alone, so unsure and without any—I don't know exactly how to describe it—without any supports or foundations I guess. After the ride here, bicycling twenty thousand miles sounds impossible. I don't think I can go through with this."

I began backing away from the train. But Ann smiled and gently pushed me forward.

"You'll do it," she said. "Just remember that you can do anything you really set your mind to, anything. You'll do it all right. I know you will."

I squeezed Ann's arm and climbed up the steps.

As the train made its way north, Larry and I sat together holding onto each other's hands and staring blankly out the window. We were too choked up to speak, so John busied himself talking with the other passengers.

There were twelve miles of low rolling hills between San Luis Obispo and the campground at Morro Bay. In that short distance I learned that the difference between the maneuverability of my bike with and without fifty pounds of gear closely resembled the difference in the handling of a Mack truck and a Porsche. The first time I turned my handlebars to miss a rock in the road my bike continued to move straight ahead, and my front tire collided with the stone. The impact nearly jarred my teeth loose.

All right, I muttered to myself after I regained my balance, next time you'll try a sharper turn. And the next time I spotted a rock in front of me I gave my handlebars a hard shove. Unfortunately that sent my bike sliding sideways and me bouncing across the pavement. But after a bit more experimentation I found that if I leaned my whole body in the direction I wanted my bike to go and turned the handlebars farther than I would without the extra weight, but not too far, I wobbled less and missed most of the rocks and sticks on the road.

When we reached the campground at Morro Bay, an hour and a half after we left San Luis, the rangers at the gate met us with some good news. Under the California Bike and Hike program, anyone who arrived at a state campground on foot or on a bike paid only fifty cents to camp, instead of the regular four-dollar fee. The rangers assigned us a huge secluded campsite full of pine trees.

John was ecstatic. "This is perfect!" he exclaimed after we set up camp. "Pine trees and fresh air everywhere, and we've still got time before it's dark to bike around the bay and pick up some fish for dinner. Yeah, this is the life! You guys are gonna have a great time these next two years."

Maybe, I thought. But I was still too nervous to relax and enjoy our surroundings. And when I crawled into our tent after dinner I couldn't sleep. The ground felt hard, and my thin sleeping mat hardly provided any padding. I kept thinking about the next day. It would be our first full day of bicycling, and Larry and I planned to pedal all the way to the Plaskett Creek campground, over sixty miles north of Morro Bay along the coast. During the final twenty of those sixty miles, we'd be tackling the treacherous grades of the southern Big Sur coastline. Sixty miles over lots of mountains—what a way to start out.

The three of us got up early the next morning and scrambled some eggs and brewed a pot of tea for breakfast. By eight o'clock, we were on the road heading north along Highway 1. A few miles from the campground, the bottom of my handlebar bag started to scrape against the top of my front tire—our cookstove and cookset were too heavy for the bag's supporting bracket. I stopped and reorganized my gear, shifting the stove and cookset to one of my rear panniers and repacking my front bag with lightweight clothing. In the next month I would make at least a dozen more such reorganizations before I'd learn how to balance the weight of my gear and how to position it for quick access to the items I used most often.

The morning of May 15 was clear, crisp, and sunny, perfect for bicycling, and John rode along with Larry and me for over an hour before he headed back to San Luis to catch the train home.

Larry and I stood at the edge of the road and watched John move back down along the coast, back to his home, family, and friends. After he disappeared around the last bend in the road we closed our arms around each other and held on tight.

"It's just you and me now," Larry whispered. "This is it."

At long last, we were alone together starting out on our adventure. Almost immediately our homesickness and apprehension dissolved, and an anxious excitement bloomed in their place. The sun beat down out of the heavens; the Pacific sparkled; the air smelled fresh and clean; the surf crashed, birds sang, cows mooed, and the garden snakes, lizards, and squirrels scampered beside us alongside the road. No phones rang; no typewriters tapped; no clients screamed. For the next two years, there would be no rent or utility payments to make at the first of each month, no more forms and government regulations, no more eight-to-five behind a desk in a room filled with stagnant cigarette smoke. Trees, streams, and wildlife surrounded us now, and we were free to wander wherever we pleased. The freedom felt great, and Larry started to sing.

The two of us sang all the way to San Simeon, some thirty miles north of Morro Bay, where we stopped to eat lunch—and then all hell broke loose. San Simeon at lunchtime turned out to be where and when the merciless coastal headwinds began, and after we finished our meal we cycled straight into them for thirteen miles over a relatively flat terrain. Larry pedaled in front to block the wind. I stayed behind him, my head down, my eyes glued to his rear fender. We crept along in our lowest gear.

It took us two hours to conquer those thirteen miles. While we struggled against the wind, the sun fried its way through our sunscreen and sizzled our faces and lips. Every twenty minutes, when my knees, feet, seat, neck, shoulders, and back screamed for me to stop, I would pull off the road and lie flat on my back on the dirt shoulder. I'd dip my bandana headband into my water bottle and spread it over my scorched face, then for five or ten minutes try to block out the pain that was needling my muscles before I gathered myself up again and pounded my pedals for another twenty minutes. At the end of two hours we were at the cliffs.

When I first spotted them up ahead—the string of mountains that plunged into the ocean—I wondered how, when we were barely negotiating flat ground, we'd ever be able to climb them in the wind. I found out soon enough.

The mountain ridges ran east to west creating inlets or bays between each other. As we approached the first mountain, the road curved inland around a deep, wide bay, then climbed up the side of the mountain while heading back out toward the ocean and the end of the ridge. The mountain protected us from the northerly wind while we pumped up the steep grade, and we found that the climbing was actually easier than pedaling on flat ground against the head winds. It felt wonderful to escape the howling wind; wonderful all the way up to where the mountain dropped off into the ocean and the road curved around the ridge's sheer, rocky face as it turned back into the next bay. Logic told us that when we rounded the curve and were no longer shielded by the mountain, the gales would be there to greet us.

Just before we hit the curve I went into a crouch and took an iron grip on my handlebars. The wind struck me the moment I swung far enough around the side of the mountain to glimpse the endless series of ridges and bays that stretched along the coast ahead of us. And when it struck me, it swept me and my bike into the air and heaved us off the road and into the face of the cliff. The right side of my sunburnt body bounced across the gravel and rocks, and the gales pelted my face with sand and dirt; then all seventy pounds of my bike and gear came crashing down on top of my legs.

Fighting the explosions of air currents, I struggled to my feet, dragged my bike upright, and climbed back on. This time the wind blasted me into the opposite lane. I yanked my handlebars back to the right, but the bike's tires continued to skitter toward the dirt shoulder on the left-hand side of the road and its menacing, vertical two-hundred-foot drop to the rocks and crashing surf below. Just before I ran out of pavement I jumped off the bike and toppled onto the asphalt. This time my bike landed on my hips.

Almost as soon as I hit the pavement I heard a car approaching. It was barreling up the grade from the next bay, and it sounded awfully close. Larry had managed to stay upright in the turn because he and his bike weighed more than I and my bike. He heard the car too. He ran to the middle of the road and motioned for it to stop.

"Get up!" he screamed. "I don't know if this guy sees me!"

I was still crawling out from under my bike when the car's brakes started to squeal. The driver slammed to a stop fifteen feet away from me, and I quickly pulled myself and my bike across the road and up against the cliff.

I wrestled my bike around the rest of the curve and partway down the incline before I climbed back on and tried to pedal again. It was all downhill to the back of the next bay, but even so, I had to pump hard to keep moving forward in the wind. Not until I reached the back of the bay was I free of the gales.

For four hours we battled the twenty miles of coastal mountains to the Plaskett Creek campground; grinding up the grades, dragging our bikes through the curves, and struggling downhill against the wind. Every half hour I had to stop, pour water over my face and lips and into my parched throat, and lie on my back to rest my aching muscles.

After our first two hours in the mountains I was physically ex-hausted, and there were very few places on my body that didn't hurt. My left shoulder muscle felt as if someone had thrust a butcher knife into it and was slowly turning the blade back and forth. My throbbing rear end refused to go numb. I was tired from not having slept much the last couple of nights, and I felt as if I'd burned up every last calorie of the lunch I'd eaten four hours earlier. The thought of two more hours of wind and mountain ridges was almost overwhelming, and to keep myself pedaling I tried pep talks. "Come on kid. You can do it. Come on now. Toughen up. It's not much farther. Just keep pedaling. Just get to Gorda."

Gorda was the dot on our map where we planned to buy our sup-plies for dinner and breakfast and gorge ourselves on enough food and drink to propel us through the last five miles to the campground. It was over an hour from the time I began my pep talks to the time we got to Gorda. The last few miles were touch and go; Larry kept telling me that Gorda was "just around the next turn," and I managed to push my pedals through turn after turn and climb back onto my bike each time the wind tossed me off it.

At six o'clock we crept into Gorda. The grocery store had closed at five-thirty. I wanted to cry, but I was too tired. Instead, I pushed my bike back out to the road and prepared to expand my upper limits for pain, hunger, and exhaustion. As we pedaled out of Gorda I hunched my shoulders against the wind and fell into a near delirious chant: "Come on Barb. Come on Barb. Come on Barb." About a mile north of Gorda the pavement suddenly gave way to a loose dirt path sprinkled with rocks. As soon as we hit the dirt, the cars that sped past blinded us with suffocating sprays of dust and gravel, and I quit chanting.

"I hate this!" I hollered. "My shoulder is ripping apart, my muscles ache, my face is scorched, my lips are blistered. I'm dead tired, and I'm shakey 'cause I haven't eaten in over six hours! I'm all scraped up 'cause these tornado winds keep chucking me off my bike, and now there's no road! And don't you dare tell me the campground's 'just around the cor-ner,' cause I know damn well it's not!"

Larry couldn't see me through the cloud of dirt that engulfed us, but he could hear my every word. He knew that I'd hit my limit and that there wasn't a thing he could say to help me. He kept quiet and prayed that I would keep pedaling. I did, and after a mile or so of the dirt and rocks the pavement reappeared.

It was seven o'clock when we reached the campground. We had been on the road for eleven hours, creeping along in our lowest gears in the blazing sun. I coasted to a stop next to the picnic table in the first empty campsite we came to and eased myself off my bike and across the top of the table. Larry set to work pitching our tent while I lay on the table staring blankly up at the sky, marveling that every ounce of my body was in pain. And I wondered why, after the last time I'd experienced such excruciating pain, the day we had pedaled from Santa Barbara to Ojai and back, I hadn't learned my lesson and abandoned bicycle touring altogether.

Once the tent was up I made my way across the grass. My legs continued to move as though they were still pushing pedals, and my torso refused to straighten up out of its hunched-over position. I "pedaled" on into the tent, curled up on top of my sleeping bag, and promptly passed out. If Larry hadn't started ranting hysterically about an hour later I would probably have slept straight through the night. He'd pedaled up the road a mile to the grocery store in Pacific Grove, a two-building town, and had just returned with a can of beef stew and a packet of won ton soup only to find that our stove wouldn't start up because it was missing a gasket. It seemed the gasket had fallen out unnoticed when he'd cleaned the stove after breakfast in Morro Bay.

"What's the matter?" I asked as I climbed out of the tent. The nap had helped. My left shoulder still felt like it had a butcher knife in it, but I wasn't feeling as drained as before. Larry explained about the stove, and I shrugged my right shoulder.

"Don't you understand what this means?" he pleaded.

To me it meant we didn't have to bother with cooking and washing dishes and we could go to bed earlier. I had passed the point of being hungry even before we got to the campground.

"It means I'm going to die of hunger right here and now before your very eyes!" he shouted. "It's been eight hours since I've eaten anything! I'm beat and I'm starved. I've got to eat something right this minute or I'll die!"

I wanted to tell Larry that he only *thought* he was going to expire; that nobody who weighs one hundred sixty pounds and is in top physical shape has ever starved to death overnight simply by skipping dinner, but I decided that wouldn't be a good thing to say at the moment. By the look in his eyes and the tone of his voice I knew he was no longer capable of rational thought; exhaustion and hunger had finally taken their toll. Larry could endure a lot more physical pain than I, but when it came to hunger—well, that was another story. I tried to calm him.

"Look, I'll go borrow a stove from someone," I said. "It'll only take a minute."

I spied a camp stove with two burners sitting on the picnic table in a neighboring campsite, and its owners were glad to lend it to me. When I carried it back to our site, Larry was sitting on one of the picnic benches rocking back and forth, whimpering softly to himself. I lit both burners and heated up the soup and the stew. The moment Larry started shoveling the hot food into his mouth, the look of hysteria began to fade from his eyes. By the end of the meal, it had disappeared altogether.

After we washed up our bowls and returned the stove, we climbed into the tent. We rolled around on our mats for a while trying to find a spot on our bodies that wasn't quite as sore as the others.

"You know," Larry mumbled just before he started snoring. "It's been one helluva day. We've sure gotten off to a thundering start."

The first rays of sunlight that filtered down through the pines and into our tent coaxed us awake early the next morning. We lay in each other's arms and watched the blue jays and squirrels and listened to the breeze dance through the pine needles. The chilly morning air felt good against our sunburned faces. Our bodies still ached, but we felt rested, and that brightened our spirits. Just as we were about to fall back to sleep someone's voice snaked in through the tent walls.

"You two asleep in thar?" a man asked in a southern drawl. It was Mr. Marston, the fiftyish fellow from Houston we'd met the night before when we hobbled into the campground. He and his wife had parked their truck camper in the site below ours.

"No, we're awake," Larry answered. "What's up?"

"Breakfast. All the eggs, sausage, toast with blackberry jam, and coffee you kin force down inta those stomachs o' yers. It'll be ready pretty quick now, so ya'll come on down as soon as yer up."

The mention of food literally shot us out the door of the tent. Larry and I sat ourselves down at the Marstons' picnic table, and Mrs. Marston dropped a huge plate heaped high with hot food in front of each of us. Nothing could have tasted better. As soon as we finished what was on our plates, Mrs. Marston piled on more. By the time we had polished off three platefuls neither of us could move, and we felt supremely indebted to our two new friends.

The four of us talked for three hours—mostly about the state and national parks the Marstons recommended that we visit while we pedaled through America—before Larry and I walked back to our campsite to pack up and start pedaling again. The head winds had died down, but we were too sore to go very far today; we decided to cycle only as far as Limekilm campground, seven miles up the road.

As we started to take down our tent one of the other campers, Pete Olsen, a middle-aged fireman from Los Angeles, came over to see what we were all about. Pete stood next to the picnic table and surveyed the mountain of clothing and gear stacked on top of it. Since we had packed everything wrong the day we left Santa Barbara, putting things we wouldn't be using very often on top of the things we would, we had had to pull everything out of our panniers to get at what we needed the night before and that morning.

"Bet you two can't get all that stuff back into your packs now that you've yanked it all out," Pete said as he eyed our books, camera, clothes, sack of toiletries, towels, tools, spare parts, cookset, silverware, candle lantern, and the two bottles of champagne our friends had given us at the station in Santa Barbara. "You must be new at this. Where you off to?"

"Around the world," I answered sheepishly, trying to stand up straight without wincing in pain. "Yesterday was our first day."

Pete didn't say anything, but I could almost hear his mind at work: You mean you two pitifully disorganized kids, who could just barely limp into the campground last night—one of you collapses inside your tent while the other one screams at your stove which you never did get to work—and who today, after only one day on the road, are too sore to pedal more than seven miles, are going to stand there and tell me you're gonna bicycle around the world? Around the world with a busted cookstove and two bottles of champagne. Well, good luck to you both. You'll need it and a lot more!

Pete took another good look at everything on the table, then shook his head and walked away.

At the store in Pacific Grove Larry and I picked up a gasket for our cookstove and supplies for lunch and dinner before we pedaled on to Limekilm. We pitched our tent among the ferns and pines and spent the day walking the beach and hiking in the hills and along the stream that flowed past our campsite. There were showers at Limekilm, and at the end of the day we soothed our aching muscles in the hot water and washed away the layers of dirt and sweat that the previous day's ride had encased us in. For dinner we cooked macaroni and cheese from a box and broke out the champagne. We were sound asleep by eight o'clock.

It took us three days to pedal the one hundred thirty-five miles from Limekilm to Larry's parents' house in San Jose. Each morning I started out slow—sore and stiff from the day before—and by midafternoon, after we had pedaled about thirty miles, I would slow down even more, almost to a crawl, as the brigade of sharp pains marched through more of my muscles and the butcher knife sliced deeper into my left shoulder.

Every afternoon I was drained of all my energy. Every incline looked like Mount Everest, and I kept checking my tires to see if they were flat, thinking maybe that was why I was going so slow. Even when I pedaled downhill, I had to struggle. The last ten miles of each day were sheer agony for me, and every night I felt thoroughly discouraged. I would pull out my map while we ate dinner, study the tiny stretch of mileage we had covered that day, then compare it to our projected route across North America and wonder how we would ever make it the six thousand miles we expected to pedal on our way to the East Coast.

"Now don't get totally disillusioned right off. It takes a while, but you'll get in shape," Larry would say to me at night. "It's just that you're not accustomed to bicycling over about fifteen miles a day, and all that extra weight makes it even tougher. Give yourself a break. You've only been at this for a few days now. It'll probably take you a month or so before you're in good enough shape to whiz through a forty- or fifty-mile day or crank out an eighty-miler. And besides, I don't think you're eating enough. You're burning up a lot of calories and you're building up muscles, so you need to eat a lot more than you normally do. I think some of your exhaustion probably has to do with you just plain running out of fuel."

When we got to San Jose I weighed one hundred seven pounds, eight pounds below my normal weight and three pounds less than what I had weighed on May 14. I felt weak, and for the first few days that we stayed with Larry's parents I spent most of my time eating and sleeping. But by the end of a week I was revitalized and even anxious to start out again.

On May 28, Larry and I left San Jose and continued north on Highway 1. Larry's parents were apprehensive about what our journey might have in store for us, but they were excited for us too.

"Do it now while you can," Larry's father whispered to us the day we left. "But be sure to be careful and take care of each other. And call us as often as you can while you're still in the States."

❦

It was a strenuous ride up the coast through Sonoma and Mendocino counties. For five days the road bounced up and down the steep coastal mountains. But the coastline and the countryside were beautiful, and I soon found myself paying less attention to my aches and pains and more attention to my surroundings. We wound our way around the countless deserted coves and bays of the Pacific. The shiny turquoise waters were dotted with rocky outcroppings where the seagulls made their homes. Sometimes the road turned inland for part of a day, and then we sailed over rolling hills and grassy farmland. The coast was sparsely populated, and we pedaled to the sounds of the wind and the waves and the sea birds. The people in the few settlements along the highway were proud of their scenic, isolated land and determined to keep it that way.

"Yep," smiled the owner of the single-room general store in Elk, a don't-blink-or-you'll-miss-it burp on the map just south of the town of Mendocino, "us folks like it just fine the way it is up here—lots of rugged, unspoiled coastline, open spaces, and not many people. Down south it's too crowded and filthy and noisy. There's nothing but cement and asphalt and people down there. Yep, I had my choice some years back. I could either buy a store in Los Angeles and live in that endless asphalt jungle and worry all the time about gettin' robbed or mugged and spend my time driving on freeways getting to and from work every day, or I could buy this place here. So I came on up here to take a look at the place, and I never left.

"Now, I just sit here and look out over the Pacific and breathe in the fresh salt air and laugh out loud every time someone from L.A. comes in here and asks me how the blazes I can stand living in the middle of nowhere. Just as soon as they ask me that I always ask 'em how the smog's been in L.A. And when they start to get all defensive, I just smile and say, 'Well, I gotta admit, we got our smog problem up here in Elk too. Why, just the other day a tourist came through and lit up a cigarette, and the health officials declared a first-stage smog alert!'"

When we set out from San Jose I decided to give Larry's suggestion that I eat more and more often a try. Instead of eating only one meal between breakfast and dinner, as I had between Morro Bay and San Jose, I started eating three. We began each day with a huge breakfast—we'd wolf down six scrambled eggs with cheese, half a loaf of bread, two bowls of granola, and three or four cups of hot tea. We'd pedal on that for a couple of hours, then around ten o'clock we would pick up a morning snack—donuts covered with chocolate, caramel, or powdered sugar; or a pound cake washed down with a quart of chocolate milk. Each noon we built ourselves a couple of cheese, tomato, and salami sandwiches to go with our fruit and cookies. That would hold us until three or four o'clock when we went for the chocolate candy bars and soft drinks. If we were pedaling through a big town, we always hit the local A&W for a rootbeer float or a frostie. For dinner we dumped a can of beef stew, chop suey, or enchiladas, or a package of macaroni and cheese, into one of our bowls and a can of corn or green beans into the other and called it dinner. Our canned-food dinners were anything but nutritious, but they were quick and easy to fix. We survived on them and our junk-food snacks for the first two and half months of our trip, before we gradually began our transition to a healthier diet.

Just as Larry had suspected, eating something every two hours made a huge difference in the way I felt. It kept me from becoming completely exhausted, and that buoyed my spirits enormously. Each day as we made our way up the coast I could feel my muscles strengthening and my endurance edging higher. The butcher knife disappeared from my shoulder, and my seat became more accustomed to the brutal treatment it received all day long. By the time we pedaled into Leggett, where we turned onto Highway 101 at the start of the redwoods, I could pedal fifty miles a day without collapsing in agony afterwards.

When we entered the redwoods we penetrated the sacred domain of the legendary logging trucks of northern California. We had heard a lot of stories about the logging trucks; it seemed that every year or so one ran over a bicycler touring the redwoods. The whole way up the coast I had tried to prepare myself mentally for the day the loggers would join us on the roads, but the first time I heard that deafening, unmistakable roar closing in behind me and turned around to see the road swallowed up by an eight-ton, sixty-foot-long logging truck dwarfed by its sky-high wall of tree trunks, I nearly croaked. I swung my head back around and edged over as close to the shoulder of the road as I could without falling into the dirt. Then I clenched my teeth and stared straight ahead, trying hard to block out the explosion of noise. I prayed to God Almighty to spare me just this once, promising that if He did I would never again bicycle on a road with a logging truck.

The trucks took some getting used to all right, and although I never managed to keep my heartbeat under control when I heard one blasting toward us from the rear, after a day or two I did learn to accept them. The drivers were always careful to pull way around when they passed us, and for that I was supremely grateful.

The day after our first encounter with a logging truck, we met our first fellow bicycler. Eric pedaled up alongside us as we were coasting down a long hill between Leggett and Garberville. His bike was making a loud flapping noise. It sounded as if he had a piece of cardboard in his spokes.

"Hi there!" he shouted.

I looked over to see what was causing the flapping noise. It was his underwear.

"Hi! Where ya from?" Larry asked.

"San Diego. I'm pedaling up to Portland to visit some relatives."

Eric looked like a typical, handsome, southern California surfer. He had a good tan, sunbleached blond hair, and a muscular build. I guessed him to be about nineteen.

"Where you two off to?" he asked.

"Oh, right now we're on our way up to Canada," answered Larry.

"You sure gotta lot of stuff there. Me, I'm travelin' light. Gotta few tools, a pair of shorts, a T-shirt and a sweater, a bowl and a knife, a fork and a spoon, and a tube tent and a sleeping bag."

He also had a pair of underwear tied to and hanging from his handlebars and when he saw me eyeing them, he flashed me a wide smile.

"Oh yeah, and this pair o' real holey underwear. I washed 'em out last night, but they were still wet when I got up this morning so I tied 'em onto my handlebars to let 'em blow dry. That works OK, tying 'em to the handlebars like this, except that they keep snappin' against my wrist when I go downhill fast, and that makes my wrists sting. Hurts like you wouldn't believe when they really get to snappin'."

"Why don't you tie them to your rear panniers instead," Larry suggested. "That way they won't bother your wrists."

Eric shook his head. "I'd be afraid they'd blow off back there and I wouldn't see 'em go. And then where'd I be? I mean, I gotta be real careful with what little clothes and gear I got."

Eric was headed for the Avenue of the Giants, north of Garberville, as were Larry and I, so the three of us rode together. Not more than an hour after we met up, we ran into the Copenhagen Kid. His real name was John Winwood. He was cycling south, and the minute he spotted the three of us coming up the road he slammed on his brakes and shouted for us to stop and talk with him.

John was a strange sight. His tanned skin had worn out long ago, his face spoke of more than its share of fist fights, and an ancient, misshapen, leather cowboy hat, stained by years of sweat and dirt, topped his five-foot, seven-inch frame. He wore a faded flannel shirt, tattered blue jeans, and crusty combat boots. As soon as we were within earshot, John began telling us all about himself.

"Howdy folks! Name's John Winwood, and I'm forty-seven, and I ain't got a real tooth in ma mouth. These here are all false. I'm a registered crazy. Was in a mental institution fer over twenty years o' ma life. I'm one real mean SOB, an' I beat the livin' daylights outta people I don't like. But don't you worry none. I like you three just fine. I like bicyclers. They're ma friends."

John was riding a Schwinn one-speed modified into a ten-speed. There were even toe clips on the pedals.

"Takes some hard jammin', but if I keep at it real good I kin get these here boots o' mine inta them there foot holders.

"Anyway, I'm ridin' fer the Jerry Lewis Muscular Dystrophy Telethon. I started in Eureka a few days back—I sleep in the bushes at night—an' I'm pedalin' to San Francisco and back. I got fifteen hundred dollars in pledges if I make it the whole way. An' I'm gonna be on TV in San Francisco! Say, you folks cycle through there?"

"San Francisco? Yep, Barb and I did," Larry answered.

"Good. I wanna know what the folks are like down there. I heard they was some real mean bastards."

"We had a tough time getting through the city," I said. "The buses kept running us off the streets, and the cars kept honking at us."

"Well, they damned well better be nice to me," John grumbled. And to prove his point, he pulled a long sharp knife out of his only pack. But before he had time to explain what he might be planning to do with it, a voice shouted at us from inside his pack.

"The bears are thick in Garberville," it warned.

Larry, Eric, and I said nothing as we stared nervously at the talking pack. John's eyes were dancing, and the grin that spread across his face displayed every false tooth in his mouth.

"I read ya loud and clear, Chain Saw," the pack hollered again. This time it was a different voice. "Ten four!"

John was laughing now. He reached inside his pack and pulled out a citizen's band (CB) radio half the size of an egg carton.

"This sucker's got eight batteries in 'er," he announced with great pride, as he attached his CB to its holder on his belt. "Yep, this here's a good one. I talk ta all the truckers all day long. Damn! You should see the looks on them big truckers' faces when they blow by me and see I'm the one they been talkin' to! Here they been thinkin' I'm some big mean dude in a big rig, and when they come by and see I'm nothing but a turkey on a pedal bike—I mean they look like they seein' a ghost!

"But ya know what? They watch out fer me. I kin hear them truckers all tellin' each other ta watch fer a bicycler on the road up ahead. Yep, everybody's talkin' 'bout the bicycler in the redwoods with a forty-channel CB. You bet. That's me, the Copenhagen Kid. That's ma handle!"

John stuffed his knife back into his pack, then reached into one of his shirt pockets and pulled out a stack of cards.

"Look, I gotta be gettin' along. But first I'm givin' ya'll one o' ma cards. Tells right there I'm ridin' fer muscular dystrophy. Now ya'll have a good time up in the Avenue. They's some mighty big trees up there. Real monsters!"

John worked for a few moments at getting his left foot lodged into its toe clip before he rolled back onto the pavement. When we wished him good luck on his ride, he tipped his hat to us, then hollered something into his CB and hurried off down the road.

There was a special camping area for bicyclers along the Eel River in the Avenue of the Giants. It was nestled in a secluded grove of redwood skyscrapers, and there were already four other cyclers camped there when the three of us pulled in. While Larry and I pitched our tent on a soft mattress of needles next to a redwood about six feet in diameter, Eric prepared to head off to the hot showers at the regular campground a half mile down the road.

"Haven't had a hot shower in a few days," he said as he fumbled through his packs for his bar of soap. "This'll feel great! I always shower and wash my clothes all at the same time. I walk into the shower with all my clothes on and suds them and myself good. Then I take off my clothes and lay 'em on the floor, and while I'm scrubbing my body I stomp on 'em with my feet. That works pretty good you know. Gets all the dirt out. Then I rinse 'em out an' put 'em back on wet, and they dry out pretty quick from my body heat. Yeah, as long as the weather stays nice and warm like it's been I don't mind wearing 'em wet for a while."

After we set up the tent, Larry and I walked over to the river for a swim and to meet the other bicyclers in the camp: Mike, Ed, Craig, and Tom. Mike was a carpenter from Florida, who had just cycled across the States, and Ed was a high-school math teacher from British Columbia on his way down the coast "to where the smog starts, and then I'll quit and fly back home." Craig and Tom were touring northern California and Oregon together. Both of them were from Fresno, California, and "like, really into health food." They grew their own alfalfa sprouts in the rows of little cloth sacks that hung from their handlebars, and they pedaled to "like, really mellow classical music" from the cassette player in Craig's handlebar pack.

"Sprouts and Mozart. You know, like, that's what I got up front," Craig nodded, pointing to his handlebars. "Ya gotta have fresh sprouts, man. Nothing's no good without 'em. Try this. This is good stuff. Great afternoon snack, man. You know, like, it's got my sprouts in it."

Craig handed us the bowl he was eating from. We looked into it, a nasty mixture of alfalfa sprouts, tofu, bulgur wheat, shredded zucchini, sunflower seeds, and a few other questionable ingredients. To a couple of junk-food junkies, Craig's snack was one of the most repulsive sights we'd ever set eyes on.

"Hey thanks," said Larry, backing away from the bowl as if it might attack him, "but I'll stick to my Hostess snowballs."

"Snowballs? Man, like, no way. Like, sugar's poison, man," Craig muttered in disgust. He shook his head and shoved a spoonful of the mixture into his mouth, then washed it down with a few swallows from his can of guava-apricot-papaya-banana-peach nectar and turned up Mozart.

Larry and I spent the rest of the day floating in the river, basking in the sun, and exploring the redwood groves. It felt good to give our bicycling muscles a rest. In the evening, Eric, Mike, Ed, and Larry pooled some money and went shopping at the campground grocery store. When they got back, they tossed a green salad in a grocery bag, chopped up a plate of fresh fruit, and we (including Craig and Tom, who ate another tofu and sprout dish) gathered around the fire, devouring food and the three bottles of wine Mike had chilled in the river.

It was a clear night; what sky we could see through the towering redwoods was a blanket of stars. Larry and I curled up together on our mats next to the campfire. The flames warmed our bodies, the smells of the redwood needles, the fresh sap, and the burning wood filled our nostrils, and the sounds of the river and the crackling fire played in our ears. A peaceful feeling settled over me, and for the first time since we started our journey my muscles were nearly free of pain. I found myself thinking that maybe, just maybe, I might make it to Oregon after all.

BEARS

◆   CHAPTER FOUR   ◆

Things fell together nicely from the Avenue of the Giants through southern Oregon. I had finally built up and toned my cycling muscles. And on our second day in Oregon, I knocked off my first eighty-mile day. Bicycling felt good by then. I enjoyed working and strengthening my muscles every day, and the constant exercise felt exhilarating, even necessary. On the days we didn't bicycle, we always went for a hike or a jog to avoid the listless or anxious moods that fell over us when we failed to exercise. Bicycling kept our bodies feeling alive and invigorated.

Now that I was in shape, cycle touring seemed like a great way to travel. We moved slow enough to see and hear things that to passing motorists were only blurs of color and sound. We took in the textures and odors of the soil and the vegetation. And because bicycling is such a quiet mode of travel, wild animals weren't frightened away when we came up the road toward them. Deer, accustomed to seeing and hearing huge, noisy boxes of accelerated steel on the roads, often loped to the edge of the pavement to find out what we were. And too, touring by bicycle made it easy for us to meet people.

Whenever we stopped in a small town to pick up a snack or food supplies at the local country stores, people always hurried over to talk with us. The Oregonians were extremely friendly folks, and shop owners always took the time to sit down and talk with us. First, they wanted to hear about our trip and how we were faring, then they would tell us what they thought we ought to know about themselves, their relatives and friends, the history of their town, and the points of interest up ahead.

It was also in southern Oregon that we discovered free camping,

35

something which made bicycle touring even more of a joy. At the end of our first day in Oregon there was no campground nearby, so we pulled into a secluded cove somewhere between Brookings and Gold Beach and pitched our tent on a grassy spot along the beach. The cove was surrounded and protected by high cliffs covered with green ferns, and a freshwater stream flowed off a cliff and down across the wide sandy beach and into the ocean. Larry and I bathed in the stream at sunset and watched the blue Pacific turn a brilliant orange and the white sea gulls float back and forth across the darkening sky. That was the first time we camped outside of a campground, and instead of being surrounded by packs of recreational vehicles with rumbling generators and the blaring stereos and televisions that some people like to take with them when they go camping, we were embraced by a quiet peacefulness, free of noise and exhaust fumes. From that night on, we stuck to free camping and stayed away from campgrounds, except when we wanted a hot shower.

The weather along the coast of California had been perfect; warm and sunny days, and cool crisp nights tailored for sound sleeping. But then, being a native of southern California, that was exactly what I expected. When we left Santa Barbara, I was confident that we'd be pedaling through nothing but clear warm weather for the next four months. It never occurred to me that there might be some places in North America where it actually rained during the summer. Therefore, I was flabbergasted by what the owner of the grocery store in Smith River, California—the last settlement before the Oregon border—said to us as we strode through the front door of his shop and made a beeline for the last package of chocolate donuts.

"Which way you folks going?" he asked.

"North," Larry answered. "Up the coast of Oregon."

"Oregon, huh? Well that's Oregon over there where the rain starts," he chuckled, pointing out one of the windows. "Least, that's how the saying goes. If it's not raining over there today, it will be tomorrow. That's what we say around here."

Larry and I stepped outside and glanced uneasily in a northerly direction. Sure enough, there were clouds up ahead. I was surprised we hadn't noticed them earlier.

"People up there have moss growing all over their bodies," the owner grinned. "And when they tilt their heads, water falls out. You can bet you're going to get mighty wet pedaling in Oregon. That's for sure."

Luckily, the rains didn't come until our third day in Oregon. The first two days were cold and overcast, but we ignored the threatening storm and savored the spectacular coastline and pine forests enclosing our route. Then, on the evening of June 10, we pitched our tent beside a lake near Reedsport and awoke the next morning to the awful sound of a downpour. I peeked out one of the tent windows and watched solid sheets of water descend from the sky. It was raining so hard I couldn't make out the edge of the lake.

"Looks like we won't be pedaling today," I said, climbing back into my bag. "What do you think?"

Neither of us had much experience bicycling in the rain. Southern Californians in their right minds would never consider doing that sort of thing. When it rains in southern California—which almost never happens during the summer—everybody hibernates. The fact of the matter was that Larry and I didn't know for sure just what might happen if we did haul off and bicycle in the rain.

"Well, you heard what the man in Smith River said. If we decide to sit it out we could be stuck here for a week waiting for it to clear. I figure we've got to plow through it. Otherwise we'll never get through the state," Larry reasoned.

I was still for waiting out the storm. I couldn't imagine it would rain this hard during the summertime for longer than a day. But eventually Larry convinced me that we should go on. We packed everything that went into the main compartment of our panniers in large plastic garbage bags and pulled another bag around the outside of each pannier to keep our extra clothes and valuables dry. Then we donned our rain jackets and climbed outside.

It took almost two hours to cook and eat breakfast, clean up our dishes, take down the tent, and pack up our gear. We had absolutely no idea how to cope with the rain. The eggs we managed to cook were one-third water by the time we ate them. I packed the wet cookset in with my dry clothes by mistake. And by the time we collapsed our tent and stuffed it into its sack, the inside of it was just as saturated as the outside. When we finally started pedaling, clad in our sweat shirts, shorts, wool knee socks, and rain jackets, we were already drenched and shivering.

It rained on and off—mostly on—for the next five days, straight through to the Washington border. And since no rain jacket is completely waterproof, Larry and I spent the good portion of those five days cold, wet, and miserable. Even when it was only drizzling, we stayed soaked, because the nylon jackets prevented our sweat from evaporating. Our shoes never dried out, even when we threw them into a dryer for two hours at the laundromat in Garibaldi. Often our hands felt as if they might freeze to our handlebars. And at the end of our second day in the rain, I noted in my journal, "Today, the only warm place on my body was the snot in my nose."

What helped us through the ordeal of bicycling and camping in the cold, saturated gloominess were Oregon's friendly people and its beautiful scenery, which we caught glimpses of whenever the skies cleared. Just when we'd think the rain was never going to end, the clouds would lift, and there, in place of the gray walls of rain, would be either a forest thick with trees, ferns, and moss, or a rugged stretch of cliffs and coves edged by the stormy Pacific.

On our third day in the rain, a hailstorm chased us into Tillamook. It was lunchtime when we splashed into the city, and in an attempt to thaw out our icy bodies, we took refuge in the Fern Cafe at the center of town. We scarfed down two piping hot, open-face roast beef sandwiches with mashed potatoes and gravy. Before our meal arrived, we walked into the restrooms, pulled off our shoes, wrung out our socks, and ran hot water over our feet and hands. Then we slipped back to our booth barefoot, buried our feet in the dry carpeting, and inhaled a couple of pots of hot tea. Gradually a feeling of warmth and contentment crept over us, and it was a long time before we were able to pry ourselves loose from the protective womb of the Fern Cafe and take on the rain and cold again.

The rain turned into a light drizzle an hour after we left the cafe. But when another downpour hit us the next morning, I decided it was time to rig up a way to keep the flood of frigid water out of my shoes. In a grocery store north of Garibaldi I bought a package of small plastic garbage bags and a box of rubber bands, jammed my feet into two of the bags, and pulled the rubber bands around the plastic at my ankles.

Except that the bags had a tendency to catch in the chain and the chain ring of my bike, picking up a thick coat of black grease, they did help to keep my feet dry. I must have been quite a sight, though, tramping through stores from then on: two beady eyes peering from a hooded rain jacket hanging nearly to my knees, and a pair of bare, muddy legs with two greasy trash bags for feet. The bags brushed noisily against one another while I shuffled up and down the aisles dripping a trail of muddy water.

It rained our last night in Oregon. We were camped in a forest just north of Cannon Beach, and rather than cook dinner in the downpour, we climbed into our tent, peeled off our wet clothes, pulled our sleeping bags around us, and polished off the supply of cookies, potato salad, and chocolate milk we'd picked up in town. After our meal, Larry poked his legs out of his sleeping bag and studied his feet.

"Look at those things," he muttered. "Have you ever seen a more shriveled pair of feet? You know, if this rain keeps up much longer they may never look normal again. Hell, they already look like they're pushing a hundred. Guess I shouldn't complain though. At least we haven't gotten sick. You'd think we'd have developed pneumonia by now, being as wet and cold as we've been for the last week. But I guess we're in good enough shape now to fight off almost anything. That's good. . . . Too bad about the feet though. Well, anyway, maybe the sun'll shine on us in Washington."

We crossed the bridge over the Columbia River from Astoria, Oregon, into Washington on June 14. We headed northeast through South Bend, Montesano, and Shelton, and around the east side of the Olympic Peninsula to Port Angeles, where we caught the ferry to Vancouver Island, British Columbia. It rained our first two days and our last day in Washington, but Washingtonians were even friendlier than the people in Oregon, and their hospitality kept our spirits up. At the one campground we stayed at to get a hot shower—near Chinook, next to the Columbia—the ranger let us camp free—"Because anyone who's bicycling through Washington deserves a free campsite and shower." After we thawed our rain-soaked bodies in the camp's hot showers, I hung our wet clothes and towels inside the restroom to dry over night. In the morning, to my surprise, they were gone. For the last month Larry and I had left our bikes unlocked outside of stores while we shopped and along back roads and highways while we hiked. No one ever touched them or any of our gear. So why, I wondered, had someone bothered to steal our dirty towel and wet smelly clothes?

I walked back to our tent scolding myself for being too trusting, but just as I started to climb inside, a hand tapped me on the shoulder. It was the middle-aged woman who was camped in the site across the park. Her arms cradled our belongings, clean, dry, and neatly folded.

"I saw these hanging in the restroom last night when I went in to take my shower, and I knew they had to be yours," she smiled. "I was going to the laundromat in town last night, anyway; so I grabbed 'em up and took 'em with me. I'm really sorry about the rain. Hope it clears up soon so you can enjoy our state."

Washingtonians were also the most considerate drivers we would encounter on our trip. They never honked at us, and when they pulled up behind us, they were so quiet we usually didn't know they were there. On winding roads they drove calmly behind us, sometimes for miles, until it was perfectly safe to pass; then they eased by slowly and cautiously, waving and smiling. Pedaling in Washington was a relaxing experience.

The ferry from Port Angeles across the Strait of Juan de Fuca dropped us off in Victoria, at the southern tip of Vancouver Island. The whole way up the U.S. coast from Morro Bay, we'd made a point of avoiding cities. It was nearly a month since we pedaled through San Francisco—a month free of smog and traffic jams. But as soon as we pedaled into downtown Victoria, we could taste its foul air. It burned our eyes and nostrils. Brakes screeched, horns honked, and dark clouds of car exhaust spewed everywhere. The pollution and noise were suffocating.

We raced through Victoria and pedaled north through the island's fairyland of bays, long sandy beaches with views of the snowcapped coastal mountains across the straits, waterfalls, lakes, and glaciers, to the end of the road at Kelsey Bay. From Kelsey Bay we caught the ferry along the west coast of British Columbia, where there were no roads, to Prince Rupert, just below the southern tip of Alaska.

Now that we'd pedaled some sixteen hundred miles northwest from Morro Bay, it was time to turn east. The Yellowhead Highway, the two-lane road that travels east across central British Columbia, covers six hundred eighty-five miles from Prince Rupert to Jasper in the Canadian Rockies. It took us ten days to pedal it. In that time we learned a lot about Canada's bears and infamous man-eating mosquitoes, about bicycling in a flood, and about pedaling over one hundred miles without passing a single settlement.

From the small frontier town of Prince Rupert, where the ferries sail north to Alaska, it was four hundred fifty-four miles to the nearest bike shop at Prince George. To make sure we wouldn't be stranded by a breakdown, we had stocked up in Victoria on spare parts—a rear derailleur, two tires and inner tubes, spokes, bearings, a cluster, some brake and shifter cables, and a complete set of tools, including a crescent wrench, screw drivers, and allen wrenches. Each of us lodged a spare tire in the space near the hub between the spokes of our rear wheels.

From Prince Rupert to the next town, Terrace, it was ninety-five miles. So before we set out on the Yellowhead in the early afternoon of July 2, Larry picked up a two-day's supply of food: peanut butter (which I scooped from its jar into a lightweight plastic container), two loaves of bread, and oranges for lunches and snacks; a package of our old standby, macaroni and cheese, for dinner; and six eggs and a box of granola for breakfast. The last sign we passed after we pedaled out of Prince Rupert and partway across the dark, barren plateau east of town read, CHECK YOUR GAS—NEXT SERVICES 90 MILES. It seemed strange, almost ominous, to think that for the next day and a half we wouldn't pass a town or even a house. Larry stopped and rechecked our food supply to make sure we had enough to see us through.

About six miles east of Prince Rupert, the road came to the end of the plateau and dropped down into the Skeena River valley. From the top of the plateau, Larry and I looked out over what appeared to be an almost endless expanse of perfect, unspoiled wilderness. Except for the road and its neighboring ribbon of railroad track, there were no signs of man anywhere. Pine forests, unmarred by logging, spread like soft green comforters through the valleys and curled around the lakes and the waterfalls. Jagged mountains patterned with snow and laced with waterfalls sprang up along the valley, creating smaller, deeper valleys and gorges, which funneled off into the distance into other panoramas of forests, lakes, and waterfalls

We glided down the face of the plateau and followed the Skeena for the rest of the day. There was almost no traffic. The birds, waterfalls, wind, and the river made the only sounds we could hear as we cycled through the grandeur and natural beauty.

At the end of the day, we pushed our bikes into the forest and found a level area covered with pine needles next to a shallow stream. It was an ideal camping spot—or so we thought. The pines would protect us from the wind, and the stream would provide our drinking water, dishwater, and bath. While Larry started pitching the tent, I leaned my bike against a tree, rinsed my face and hands in the stream, then went off to pee.

I'd just squatted down when they attacked. I thought I'd squatted onto a clump of stinging nettles. But soon a few made their way around and up to my face. Mosquitoes, I groaned. I looked down at my rear end: white skin buried in a dark cloud of insects busily sucking my warm blood. Immediately, I remembered what the man at the grocery store back in Prince Rupert had said.

"The skeeters get pretty thick between here and Terrace," he'd cautioned Larry and me. "Once you get past Terrace, you should be all right until you get up into the Rockies. But let me warn you. These aren't your ordinary skeeters we've got up here in central B.C. They're what you might call our genuine Royal Canadian Mounted Mosquitoes. They're bigger and meaner than any you've met up with so far, and they fly in swarms as big as a house. Yessir, us Canadians like to consider our mosquito belt our first line of defense against any ground attack by the Soviets."

I grabbed up my shorts and fled, but the cloud stayed with me. I didn't want to lead them back to our camping spot, so I ran to the road and back in an attempt to lose them. It was no use. These critters were not only bigger and meaner than any I'd ever encountered before, they were also one hell of a lot smarter. They stayed right behind me no matter where or how fast I ran. When I turned back to the stream, I found Larry battling a swarm of his own. He'd just finished pitching the tent, and the two of us dove inside. Within a few seconds, hundreds of mosquitoes were bouncing against the netting over the four tent windows, trying to plunge through the mesh.

Both of us pulled on our long socks, our sweat pants and sweat shirts, and closed our hoods over our heads, so that only our faces and hands were exposed, and over them we smeared a thick layer of Cutter's mosquito repellent. Then we went outside to cook our dinner. The smell of food instantly brought what must have been every living bloodsucker within a one-mile radius. The air was so hazy with hovering bodies that we could barely see to cook. While we ate, insects flew into our eyes and mouths and caught in our eyelashes and teeth.

By morning, my behind had turned into a speckled mass of welts. It stung to bicycle on a butt full of itchy bites, but fortunately, just as the man in Prince Rupert told us, once we got past Terrace the mosquitoes thinned out. They never bothered us much after Terrace, except for a few times in the Rockies and again near the Idaho border.

During our first four days on the Yellowhead, until we reached Houston, two hundred sixty miles past Prince Rupert, we were surrounded by timber, lakes, rivers, and mountains crowned by snow or glaciers. The road followed along the Skeena and Bulkley rivers, which made for easy pedaling. There were no steep climbs, and we had a tail wind the whole way. We covered around eighty miles each day, pedaling from ten in the morning to seven at night, and we stopped often to fill our water bottles in the icy streams and scout the waterfalls and Indian settlements in the forests. The few times we came to a town, we pulled into the local coffee shop for a milkshake and an earful of small-town gossip.

There were a few minor mishaps during those four days. On our third day, during the ninety-mile stretch between Terrace and Hazelton, we overestimated our supplies and ran short of food. By the time we reached Hazelton, we'd both developed a bad case of the shakes from bicycling for seven hours without eating anything. After that experience, we kept an extra supply of peanut butter and bread and an extra box of macaroni and cheese on hand.

The next day, when we pedaled out of Hazelton, the metal rack that supported Larry's handlebar pack broke. Larry tied the pack and the damaged rack to his handlebars with one of the two nylon straps he used to secure his sleeping bag to his rear rack. The setup held together for twenty miles, until we reached Smithers, where he had the rack welded. Then that afternoon, exploring an unpaved side road, Larry lost control of his bike in a loose patch of gravel, slammed into a rock, and bent the rim of his front wheel.

Yet, apart from those problems, the ride from Prince Rupert to

Houston was ideal. The weather stayed hot and sunny, and the traffic kept to a trickle. Every evening, after having worked out for eighty miles, our muscles felt tired, but they didn't hurt like they had when we first started out. We'd now come to crave that tired, fulfilled feeling we experienced after a long day of bicycling.

Each night we set up camp in a forest near a river or a stream. Woodpeckers, gray jays, and Clark's nutcrackers bounced along the boughs over our heads, while we pitched our tent on spongy mattresses of ferns, pine needles, and wildflowers. Once our tent was up, we would start dinner cooking and bathe together in the frigid water, which as often as not came from a nearby glacier. The smell of dinner cooking and the feel of the water cutting away the film of sweat that coated our bodies made a wonderful combination. And because darkness never set in until eleven o'clock, after our meal we'd stretch out in the ferns, dangle our feet in the water, and read a book or reminisce about the day. I always looked forward to the evenings those first four days on the Yellowhead; I treasured the special closeness Larry and I felt toward each other and the wilderness.

Past Houston, the streams and waterfalls disappeared, the trees grew shorter and scruffier, and the mountains and valleys turned into monotonous, low rolling hills. It was near Houston too that we came upon Chris, a Canadian, and the only other bicycler we met on the Yellowhead. Chris was a tall, skinny fellow in his late twenties. He was on his way across Canada to Newfoundland; he had started out from Prince Rupert less than a week ago.

"Looks like you two are headed to the Rockies too," he smiled. "Mind if I tag along? I don't much care for bicycling by myself. It gets pretty boring most of the time."

"Not a bit," Larry nodded. "We'd be glad to have some company."

Chris rode and talked with us for only about an hour (explaining how he was taking the summer off from work to tour his country) before he determined that he couldn't keep up with our pace and told us to go on.

"Listen, you're biking a lot faster than I'm able to, so why don't you go on ahead? You wouldn't have any fun going at my rate, anyway. I plan on staying at the campground at Burns Lake tonight, so why don't you camp there too, and we can talk when I get there."

Larry and I reached Burns Lake around six o'clock. Three hours later, Chris dragged in. I felt sorry for him. He looked a lot like I had at the end of each day during the first week of our trip; exhausted and hunched over in pain. I tried to offer him some sympathy after he'd slouched onto the picnic table in our site, but he refused to admit that he was worn out or riddled with aching muscles. Instead, he asked if we had any food we could spare. All the grocery stores had closed by the time he came into

Burns Lake, and he was out of provisions.

"I just need a little bit to eat, that's all," he said to Larry. "If I eat something I'll be fine."

Larry handed Chris the pannier with all our food in it and told him to help himself. That, we quickly found out, was a big mistake. Chris helped himself all right—to everything we had except for the half dozen eggs and the tea bags. After he'd nearly wiped us out of food, he rolled out his sleeping bag next to our tent, crawled inside it, and pulled his waterproof cocoon around him. He didn't thank us for the meal or offer to share the camping fee.

In the morning Chris asked for a bite of our eggs. He polished off half the batch and most of our tea. I tried to be understanding about the whole situation. After all, I told myself, he's been touring for less than a week now, so he's plagued by all the beginner's aches and pains and that gnawing combination of exhaustion, depression, and constant hunger.

"Today I'm going to try and stay up with you two all day," Chris announced as we pulled onto the highway after breakfast. But in less than a half hour, he started to lag behind, and we didn't see him again until late that evening, when he limped into the free campground at Vanderhoff. Pain and fatigue were etched even deeper into his face. He leaned his bike against our picnic table, dropped onto one of the benches, and lowered his forehead and arms onto the table. I sat down beside him and attempted once again to console him and offer some words of encouragement.

"Chris, don't get too down on yourself about the way you feel. It's hard at first. I know; it took me a while to get in shape too. I started out slow just like you, and every night I felt like I didn't have an ounce of energy left in me. But what you've got to do is to try and—"

Chris's head popped up off the picnic table, and the look in his eyes froze my vocal cords. I thought he was going to cry.

"Listen," he said, almost in a whisper. "It's not the beat up, sore, dead tired way I feel all the time. That I can handle. I know that'll go away eventually. What's really eating me up is the fact that you, a woman, can bicycle harder and faster than me, a man. Look, I don't care if I'm just starting out and you've been at it for a while now. I'm a man; I should be able to keep up with any woman, no matter how out of shape I am. But you know what? The ugly fact of the matter is, you can bicycle twice as fast as I can. Now, do you know how frustrating that is for me? Do you? I'm telling you, my ego will not accept the notion that a woman can bicycle better than I can. It just won't accept that. Hell, I started out this morning pedaling as fast as I could, and you blew by me like I was standing still."

Chris rocked his head in his hands, then lowered it back onto the table. I don't remember exactly how I felt toward him right then. Maybe I pitied him, maybe I didn't. There hadn't been any anger in his voice, only remorse and frustration. Neither of us said anything to each other for the rest of the evening.

It turned cold during the night and rained, and Chris emerged from his cocoon in the morning looking a lot like a drowned rat. His hair was matted, his clothes were sopping, dark troughs underlined his eyes, and his lips had taken on a bluish tint. He was too proud to admit it, but his cocoon hadn't done its job.

"You look like you're on the verge of icing over. Come over here and drink some of this hot tea. It'll help defrost you," Larry said as he placed a cup on the table.

"I-I'm f-fine," Chris stammered, unable to control his shivering.

"Well you don't look fine to me," answered Larry, "so go ahead and drink this stuff."

Chris moved his right hand next to the plastic cup; the skin was bright pink, and his fingers were so stiff they refused to clasp. Larry reached over and molded Chris's hand into a half circle, then inserted the cup and closed his fingers around it. The moment Larry let go, Chris's trembling palm shook the scalding tea into both of their faces. Chris was still trying to rally his body temperature when we pedaled out of the campground after breakfast, and he didn't catch up with us until after the flood two days later.

The flood hit on July 10, the day before we reached the Rockies, and it caught Larry and me at a bad time. We'd already pedaled seventy miles that day, and we still had another twenty to go before we would reach the town of McBride. It had been a day and a half since we passed a town, and we were down to the very last of our food.

At four o'clock we stopped alongside a stream to rest and eat a snack before tackling the final twenty miles into McBride. This would be our first attempt at pedaling more than eighty miles in one day. Our butts and muscles were already sore, but since there were seven hours of daylight left, we figured we could take it easy the last twenty miles. We figured wrong.

Four miles past the stream we saw the wall. Up ahead, the clouds that had sat overhead all day, without dropping any moisture on us, blended in with the trees and the road to form a single dark barrier.

"It's dumping up there," Larry groaned. "We'd better get out our rain gear. We're headed straight for it."

I pulled on my rain jacket and wool socks and cycled into the darkness. As the clouds closed in around us, water tumbled out of them in

45

a solid pounding torrent. The temperature fell, and within a mile our bare hands were so cold and rigid we could barely steer. Sections of the road disappeared under the water, and our brakes quit functioning. The rain filled our shoes, turning our feet into heavy bricks of ice. Passing cars and trucks dumped mud and more water over us; the brown water gushing into our mouths and penetrating every thread of our clothing.

After fifteen or twenty minutes, we were too wet, cold, and exhausted to keep pedaling. The cold had sapped our energy and stiffened our joints.

"Let's pitch our tent and wait out the storm," I shouted over the roar of the deluge.

"Fine with me," Larry hollered back. "Pull off and we'll set up in the forest."

But when I turned onto the shoulder of the road, my bike slammed to a stop as the bottom half of my front wheel sunk into a foot of water. I climbed off the bike and waded to where the forest started, hoping we'd find dry land. But even under the shelter of the trees, the ground was flooded.

"We're had," I muttered. "I haven't got the strength for another twelve or thirteen miles or whatever it is we've got left to McBride."

"Me neither. But we've got to do it," shrugged Larry. "We'd drown camping here."

I knew there was nothing else we could do, so I waded back to the road and started pedaling again. Every time I coasted down an incline, blasts of arctic air whipped my body and threatened to freeze my legs into place. Pushing the pedals and holding onto the handlebars became incredibly painful work. Out of pure desperation I started to sing. It was a long rambling song, which I made up as I struggled to keep my legs moving. I called it "The Ride to McBride," and it talked a lot about what stupid idiots we were for not stopping and setting up camp when we first saw the storm coming toward us; about the quart of frozen water in my shoes; about the tears streaming down my already saturated face.

While the storm loosed its fury upon us, Larry and I had a tough time hearing or seeing much of anything. If I wanted to say something to Larry I had to pull up alongside him and yell. But even then he couldn't catch all I was saying. So it surprised me when, not more than a half hour after I'd started singing, I heard a faint rustling sound. I turned my head to the right, toward the shoulder of the road where I thought the noise came from, and there, thirty feet away and charging straight for us, was a gigantic black bear. A split second after its massive image registered in my brain, I remembered that someone somewhere had once told me that bears can run at speeds up to thirty miles an hour. I opened my mouth and filled the air with a deafening, bloodcurdling scream.

The bear froze. It was now about fifteen feet to the side and slightly in front of us, and it looked taller and wider than I'd ever imagined a bear could grow. It lifted its head and strained to peer through the sheets of water that separated it from us, and I suddenly realized that it hadn't been coming after us—it had probably only been trying to get across the highway before a car came by. Since we didn't have any headlights or noisy engines, it hadn't noticed us coming up the road.

The beast made out our outlines almost instantly, and the sight of us—bizarre creatures, half human and half machine—was enough to send its five hundred pounds into the air. While airborne, the body turned one hundred eighty degrees and landed facing the forest. Its legs were running even before they contacted the ground, and the moment they did, the animal barreled off into the forest at full speed. Over the downpour we could hear it crashing into the trees.

Fifty minutes later, drenched and unable to steady our shivering bodies, Larry and I crept into McBride. We knew the local campground would be flooded, so we pulled ourselves and our bikes through the front door of the aging Hotel McBride. There was no one in the lobby, but I could hear people talking in the dining room as I peeled off my rain jacket and watched a giant puddle form around my feet.

"Well, I'll tell you one thing for sure. It's the worst storm I've ever seen," said one of the voices from the dining room. "Even old man Evans says it's the worst."

"Has to be. Didn't you hear the news? It's flooded out Edmonton. They're in a real mess over there."

"Yeah, I'll bet. Well it better quit pretty soon or there's gonna be real trouble here too. My yard's already under more than a foot of water."

The manager appeared at the front desk. He took a quick survey of us and our bikes, then shook his head.

"Caught you on the road did she? Looks like you two took quite a beatin' out there. Don't know how you survived it. Myself, I've never seen a rain worse'n this one. I'd a' thought she'd a' washed you two right off the pavement. You're in luck though. I got one room left and it's all yours. Room 20. The bath's across the hall."

We hoisted our bikes onto our shoulders and carried them up the creaking stairway to our room on the second floor, pulled out some dry, clean clothes, and walked across the hall to the bathroom.

I'll never forget the bathtub in the Hotel McBride. It was deep and long enough to swallow up the two of us. I filled it to within a foot from the top with steaming water; then slowly, ever so slowly, we eased our frozen bodies in. My feet and hands felt as if they'd crack when they hit the water.

"Heaven," Larry moaned.

The hot water and steam soothed our strained muscles, stiff joints, and aching behinds. And after five or ten minutes, we stopped shivering. It felt wonderful to be warm again. Larry and I sat smiling dreamily at each other while the dirt, sweat, mud, and chain grease melted off our bodies, turning the water a grayish brown. It was the greatest bath of my life.

By morning, although most of the streets and sidewalks in town were still under water, the rain had stopped. We headed to the local laundry to wash and dry our clothes. Afterward, we picked up a two-day's supply of food at the grocery store to see us through to Jasper, one hundred four miles away. Just as we finished packing the supplies into our panniers, Chris came splashing into town. It was obvious that he and his cocoon had been exposed to the full force of the storm, and it made my stomach queasy to look at him.

"D-Don't ask m-me about l-last night," he chattered. "I d-don't w-want to discuss it. OK? I'll just t-tell you t-that I slept in m-my cocoon on a p-picnic t-table in a r-rest stop."

Chris did mention that a couple in a van had pulled into the rest stop shortly before the deluge began and tossed him a few joints to help him get through the night.

"I t-think I'll c-climb into a d-dryer and stay t-there for t-the rest of t-the d-day," he stuttered as he waded off in the direction of the laundromat. Larry wished him luck.

Traveling by bicycle, Larry and I often found ourselves bouncing between super highs and rock-bottom lows. While we were battling the storm, I was convinced that bicycle touring had to be the ultimate in masochistic travel. But the next day, when we climbed into the Rockies and were greeted by the awesome sight of Mount Robson, the tallest point in the Canadian Rockies, I was ecstatic. And, except for the day we cycled to the Columbia icefield, I remained that way for the next week and a half, while we camped amid the glaciers, elk, moose, marmots, and chipmunks of the Canadian Rockies. We did some steep climbing in the Rockies, but our muscles were strong enough then that we could cover our usual sixty to eighty miles each day even with two or three passes along the way.

It was July 14 when we came into Jasper, a date that marked both our fifth wedding anniversary and the start of the third month of our journey. To celebrate, we splurged and stayed the night in a motel. Our room came with a complete kitchen, and as soon as we checked in in the afternoon, we went out and bought the fixings for a steak dinner—something we'd dreamed about the whole way across British Columbia while we survived on peanut butter and macaroni and cheese. On our way into town, we ran into Chris. He looked like he'd fully recovered from his night under water.

"Hey, I didn't think you two were in Jasper. I couldn't find you in the free camping area outside of town. Where you camping out?" he asked.

"It's our wedding anniversary, so we're splurging. We're staying in a motel," Larry answered, without giving the name of the motel.

"Oh, I see. Yeah, OK. Well, I'll be seeing you around. I'm sticking around here for a few days to do some hiking. You too?"

"We'll probably pedal south a ways to hike. Jasper's too crowded," I said.

"Yeah. Well, maybe I'll catch up with you down south. I'm going as far as Banff before I turn east."

It had been three days since Larry and I bathed, and as soon as we got back to our room, we soaked ourselves in the bathtub. I built a fire in the fireplace, and we stretched out in front of it on the soft thick carpeting and opened a bottle of wine. Lying next to the fire, we talked for a long time, mostly about how we'd been drawing closer together since the beginning of our journey.

"Sure we get mad at each other sometimes," Larry said, "especially when we get irritable when it rains—it seems like we *always* yell at each other when it rains, or when we're tired or hungry. But what couple wouldn't? But you know, it seems like the more experiences I share with you and the more hardships we overcome together, the closer I feel toward you, and the more I respect you. Like the night we pedaled into McBride. After we'd gone through that storm together, bear and all, I could feel the bond between us tightening. And we're learning to support each other, too. We complement one another now: your strengths compensate for my weaknesses, and my strengths help make up for your weaknesses."

Larry and I talked and made love through the afternoon. In the evening we prepared our feast of steak, baked potatoes, tossed green salad, and chocolate pudding. It had been so long since we'd last eaten these kinds of foods that I almost forgot what they tasted like. Larry spread out the meal on the carpet in front of the fireplace, and just as we nestled onto a cushion together, someone knocked on the door. I opened it, and there stood Chris.

My first thoughts were that someone had stolen his bike or all his money, and he'd searched us out for help. It's gotta be something really bad, I figured. Why else would he have gone to all the trouble of checking through the dozens of hotels and motels in Jasper to find us? And besides, he wouldn't be bothering us unless it was something important. He knew that today was our anniversary, that we wanted to be alone. I stepped aside to let him in and waited for the terrible news.

"Nice place," Chris mumbled as he walked through the room and sat down in the chair next to the fireplace and our meal.

I sat back down on the cushion with Larry, and we watched Chris scrutinize the food on the floor in front of him. While he spoke, his eyes never moved from the piece of steak on my plate.

"Yeah. Well, I just thought I'd stop by and say hello. My bike's downstairs. Went for a hike this afternoon. That was nice. But you know, the free campground doesn't have any showers—which is too bad, 'cause I sure could use a shower. Yeah. Well, anyway, this sure is a nice place you've got here. And it looks like you've cooked quite an extravaganza."

Chris looked sideways at us and grinned.

"Is everything all right with you?" I asked.

"Oh sure. Everything's fine. Like I said, I just thought I'd stop by and say hello."

Say hello and see if maybe we'd invite you in for a hot shower and a free meal, I bellowed to myself. Larry sensed that I was just about to say something really nasty to Chris, so he spoke before I got the chance.

"You know, Chris, there are some hot showers downstairs by the pool. Why don't you help yourself. And here, I'll wrap up some of this steak and stuff and you can eat it back at the camp. Sorry to rush you out like this, but Barb and I would like to be by ourselves right now. You can understand that, can't you?"

"Hot showers downstairs? Great!" Chris beamed, while Larry scraped off part of our meal into a couple of plastic bags. "Hey, maybe I'll catch you two later this week, when I head south."

As it turned out, we never ran into Chris or another cycler like him again, although we did meet a number of bicyclers who had their own encounters with what they referred to as "real pain-in-the-butt sponges."

Larry and I left Jasper the next morning and pedaled south on Route 93, through the heart of the Rockies, to the Columbia icefield. Less than halfway to the icefield, it started to pour. Since we didn't have our rain jackets on, we pedaled for the nearest shelter, the outhouse in a road-side rest stop. We leaned our bikes against the wooden cubicle, pulled out our jackets, some bread, peanut butter, and oranges, and dove inside. I propped the door open to let the fresh air in and the bad air out, and we huddled together on the toilet seat and ate our lunch. Occasionally, a motorist with an urgent need to relieve himself turned into the rest stop, leapt out of his car, and made a frantic dash for the toilet. But once he came to within ten yards of the outhouse and spotted two bikes and two figures inside chewing on sandwiches, every one of them ran back to his car and blazed off for the next nearest site of relief.

When we started cycling again, the air temperature had fallen and the rain felt like chips of ice. After a quarter of an hour I realized that, even though I had been working hard climbing the grades, my body couldn't warm up. I shouted to Larry that I was going to pull off the road and put on my sweat shirt and the wool mittens I'd bought in Jasper. Larry was cold too, but he was in no mood to stop. He hated stopping in the rain. No matter how cold or wet he got, he never wanted to stop and change his clothes, as I always did. We still had another forty miles to pedal before we would reach the icefield, and the prospect of spending the rest of the afternoon bicycling in the cold rain started us arguing.

"Why didn't you put on your mittens and sweat shirt before we left the outhouse?" Larry yelled at me.

"Because I didn't think I'd need 'em. I didn't know it was this cold out here."

"You'll only get colder and wetter if you stop," Larry yelled. "All your other clothes'll get wet when you open up your packs to fish out your sweat shirt. Keep pedaling. You'll warm up."

"No I won't!" I protested. "I'm getting colder, not warmer!"

"So let's pedal faster. That'll warm you up."

"Pedal faster? I can't pedal any faster! I'm freezing!"

And so went the argument until Larry gave in. But by then I was raging mad, and I wasn't stopping, no matter what. I'll just keep right on pedaling, I shouted to myself. I'll keep right on pedaling without those mittens or sweater, and pretty soon I'll freeze to death and that'll show him!

"I'm not stopping!" I yelled out loud. "I'm gonna prove I can be tough, too."

"Forget it, Barb. I don't want you complaining; so pull over and put on whatever you want."

"*I am not complaining and I am not stopping!*"

I was shaking now from anger and the cold. My hands and feet stung, and the water was already coming through my jacket. Then suddenly, just when I was about to holler something else at Larry, a stream of blood splashed onto my handlebar bag. I stared at the bag a few seconds, trying to comprehend what I was seeing; I watched in horror as more blood poured down the front of my jacket and over my legs and the front of my bike. It seemed that the blood was coming from me. I touched my face. My mouth and chin were covered with the warm, red liquid. I must have let out a shout when I felt the blood, because just after I brought my hand away from my face, Larry pulled up alongside me. Panic shot into his eyes.

"Quick! Pull off the road!" he screamed, as he started to do so himself.

"No! I don't care if I bleed to death! *I am not stopping!*" I fired back automatically. But the blood scared me, and after a few yards I turned into the mud at the side of the road.

A vein had burst inside my nose, and a steady flow of blood was gushing out of my right nostril. I sat down in the puddles, tilted my head back, and pressed my fingers against the side of the nose. The passing cars and campers sprayed me with mud and water. While I waited for the pressure to stop the bleeding, Larry pulled my sweat shirt and mittens out of my packs and helped me into them. Then he put his arms around me to shield me from the rain.

"How come when it rains I always forget how much I love you?" he whispered. "Do you think we'll ever learn to control our emotions when the weather turns lousy? You know, it seems like the minute I feel a raindrop, I start to get upset. I know you're going to want to stop and put on warmer clothes, and you know I'm going to want to start pedaling faster, and right away we're at each other. It's so hard to stay calm in the rain, but we've got to keep trying. Maybe some day we'll get the hang of it."

After my nose quit bleeding, we pedaled for another three hours in the downpour before we hit the six-thousand-six-hundred-seventy-six-foot Sunwapta Pass, only three miles north of the icefield. From the foot of the pass, the road looked nearly vertical; it shot straight up from the flat Sunwapta riverbed and disappeared into the clouds. Traffic crept up the climb at a snail's pace, and motorists coming down shouted to us that the road was too steep to bicycle. We felt defeated even before we started; our muscles were already sore, and we were shaking from the cold. We stood at the edge of the road and polished off a couple of peanut butter sandwiches, shifted into our lowest gears, took a good hard grip on our handlebars for extra leverage, and started grinding the pedals.

As the road turned skyward, every muscle and all the weight and energy in my body went into each slow, deliberate stroke of my legs. One—two, one—two. First one leg crushed down, then the next bore down, just as solidly. One—two, one—two. We moved up into the clouds, and even though there were glaciers next to us and the icy rain continued to pelt down, perspiration spewed out of me. I peeled off my jacket and sweat shirt and struggled on in only a T-shirt, shorts, and wool socks. For what seemed like an eternity, we inched upward at a rate that felt slower than a walk. I needed all my strength and concentration to maintain my rhythm and keep from teetering to a standstill.

When I reached the top of the pass, a feeling of triumph and relief washed over me. It had been a long seventy miles. We pitched our tent next to the icefield, which was almost totally obscured by the low-lying clouds. Camping beside a flow of glaciers is a lot like camping in a freezer. I climbed in the tent, yanked off my wet clothes, and pulled all my dry clothes—two T-shirts, down jacket, sweat pants, two pairs of socks, and a stocking cap—over my sweaty, muddy body. Then I slid into my down sleeping bag, zipped it around me, and stayed that way for the rest of the night.

By morning the rain had diminished to a drizzle—a Canadian spit, as the locals called it—and the mountains were dusted with a thin coat of freshly fallen snow. The clouds began to clear shortly after we got up. Within a couple hours the glaciers were glistening in the sunlight. It was a spectacular sight, and we made a quick rebound from the previous day's rain-soaked low. For half the day we hiked around the icefield in the warm, glorious sunshine. The other half we spent pedaling forty-five miles south to the campground at Waterfowl Lake. There were no clouds that afternoon to obscure our view of the chain of mountains that towered over both sides of the road.

The campground at Waterfowl Lake nestled in a forest beside a clear turquoise lake, which reflected the surrounding glaciers. Because we arrived on bicycles, the ranger let us camp free. She gave us a campsite near another couple who were bicycling through the Rockies. She warned us that bears sometimes wandered into the campground looking for food, so before we went to bed, Larry gathered all our food, put it into a pannier, and hung the pannier from the middle of a cord he'd tied about ten feet off the ground between two trees.

At three o'clock in the morning I awoke out of a sound sleep, startled. While my eyes adjusted to the darkness, I listened for the noise that might have awakened me. At first I thought I heard a rustling sound, but then everything was still. I rolled over and looked at Larry. He was sitting up. His body was tensed and rigid, and his eyes were the widest I'd ever seen them. He was straining to listen to something.

"What's the matter?" I asked.

"Shh," he answered in a barely audible whisper. "Listen."

I did, but I couldn't make out any peculiar sounds. Larry sat motionless for several minutes, listening, then he leaned forward and put his face up against one of the windows. He carefully surveyed the outside world before he sat upright again and listened intently for another few minutes. Still there was no noise.

"A little before you woke up, I heard something moving beside the tent," he whispered. "Then it sounded like something brushed the tent, so I rolled over and looked out that window. I put my face up against the mosquito netting, and right there at the very tip of my nose, staring right back at me, was a bear. I could feel him breathing on me! I half jumped out of my skin, and my heart started pounding in my throat so hard I thought I was going to choke. Well, thank God the sight of me scared him as much as he scared me. He jumped away from the window and took off running. He made a lot of noise when he went, too, and that's what woke you up."

Larry stopped talking, listened to the stillness, and looked through each of the tent's four windows. I was too nervous to move.

"The food," I whispered. "Are you sure you put all the food in the pannier outside? What if there's a candy bar or some fruit still stashed in one of the packs in here?"

"I think I got it all, but we'd better check everything to make sure. If another bear comes by that's not as skittish as the last one and smells something in here, we'll be in real trouble."

Our search turned up nothing, but even so it was an hour before either of us fell back asleep. We lay in our sleeping bags, our ears straining to pick up the slightest movement outside, our bodies tensed and ready to bolt out the door.

In the morning Larry checked over the tent. He was convinced he'd felt the bear swat it last night, and sure enough, he found a cluster of holes in the rain fly above one of the windows.

"Looks like he was getting ready to claw his way in," I winced. "It's a good thing you sat up and looked through the window when you did."

While Larry started breakfast, I pulled the plastic water bottles off our bikes and walked to the nearest faucet to fill them with water for tea. When I turned on the water into the first bottle, it became a sprinkler head; as fast as the water flowed into the bottle, it came shooting out through a half dozen holes near its base and splattered over my legs and shoes. The bear had sunk his claws into our bottles as well as our tent.

Larry was talking with Karen and Dave, the bicyclers from San Diego who were camped near us, when I got back to the campsite. Dave was doing most of the talking, and he was jumping around a lot, waving his hands in the air. Karen stood next to him staring at the ground, mumbling long nervous groans.

"I'm finding out what happened after the bear left us last night," Larry explained to me. "Turns out my ugly mug scared him so bad that, when he took off, he didn't even take the time to look where he was going."

"You bet," Dave nodded. "He was makin' for home for all's worth, and I guess our tent was dead center between yours and home. When he came flyin' by us, he tripped over one of our guy lines and crashlanded into the top of the tent.

"I'll tell you something, wakin' up inside of a collapsed tent and feelin' a bear on top of you is one horrifyin' experience. I knew it was a bear right off, 'cause one of its paws was spread out over my face, and I knew that only a bear could have a paw that big. It was a soft paw—no claws. But I knew they were comin'. I lay there frozen in sweat waitin' for those damn claws to pop out. 'It's just a matter of seconds now,' I kept sayin' to myself. 'A few more seconds, Dave, and those claws'll be slicing your face apart.'

"Then all of a sudden I hear Karen whisperin' something to me. She wasn't movin', but she kept whisperin', 'Dave, there's a bear on us. We've got to do somethin', Dave. Dave there's a bear on us!' Do somethin'! What the hell were we supposed to do? I couldn't talk; not with a paw in my face. It felt so soft and harmless when its claws weren't out. Like the calm before the storm, I figured.

"You know, it seemed like half the night went by before that paw finally moved to more stable ground. Then the bear's mass started to rise up off of us. And once he got himself up, he lumbered off into the forest."

Dave paused here long enough to spread his right hand apart and cover his face with it. He rolled his eyes and lowered his head.

ROUTE 212: THE ENDLESS ROAD

◆ CHAPTER FIVE ◆

From the Canadian Rockies we pedaled south through southwestern British Columbia and into Idaho at the end of July. Both of my parents were raised in Idaho, and many of my relatives still lived there. All my life Dad had told Idaho huntin' and fishin' stories and had talked a lot about the wilderness—and a little about rattlesnakes. As Dad put it, "The first time you hear a rattlesnake cut loose, you know exactly what it is. No one has to tell you it's a rattler."

But Larry and I entered Idaho with more fear of its ranchers, cowboys, and farmers—the fabled western rednecks—than of its rattlesnakes. We'd agreed never to tell anyone in Idaho or Wyoming that we were from California—that decadent, overpopulated strip of America, teeming with drug addicts, perverts, hot tubs, and super-slick real-estate agents. And we prayed that the hair hanging over Larry's ears might pass unnoticed.

The first time one of Idaho's countless two-ton American-made pickups with a gun rack mounted in its rear window eased past, then pulled off the road in front of us, I was sure the man inside wearing a cowboy hat had decided to personally decrease the traveling California freak population by two, or at the very least blast a few holes through their panniers just for the hell of it. I died a thousand deaths before we came up to the truck, and its burly, tough-looking driver stepped out.

"There's a steep climb comin' up," the rancher smiled when we slowed to a stop. "Need a lift?"

"Thanks a lot," I smiled back, "but we ought to be able to make it all right."

"Well, it's good to meet some tough, adventurous sorts. Have a good ride!"

After a few more encounters with the Idaho rednecks, we realized our preconception was totally false. They didn't seem to care where we were from or that Larry's hair was a lot longer than theirs; they were more interested in what we were doing than what we looked like. Wherever we went in Idaho, people pulled us over to offer a ride or food. One woman, Mrs. Thurber from Sun Valley, threw her shiny new van into a sideways skid across the gravel shoulder of the road when she spotted us resting at the top of a pass in eastern Idaho. She and her two teen-aged daughters leapt out of the van and handed us two boxes of donuts and a jar of ice-cold grape juice. Things like that happened all the time in Idaho. Its generous, kindhearted people and its ample National Forest (sixty percent of its area) made Idaho our favorite bicycling state. We encountered little traffic (the population of the whole state was less than that of the city of San Diego), not a single NO CAMPING sign, and plenty of dirt and gravel roads on which to explore the isolated wilderness of the northern and central regions.

In Idaho I not only changed my opinion of ranchers and cowboys but also of health food. I don't remember exactly why I decided, in northern Idaho, to try out yogurt, that rotten-tasting fermented-milk concoction, which most true junk-food aficionados detest more than anything else. I was shocked to find that I actually liked the stuff; after a week I even developed a craving for it.

My addiction to yogurt proved to be the first step on the road to a major change in my diet. Pretty soon I was creating all sorts of healthy and hideous mixtures. I stirred granola into my yogurt. I sliced bananas onto my peanut butter sandwiches, then sprinkled on sunflower seeds and raisins. I opted for fruit instead of chocolate bars, and I switched from soft drinks and chocolate milk to fresh-squeezed orange juice. The only drawback was that the sudden change in diet gave me a monumental case of the runs. My stomach didn't know quite what to do with all the new, strange foods I was feeding it, and for the first ten miles after I'd eaten, the meals would churn and gurgle inside my belly, then dive for the escape hatch. But even so, I stuck to my new diet, and after a few weeks my stomach agreed to accept it.

At first Larry was repulsed by what he viewed as my "sudden, unfathomable fetish for the inedible." Eventually, though, he too began to change over, and we started to eat other things besides canned foods for dinner. We steamed vegetables, melted cheese over them, and mixed in sunflower seeds; we cooked vegetable stews and simmered thick spaghetti sauces. Canned meals were still the most convenient and the easiest to carry and prepare, but the more nutritious the foods we ate, the better we felt and the fewer stomachaches we had. By the time we reached Florida we were no longer belting down daily fixes of candy bars, pound cakes, donuts, and ice cream, although we did continue to indulge in an occasional junk-food pork-out every now and then.

Uncle Bill and Aunt Marge, my father's brother and his wife, owned a cabin at Cascade Reservoir near the town of McCall, in central Idaho. Larry and I arrived there on July 29, and planned to stay a week to give our seats a much needed rest.

About midnight on our second night at the cabin, Aunt Marge barged into our room yelling for us to wake up. Then I heard a second familiar voice say something to me, and I parted my eyes a crack, just wide enough to recognize my father standing at the foot of the bed.

"Wake up! You're having a bad dream!" he laughed.

Seeing Dad standing there with a gigantic, mischievous grin splattered across his face was a wonderful surprise. He'd decided on the spur of the moment to fly up from San Diego to spend the week with us. Mom had stayed home to run their gift store, but in May she and Dad planned on joining us in Spain.

For the first few days, Larry and I bent Dad's ears with our stories while we sat on the front porch of the lakeside cabin, cleaning and adjusting our bikes. Three times a day Aunt Marge cooked up a colossal feast, and by the end of the week, I'd put on ten pounds. On the weekend, sixteen of my aunts, uncles, and cousins rendezvoused at the cabin for two days of swimming, waterskiing, canoeing, sailing, hiking and endless talking.

Monday morning Larry and I awoke to a lonely silence inside the cabin and inside ourselves. The festive, secure feeling was gone. Everyone else had gone home. After breakfast we packed our gear, but we were so homesick we couldn't force ourselves to climb on our bikes. Instead, we walked down to the lake and sat on the shore and wondered if maybe it wasn't time for us to go home, too. We sat and watched the empty canoe bob in the water, listening to the echoes of the voices of our family. Now, once again, it was just the two of us, and that day proved to be a long, lonely one.

We left the cabin early the next morning. Within a couple of hours, our homesickness subsided, and we were content to be back on the road again, meandering through the mountains, past waterfalls and meadows, headed southeast toward the Sawtooths, the Grand Tetons, and Yellowstone.

In the late afternoon of August 10, Larry and I found ourselves in a desolate stretch of central Idaho, just south of the town of Challis. By now, after nearly three months of pedaling and camping, we'd learned a few things about the ways of nature, including how to smell a rainstorm approaching and how to spot a distant stream by its surrounding vegetation. This afternoon we were especially dirty and sweaty and in need of a bath; while we pedaled, we scanned the barren landscape for a telltale row of trees or bushes that indicates the presence of a stream.

The creek I found was in a shallow ravine about fifty yards from the road, and there was a plateau nearby large enough to hold our tent. To get to the plateau we had to climb over a six-foot-high wooden fence, hop the little creek, and hike uphill some fifteen yards. We carried the tent, mats, sleeping bags, and our handlebar packs to our campsite. Then, while Larry pitched the tent, I began to haul over our bikes and the rest of our gear. I was retracing my route between the road and tent for the third time, carrying a rear pannier in each hand, when, a couple yards from the creek, a sudden noise at my feet halted me. No one had to tell me what it was I'd heard. Dad was right; I knew there was a rattlesnake at my feet.

I knew it was a rattlesnake. But I couldn't make myself accept that fact; so instead, I decided to believe that what was slithering next to my feet was a harmless garden snake. This was an unreasonable decision based on what I'd just heard; but it was a comforting one, and it calmed me enough so that I could force myself to look down. Six inches from my right foot lay a rattlesnake. It looked to be about three feet long and had thick brown scales, dark markings, and a mean, arrowhead-shaped head. While it watched me, I had the distinct sensation that snakes were slithering up the backs of my legs.

Finally, I bolted into the air. I heaved the panniers out of my hands and ran for the road. When I got to the fence, I grabbed the top rung and flipped myself over. Larry had looked up from his work just in time to see the panniers soar through the air and me fly over the fence. He ran to the edge of the plateau, and as he started down the incline toward the creek, I screamed a warning from the road, "Don't go down there! There's a snake!"

"You and snakes," he laughed. "As many as we've run into these last few months, you'd think you'd be used to them by now."

"This one's a rattler!"

"Rattlesnake, huh?" Larry hesitated for a moment then continued moving down the slope. When it came to snakes, I usually blew things way out of proportion, so he figured he was perfectly safe. At the bottom of the hill, he calmly stepped across the creek.

Larry spotted the rattler—it was now partially hidden beneath a shrub—a moment before it coiled. When the ugly hissing sound cut through the air, he screamed something unintelligible, grabbed up a rock, and fired it. The rock hit its mark, and the serpent shot out from under the shrub. Next, Larry ripped a limb off a tree beside the creek, and when the snake coiled again, he let out another high-pitched wail and swung the branch. The limb missed the snake. The serpent slithered to the right a few feet and prepared to strike. And again Larry cried out and brought down the branch. On his fourth swing he connected with the rattler's head. He lifted the dead snake with one end of the branch and carried it well away from the path and the tent.

Convincing myself to walk back down the path took some doing. Larry brought me a branch of my own, and as I made my way toward the tent, I swatted at the bushes with it while my feet did a fast jig.

After dinner, Larry went off to take a picture of the snake, but when he came to the spot where he'd left it, it was gone.

"When I saw it was missing," he explained afterward, "for a fleeting moment, I thought maybe it'd come back to life and was coiled up right behind me ready to strike. That was an awful scary experience. But then I found it not too far from where I'd set it down. It was dead all right. I guess it had crawled over there by some sort of reflex movement."

For over a week after the rattlesnake incident, I suspended my practice of walking back into the bushes and trees alongside the road to relieve myself. Instead, I would wait until we came to a town or a gas station and use the public toilets. Sometimes, when the toilets were few and far between, I thought for sure my bladder would burst; but nonetheless, I refused to go into the bushes.

A lucky thing happened when we pedaled out of Idaho and into Yellowstone National Park—it snowed. The tourists fled the park in droves, leaving it nearly deserted at the peak of the tourist season. It was extremely cold cycling the park. The mountains were covered with snow, and every time we pumped over a pass snowflakes sprinkled down on us. But we had the mud pots, the geysers, the hot springs, the canyon, the deer, the moose, and the rest of the wildlife, almost all to ourselves. We could hardly have asked for more.

It took almost an hour to cycle over the eight-thousand-five-hundred-thirty-foot Sylvan Pass at the east exit of Yellowstone. When we came down off the pass and out of the Rockies, we figured we had a long, relatively flat haul to the East Coast. As far as either of us knew, there weren't any real mountain ranges along our tentative route through Wyoming, South Dakota, Minnesota, Wisconsin, Michigan, lower Ontario, and New York—only flat lands or rolling hills until the Appalachians. No one had said anything to us about Wyoming's Bighorn Mountains, and we failed to notice them on our maps. The first person to mention them was the owner of a sporting-goods store in Cody, where we picked up white gas for our cookstove.

"So yer headed east are ya? Which pass ya figure on tacklin'," the man asked.

"Pass? What pass? We're going east, not west," Larry answered.

"Well, I'll tell ya folks somethin'. Goin' east from here, yer headed straight fer the Bighorns. They're only 'bout eighty miles away, and they've got some of the most treacherous passes you'll find anywhere. Worse than that part of the Rockies ya just came through, that's for sure. I'd recommend ya turn south up ahead at Greybull, go down to Worland, then head over the Powder River Pass into Buffalo. If ya keep on straight at Greybull, you'll be headin' over the Granite Pass road into Sheridan, and that's a bad stretch in there. Powder River's a higher pass, but it's a better road."

At nine thousand six hundred sixty-six feet, Powder River proved to be the highest pass of our entire journey. In the fifty-five miles between Worland and the summit, the road climbed fifty-six hundred feet, most of it during the switchbacks in the last fifteen or twenty miles.

We started up the switchbacks in the early afternoon on August 24, when the air temperature hovered in the high eighties. For three hours we ground up the grade. The climb was slow, hot, and tedious, and along the way we passed two giant recreational vehicles that had conked out. From the summit we plunged down into Buffalo, then set out across eastern Wyoming.

Two days later we entered South Dakota. We'd heard a lot of stories about South Dakota from other bicyclers.

"Nothing but flat or rolling empty prairie," one of them had told us. "You'll die of boredom."

"I've never heard of a bicycler catching a tail wind in South Dakota. Everyone has head winds no matter which direction they're pedaling," said another.

"South Dakota? It'll test your ability to remain sane and married," someone else had assured us. "Head winds and nothing to look at. I read a newspaper article while I was there that said some Russian scientist that was visitin' South Dakota thought the terrain looked just like Siberia! And there's lots of mosquitoes, too. They're the state bird."

We came into South Dakota at Belle Fourche and followed Route 212, the scenic route, as someone in town referred to it, for four hundred miles, straight across the state to Minnesota. The first twenty-five miles, from Belle Fourche to Newell, weren't too bad; there were some farms to look at. But the next thirty-five miles, from Newell to Mud Butte, lived up to everything anyone had told us about the state. We had a head wind the whole way and were surrounded by rolling hills so barren there wasn't a single tree to break up the monotony. I'd never seen land so empty. There were no crops, no livestock, and no vegetation except for short golden grasses here and there. The bare hills rolled, one after the other, for as far as I could see. From the top of each rise, I usually could count eleven more ahead. And so it went for the entire afternoon—up and down, up and down, up and down; boring, boring—boredom at its finest.

It would have been nice to have been able to stop and rest our muscles, or eat a snack, or read a little, to break up the tedium of the empty landscape, but the mosquitoes wouldn't allow that. When we stopped they swarmed over us. They also determined our speed, because when we slowed down below ten miles an hour, they were on us and biting.

We pedaled nonstop for three long painful hours against the stiff winds and over the low, but steep, hills. To keep my speed up and help block out the monotony and fatigue, I tried daydreaming about South Sea islands. But I tired of that after an hour and went back to staring blankly at the bare land around me and the ribbon of asphalt that stretched on and on and on to the horizon without making a single turn and without passing a tree, or shrub, or animal. When we came into Mud Butte, after three hours in the prairie, the two of us had our doubts as to whether we'd be able to endure another three hundred forty miles of head winds, mosquitoes, and nonexistent scenery without going completely batty.

Booming downtown Mud Butte, South Dakota (population two), consisted of a rustic coffee shop on one side of Route 212 and a one-room volunteer fire station on the other; if a fire broke out in the coffee shop, the McGillivrays, the middle-aged couple who ran the coffee shop and lived in the cottage connected to it, would, I suppose, dash across Route 212, jump into the fire engine, drive back across to the coffee shop, and put out the fire. As Larry and I stumbled through the front door of their shop, the McGillivrays took a look at our long faces and heavy bikes and shook their heads knowingly.

"The last bicycler that rolled in here hitchhiked out," Mrs. McGillivray shrugged as she slapped our iced teas onto the counter and straightened her cotton dress. "He dragged in here 'round noon a few months ago, and he was a real wreck. That long dry stretch between Newell and here 'bout drove the poor kid to despair. He was a real nice boy, though. Was bicyclin' from somewhere on the West Coast to his home on the East Coast somewhere. Boston, I think it was; somewhere big, anyway. And he had his heart set on bicyclin' the whole way; and up until South Dakota he was farin' just fine.

"When he pulled in here, he wanted to know how much longer the type of terrain he'd just come through lasted, and I had to tell him that at the rate he was movin' he had another seven or so days of empty, wide-open spaces ahead of him. I figured seven days was how long it'd take him to get out of South Dakota and into Minnesota, where there's lots of farms and towns and green grass. When I told him the scenery got even more borin' east of Mud Butte, 'cause it flattened out and then there weren't even rollin' hills to look at, he looked like he was gonna cry.

"From what I hear, it's real crowded back East—people and buildings everywhere—and I guess folks from back there can't take to travelin' for hours and hours for a bunch of days without seein' anythin' but rollin' or flat dirt. In a lot of South Dakota the only time ya see a buildin' or a tree is when ya come to a town, and a lot of times there just aren't a lot of those around. I'm used to it though. I like it here. No sir, I wouldn't want to live back East, where there's people all over everywhere and everythin'. I need room to move around and be by myself.

"Anyway, me and my husband talked with the kid for a long time. He was all torn up. Didn't want to get back out again into that 'lonely emptiness,' as he called it. But he didn't want to cheat and hitchhike, either. He sat and argued with himself for hours.

"After a bit, a rancher from over there by Watertown, almost to the Minnesota border, came in for somethin' to eat. He was on his way back home from Wyomin' in his pickup, and he offered to give the kid and his bike a lift. Well, I'll tell ya, that boy hemmed and he hawed a good bit, but finally he decided to take up the offer, and off he went.

"A month later we got a letter from him. He was back home in Boston or wherever it was. Said, after he got to Watertown he cycled the whole rest of the way to the East Coast. Never had to hitchhike again after South Dakota. Guess that says somethin' 'bout this here state. It does in the best of folks."

"Yeah—I'll bet it does," Larry grunted while he stared out the window.

That evening Larry and I pitched our tent behind the coffee shop in the only patch of green grass in the seventy-five miles between Newell and Faith, forty miles up the road. The mosquitoes were so thick that we ate dinner inside our tent. We were exhausted from battling the head winds all afternoon, and we fell asleep early.

The ripping and chomping started around two o'clock in the morning. I was the first to wake up, and I listened to the sound—*rip—chomp, chomp, chomp, chomp—rip—chomp, chomp, chomp, rip, rip—chomp, chomp*—for a few moments until the ground began to vibrate under the weight of heavy footsteps, and something snorted. I looked out the window; we were surrounded by six steers, each with a pair of two-foot-long horns. The animals were grazing on the grass around our tent. While I watched them graze, one of them tripped on something and nearly put his horns through the side of the tent.

By now the chomping had awakened Larry, and we agreed that we'd better chase off the steers before a couple of them accidentally stumbled into the tent. We shooed them off fifty yards, then climbed back into the tent, squished the half dozen mosquitoes that followed us in, and fell asleep.

Ten minutes later the *rip—chomp, chomp, chomp* started again. And again we chased the steers away, and again they came back. We chased them away four times, and they stumbled back four times. The fifth time that they wandered back, Larry bolted out the tent door without taking the time to pull on any clothes, grabbed up a stick, and herded the steers across the prairie. Had the McGillivrays wakened and looked out their bedroom window just then, they would have witnessed the peculiar sight of a human form, stark naked and glowing in the moonlight, chasing behind a group of trotting, four-legged, long-horned beasts. I watched Larry and the steers top a rise in the plain and disappear. Eventually Larry came back, but the steers never did.

"Rodeo steers!" Larry grimaced when Mrs. McGillivray gave him the news in the morning. "You mean the kind that gore the cowboys in the rodeos?"

"That's them," she nodded. "They're a tough bunch, those six. Real prizes, too. I can't figure how the blazes they got out of the corral last night. But there's no need to worry. My husband'll catch 'em. 'Round this country, there's no place to hide."

Mr. McGillivray was still off searching for his steers when we left Mud Butte to start our second day in South Dakota, and Larry was feeling quite lucky to be in one piece.

We cycled eighty miles that day, and they all looked exactly alike. It was as though we were pedaling yet standing still. Our surroundings never changed, and the boredom grated on our nerves. We felt trapped. All day we argued and complained about trivial things.

The next morning both of us agreed that we'd better make a real effort at getting the hell out of South Dakota, because if we weren't out soon, our mental health would disintegrate altogether. We started out from Eagle Butte at seven-thirty. One hundred ten miles and fourteen hours later, the two of us collapsed in a deserted camping area outside of Faulkton. This was the farthest and longest we'd ever pedaled in one day, and except for the Missouri River, which we crossed at midday, the landscape remained just as monotonous as it had been for the last two days. We battled a head wind the whole day, and by evening every part of my body hurt. I couldn't pedal fast enough to keep ahead of the mosquitoes, but I was too tired and sore to care.

When we pulled off the road at nine thirty, our knees had given out. Standing was painful and squatting proved impossible, so we pitched the tent while sitting down. Our aching bodies kept us awake all night.

In the morning I awoke to the terrible realization that I was still in South Dakota and that the sharp pain in my knees hadn't gone away. Always before, when I'd gone to bed with sore knees, they felt fine by the next morning. We hoped to put in another one hundred-plus miles this day, which would take us as far as Watertown, so that by the following morning we'd be out of the state. But with my knees as sore as they were, I wasn't sure I'd last that distance.

We pedaled into Faulkton after breakfast and bought our day's supply of food. Faulkton turned out to be a kind of oasis. Unlike the other towns we passed through in the last three days, it was a pretty place with lots of greenery. It had neat, well-kept houses, lawns, and flowerbeds, and there weren't any mosquitoes in the city park. We locked our bikes outside the grocery store and spent an hour walking around the town, looking at the grass, and standing in the shade of the trees, pretending we were someplace far away from South Dakota and its barren plains.

This was our fourth day in South Dakota; August 30, the day that state nearly conquered us. We pedaled for six hours and covered a grand total of forty-one miles, thanks to the howling head wind that was waiting for us at the edge of Faulkton. Larry cycled in front, to block the wind, and he cursed it for the whole two hours it took us to go the twelve miles from Faulkton to one of those rare points of interest in South Dakota—a turn in the road.

At the turn, we stopped to eat lunch. The terrain offered no trees or bushes to block us from the wind, and it occurred to me that I'd forgotten what it was like not to hear wind all day. Frustration and depression overcame us as we stared at the empty land. There were one hundred twenty-five miles of Route 212 still before us, and it appeared as if we were going to have to fight through each and every yard of them. Larry talked about hitchhiking to Minnesota, but as sick as we were of the head winds and the never-changing plains, we couldn't bring ourselves to admit defeat.

After the turn, the wind hit us at a slight angle instead of straight on, but even so, it was tough pedaling. In the next two hours we could only manage to cover fourteen miles. We argued a lot during those two hours, mostly out of frustration and pain. Larry didn't think we were moving fast enough, and I thought my knees would fall apart. There was nothing to look at except each other, as had been the case all morning and for the last three days, and by now we could hardly stand the sight of one another. To escape the other person's constant griping, we began cycling farther and farther apart. Two hours after the turn we inched into Zell—the first sign of civilization since Faulkton—another Mud Butte minus the fire station. We hadn't spoken to each other in well over an hour. Even so, we both entered Zell's lone store and coffee shop with the same idea in mind: to get drunk quick.

There were two wooden benches outside the store, one on either side of the front door. I dropped onto one with my three cans of beer, and Larry sat down on the other, as far away from me as possible. I popped open one of the cans and looked over to my left, toward the east, at the long, straight, flat band of pavement that cut through the flat featureless plain. The wind picked up the pop top and whipped it out of sight. For forty minutes I drank beer, watched the road, and let the wind spray me with dirt. My knees never quit aching. When all three cans were empty, I climbed back onto my bike. I didn't feel any different mentally or physically from when I arrived.

It took us almost another two hours to pedal the ten miles to the town of Redfield. By the time I could make out Redfield's cement buildings, the dry heat and the wind and dust had cracked my lips and parched my throat. We stopped at a hamburger stand at the edge of town and ordered a snack, and Larry asked for two cups of cold water so we'd have something to drink while we waited for the food.

"Sorry, you'll have to pay for water just like you would soft drinks," grumbled the man behind the counter.

Larry canceled our order, and we pedaled to the grocery store in town.

Redfield had a bad feel to it. The people on the sidewalks looked away when we cycled toward them, and no one returned our greetings. As soon as we picked up cold drinks at the store, we headed for the state campground eight miles to the east.

Just outside of Redfield, Larry stopped at the Wilson Motel, which had an adjoining camping area for trailers and recreational vehicles. And for the first time in half a day, he spoke to me in complete sentences.

"What do you say we call a cease-fire? I'll apologize for saying you're the world's slowest bicycler, and you can tell me you didn't really mean it when you said you didn't care if I disappeared off the face of the earth and you never saw me again 'cause you've never had a good time doing anything with me anyway. OK?"

"Look, I'll tell you what let's do. It's been three days now since we washed last. We're both getting pretty ripe, so let's go in here and ask the manager if the campground up ahead at Fisher Grove has showers. I got to thinking maybe it doesn't, and that'd mean another night of sleeping with our sweaty legs sticking to each other and our arms sticking to our sides. If the manager tells us there aren't any showers up ahead, maybe he'd let us wash up here. I figure a nice cool shower'd pick up our spirits a lot, and this way we'd make sure we got one today. What do you think?"

The owner of Wilson's assured us that there weren't any showers at Fisher Grove. "I don't usually let people who aren't stayin' here use our facilities but since we're not really set up for tent campin', and seein' as how you two look like you could really use a shower, especially after a hot day like today, I'll do you a favor and let you use our bathrooms for two dollars for the two of you. How's that?"

As Larry suspected, our outlook on life took a sharp turn for the better after we got out of the wind and ran some cold water over our burnt, sweaty bodies.

Real, honest-to-goodness green grass, bushes, and trees covered the campground at Fisher Grove, and we decided to stay there rather than free-camp out on the prairie. The wind was blowing too hard to set up our tent without a windbreak, and here we could pitch our tent behind the shrubs.

When we checked into the campground, the ranger informed us that the restrooms had showers.

"Too bad the man at the Wilson Motel didn't know that," I shrugged. "He said there weren't any here, so we paid him two dollars to use his."

The ranger shook her head. "Oh, he knows all right. He and his family camp here every year. He just saw an easy two bucks in the wind, and he took you for it. Some folks are like that, you know. Even so, it's hard to imagine someone takin' advantage of a couple of worn-out bicyclers."

This news capped our day. And all through the night, the wind roared past the trees and bushes and made our tent walls jump and snap so loud we couldn't sleep. It sounded as if the whole tent was being ripped to pieces.

"If this wind keeps up, it's going to take us another three or four days to get out of the state," Larry grumbled. "Three or four more days of poking along at six miles an hour with nothing to look at, the sun frying our skin, and the wind howling in our ears."

I spent all night contemplating that sobering thought. But by morning the wind had died down somewhat and had shifted its angle, so that it hit us more from the side than straight on. Any place else we'd have thought it was a bad day for cycling, but in South Dakota, the lack of a full-blown head wind was a relief. Around midday the wind shifted again and angled almost to our backs. We took advantage of this and pedaled as fast and hard as we could for the rest of the day. We rode until dark, to within fifteen miles of the Minnesota border.

On September 1, a tail wind picked us up at the Minnesota border and blew us halfway across the state. It was one hundred degrees and ninety-eight percent humidity, but Larry and I were in heaven; we'd escaped South Dakota. Two weeks later, with Minnesota and Wisconsin behind us, we pedaled into Michigan, where practically everyone, it seemed, was waiting for the opportunity to invite us into their homes.

NORTHERN HOSPITALITY

♦ CHAPTER SIX ♦

The first ones grabbed us at the end of our first day in Michigan, outside the bike shop in Escanaba on Lake Michigan on the Upper Peninsula. We'd just ridden into town and were standing in front of the shop, which had closed an hour earlier, checking our maps to find the nearest campground with hot showers. We were cold and muddy from cycling in the rain all day.

Before I had time to put away my map, a woman and a man approached us from opposite directions. The woman got to us first. She looked to be in her early thirties, and she was plump, with short dark hair and a wide smile.

"I saw you standing out front here, and I saw the CLOSED sign, so I decided to stop and see if I could help you out," she said. "I've got some spare bicycle parts in the basement if you need something."

"Thanks a lot, but we were only going to buy a couple spare tires, and there's no rush. We can make it to Bay City on what we've got and buy the spares there. Thanks for stopping though," Larry answered.

"How far you cycled from on your trip so far?"

"California."

"California?! I thought maybe you'd come from Wisconsin. How much farther you going?"

"Hopefully, around the world."

"The world! That cinches it. You're staying at our place tonight. I've got to pick up my son at nursery school right now, but my house is really close. Go up to the corner and turn right. Go three blocks, and it's the brown house on the corner. Have a look 'round town first, and I'll see you there in five minutes."

The woman started to rush off.

"Wait a minute," I yelled after her. "What's your name?"

"Cinda," she shouted as she climbed into her car. "I'll hurry, so I'll be home when you get there!"

"I'm Barb and this is Larry," I called back, but she had already barreled off.

Now the man who had walked up just after her started talking.

"Well, I guess she beat me to it—I can't have you over to my house tonight. But if you're looking for tires, the auto supply store down the street about five blocks on the right carries bicycle tires, and they're open 'til six."

"Thanks! We'll check there."

"No problem. Have a good time in Michigan."

Cinda Eltzroth and her husband, Elmore, were eager to find out all about Larry and me, and the four of us sat up half the night talking. Cinda and Elmore made us feel right at home in their roomy two-story house, and by the end of the evening Larry and I felt as if we'd known them for years.

"So what do you think of Michigan so far?" Cinda wanted to know right off.

"Great people," I answered. "When we came over the border from Wisconsin today, we stopped at a gas station at lunchtime over in Spalding to ask where the nearest grocery store was, and the man that ran the place hauled us in out of the rain and had us sit in front of the heater in his office and tell him all about our trip. He asked us a whole slew of questions, then afterwards he directed us to the supermarket. And just after we got there and started shopping, the local reporter for the Escanaba *Daily Press* came looking for us with a camera and note pad in hand. Turned out the man at the gas station had called her and told her about our trip.

"And that's the way it went all day today. Everybody we met took a genuine interest in us and our undertaking. It's funny, even though it was raining all day I had a warm feeling inside because of the way people were treating us. People are really nice around here."

"Just your routine Michigan hospitality, I guess," Cinda smiled.

The next morning, after Elmore, a geologist for the state, went to work, Larry and I talked with Cinda until eleven o'clock. When we left, Cinda told us to be sure to give their address to any bicyclers we met who would like a place to stay for the night in Escanaba.

From Escanaba we pedaled east along Lake Michigan on Route 2. It rained all day, and by four o'clock the wind was blowing so hard that the lake was a patchwork of huge whitecaps. We found a deserted motel-campground beside the lake outside the miniscule town of Thompson, near Manistique, and pitched our tent behind the motel building. The building blocked the wind, and the grass provided a perfect mattress. Once we set up camp, I climbed inside the tent to arrange our mats and sleeping bags. I'd almost finished when I heard Larry speak to someone.

"Oh—H-Hello." Larry stammered. His voice sounded edgy. "Ah, Barb. Ah—I think maybe you'd better come out here now."

"But I'm all warm and settled in here. What's the problem?"

As I spoke, a pair of black shoes appeared at the tent door and a man's face peered in. I leaned forward and glanced at the stranger. He was holding a gun in his right hand.

"All right, ma'am. Why don't you come on out now," he said sternly.

Why? Why, because I'd much rather be shot to pieces right here in the warmth and comfort of my own tent than out there in the cold, I muttered to myself as I cautiously climbed through the tent door. So we're not even going to make it across America, I breathed. This is it—the end.

"All right now, may I see some identification please," I heard the man say as I looked up at him. He was a state police officer. Even so, I didn't know whether to feel relieved or not. The gun made me nervous.

The officer ran his eyes over our driver's licenses and jotted down the information on a pad of paper. Then, after he studied Larry and me and our tent and bikes for a moment, and listened to us explain that we were bicycling around the world, he shoved his gun back into its holster. He gave us a slight smile and heaved a long sigh. The man didn't appear to have any idea what he should do next.

"Some people down the road saw you two looking in the windows here and figured you were burglars—guess they didn't see your bikes—and they called the police," he said, finally.

"Now I know you're both perfectly innocent and you're not gonna steal anything, but I can't allow you to stay here," the officer continued. He was young, maybe in his mid-twenties, and seemed like the jumpy sort. His name was Mike Sweeney.

"This is private property," he said, "and someone has made a complaint. I can sympathize with the situation you're in, though," he went on after a short pause. "You're not gonna want to take down that tent and pack up and look for another campin' place in this weather. The nearest campground that's open is the state park. It's only three miles away, but the road to it's out, so that's no good.

"But don't worry, I've got a solution. You two are gonna stay with me tonight. My house is only a half mile from here. I'll call Tony—that's my wife—and let her know you're comin'. I've got some paper work to finish up before I go home, but that shouldn't take me more than an hour. What do you say?"

"Fine," said Larry, "except what's your wife going to say when you call her up and tell her you've invited two total strangers that somebody thought were burglars to stay the night, and that they'll be right over but you personally won't be home until later? You sure she'll go for that?"

"Yep. Ya see, there aren't many people to visit with up here in backwoods Michigan. We just moved up here from down south—Kalamazoo—and Tony's been pretty lonely and homesick lately. We'd both be excited to have you stay the night with us. It's not every day we get a chance to talk with someone who's bicyclin' 'round the world."

"Well, we really appreciate the offer. We'll just pitch our tent in your backyard."

"Hey, no way you're doin' that. We got plenty of room in the house. You're stayin' in the spare bedroom. Besides, there's a special reason why you wouldn't want to camp in the yard, but we'll talk about that later. Right now, I've got to get back to the station. I'll see you at the house in an hour or so."

Our fear that Tony might not approve of Mike's idea proved totally unfounded. Tony had two cups of steaming hot chocolate and a hot bath ready for us when we arrived. As Mike predicted, she was glad to have some "city types" near her age to talk with. She greeted us at the door wearing a pair of jeans and a bright green blouse.

When Mike strolled in a half hour later, he was famished. Larry assured him that he and I had already eaten dinner, a salad and some spaghetti that we'd cooked up behind the motel. But Mike figured our stomachs could hold more.

"I hate to eat alone, and Tony's always on a diet, so you're just gonna have to join me—that's all there is to it. Besides, I always fix more than I can eat. Now that's where you two come in. Doin' all that bikin', you must have huge appetites, so tonight there aren't gonna be any leftovers, 'cause you guys are gonna eat 'em all!"

Larry and I were already full, and I had this funny feeling that we were letting ourselves in for more than we could handle, but Mike stood his ground. He started out by baking two frozen pizzas. Of them, he consumed four small pieces; then he allowed as how Larry and I were to eat the rest. While we struggled through the cheese, pepperoni, tomato paste, onions and pasta, Mike began popping popcorn and heaps of it. Even Tony was recruited to help devour it. She and Mike polished off two medium-sized bowls, while Larry and I, making a slow rebound off our first course, were each handed a bowl which measured a foot in diameter and six inches deep. Luckily, we both love popcorn, and we set to work on our portions while Mike and Tony talked about Mike's job, the difference between "fast city livin'" in Kalamazoo and the slow pace of the sparsely populated Upper Peninsula, and the incredibly harsh winters in Thompson. They finished talking about the time Larry and I entered the bottom quarter of our bowls.

"OK, now you tell us all about your trip so far and about your plans from here on out," said Mike. "And I'm goin' to dish up some rice puddin'. Now don't bother complainin' that you're full. I know two hungry bicyclers can eat a lot more than what you've eaten so far. Hell, I'm still goin' strong, aren't I? And I didn't pedal any forty some miles this afternoon."

"But like I said Mike, we already ate dinner before we pitched our tent. And anyway, you're giving us a lot more food than you're eating yourself!" Larry protested.

"That's all right. Food's good for ya. And you wouldn't like me to be stuck eating alone after the favor I did you both not tossin' you into the clink, would you?"

There was a twinkle in Mike's eyes, and I knew that arguing with him would be futile. He set the pudding next to our bowls of popcorn, and somehow we managed to plug through them both while we talked. No sooner had Larry and I finished our pudding and stories, than Mike jumped up and turned on the television.

"Time for the late evening news! Great timin'! You finished the popcorn and puddin' just in time for the news! That's good." Mike raced into the kitchen.

I leaned back on the couch and patted my stomach and prayed that it wouldn't explode during the night. Well, I did my duty, I said to myself. I helped keep Mike company while he ate. Think I'll skip breakfast in the morning. I closed my eyes and took a series of long, deep breaths to help force the food farther down into my stomach. When Mike came back into the room, I nearly bolted off the couch in horror.

"Yep, there's nothing I like better than a couple of tuna fish sandwiches while I'm listenin' to the news," he grinned as he plopped the two plates of food down in front of the couch. "You bet; tuna fish and news. Now there's a great combination for ya!"

I took one look at the plate in front of me, and everything inside me started to rise to my throat. Larry looked as if he was about to pass out. Fortunately, Tony noticed our agony and came to the rescue. If she hadn't, I doubt I could have survived the tuna fish.

"Mike, a lot of people can't stand the taste of tuna fish. Maybe Barb and Larry don't like it either," she commented.

"Actually, we're both allergic to tuna fish. We get really sick when we eat it," Larry claimed, in an all out effort to keep from being forced to cram more food into his stomach. "And anyway, we're pretty tired from our ride today, and we want to get an early start in the morning; so I think we'll pitch our tent out back now and get to sleep," he added, jumping to his feet.

"No you're not!" Tony insisted. "You'll sleep in the extra bedroom. Mike, didn't you tell them about the backyard?"

"Well, I started to, but I had to get back to the station and I never finished," Mike answered as he moved the plate of tuna fish closer to himself. "You see," he said turning to us, "I've been baitin' this bear back there for a week or so now; you know, leavin' hunks of fresh meat out in the yard every night so the bear'll make it a habit of comin' by each night for a free meal. Huntin' season starts next week, and I plan on gettin' that bear the first night.

"Anyway, what I'm gettin' at is, if you two are out back in your tent tonight when the bear comes by, he just might mistake you for the bait. So you've got your choice: you can sleep inside in a nice warm bed out of the cold and rain—there's supposed to be some thunderstorms through here tonight—or you can pitch your tent out back and spend the night worrying about bein' eaten alive. It's up to you."

Mike flashed us a wide grin, and an entire tuna fish sandwich disappeared behind his teeth.

Larry and I found it extremely difficult to spend money in Michigan. The few times we pulled into a campground for a shower, the rangers refused to charge us. At the fruit and vegetable stands along the roads, we were given more than we asked for and never charged for any of it. In a laundry, in the small town of Vassar, southeast of Bay City, Bonnie Wagner, who worked there, insisted on washing and drying our clothes free.

"You two go on up to the store and get yourselves some lunch, and I'll have your things finished before you know it," she said.

When we got back to the laundry, Bonnie had an invitation for us. "The weatherman says there's a hailstorm coming through here pretty soon, so I don't think you should bicycle anymore today. I'd like you to come home with me and stay the night. I'll feed you a good hearty dinner, and you can have a hot shower and sleep in a real bed. My husband's been gone for almost six years now, and my youngest just moved into an apartment of his own; so I'm living by myself now, and I've got plenty of room, and I'd really enjoy your company. But mainly it's just that I'd like to do a little something for you two because I think what you're doing is wonderful, and I'd like to share in it—contribute a little something to it. We'll spend the rest of today visiting, and you can start out again tomorrow, when the weather's cleared."

Bonnie's enthusiasm and good-natured laugh, along with her kind, caring way, won us over right away. The three of us talked and joked all afternoon and evening. Bonnie told us about her life, her thoughts, her emotions, and her opinions, and she had us tell her about ours.

Bonnie made people feel good about their fellow human beings. She took the time to care about other people, to take an interest in what they were doing, to help them out. When we said good-bye to her in the morning, I felt as close to Bonnie as I did to my friends back home. She wrote to us regularly throughout the trip, and we wrote to her.

We would meet a lot of people like Bonnie in the next nineteen months, people who opened their homes and their lives to us and helped ease our bouts with homesickness and loneliness. They gave us a home and a family away from home.

FROSTS

CHAPTER SEVEN

We knew the frosts were coming—the geese had been flying south for days—but we weren't sure what to expect from them. We were as apprehensive of fall weather in the East as we had been of rain in the Pacific Northwest.

It was late September. We'd crossed Michigan and lower Ontario, Canada, and we were having a great time weaving from winery to winery in the Finger Lakes region of New York State. In the late afternoon on September 25, feeling warmed and numb from an hour of serious wine tasting, we left the Widmar Winery in Naples, at the base of Canandaigua Lake, and pedaled east into the hills between Naples and Keuka Lake. We were headed for the wineries at Hammondsport.

As we climbed up into the hills, the air temperature suddenly took a nose dive, and we had to stop and pull on our jackets, sweat pants, and mittens. Halfway to Keuka Lake we turned into the village of Prattsburg to buy food for dinner. Everyone in the local grocery store was talking about the snap in the air. Tonight would be the night, they all agreed; the first frost of the season. It was time to bring the potted plants inside.

Larry and I pitched our tent in the woods at the edge of town. The air felt icy and I kept on my wool socks and stocking cap even in my sleeping bag. In the morning the air seemed even colder, and the steam from our first words hung suspended inside the tent. I dressed inside my sleeping bag, then climbed out of the tent to see if the people of Prattsburg had guessed right.

The grass and our bikes were white with frost. Our aluminum pots had frozen to the board they were resting on, and the water in each of

76

our bottles was a solid chunk, as was our carton of milk. Larry tapped the rain fly of the tent with his hand, and the sheet of ice that encased it shattered and slid off onto the ground. We worked for fifteen minutes coaxing our stove to life. Since my fingers refused to flex in the cold, I wore my mittens while I cooked and ate breakfast. Afterward, Larry filled one of our pots with the chunks of ice from our water bottles and warmed it on the stove to wash the dishes in. As the frost began to evaporate in the sunshine, a fog rose off the ground and obscured the grass and trees around us.

When we started cycling we had a tough time grasping our handlebars, shifting the levers, and pushing the pedals. We cycled for two hours before the stiffness finally went away. For the next month and a half, until we got to Georgia, a frost would greet us almost every morning, and at times the walls of our tent would be frozen stiff by seven o'clock in the evening.

Four and a half months and six thousand four hundred fifty miles from the start of our journey we arrived on the East Coast. On October 2, Larry and I rolled into Storrs, Connecticut, twenty miles east of Hartford, and spent the next three weeks with Fritzi Batchelor, a friend of ours who had moved to Connecticut from Santa Barbara in 1975. I had worked for Fritzi at the university library while I was going to school. She was now working at the University of Connecticut. She lived alone in her house in the woods with her dog and cat.

When we reached Connecticut, Larry and I were good and ready for a break from pumping pedals all day and constantly being on the move. We pushed our bikes into Fritzi's garage, closed the door, and vowed not to set eyes on them for at least two weeks.

The livin' was easy at Fritzi's. Everything in her house was a luxury to us—the stove with its four burners, the oven, the refrigerator, the washing machine and dryer, the carpeting, and the pillows and clean sheets on the perfectly even surface of our bed. I'd almost forgotten just how pampered life could be. When I woke up in the middle of the night with an urge to go to the toilet, there was no need to struggle into shoes and layers of clothes, feel blindly for the toilet paper, fumble with the tent door and the rain fly, trip over rocks and ferns, and squat in the cold or pouring rain; then climb back into the tent and search out and squish any mosquitoes that had flown in while I was opening and closing the door.

Every morning, Larry whipped up pancakes and bacon, and when it rained or the wind kicked up we stayed inside the house all day and listened to the stereo or took a nap in front of the fireplace. When the weather was nice we went jogging or hiked in the woods. In the evenings the three of us sat in front of the fireplace and talked and shared a few bowls of popcorn. On the weekends Fritzi drove us around Connecticut to see the fall colors and the lakes and look through the antique shops.

In all, our first two weeks in Storrs provided a peaceful, relaxing end to our trek across the States. Only one thing worried me—I could barely squeeze into my only pair of pants. I now weighed one hundred thirty-five pounds, twenty-eight pounds more than when I began our journey. Some of the extra weight, maybe ten pounds of it, was due to the muscles I'd built up, but the rest fell into the category of plain ol' fat. This was the first time in my life that I'd been anything but thin.

By the time we had reached eastern British Columbia, my upper body was heftier from lifting a sixty-five-pound bike over sand and bushes. Climbing passes in the Rockies had made my leg muscles bulge. So when we had dropped down into Idaho I was muscular—but definitely not overweight. Then had come Aunt Marge's cooking, nine days of nonstop pork-outs, and no cycling. I left the cabin weighing one hundred thirty pounds, almost fifteen pounds more than when I arrived.

I figured the extra pounds would disappear after a couple of weeks of bicycling, but that assumption proved completely false. By Minnesota I was up to one hundred thirty-five.

The reason I didn't lose any weight between Idaho and Minnesota even though I was cycling every day was simple enough. After my body adjusted to the daily exercise, and my muscles were built, and we left the mountains, it no longer needed the huge amounts of food I had been eating during the first few months of the trip. I should have cut down on my food intake as we came across Wyoming and South Dakota; but unfortunately, my appetite never changed, and I continued to eat just as much as before.

It wasn't until Minnesota that I realized the time had come to start dieting. I quit eating bread, sweets, and milk altogether, and I cut down the size of my meals. For the next month, my lunches consisted of a small container of yogurt and some granola. The diet kept me from gaining any more weight, but I didn't lose any either, and I was always hungry. Larry, however, never gained a pound. No matter how much he ate, he burned it up.

At the start of our third week at Fritzi's we brought the bikes out of seclusion and gave them an overhaul. Larry put a new rim on his rear wheel and respoked his front wheel. We regreased our hubs and bottom brackets, cleaned and oiled our chains, clusters, and derailleurs, and replaced our brake and derailleur cables. After we finished the bikes, we sewed ourselves waterproof nylon booties, which came up almost to our knees, to wear over our shoes and wool knee socks when it rained, and some waterproof overmittens and seat covers. On October 23, we packed up our bikes once again, said good-bye to Fritzi, and started out for Florida.

From Storrs, we headed southwest, back into New York State. Staying north of New York City, we crossed over the Hudson River at Peekskill and cut through northwestern New Jersey into Pennsylvania. We followed the Blue Mountains southwest on Route 443 as far as Harrisburg, then turned directly south and braved bicycling into Washington, D.C., to do some sightseeing. After meandering along backcountry roads for the past two weeks, the crowds and traffic in the capital made us nervous and claustrophobic. We lasted only a couple of days, then headed west to Front Royal, Virginia, where we climbed up onto the ridge of the Appalachians. We followed the Skyline Drive and the Blue Ridge Parkway through Virginia to Asheville, North Carolina.

In Front Royal everyone we talked with voiced the same warning when they found we were headed onto the Drive and the Parkway. "It's too cold fer ya'll ta be cyclin' up there this time o' year. Why we're already inta November. The first snow'll be acomin' pretty quick now. The leaves've all fallen off the trees, and the facilities in the Parkway campgrounds 'er 'bout all closed down fer the winter. Ya'll won't be findin' nothin' but a couple o' pit toilets and one workin' water faucet in any o' them campgrounds."

Most of the cyclists we'd met in New England also cautioned us about the Drive and the Parkway. They insisted that the ride was difficult even for an experienced bicycler without panniers because of the long, steep grades.

But despite all these warnings, Larry and I were anxious to get up into the Appalachians. Trucks weren't allowed on either the Drive or the Parkway, and now that the leaves had fallen, there would be few tourists. We were hoping for so little traffic that it would seem like a six-hundred-mile bikeway.

After the sparsely populated, wide-open spaces of the West, we'd had a tough time getting accustomed to all the traffic on the roads in the Middle Atlantic states. It seemed as if all eastern drivers possessed the nasty habit of honking at us to let us know they were approaching. And too, there weren't many shoulders to ride on in the East, which meant, instead of having our own lane, we rode with the semis and cars. Our desire to bicycle where we wouldn't be forced to dodge traffic and listen to honking horns all day, day after day, far outweighed any concern about the cold and the grades.

As it turned out, the twelve days we spent pedaling the ridge of the Appalachians from Front Royal to Asheville provided some of the most difficult bicycling of our entire trip. There were very few stretches where the road remained level for longer than an hour. Most of the time we were struggling up grades that took us anywhere from fifteen minutes to two hours to climb, depending on their angle and length. Once we reached the top of a grade, we would fly down the other side in a couple minutes, only to be faced by yet another steep climb.

Because of the cold weather our knees and leg muscles stiffened up when we coasted down the hills. At the foot of each grade, we had to slide off our bikes and walk for a while to loosen up the muscles before we could start up the next grade. By the end of every day, both of us had sharp pains in our knees, and by the time we reached Asheville, we'd already decided that when we got to Florida we would change our gearing to fifteen speeds to cut down on the wear and tear on our knees. We needed an extra low gear—a grannie low—so that our legs could spin faster when we hit a steep climb.

The grades weren't the only problem. There weren't any stores on the Parkway, so when we ran low on supplies, we had to come down off the ridge into one of the valleys where the towns were, buy our food, then climb back onto the Parkway again. Sometimes it took us an hour to get down and back up. Each time we hit a grocery store we bought as much food as we could cram into our packs, usually a three-days' supply, and we stretched our provisions by keeping our food intake at a minimum. The extra weight in food, and especially climbing back up to the ridge with it, made cycling even more difficult. But after twelve days of eating a hunk of cheese and some sunflower seeds for lunch and steamed vegetables and a handful of granola for dinner, coupled with the rigorous, calorie-consuming hill climbing, I finally lost the layers of fat I'd been carrying since Idaho.

As we had hoped, the Parkway did turn out to be almost deserted, although there were plenty of deer, skunks, bears, raccoons, foxes, and owls to keep us company while we camped. We enjoyed the quiet solitude of the Appalachians, and we fully expected to follow the Parkway all the way to the Great Smoky Mountains; but the day before we pulled into Asheville, the weather turned foul. In Asheville we were told that the forecast called for three or four more days of cold rain and possibly some snow, and we decided then that it was time to turn south.

During the third week of November we shot across northwestern South Carolina and headed into Georgia. The seventy-degree days felt wonderful after two months of frosts. What didn't feel wonderful about Georgia were its people.

Almost everyone in the small towns along the Georgian backroads was disturbed by Larry and me, our bikes, and our undertaking. We were met by bewildered stares when we rode into towns, and by concerned, uneasy looks on the days when our socks and underwear were hanging from our panniers to dry. If we explained that we had ridden from California and were headed down into Florida, people looked at us as though we had taken complete leave of our senses. Why anyone would do such a "plain crazy thang" was beyond them, and we rarely told anyone about our plans to bicycle around the world for fear they might lock us up. When we walked out of a store in Georgia, the owner usually managed a strained "Ya'll come back now, hear?" but the voice conveyed anything but sincerity.

The prospect of spending Thanksgiving—which in my family always meant a big celebration with a group of close family friends—in a place where I was viewed by nearly everyone I met as a suspicious character, weighed on me as we pedaled from Royston through towns like Lexington, Crawfordville, Louisville, Midville, Swainsboro, Reidsville (west of Claxton, home of the annual rattlesnake roundup, and just north of the miles of boiled-peanut stands along Route 23), and Ludowici. By the time we came into Brunswick on November 22, Thanksgiving eve, the old, gnawing homesickness was back. We pulled into Weathering Oaks campground in Brunswick just before dark to get cleaned up for the next day, when we planned to go into a restaurant for the first time in a long while and have a turkey dinner—by ourselves.

In the office at the Weathering Oaks campground we found ourselves face to face with a two-hundred-pound, muscle-bound Samoan wedged into a short-sleeved flowered shirt and a pair of cotton shorts. His face broke into a massive smile the moment we stepped through the door. Georgia was the last place I would have expected to encounter a Samoan; but there he was, an easygoing, goodnatured, transplanted islander from the South Seas, who had only recently moved to the Deep South.

"Howdy folks! My name's Samani, but you can call me Pineapple— Apple for short. Looks like you two've come a long way on those bikes. Mind if I take a look at 'em?"

"Help yourself," I nodded.

"Where ya comin' from?"

"California."

"Hmmm. Georgia puts you a long way from home, doesn't it? Ever get homesick?"

"Sure, lots of times."

"Bet you're real homesick right now with Thanksgivin' bein' tomorrow, aren'tcha?"

"Yeah, I guess we are."

"Well, look a' here. We're havin' a big feast tomorrow, so how about you two joinin' me and my wife, Sharon, and my five kids, and some of our friends from around here for Thanksgivin' dinner. We're havin' it right here at the campground, and we'd sure like to have you if you could spare the time. I've made up a big batch of my Samoan chop suey for the occasion; but don't worry, in case you don't like chop suey, there'll be heaps of turkey, dressin', yams, fruit salads, cranberries, jello, rolls, and pumpkin pie, to go along with it."

Larry and I were quick to take Apple up on his offer. And the next day, as Apple's family and friends and Larry and I sat down to Thanksgiving dinner together, Sharon put her arm around me and giggled, "Well, I bet when you started out your trip you never figured you'd be spendin' Thanksgivin' in a campground in Georgia, eatin' chop suey with a Pineapple sayin' grace in Samoan, now did ya?"

DIVE OR DIE

When a park ranger in the Florida Keys told us that once while he was bicycling in central Florida a car pulled up alongside him and the woman driver tossed a dirty diaper in his face, we knew he was telling the truth. And we weren't surprised in the least that in southern Florida a motorist heaved a cupful of crushed ice into his eyes. After pedaling nearly the full length of Florida, Larry and I knew all about that special experience called Surviving on a Bicycle in Central and Southern Florida. And we had a few tales of our own to tell as well.

Northern Florida had been a different story. From the Georgia coast we had pedaled southwest into the Okefenokee Swamp, where we paddled a canoe next to and over alligators for a couple of days. Then we climbed back on our bikes and wound our way through the back roads of northern Florida, headed toward New Port Richey on the Gulf of Mexico, near Tampa.

The days were hot now. The temperature hung in the eighties, and the humidity was so high that our sweat turned sour, and what little clothing we wore was always sopping. As in Georgia, the traffic on the Florida back roads was sparse and the drivers were considerate. We took our time. We no longer needed to worry about winter catching up with us. And, unlike the Georgians, the people in the towns we passed through did not make us feel uncomfortable or anxious to keep moving. Each day at lunch we would pick up a newspaper and sit in a park for a couple hours reading, eating, and napping.

Larry and I were headed for New Port Richey to visit my great uncle and aunt. At eighty Uncle Clarence was still going strong. Every

November he would jump behind the wheel of his car and drive himself and Aunt Evelyn some eight hundred miles from their home in Huntington, West Virginia, to the Deep Lagoon Mobile Home Park in New Port Richey, where they spent their winters.

After his first wife died when he was in his mid-seventies, Uncle Clarence discovered that living alone was a lonely experience. To remedy the situation, he submitted a card with his name and information on his background and interests to a computer dating company.

"I'd just bought a mobile home, but I didn't have a lot picked out to put it on yet. So when Evelyn's name popped out of the computer, and we got together, and it turned out that she had a lot but no mobile home, well then, we just put one and one together and got married. That was one smart computer!"

I called Clarence and Evelyn the night before we pedaled into New Port Richey, to let them know about what time we expected to get in. The following day, when we came to within five blocks of the park, Uncle Clarence was waiting for us at the edge of Highway 19 with his two-wheeler. It had been a few years since I had seen my great uncle, but I knew the person at the corner was Clarence the moment I set eyes on him. He was standing straight as a flag pole and sported neatly pressed light-blue bermudas, a white short-sleeved knit shirt, tennis shoes, and a baseball cap.

I chuckled to myself when I spotted Clarence standing there looking as spry as ever, eager to bike along with us. Twenty years ago, when Clarence drove out to San Diego to visit my family for a summer, Dad had installed a railing beside the front steps to our house for his uncle, but Clarence, completely ignoring the railing, hit about every third step as he bounded up the stairs to greet us. And now, here was Uncle Clarence still in good enough shape to bicycle to the grocery store, the laundromat and the beach. I knew Clarence felt proud to see his great-niece pedal up after bicycling some eight thousand five hundred miles across America; but I was just as proud of my great uncle. With eight decades behind him, Clarence had a zest for life that most people lost long before their fortieth birthday.

"Hey Clarence, I'm pretty beat. How about carrying my packs for me the rest of the way?" Larry hollered.

"Oh, I think you can make it another five blocks. There aren't any steep passes between here and the park," Clarence laughed.

Sitting perfectly erect, a beaming smile on his face, he escorted us into the park. Thanks to him and Evelyn, everyone there knew all about our trip, and we were treated to an enthusiastic welcoming by some one hundred old-timers.

Larry and I stayed in New Port Richey for a week. They were seven busy days. Since most of our clothes were now near shreds, we spent one day shopping for shorts, underwear, socks, and T-shirts. The next morning we washed out our down sleeping bags and jackets by hand in the bathtub, stuffed them into a commercial dryer, and fed in dimes all afternoon. Another day, we hit the travel agencies in town. We hadn't decided yet what to do during the winter months ahead: whether to crew on a sailboat in the Caribbean, bicycle in the Yucatan, or fly right to Spain.

After we talked with the travel agencies and found out about cheap flights to both Europe and the Yucatan, we started shopping around for bicycle parts. Larry found the clusters and chains and the bottom-bracket tool we needed, but he was unable to locate a triple crank. He ended up phoning a Palo Alto bike shop in California and having them mail us the parts we needed to change our gear sets from ten to fifteen.

On the days we weren't shopping or repairing and adjusting our bikes and gear, Clarence and Evelyn took us sight-seeing. And every evening Clarence had us up talking until almost midnight. "I could listen to your stories forever," he kept saying. "And I love to watch you work on your bikes. This sure is a big treat for me!" Before we could go to bed, Clarence would haul us outside for a brisk walk five times around the park.

Almost all the people in the park lived in New England or the Midwest, and traveled to Florida to escape the harsh winter weather. Surprisingly enough, many of them came from the same small towns Larry and I had passed through or stayed in, and they were anxious to talk with us and take us under their wing. While we worked on our bicycles and put on our new fifteen-speed chain rings and crank assemblies, people constantly came by to offer us their wrenches or just to sit and watch us work.

Two nights before we left New Port Richey, Larry and I put on a slide presentation for everyone in the park. As we came across America, we mailed our film to my parents for developing and safekeeping; so when Clarence told me that the people in the park wanted to see our slides, I called my parents and asked them to send them to us. The day after our presentation, Ann Turnbull, the park's oldest resident, walked into Clarence's mobile home and handed me an envelope.

"Well, you two sure have livened up all us old folks around here," she grinned. "All anybody's been talking about today is your adventure. Yessir, thanks to you two, now we've all got a lot of invigorating and vicarious daydreams to fill our lonesome moments with. Here, I want you to take this envelope. It's got some money in it. A group of us wanted to give you a little something so that we could feel like we were helping you out a bit, like we were sharing in your trip. And it's a thank-you too for the way you've brightened up our lives, giving us all something exciting to think and talk about."

For the rest of the day people stopped by to say good-bye and wish us luck. A couple from Michigan, the Zieglers, gave me a necklace as a keepsake, and another couple brought over a Christmas card with a twenty-dollar bill slipped inside it for us to buy Christmas dinner with— wherever we might be.

Before Larry and I left the park on the morning of December 9, we spent an hour thanking everyone for all their help and kindness and gifts. It was especially hard for me to say good-bye to Clarence; when I went to hug him he put an arm around my shoulders and told me that what Larry and I were doing made him very proud and that he would never forget our week together for as long as he lived. At the exit to the park I stopped and looked back; Clarence was standing as straight as could be next to his two-wheeler, waving to us with tears in his eyes. That was the last time I would see my great uncle alive.

From New Port Richey Larry and I headed east on Route 54, to swing out around Tampa before turning south toward the Keys. The first sign that things were going to be different in central Florida came only fifteen miles outside New Port Richey. A middle-aged woman in a gigantic gas guzzler pulled up directly behind us, revved her engine, and blasted her horn. The car sounded as if it was just about to barrel over the top of us, so we both turned off the pavement. There was no shoulder, and when our tires buried themselves in the sand at the edge of the asphalt, the bikes slammed to an abrupt halt, sending us soaring over our handlebars. As I landed with a thud in the sand in front of my bike, I looked up to see the woman slowly edging by me. She had a boy, seven or eight years old, with her, and she was pointing at us so he could appreciate what she had done. The two of them burst into laughter. When Larry and I jumped up and started for the car, the woman hit the accelerator and sped away, still laughing.

"Now that's one weird lady. Hope there aren't any more like her around," I shrugged. Had I only known.

For the rest of that day and all the next, the traffic was heavy, even though, according to our maps, we were traveling on back roads. We followed Route 54 as far as Zephyrhills, then took Route 39 south. There were no shoulders on either route, and no one made any effort to move over when they passed us. This was the first time on our trip that cars whizzed by us without giving an inch, and we made sure never to wander from the thin strip of pavement between the sides of the cars and the tire-jolting sand.

On our second day out of New Port Richey, part way down Route 39, somewhere north of a handful of buildings called Fort Lonesome, we stopped to buy food for dinner at a small grocery store. The heavyset woman behind the counter looked up at us curiously when we walked through the front door of her store.

"Don't see many folks travelin' like you 'round here. Where you folks from?" she asked.

"California," I answered.

"California! You from California?"

"Yes."

"Hell's Angels. That's all they got in California, Hell's Angels. You two Hell's Angels?" The woman glanced nervously outside at our bikes.

"No," I said. "Actually not everybody in California's a Hell's Angel. There aren't really all that many around, especially outside of the Oakland area."

"Now that's gotta be a lie!" the woman shot back. "My neighbor went to California once, and she told me them motorcycle types was everywhere, and they's lots of 'em!"

"Well, you see, it doesn't automatically follow that a person who rides a motorcycle in California is a Hell's Angel. There are—"

"Well it does 'round here!" she cut me off. "You bet it does. We hate motorcycles. 'Round here, our men like to take potshots at any motor-cyclers that come through these parts."

The woman paused for a moment and eyed our bikes again. She was a short person, in her forties, and she had tucked her rotund body into a printed house dress. Her dark hair was cropped short.

"We're riding bicycles, not motorcycles," Larry reassured her.

"Well, I don't know. The men might take a shot at you folks, too. That's a pretty strange setup you got out there."

While the woman went on scrutinzing our bikes and gear, Larry and I were both thinking the same thing. Why hadn't someone warned us? We had heard a lot of stories about the rednecks in Texas, Alabama, and Mississippi taking a dim view of bicyclers. One cycler told us that while he was pedaling through Texas a rancher driving by in his pickup shot a few holes into his rear panniers. But no one had ever mentioned Florida.

After a brief silence, the woman began talking again.

"Say, why would a lady wantta go an' bicycle all the way from California to Florida anyway? Normal women don't do things like that. You makin' her do it?" she glared at Larry.

"No way! This was all her idea," Larry chuckled before I had time to open my mouth.

"Now there you go tellin' lies again. I kin tell by lookin' at her it weren't her idea. The poor thing; she's too skinny to be pedalin' a big, heavy bicycle like she's got out there. You're makin' her do it, and you should be 'shamed o' yourself! All I gotta say is, you folks better take real good care of yourselves 'round here. 'Member what I telled ya! We don't like no motorcycle sorts."

On that note Larry and I exited the store and took off down Route 39 again, clinging to our narrow line of asphalt while the trucks, pickups, and cars scraped past us. By late afternoon, about the time we were ready to quit pedaling, we found ourselves surrounded by swamps, barbed-wire fences, and NO TRESPASSING signs, which ruled out any chance of free-camping for the night. Neither of us had any desire to hop a fence in central Florida and pitch our tent. We knew that if the alligators didn't get us, some angry rancher would fill us full of bullet holes. We kept on pedaling, hoping we might come to a dry, unfenced area.

It was nearly dark by the time we turned onto Route 62 and rolled into the speck on our maps labeled Duette. Duette, Florida, consisted of two buildings—a one-room schoolhouse with a NO TRESPASSING sign posted at the end of the school yard, and the Dry Prairie Baptist Church. Directly behind the church stretched a huge expanse of lawn, a perfect spot to put our tent.

It was Sunday evening, and according to the sign on the front of the church, services would begin at eight o'clock. Once before on our journey, we had asked permission to pitch our tent on church grounds—at the Episcopal Church in the village of Oxford, Connecticut. The church members not only offered to have us stay the night in their homes but fed us dinner and breakfast and packed a lunch for us to take with us when we left the following morning.

Larry and I cooked and ate our dinner, then sat on the steps of the Dry Prairie Church waiting for the members to begin arriving. The first person to appear was the Reverend Max Durance, a flawless stereotype of a southern preacher. He was a stocky man, his belly hung over his belt, and he spoke with a southern drawl. His right hand held a Bible, thick and black, while his eyes penetrated us with a disapproving squint. Larry did the talking.

"Hello, my name is Larry Savage and this is my wife, Barbara."

I smiled and nodded to the reverend. He glanced my way suspiciously for a moment, then turned his eyes back to Larry.

"We've bicycled here from the West Coast and we're on our way to the Keys."

Good idea, I thought. Don't mention California; not to this guy, anyway.

"We camp out every night in our tent, and we were wondering if we could pitch it tonight somewhere around here where it's dry."

The reverend was slow to respond, and the harsh expression that had settled over his face when he first spotted us never faded.

"So ya'll need a place to camp do ya? Well, thar's no place 'round here with facilities," he said, finally.

I eyed what was obviously a restroom connected to the church building, but the reverend kept his gaze focused on Larry.

"But if ya'll just want some place to pitch yer tent fer the night, thar's a dry patch o' land with some trees on it 'bout three quarters o' mile on the right up that road, over thar 'cross the highway."

The reverend paused here for a moment as a smile crept onto his face.

"A lotta people drive thar trucks 'round that patch o' land at night, so ya'll might have to put up with some noise and some headlights shinin' in yer tent, but I don't 'magine ya'll will be bothered much more'n that. If somebody wants to know what the heck yer doin' thar, ya'll just tell 'em Max Durance gave ya'll permission to camp thar. Ya see, I own all the land 'round here. I lease it out, so everybody 'round here knows the name Max Durance all right."

I looked across Route 62 and tried to make out the road he was talking about, but by now it was too dark to see that far. There was a big, winning grin on the reverend's face now as he watched us stare across the asphalt into the darkness, and I sensed that we were in for it. Larry managed to smile back at the man and utter a polite "thank you very much."

The churchgoers and their leader stood by watching in silence as we grabbed up our bikes and pedaled across the street. A few yards down Route 62 we came to the road, but when we turned onto it our tires sunk. The reverend had sent us into the sand. For nearly a mile we carried and pulled our bikes through the sand, keeping our eyes on the fence that stretched along the right-hand side of the road. We were searching for the break in the barbed wire that Reverend Durance assured us was there, and through which we could push our bikes and follow the trail to the camping spot. We plodded through the sand for forty minutes until we were forced to admit that what we suspected from the moment we left the church was true: the reverend had sent us on a wild-goose chase.

There was nothing to do but drag our bikes back to Duette. Part way back, a truck sped by spraying us with sand. The driver didn't stop or slow down to find out why a couple of bicyclers with heavy panniers would be carrying their bikes down a sand road at night in the middle of nowhere in Florida, and I was sure he couldn't have cared less.

When we got back to Duette, we could hear the people singing inside the church. We pitched our tent behind a tree next to the school-house. The darkness and the bushes hid us from the church members, who climbed into their cars and trucks after the service and headed home. In the morning we hurried to have our tent down and our bikes loaded up before daylight; then we strolled over to the picnic tables behind the church and cooked breakfast. While we were eating, a man pulled up in his pickup. He jumped out of the cab and walked directly toward us.

"Mornin', he smiled.

"Hello," I smiled back.

"Where ya'll from and where ya'll goin'?"

"California and the Keys."

After that, nobody said anything for a few moments. The man stared at Larry and me, then looked down at his feet and back up again.

"Well say, where did ya'll spend the night last night?" he asked. His eyes were scanning the lawn behind the church building, but there was no sign of a tent having been pitched anywhere.

"Up that road over there, right where the reverend told us to. You know, that dry patch with the trees three-quarters of a mile up," I answered as innocently as he had asked.

"Oh."

The man looked back down at his feet. He moved away from us and checked inside the church and the small hall alongside it. When he finished, he climbed back into his truck, and as he drove away, he shouted, "Ya'll have a good day now, hear?"

Larry and I packed up and took off for Fort Myers, eighty-nine miles away. From Duette we continued east on Route 62, then turned south through Wauchula and Arcadia, following Highway 17 and Route 31. The drivers on 17 and 31, which were not main highways but were heavily traveled, proved to be a special breed. We both fully expected to be killed. The basic philosophy these drivers adhered to was simple enough: all roads are constructed solely for motorized vehicles; therefore, bicyclers have absolutely no right to use them. When the drivers on 17 and 31 spotted us up ahead pedaling along the edge of their lane, the overwhelming majority of them responded in one of three ways. They either rode behind us and honked for what seemed like an eternity before roaring by as close as possible; or they pulled alongside us and filled the air with raging obscenities; or they opted for the silent, direct approach and tried to hit us. With this last group there was never any warning. They never honked or shouted; they simply plowed straight for us. Luckily, we always heard their engines and dove off the road just before they ran us over. Upset that they had missed their opportunity, the drivers would shake their fists or give us the finger as they barreled past.

Although we turned onto Route 31 to get away from the deadly motorists on Highway 17, Route 31 proved to be a thirty-seven-mile commercial truck route, which made the highway tolerable by comparison. A few of the route's truck drivers, who swept past us in rapid succession, pulled slightly to the left as they came by, but the majority did not, even when there was no oncoming traffic.

Unfortunately, there was not enough room in the one southbound lane for a semi and our bikes, so we were quick to devise survival tactics. Larry stayed directly behind me and yelled out what he thought we should do every time he saw a vehicle coming up on us. Pedaling in front, I watched for potholes and rocks in the road and listened for Larry's commands. Each time I heard a truck behind us, my stomach knotted up; I tightened my grasp on my handlebars and prayed that Larry wouldn't misjudge the driver.

If the truck appeared to be pulling over the left to pass us Larry would yell at me to stay on the road, in which case we'd both squeeze over as close as possible to the edge of the pavement and hope for the best. If, on the other hand, the truck kept right on target, he'd scream, "Dive!" And depending on how close it was to the time of impact, he'd follow the "Dive!" with either a "Now!" or a "You've got time." "Dive! Now!" meant I should turn my bike into the sand immediately, while "Dive! You've got time" told me that I could brake first, then turn. If we had enough time to brake, we could usually keep our balance when we hit the sand, and often we'd manage to wobble back onto the road before the sand slowed us to a standstill. But the times we dove into the dirt at full speed we were inevitably transformed into airborne projectiles.

Sometimes Larry read a driver's intentions wrong. He would look back and see a truck moving over to pass and tell me to hold steady. But when he glanced back a second time and saw that the truck had pulled back in behind us and that we were about to become one with the vehicle's undercarriage, he'd scream "Dive! Now!" in such a hysterical tone that I'd leap sideways off my bike even before it hit the sand.

At the end of the day, when we came into Fort Myers after sixty miles of dodging cars and trucks and listening to an almost constant spew of obscenities, it took us a full hour before we could bring our nerves under control and stop our bodies from shaking. That night both of us had nightmares about being run over by trucks. The next day there was more of the same; more shouting, honking, screaming engines, near misses, and crash landings in the sand as we battled our way south toward the Everglades on Highway 41. At one point we had to jump into the sand five times in a half hour.

It wasn't until the following day, our fourth day out of New Port Richey, that our frayed nerves were given a reprieve. We entered the Everglades, the traffic diminished to a trickle, and the motorists permitted us to coexist with them. For the first time since New Port Richey we were able to take our eyes off the road and the traffic and be aware of our natural surrounding. We spent our time watching the herons, sandhill cranes, egrets, water turkeys, buzzards, hawks, eagles, and alligators in the swamps lining the road. Because they couldn't hear us coming we could often get within a few feet of them before they were startled away.

At the end of our first day in the Everglades, we pulled into Monroe Station, one of the only two settlements in the swamps along Highway 41. Monroe Station was a small dry patch of land that held a cafe and a gathering of about twenty Seminole Indians. I asked in the cafe if there was some place we could pitch our tent for the night, and the waitress directed us to a forestry station a quarter mile into the swamp along a dirt road a foot above the murky water, alligators, and water mocassins.

There was no one at the station, but we could hear voices coming from the other side of the fence next door, which had a sign EVERGLADES CONSERVATION SPORTSMAN'S CLUB. Larry knocked on the front gate of the club and asked the man who opened it if it would be all right for us to camp at the station.

"Sure. But look, there's no reason for you two to camp over there when you can set yourselves up inside here," the man smiled. "You'll probably be wantin' a shower after cyclin' all day in this heat, and that's somethin' we've got and the station doesn't. Oh say, I haven't introduced myself. My name's Butch, Butch Dempsey, and this is my wife, Ally. We're the caretakers here at the club. Come on in and pitch your tent over there on the grass next to the house. After you get your tent up, we'll get you something cold to drink and give you a tour of the place."

Butch shrugged off our thank-yous as he led us to the spot he thought would be the best place for our tent. Both he and Ally looked to be in their early thirties; they were dressed in jeans and work shirts.

"Now there's one thing you've got to be sure and do 'round here, and that's keep an eye out for snakes, 'specially in the grass," Butch warned us. "You've probably already been hearin' a lot about the eight-foot diamondbacks down in the Keys, and about the pigmy rattlers, and the massasaugas, the copperheads, and the coral snakes. But to tell you the truth, there are only four types of snakes you've got to watch out for here in Florida, so that should make it pretty simple."

"Four, huh. What are they?" I asked.

"The big ones, little ones, live ones, and dead ones!" Butch's laugh was deep and infectious.

"Actually, I *am* serious about watchin' out for snakes. Don't go walkin' 'round outside your tent after dark without a big flashlight. And there's somethin' else I should warn you 'bout—the panther. She comes by sometimes in the middle of the night and lets out a real shrill scream. The scream'll scare the hell out of you; but don't worry, our German Shepherd'll frighten her off."

Before it got dark, Butch and Ally showed us around the club. There was a meeting hall, a camping and barbecue area, and a swamp-buggy corral.

"The club members go out huntin' wild boar in these buggies, and sometimes they break down out there in the swamp," Butch explained. "The buggies all have radios on 'em, so the folks'll call me, and I'll go out and get 'em. One time though, I took a group out in one of these buggies and we broke down and I couldn't get anybody to answer my call. So me and another guy had to wade back here to get another buggy. None of the snakes or 'gators bothered us the whole way back; so we did all right."

At seven the next morning, Ally stuck her face up against one of our tent windows.

"Hey you two," she whispered, "how about joinin' us for breakfast this mornin'? It's just about fixed, and I've made gobs of food, so I hope you'll come and help us finish it off."

Larry and I nearly trampled each other trying to be the first one into the house.

Butch was sitting at the kitchen table listening for distress calls on his radio, and in front of him rested heaping platefuls of baking-powder biscuits, grits, fried eggs, bacon, and some just-out-of-the-oven banana nut bread. While Larry and I inhaled the food that Ally kept loading on our plates, she and Butch told us about the Seminole Indians who lived back in the swamps; about how that was the one Indian tribe that had yet to sign a treaty with the U.S. Government, and about how some Seminoles had never once ventured outside of their particular section of the Everglades.

After breakfast, Ally slipped a paper bag with a loaf of banana nut bread and a batch of biscuits into our packs, then she handed us "your Christmas present from me and Butch"—a box of homemade sugar cookies wrapped in Christmas paper.

On December 15, Larry and I rode out of the Everglades and into the Keys. We were headed for Key West, at the end of the one-hundred-sixteen-mile-long string of keys and bridges, to see about crewing on a sailboat into the Caribbean.

As soon as we hit the first key, the mood of the drivers turned ugly again. We tried cycling on the bike path, which ran along the opposite side of the road, but found it so littered with rocks, sand, potholes, curbs, broken bottles, and parked cars, that it proved even more dangerous to bicycle on than the road itself. Since we only had four miles to go to the state campground on Key Largo, we decided to pull back onto the road. A half mile before the campground entrance, a Florida couple in a big, flashy van slowed alongside Larry and motioned for him to pull over.

"Hey buddy!" the driver shouted as Larry eased to a stop at the edge of the pavement. The fellow was wearing a John Deere cap, a cowboy shirt, and seemed to be about our age. "There's a bike path over there you're supposed to be usin'. My hard-earned tax dollars went to buildin' that thing to keep you people off the roads, so you goddamned better use it!"

To my amazement, Larry, who usually lost his temper in situations like this, remained calm. He politely explained that we had already attempted to bicycle on the path, but that it was too hazardous; that we had to keep getting off and walking our bikes over the curbs, and that cars kept pulling out of the driveways in front of us.

"We got back on the road because we were going too slow, dodging all the obstacles in the bike path, and we wanted to get to the campground up here as soon as possible to be sure and get a campsite before they all filled up this morning," Larry explained.

"Say, where you two from?" the man demanded to know, ignoring Larry's explanations.

"California."

"Well us folks here in Florida hate people who obstruct traffic. You understand what I'm sayin'? Roads here in Florida are for cars and trucks; so if you want to ride your bikes on a road, then get the hell out of this state! Go on back to California! You bikers aren't welcome here, acting like you own the place!"

"That's right!" his wife chimed in. "If ya won't ride in a bike path that we went and spent thousands of dollars buildin' for ya, then ya never shouldda come to Florida! So get outta here!"

Before Larry had time to respond, the man gunned his motor and roared off.

The campground at Key Largo was crowded and noisy, and we left the next day for Long Key, thirty miles up the road. Because it was a Sunday, there were no commercial trucks on the road, and the car traffic was light, so the ride went smoothly.

The state park at Long Key was a secluded and peaceful place. Our site sat right on the water's edge and was shaded all day by a cluster of tall pine trees. We spent three days at Long Key, resting, reading, swimming in the clear turquoise water, and watching the giant herons wade near our tent.

It was a weekday when we left Long Key for Key West. As we rode through the gate at the exit of the campground, a park ranger stopped to talk with us.

"Where you going?" he asked.

"Key West."

"That's a tough ride," he grimaced, shaking his head. "Narrow, two-lane bridges the whole way and lots of traffic. I did it once, but I'd never do it again. The seven-mile bridge up there past Marathon is a nightmare. It's real narrow, and the only time I cycled it I found out real quick that there really isn't enough room for two cars and a bicycle side by side to each other on it. The first time I was alongside two cars passing each other, I almost got myself squished into the railing and bumped into the Gulf. After that, I rode smack in the middle of the lane so that the cars could pass me only when there wasn't any oncoming traffic.

"No, I'd advise you to skip bicycling to Key West. It's too dangerous. People don't just get hurt doing it, they get killed. There's been some cyclers hit recently. Personally, I won't bicycle anywhere in southern or central Florida anymore. I used to do it, but I've had too many bad experiences. The way I figure it, the people in central and southern Florida make up the largest collection of bicycle haters to be found anywhere on the face of the earth. If you want to bike in Florida, stick to the north. I do."

Unfortunately, Larry and I were too stubborn to heed the ranger's advice, and we took off for Key West anyway. For the first thirty-seven of the sixty-eight miles between Long Key and the end of the road, the drivers were relatively considerate, and no one yelled at us for not cycling on the bike paths that sprang up on some of the larger keys. It was a beautiful ride. We hopped along tiny keys thick with low green mangroves and edged by white sandy beaches. The bridges between the keys were built so low to the water that we felt we were pedaling on the surface of the Gulf itself, and we could watch the fish swimming over the Gulf floor. We even managed to cross the seven-mile bridge without a mishap by following the ranger's advice and pedaling down the center of our lane. It wasn't until after Big Pine Key that the trouble began.

Once we passed Big Pine, the bridges grew shorter, but all of a sudden everyone was in a big hurry to get to wherever it was they were going, and no one had the time or patience to put up with a couple of bicyclers on the road. Instead of waiting behind us until it was safe to pull around, drivers tried to squeeze by, forcing us against the railings. And then came the dump trucks.

There was some construction going on in the last twenty-five miles before Key West, and the dump trucks that barreled up and down the road waited for no one. For the first half hour we pedaled among them we managed to hold our own. Then, on one of the bridges, two of them bore down on us from the rear, one behind the other, while a big RV approached from the opposite direction. The driver of the first dump truck, figuring he had enough time to get by Larry and me before the Winnebago came by, pulled out into the oncoming lane to pass us. Unfortunately, he calculated wrong, and just as he passed Larry and was coming alongside me, he realized that he either had to move back into his own lane right then or collide head-on with the mammoth RV.

As he came up beside me I was watching the Winnebago, but I knew what he was about to do. The rumbling of the two dump trucks, one beside me and one behind us, was deafening. I felt my knees and feet start to go weak, then they began shaking so much I could hardly push my pedals. I sucked in a deep breath, but I didn't have to wait long. Almost as soon as I first glimpsed it out of the corner of my left eye, the dump truck turned into me. I hit my brakes and watched in horror as eight tons of steel dove into the space I would have been occupying had I not thrown a hard, solid grasp onto my brake levers. I was almost slowed to a stop when I heard Larry scream behind me.

"Go!" he shrieked. "Move!"

I tried to resume pedaling, but my trembling legs refused to cooperate.

"Move now! Move! The truck won't stop!"

I hadn't been thinking about the dump truck still behind us.

I summoned all my willpower and started pounding my pedals. Larry kept screaming hysterically for me to pedal harder, and I forced my legs to move faster than they ever had before. I powered myself to the end of the bridge, threw my handlebars to the right, and swerved off the road. Larry followed me. When our bikes hit the sand, we shot over our handlebars, an occurrence which had become quite common for us in Florida. I could feel my heartbeat in my ears as the dump truck screeched by.

"Damn, Barb!" Larry hollered. "Don't ever hit your brakes when you're on a bridge and there's a dump truck behind us! When you slammed to a stop back there, that truck just about came right over the top of us. I swear it would have flattened us for sure if you hadn't started pedaling right when you did and as fast as you did. These dump-truck drivers are absolute maniacs! They'd plow us over and never think a thing about it. This is insane!"

"But I had to brake!" I yelled back. "The truck next to me would have hit me if I didn't. What was I supposed to do?"

Larry shook his head in frustration, and we gathered up our handlebar packs, which had been jarred loose during the fall, attached them to our bikes, and rolled back out onto the road. My legs were shaking again, and it was a few miles before I could start to pick up my speed.

On a bridge eight miles outside of Key West, after another half hour of dodging dump trucks, a van coming toward us pulled out to pass the car in front of it. Once again I was pedaling in front, and once again I was faced with the choice of braking or being hit. As the front end of the van proceeded to fill up my entire field of vision, I squeezed my brake levers. This time there wasn't a truck behind us, and the van swerved back into its own lane, missing me by no more than a foot as it sliced past my handlebars at fifty miles per hour. Larry shook his fist at the driver.

Another mile down the road a car sideswiped Larry's left rear pannier, bumping him off the road and into a boulder. The stone's jagged edges gashed his right arm and thigh and flattened his bicycle pump. When he stood up, the right side of his body was covered with blood, and I could sense the anger and frustration streaming through his veins. Just as he commenced to unleash a torrent of curses at the passing traffic, the van that had nearly hit us head-on on the last bridge pulled off the road next to us, and out jumped its driver—who had turned around and driven back looking for us.

"Hey, I'm the guy you shook your fist at on the last bridge back down the road," he shouted. "What did you do that for? I didn't do anything to you!"

I guessed the man to be in his fifties; his shiny new van had Michigan plates. Just great, I thought; now even the tourists are screaming at us. The man explained that he was a sociology professor from Michigan, that he was taking a vacation in Florida, and that he didn't like people to shake their fists at him.

"Oh, so *you're* the idiot who nearly killed us back there!" Larry shot back. "Haven't you noticed the NO PASSING signs at the front of all the bridges?"

"Hey, don't you raise your voice at me! I had plenty of time to pass that car and get back into my own lane before I got to you two. I ought to know. I'm a safe driver. I knew what I was doing. I had plenty of time!"

"You did not!" I shouted back. "If I hadn't braked, you would have hit us. You misjudged our speed and our position. Hell, you nearly hit us even after we'd stopped!"

"You don't know what you're talking about! I had plenty of time. And look, don't go telling *me* how to drive. You bicyclers are so egotistical, you expect all the cars and trucks on the road to bow to you. Well, roads are for cars. Cars have the right-of-way at all times, and you bikers should get off the road whenever us drivers need the room. It makes me furious when you don't pull off and let us by. Hell, if it weren't for cars, there wouldn't be any roads for you to pedal on!"

"So what did you want us to do back there? Get off the bridge? Which means jump into the ocean, so you could pass illegally without bothering about us!" Larry hollered into the man's face. But no sooner had these words left Larry's lips, than the man threw his fist into the side of Larry's head and sent him reeling back onto the ground next to his crashed bicycle.

What happened next surprised all three of us, because none of us had noticed the other van pull up. The driver had seen Larry get bumped off the road, pulled over, and stood off to one side listening to the three of us argue. But when the man punched Larry, Susan, who had long blond hair, flashing dark eyes, and about my build, grabbed the man from behind, around the neck, and shouted, "If you want a fight, you'll have to fight me too!" Then she tightened her solid grip on his neck. As his face started to turn a deep red, he motioned that he wouldn't swing any more punches. Susan released her hold, glared at him, then turned to us.

"I moved to Florida—here to the Keys—two weeks ago, and the first and only time I tried to ride my bicycle here I couldn't believe the mentality of the drivers. It was disgusting. They'd come at me like I wasn't even there. I've only been here two weeks, and I've already seen a person run over and kill a small child. That guy could have missed the little girl easily enough, but he didn't really try to. He probably thought he had enough time to get around her, just like this guy here thought he could get around you two. You know, this place makes me sick, the way people drive with a total disregard for human lives."

Larry stood up and stepped toward the man, who by now had decided that it was time to do some fast talking. Words started popping out of his mouth like ammunition out of a machine gun.

"Now let me explain this," he sputtered. "I'm a fifty-three-year-old sociology professor from Michigan, and I don't want to make anybody unhappy. I'm an intelligent, conscientious person. I'm also a very safe driver, and I'll tell you again, I am positive I had enough time to pass that car without hitting you two. I can see why you're upset about the drivers in Florida. I agree they're terrible here in the Keys. But the reckless ones are all young kids on dope. That's who's running you off the road, not people like me."

"Oh, so now you're trying to tell us that all those commercial truck drivers and middle-aged, so-called rednecks in their pickups, vans, and cars who have been running us off the roads and yelling at us all the way through central and southern Florida, and the dump-truck drivers here in the Keys, are really a bunch of teen-aged dope addicts in disguise," Larry commented sarcastically.

The man chose to ignore Larry's statement and instead went on to advise us on how to ride a bicycle safely.

"You probably haven't bicycled much, and that's why you're so nervous," he said. "So I'll give you a few tips. I don't do any bicycling myself, because I don't have the free time and I don't have the money to buy nice bikes and gear like you two have, but I can still make a few suggestions:

like, don't bicycle at night, pull off the road for cars, and watch out for kids who smoke dope and drive. That'll make your ride safer and more enjoyable. I just want you to be happy and not yell and shake your fists at people like me."

I could hardly believe what I was hearing. But just before I started to feed the man an earful of insults, a sheriff's car pulled up, and I decided to keep quiet.

"What's the problem here?" the deputy called from inside his car. "The folks at the gas station over there called and said there was some fightin' goin' on here."

The professor shook his head and Larry and I remained silent. Both Larry and I figured that the chances of a southern deputy siding with a couple of transient bicyclers against an upstanding citizen and prospective contributor to the state's all-important tourist industry sat well below the zero mark.

"Well, if there ain't no problem, then I've got myself plenty of work to do someplace else," the deputy growled as he drove away.

The professor jumped into his van and disappeared almost as quickly, and Susan sat down and talked with us while I washed the blood off Larry's arms and legs.

After Susan left, Larry and I pulled our bikes back out to the road and braced ourselves for the last eight miles of the day. And as I rolled out onto the pavement, I promised myself that if we did make it to Key West, these final eight miles would also be the very last I'd ever pedal in Florida. There was absolutely no way I would bicycle back through the Keys. If we couldn't find a boat to crew on out of Key West, I planned to catch a Greyhound bus to Miami.

The eight miles melted into a blur of noise and near misses, and by the time we pedaled into the campground at Key West and collapsed, my body and soul felt like a quivering lump of jello. Fright, anger, physical and mental fatigue, and the heat and humidity had taken their toll, and it seemed as if Florida had won the duel. She had beaten Larry and me into submission—we would never again bicycle on her roads. And yet at the same time there was a subtle sense of victory in knowing that we had survived the horrible ordeal of bicycling the full length of Florida; a "Ha! You didn't get us after all" feeling.

In the morning we made the rounds of the marinas in Key West, but everyone we talked with had the same advice: "Try in Miami and Fort Lauderdale. That's where people pick up their crews." So we went back to the campground and packed up our gear. Rather than going to all the trouble of disassembling our bikes and putting them into cardboard bike boxes for shipment on the Greyhound bus, we decided to hitchhike into

Miami. At one o'clock we picked out a spot at the edge of Key West and threw out our thumbs. Considering the low opinion the people in the Keys had of bicyclers, we knew we would have a tough time getting a ride.

When five thirty rolled around we were still standing with our bikes. Only two pickups had offered us rides, but neither of them was headed off the Keys. It was five forty-five when the third pickup stopped.

"You two hitchhiking with those bikes?" the young driver asked. He introduced himself as Ted.

"Sure are. How far you headed?"

"Massachusetts. I'm going up there to spend Christmas with my family."

"Are you picking up the Interstate in Miami?"

"Yep."

"That's where we're headed, Miami."

"Fine, throw yourselves and your bikes in the back, and I'll have you there in a few hours."

At Long Key, Larry and I had met a young nurse, Joani Auerbach, who offered to have us stay with her in Coral Gables. Ted was kind enough to wait for us to call her before we left Key West, and to drop us off almost at her doorstep.

The next day, December 22, Joani drove us around the marinas in Miami, but we found most of the boat owners hesitant to take on crew members they didn't know.

"The piracies have made things pretty tight around here," one owner explained. "People have been hiring themselves on as crew, and then after they get out to sea they kill the owner and seize the boat to use for running drugs up from South America. But you'll get taken on eventually. It's just a matter of being in the right place at the right time—being there when someone needs a couple extra hands. It might take you a couple of weeks, though, before you make a connection. And I'd go up to Fort Lauderdale. You'll probably have better luck up there."

The idea of hanging around Fort Lauderdale for a few weeks didn't set well with Larry or me. We were anxious to get out of Florida, and when Larry suggested that we forget scouring the marinas and start checking into flights to Spain, I quickly agreed. I was looking forward to seeing our Spanish friends in Barcelona.

Back at Joani's that afternoon, I made some phone calls and determined that the cheapest way to Spain was to fly to the Bahamas, pick up Air Bahamas to Luxembourg, then take the train to Barcelona. The whole package would run about five hundred and eighty dollars for the two of us, and I made reservations on Air Bahamas for the night of the twenty-sixth.

It felt wonderful to know that we were finally about to get out of Florida.

HOT COALS & BRANDY

◆ CHAPTER NINE ◆

After our gear had rolled onto the baggage conveyor belt at the Luxembourg airport, we waited forty-five minutes before our bicycles appeared. It wasn't until long after our fellow passengers had claimed their luggage that the double doors leading to the back baggage room flew open and a pair of burly baggage handlers stepped out and heaved two bike boxes across the baggage area. The cumbersome cardboard containers sailed through the air for fifteen feet, smashed into a railing at one end of the room, bounced onto the floor, and skidded along the wall toward the stairs leading to the lobby on the floor below. Larry and I leaped across the conveyor belt and grabbed the boxes just before they took the plunge.

We wrestled open the containers and looked over the bikes to see what damage they had sustained during the flight and their airborne hand-delivery into the baggage area. There were a few scrapes on the frames but nothing major. We reattached our pedals and front wheels, raised our seats and turned our handlebars, loaded on our gear, and rolled our bikes outside.

After the heat and humidity of Florida, the bitter cold that met us at the door of the terminal felt like the North Pole. We pulled on our sweats and down jackets before pedaling into the city. Three hours later we began our twenty-one-hour train ride, which included three train changes, to Spain. Our gear stayed with us the whole way, but the bikes traveled unboxed on a separate baggage train.

By the time we reached Barcelona, after a transatlantic plane flight and an all-day and all-night train ride, we felt like zombies. I staggered into the baggage office at the station and presented our claim stubs to the

101

officials.

"*Bicicletas?*" No here. *Mañana, mañana,*" the clerk shouted at me as he waved me away.

When we checked back the next day, our bikes still hadn't arrived, and our hearts sunk.

"They should have been here by now," said Larry. "Looks like they're either lost or maybe someone stole them."

We checked again the next day, and again it was "*Mañana, mañana.*" But on the fourth day, the baggage guard's face broke into a wide grin when he saw us come through the door. He hurried into the back room and returned with our trusty companions. They'd survived their journey from Luxembourg without a scratch.

Our first two weeks in Spain were spent with Dolly, the young woman I had become close friends with while she and I worked together at a Barcelona importing firm for nine months in 1974. She now lived in a Barcelona apartment with her husband, Santy, and their two-year-old daughter, Alicia. For fourteen days Dolly stuffed us full of her rich Spanish cooking—paella, lentil stews, chicken in tomato, prune, and honey sauce with pine nuts, and stewed artichokes with sausage—and liters of wine and gobs of Spanish brandy. Santy and Dolly had a lot to tell us. Now that Franco had died, there was freedom of speech in Spain, and everyone talked nonstop about politics, the civil war, and the Catholic Church, subjects about which many Spaniards hadn't been able to speak truthfully for decades. The four of us talked and joked together for hours on end, went sightseeing, and visited with Dolly's and Santy's endless stream of relatives.

It was great to be with our friends again, but by the end of our second week in Barcelona Larry and I were anxious to escape the big city. After seven months of living in the out-of-doors, breathing plenty of fresh air, and getting lots of exercise, staying in a crowded city of three million felt suffocating. There was too much congestion, pollution, and noise in Barcelona. The streets were so clogged with traffic and smog that we couldn't do any serious cycling or running to keep in shape. And the change in our diet from simple to rich foods and large quantities of alcohol coupled with a lack of exercise kept us feeling nauseated. We knew it was time to pack up our bikes and head out to the countryside.

It rained the morning we left Barcelona. Dolly and Santy tried to convince us to wait and leave another day, but we assured them that we had plenty of experience cycling in the wet. And besides, we yearned to be on our way. Our only concern as we pedaled out of the city was the

Spanish drivers. I prayed that they would in no way resemble Floridians. Negotiating Spain's single-lane back roads full of potholes and rocks would be tough enough; we didn't need maniac drivers to make things worse.

Even with the rain, it felt great to be outdoors and pedaling, to get away from the crowds, breathe the fresh air, and feel our muscles working again. We headed north along the Mediterranean coast toward Cadaqués, a tiny unspoiled fishing village two hundred miles north of Barcelona, where we planned to spend the next month or so waiting out the remainder of the cold winter weather. The narrow coastal roads between Barcelona and Cadaqués were steep and winding, and we made good use of our extra gears, which took the knee-wrenching strain out of climbing and allowed us to relax and enjoy our spectacular surroundings. The rocky coastal mountains were spotted with pines. Herds of goats wandered across the road. Sandy beaches curled up at the foot of the sheer cliffs, and the turquoise and deep-blue waters of the Mediterranean were sprinkled with fishing boats.

There was very little traffic on the roads. The deluge of tourists from central and northern Europe wouldn't begin to arrive for another three or four months, and the commercial traffic kept to the inland *autopistas*. The occasional trucks and cars that did pass us only added to our already high spirits. The drivers never honked impatiently or tried to squeeze past when they approached us from the rear. Instead, just like the folks in Washington, they slowed down, shifted into their lower gears, and crept along behind us through the twists and turns until it was perfectly safe to pass. When they eased by, they always waved hysterically and called out words of encouragement.

The drivers weren't the only people who shouted and waved to us In Cataluna, the northeastern section of Spain. Whenever the Catalan farmers or villagers spotted us pedaling up the road, they stopped their work and yelled: *Estupendo! Fabuloso! Qué coraje!* or *Vaya con Dios.* I rode in my black cycling shorts, but no one seemed offended by my exposed legs. Everyone was too excited about meeting the two foreigners touring Spain on bicycles to pay any attention to what I was wearing.

We took our time getting to Cadaqués, stopping at most of the beaches and pueblos along the way and talking with the people we met. At lunchtime each day we would pull into a town or village and head straight for its open-air marketplace to buy oranges, tomatoes, and cheese, then hit the bakery for a loaf of crusty white bread, and one of the dozen tiny grocery shops for yogurt.

The marketplaces were always jammed with women, dressed in dark sweaters and skirts, who pushed and squeezed their way from one vegetable, fruit, meat, poultry, or cheese stand to the next, in search of the day's best bargains. Each woman pulled her own shopping cart, a nylon rectangular basket on wheels. The women bargained and gossiped and discussed the morning's local news at each stand, which made shopping a time-consuming process. Many of the women, trailed by their *niños*, spent an hour or more every day shopping at the marketplace and the stores around town.

When Larry and I pulled into a marketplace, scores of women closed in around us to see what it was that foreigners liked to eat. The Spaniards were proud of their fruits and cheeses, and it always pleased them that we asked for Valencia oranges and goat cheese. And when they discovered that we could speak Spanish, they quickly set to work digging out of us all they wanted to know. The women standing closest to us did the asking, and our answers were passed along to those at the back of the crowd. Within a matter of minutes, every human in the marketplace knew where we were from, where we were going, how old we were, and what our marital status was. The women invariably asked if we had any children, and my response made them frown and shake their heads.

"No children? What a shame," they would all mutter. Then someone would pat me on the arm and tell me not to worry, there was still time; the children would come.

We ate our lunches on the benches in the towns' tree-lined plazas, crowded with elderly Catalan men dressed in their traditional black berets, black pants, and dark sweaters. As soon as Larry and I pulled into a plaza, the old men would hobble over to examine our bikes and find out what we were all about. They usually asked if we were French, since the French were such bicycle fanatics and we were too fair to be Spanish. When they discovered that we were Americans, they would start in on how uncle so-and-so and cousin such-and-such had gone to the New World to seek their fortunes in places like Chicago, Miami, and New York City. The old Catalans talked about the civil war and the atrocities Franco had inflicted upon Cataluña, while younger people discussed inflation, unemployment, and the Basque terrorists, and asked us about everything from the CIA to *Playboy* magazine.

Each night we pitched our tent on a sandy deserted beach and fell asleep curled up in our warm down cocoons listening to the rise and fall of the swells and the splash of the waves against the rocky cliffs. In the mornings, before it was light, the muffled putt-putt-putt sounds of the fishing boats coaxed us awake, and we would climb out of our tent and watch the lights from the boats' huge kerosene lamps drift farther out to sea and the sun rise from behind the water's horizon. After stretching exercises and breakfast, we scrubbed our dishes with handfuls of sand and rinsed them in the sea while a salty breeze showered us with mist. The few fishermen still floating close to shore waved good morning to us, and the seagulls flew in to devour our scraps.

The nightmare of cycling in Florida was over now, and we were free of the planes and the trains and big cities. We felt unconfined and independent once again.

On January 26, Larry and I pumped over a ridge in the steep coastal mountains near the French border and glided down into the village of Cadaqués. We had visited Cadaqués several times in 1974, when we were working in Barcelona, and we figured it would be a perfect place to spend the next five weeks. The village was surrounded by terraced mountains and miles of jagged, unspoiled coastline, perfect for hiking. Its tough, proud fishermen had fought to prevent ugly, tourist highrises, which littered much of the Costa Brava between the French border and Barcelona, from swallowing its tiny niche of the Mediterranean coast. And too, Cadaqués was home base for the surrealist painter, Salvador Dali. Artists from all over the world journeyed to his village to live and work.

Cadaqués nestled between its narrow, deep bay and the hills that began nearly at the water's edge. Behind the hills rose higher terraced mountains, which encircled and protected the village. Years ago, vineyards covered the terraces; after a disease destroyed the vines, the people planted olive trees. Then in the winter of 1956, a frost split and killed the olive trees. Now, except for the few that had been replanted, most of the terraces were barren.

After we rolled into Cadaqués, we decided to look for a cheap pension rather than pitch our tent on the outskirts of town, since we were expecting weeks of cold rainy weather. We left our bikes at the waterfront and walked back along the steep, narrow cobblestone pathways that ran from the bay up into the hills. The pathways were lined by one- and two-story whitewashed houses; women sat out front in their wooden chairs, sewing and mending clothes. As we walked, I stopped to ask the women if they knew of any private pensions where Larry and I could stay; but for the first time since we arrived in Spain, we were greeted by suspicious stares. The women shook their heads and looked away without smiling or speaking a word. After twenty minutes I had gotten nowhere, and we headed back to our bikes. Just as we reached them, a woman we had questioned came walking down one of the pathways on her way to the store. The moment she spotted our bikes, her gruff expression vanished, and she hurried toward us.

"So you're bicycling," she smiled cheerfully. "That's why you're wearing shorts in the middle of winter! We didn't know. We all thought you were crazy people. Only crazy people wear shorts in the middle of winter. There are so many strange hippie artists that come here and want to stay in our pensions. But they spend all their money on drugs, and then they can't pay their bills; so no one wants them in their pensions. We thought maybe you were one of them.

"But now that I can see you're bicycling, well then, I've got to figure you're probably all right. Look, I know just the place for you two," she nodded as she gestured for us to follow her. "I don't know if you know it, but Spanish pensions are usually so noisy it's impossible to sleep in them. The Spaniards who live in them stay up late and talk loud and turn their televisions up loud. But this place is different. It's small and quiet and clean. It'll be perfect for you. You'll see."

The woman led us up a pathway that opened into a courtyard with a stone floor edged by gigantic earthern flowerpots. The whitewashed houses that surrounded the courtyard all had varnished doors and wrought-iron balconies crammed with more potted flowers and cactus.

The woman rapped on one of the doors, and a short Catalan lady dressed in a black skirt and a dark-green blouse emerged. The two women jabbered together in their Catalan dialect for a couple of minutes, then the woman who had brought us introduced us to Señora Nadal.

"My friend here has a few vacant rooms she will show you. I'm going shopping now, but I'll be seeing you later. I live in the house across the alley to the left. Oh yes, and my name is Señora Casañas. *Adiós!*"

Larry and I followed Señora Nadal into the house adjoining hers, upstairs, and into a living room full of antique furniture. Huge earthen tiles covered the floor of the room, the walls were whitewashed, and the balcony looked down onto the courtyard below. A long hallway led from the livingroom, past three bedrooms and a bathroom, into a large kitchen. All of the bedrooms were vacant, and I chose the far one, with the window that opened onto the cobblestone alley behind the pension. During the five weeks that we would spend at Señora Nadal's only once was one of the other bedrooms occupied; a woman from Barcelona came one Saturday morning, but left the following afternoon. Señora Casañas was right; the pension was perfect for us. Our room was small but cozy and crammed with antique bureaus and chairs. And Señora Nadal brought us a small butane heater.

By the time Larry and I unloaded our bikes and moved in, we were starved. It was still siesta time, though, which in small Spanish villages like Cadaqués lasted from one or two o'clock until five or six, and all the grocery shops were closed. So we headed for the Marítimo, the local bar-cafe on the waterfront at the center of town, for a couple of beers and a fried egg and potato sandwich.

The Marítimo boasted a huge single room jammed with wooden tables and chairs. On the west side of the room, the windows faced the collection of cement and wooden benches and clusters of bare trees that made up the central plaza of Cadaqués. On the east side, the windows looked out across the Mediterranean. A long wooden bar butted against the north wall, and mounted into the south wall squawked one of Spain's ever-present, blaring televisions. Since it was siesta time, the Marítimo was deserted except for a handful of retired fishermen snoozing at two of the tables, with their bottles of wine resting next to their heads. Larry and I ate our meal on the patio overlooking the sea, then set out to explore the village.

In front of the Marítimo was a short stretch of sandy beach. We walked along it, peering into the brightly painted fishing boats beached there; they resembled large wooden dinghies. Each was filled with nets and had a kerosene lamp mounted in the rear.

When we came to the end of the sand we climbed back onto the road that paralleled the waterfront. Up ahead a young man was white-washing one of the houses; he looked like an American.

"Howdy," called Larry from the foot of the man's ladder.

"Well, hi to you both!" came the response.

"Where you from?" Larry asked.

"Santa Barbara."

His name was Tom Bishop. Three months earlier Tom quit his job as a designer for an electromechanical firm in Santa Barbara and flew to Spain to be with his Spanish girlfriend, María José, whom he had met a couple years ago. María José was a student at the university in Barcelona, but since Tom hated the smoggy city, he was staying in Cadaqués, and María José came up on weekends.

Like most of the foreigners in Cadaqués, Tom now found himself nearer to broke than he wanted to be. He had arrived in Spain with what he thought would be enough money to see him through the summer, but he'd quickly discovered that inflation had hit hard in Spain over the last two years. Less than three months after he arrived, his resources were near depletion. To support himself, Tom painted houses and prayed for a good weekend at *La Galería Sirena*, a local art gallery, which he owned with Roland, a German. At least once a month, Tom would hop a ride into Barcelona to take María José out for a hot night on the town. He could spend exactly twenty-five dollars, the amount he received from the Barcelona blood bank for a half liter of his blood.

"Hey listen," said Tom, after we had been talking for almost an hour at the foot of his ladder. "I've got to get back to my whitewash, but there's a party tonight. Us foreigners are all gettin' together for some singin' and dancin' and eatin' and drinkin'. Meet me at the Marítimo at seven and we'll go from there."

For the remainder of the afternoon, Larry and I meandered through the tiny pathways that crisscrossed Cadaqués. We looked in at the few shops in town, then walked away from the village along the waterfront to the end of the bay. It was dusk by the time we reached the edge of the bay, and the Mediterranean and the whitewashed buildings no longer glared in the sunlight. The village was bathed in pastels. Reflections of the lights from the plaza and the houses danced on the dark, glassy sea, and the lights that speckled its old, uneven buildings turned Cadaqués into a patchwork quilt cradled between the sea and the mountains. While we sat and watched our new home, we could hear the sea slap gently against the rocks below us. In the distance was the lonely putt-putt-putt sounds of the early evening fishermen.

At seven thirty Tom strolled into the Marítimo. He was a tall man, thin, with short, curly brown hair. I guessed him to be in his late thirties. A pair of flat weather-beaten lips formed his wide smile, and from one of his earlobes hung a tiny pierced earring. The three of us walked uphill from the bar toward the cathedral, which was perched atop the highest hill in town. Before we reached the cathedral, we stopped at a three-story house and climbed the stairs to the top floor.

There was one room on the top floor. It was crammed with people—Señora Casañas' strange hippie artists, I figured—and Tom introduced us to everyone. There was Carlos, the gay Colombian painter, model, and Dali protege, in his long black coat. Phil and Karen Clarke were Australians. Phil was preparing for his upcoming watercolor exhibit at *La Galería Sirena*. Roland, Tom's business partner, who, we were told, never worked much but seemed to have a constant and sizable supply of money, was sitting next to Colette, a British woman who had stumbled into Cadaqués years ago flat broke—and broke she'd remained. Colette had sizzled her mind on LSD back in England, and now she struggled to support herself by selling her homebaked pastries. Across from Colette stood the twin male British sculptors who always dressed in black and lived in an old house at the center of town. They looked after Colette and let her stay for free in the extra room in their house.

Chico Hansen, an artist, had his oil paintings on display at the gallery. Chico was of Cuban-Norwegian descent—a strong handsome man of fifty, who looked about thirty-five. Dressed in a flannel lumberjack shirt and new blue jeans, Chico looked to be the straightest member of the group.

"I'm really into est," he explained as soon as Tom introduced us. "Est has raised my consciousness, and through it I've finally managed to get it all together." During our stay in Cadaqués, Chico did in fact seem together, especially in comparison to the other foreigners in town.

While everyone at the party drank wine and talked (in English) about who was doing what, when Dali would be in town, what cheap houses were coming up for rent, and how the art gallery was faring, a Yugoslav guitarist played American Negro spirituals and sang in his thick Croatian accent. Two drug-dazed members of the British rock group that lived in a bus parked in the hills above town accompanied him on their banjos and Jew's harp. Carlos danced by himself outside on the balcony overlooking the bay.

By midnight, everyone was thoroughly drunk or stoned. Larry and I stumbled down the three flights of stairs and wound our way through the narrow, rocky pathways to the beach, across the plaza, and up the uneven alley to our pension.

We spent a month and a week in Cadaqués, cleaning our bikes and gear, hiking through the mountains, bicycling to the other villages along the coast, reading, and inhaling liters of mouth-puckering forty-two-cent wine in the plazas around the waterfront. We hunted out the plazas protected from the brisk sea breezes. During the middle of the day the sunshine reflected off the whitewash and kept us warm. The old-timers who frequented the plazas—often nothing more than two or three benches against a wall—taught us their names.

Mondays were market days in Cadaqués. By seven in the morning the trucks came rumbling down the mountains and parked in the central plaza next to the Marítimo. Stalls were quickly set up, turning the plaza into a maze of fruits and vegetables, nuts, candies, clothes, shoes, linens, and kitchenwares. For two hundred twenty-eight *pesatas* (four dollars) Larry and I came away from our first market day with two pounds of oranges, two pounds of bananas, six tomatoes, three onions, a carton of brussels sprouts, a bag of green beans, six potatoes, six eggs, a giant zucchini, and a bag of artichokes and eggplant.

Every morning, as soon as we got up, Larry and I went for a run along the waterfront to the end of bay. The first morning the village fishermen, preparing their boats and nets for their day at sea, stared at us curiously. We waved and smiled; they waved back, but hesitantly. The next we waved and wished them good luck; they waved back more enthusiastically. The following morning they shouted and waved to us first. From then on the fishermen cheered us on every morning and stopped to talk with us whenever they spotted us in town.

After our jog I would pick up a couple of loaves of hot, freshly baked French bread at the bakery, while Larry put together a cheese and onion omelette and brewed a pot of tea in the kitchen at the pension. Then we'd settle back for a leisurely breakfast followed by a long hot shower together.

In the late afternoons we usually joined Tom and the other foreigners at the gallery for the daily song, drink, and gossip sessions. It was at one of these get-togethers during our third week in Cadaqués that Tom announced he was flying home in two days.

"I'm tired of livin' hand-to-mouth the way I have for the last month. I've got to get back to my old job in Santa Barbara and save some money."

The Yugoslav guitar player shook his head.

"Hand-to-mouth? I've been living that way for years now. If I pick up some *pesetas* at L'Hostal playing guitar and singing, then I eat. If no one tips me, well then I don't eat. That's OK. I'm used to it. It don't worry me. When times get bad, something always turns up."

"I'd worry," Tom objected. "I need a little more security than that."

But most everyone in the room sided with the Yugoslav. They'd been living on the fringe for so long they had learned not to worry about where their next month's rent money would come from.

"Say, there," chirped Carlos, "you'll be leaving the same night Phil opens here. Oh, that's simply delightful! We'll have your going-away party and the opening celebration all in one big, beautiful extravaganza. Oh, how I *love* parties!"

Carlos danced in anticipation; Colette nodded dreamily and promised to bake pastries for the party; and Chico, the only member of the group who owned an automobile, offered to give Tom a lift into Barcelona.

That evening when Larry and I returned to our pension, Señora Nadal stopped us in the courtyard. She hadn't spoken to us much during our first weeks in the village, although she always waved to us when we went for our morning runs and once gave us directions to the best hiking areas along the coast. Tonight, however, she initiated a conversation; she wanted to know how we liked Cadaqués and how our hikes had gone.

"I've heard that you two sit in the plazas with the old people and talk with them. I like that. The fishermen like you too. You talk to them when you run in the mornings and when they come in at night. Come inside my house and let's visit."

Señora Nadal led us into her living room, which, like our pension, was full of antiques. Larry and I sat down at the huge wooden table in the middle of the room and looked around at the family photos that decorated the walls.

"I never married," she continued. "I'm in my fifties, and I live alone here in this big house. To fill my time I sew and embroider clothing, linens, and drapes with a small group of my friends. We sell our work here in the village and in Barcelona. When the days are warm and sunny, we work outside in the courtyard. When the weather is bad, we all gather around this table.

"The house attached to mine, your pension, belongs to my brother. He lives in Barcelona with his family. It was built in 1730, and mine—it's an extension of the original house—was built in 1881. Both of the houses were built by Nadals, and they've always been in our family."

Señora Nadal pointed to a picture of an elderly woman hanging near the fireplace. "My mother was born here in Cadaqués, and never once did she travel outside this village. My father ran trading boats between Spain and Italy. All these beautiful hand-painted ceramics you see here and there around the room are from Italy. I was a little girl when my father ran the trading boats, and Cadaqués was a different place then. There wasn't any heat, electricity, or running water in the village. We didn't get any plumbing in here until recently.

"Do you remember seeing that big earthen jug outside the front door? The one with the small hole in the top, and a handle and a spout? Well, when I was little, all us girls used jugs like that one to fetch water in from the fountain over the spring near the center of town. We'd fill the jugs with water and put a roll of cloth around the top of our heads and balance one of the jugs on our heads and carry another jug or two in our hands and walk back home. We used the water for cooking and washing our clothes and dishes. We didn't bathe much back then. During the summer, when it was hot enough, we washed ourselves by swimming in the sea. That was a long time ago when we did that; but I can remember it like it was yesterday. And I can remember the civil war too.

"Yes, we were lucky here in Cadaqués during the war. We still had our olive trees then. The war was between '36 and '39, and the frost that ruined the trees didn't come until '56; so we had our olive oil.

"Everyone in Cadaqués, and most of Cataluña for that matter, was anti-Franco, except for the police, of course. Franco tried to starve out all us Catalans by rationing our food; but here in Cadaqués we had our oil, and that was what saved us. The oil was like gold. When Franco cut off Cataluña from the rest of Spain, the Catalans lost their supply of olive oil from the South. And you know how fanatical us Spaniards are about oil. We can't cook without it. So everyone looked to Cadaqués for their oil. We smuggled it out hidden in hay carts and traded it in Llansa for tomatoes, onions, rice, wine—almost anything. And then of course we had our fish too. Thank God Franco never bombed our fishing boats. We worried that he would. They bombed some in the other villages, but not ours. But even with our oil and fish, things got pretty bad here near the end of the war, and eventually some of the people in town ran out of money and didn't have any food to eat.

"At that time, a very rich and influential Catalan family lived in that big deserted house across the patio. The place was a palace inside and out. But now, well, as you can see, it's been boarded up and abandoned. You've probably wondered why such a grand house like that was ever abandoned and left to decay. Well, you see, the wealthy man who lived in that house with his family and servants began supplying food and money to the poor people in town. That's how it was near the end of the war. On the one hand we had Franco trying to starve us out, and on the other we had the richest man in our village trying to save us. And then one day someone told the police what was going on. No ones knows for sure who the traitor was, but of course we all suspected the man's servants. Who else would have told?

"Anyway, as soon as the soldiers found out about the food and the money, they immediately went into the house and shot the man. He died there inside his home, and his family fled to Barcelona. According to the rumors, the man's body was never removed from the house. His children eventually went in and cleaned out the furnishings, but then they boarded the place up and left it as a tomb for their father."

❧

The day Tom departed Cadaqués and Phil opened at the gallery, the foreigners in town threw a twelve-hour party. People, beer, wine, brandy, dope, and food began to appear at the gallery around noon. Phil went about hanging his pictures, while Tom tried to cram everything he'd collected in the last four months into his one backpack. What didn't fit, he gave away. Colette passed out pastries, Carlos danced, and the Yugoslav belted out renditions of "Bonnie and Clyde," "When The Saints Come Marching In," and "If I Had A Hammer," with some Jamaican calypso and even a bit of classical guitar tossed in.

Late in the afternoon Tom decided he wanted hamburgers for his going-away dinner. The whole group filed down through the cobblestone alleys to the Marítimo, where someone talked the owner into cooking the meat patties we'd bought at the butcher shop along the way. María José picked up a dozen small loaves of bread at the bakery, and some lettuce and tomatoes at a grocery shop, and we all sat on the beach and assembled *hamburguesas*, which we washed down with more beer, wine, and brandy. The beach was deserted except for a few fishermen preparing their boats for a night run. The rest of the fishermen were in the Marítimo, crowded in front of the television, watching part three of the American television special "Roots." After the hamburgers, all the foreigners except Larry and I (who owned no fancy clothes), went home to dress up in their "opening best."

At eight o'clock the gallery reopened, and pictures, foreign artists, musicians, and weirdos all went on display. Tables were crammed with bowls of champagne punch, quiche, cheeses and crackers, vegetables and dips, and, of course, Colette's pastries. Phil stood by the door and personally greeted each guest as he or she arrived. The twin British sculptors showed up dressed completely in black as usual. Two Valencian women, who lived in a tiny *casita* at the edge of town, had piled on makeup and slithered into their long billowing skirts and skimpy silk blouses with plunging necklines. The one successful artist in town, an American who drew nothing but line designs, strutted in wearing a floor-length black cape that matched his long, greasy black hair. Carlos, who had donned a see-through white blouse and black gauze pants gathered at the ankles, arrived arm in arm with an Australian ballet dancer in purple tights and a red leotard. After the foreigners had crowded into the gallery, a few brave, neatly and conservatively dressed Spanish families ventured in to have a look at the pictures and possibly to buy one or two.

It was midnight before the party wound down. Phil and the gallery owners counted their profits and declared the opening a huge financial success, which was especially good news in Cadaqués, as it meant that Tom would be able to pay off his debts around town before he took off. All in all, it was one of the best openings anyone could remember.

After Tom left Cadaqués, Larry and I quit going to the afternoon get-togethers at the gallery. Instead, we spent more time getting to know the locals. It didn't take long for the Spaniards to open up to us. It was nice, they told us, to have foreigners in town who could speak fluent Spanish, and who knew something about Spain's politics, history, and literature and wanted to learn more. And the fact that we ran every morning to keep in shape pleased them too, although they thought we were crazy for wanting to bicycle around the world.

"Why would an American travel outside of America?" they asked. "It's so luxurious over there. We know. We see America in the movies and on television all the time."

Things changed once the Spanish community decided that we were all right. The locals stopped to talk with us more often, and the owners of the tiny food stores began selling us the cheaper brands of staples that they kept in their back rooms and brought out for the Spanish locals—the expensive brands were set out front for the foreigners and tourists. The middle-aged woman and her aging mother who owned the fifteen-by-ten-foot shop where we bought our eggs, cheese, yogurt, raisins, nuts, and pasta taught us their favorite recipes and gave us spices.

And too, we became friends with Andreu, the owner of one of the two liquor shops in Cadaqués. He lived with his wife and their four children in the house attached to the back of the shop. Andreu loved to talk, and one morning after we had been coming to his store every other day for three weeks to fill our plastic one-liter bottles with his forty-two-cent special, he cut loose. He was concerned about the reports of a storm headed our way.

"I bought this shop fourteen years ago," he began. "The first year I was here, there was a terrible flood. The sky clouded over one day, and the rain began to fall, and it fell for days. The water started gushing down the street out there in front of my shop, and it carried in a lot of debris, mostly limbs and sticks. And pretty soon the debris got all clogged up under that little bridge at the end of the street, and then the water started backing up, and the next thing I knew, it was gushing into my shop. We must have had nearly a meter of water in here that year.

"Well, you know, everybody in town acted real surprised about that flood. They all swore they'd never seen anything like it before; so I figured it was a freak storm, and I'd never live long enough to see it happen again. I didn't take any precautions against another flood. 'No need to,' everybody told me.

"Well, now, let me tell you something. In the fourteen years I've been here, it's flooded exactly nine times. Nine times! When it flooded the second time, and everyone acted all surprised again like they'd never seen a flood before, I learned my lesson. From then on, I've always made sure to board up the bottom half of the front door whenever it starts to rain hard.

"I'll tell you one thing. You can't trust a lot of what people tell you around here. That's for sure. The old-timers here don't get out much, and they've gotten real thick in the head. I mean *real* thick. They go around talking like they know what's going on, but they're really making most of it up. And then they go and believe it after they've come up with it! I figure a person's got to get out and travel a bit to keep from getting thick. I traveled some when I was going to school; so maybe I won't go dumb like the others when I get older."

The next day, as we were coming back from a hike to the lighthouse, Lorenzo Riera motioned for us to sit down beside him on the wooden bench he was occupying. Lorenzo was one of Andreu's "thick old-timers";

one of the dozens of ancient Catalans who spent each day following the sun from plaza to plaza. Neither Larry nor I had met Lorenzo before, so we were anxious to hear what he had to say.

"My house faces your kitchen window in Señora Nadal's," Lorenzo explained. "I've heard you two in there speaking Spanish, so I know you can understand me. I've seen you sitting in the plazas. You know all the right ones except for this one here. You should sit here after five o'clock and not over there in the Torradet where you usually sit. Anyway, I've decided you're all right. You're not like those other foreigners that are always getting wild on drugs. I'd like to talk to you."

"Fine," grinned Larry, "then why don't you sit right there and tell us something about yourself."

That of course, was exactly what Lorenzo had in mind, and as soon as Larry made his request, a wide, toothless smile shot across the old man's wrinkled face. He patted his beret, then leaned his head into Larry's to get a better view of who he was talking to. Lorenzo's eyesight wasn't what it used to be back in the twenties when he was a young man.

"How old do you think I am?" he asked.

"Sixty," I answered. I was lying, but I knew sixty would please him.

"I'm eighty-one years old," he declared triumphantly.

"No kidding. You sure don't look it!" Larry whistled.

Lorenzo leaned back in the bench and smiled. He patted his beret again, and then he put his face back up against Larry's and continued talking. He spoke in a mixture of Castillian Spanish and Catalan, but we managed to understand most of what he said.

"I was a barber when I was young. That was a *very* long time ago. Back then, being a barber was terrible on account of the lice. I hated the lice," he muttered, shaking his head in disgust. "They were always in everybody's beard and hair.

"Thirty *centimos*. That's what I got for shaving a fellow twice a week for a month. Nowadays thirty *centimos* ain't worth nothing. Why there's a hundred *centimos* in a *peseta*, and you can't buy nothing nowadays with a *peseta*, except maybe a piece of candy.

"I worked hard all my life to make a living. Folks worked hard back then when I was younger, and almost everybody was poor. Back then, buying a cup of coffee in a bar was a big expense. But now it's all different. Folks don't know what hard work and poverty is anymore. They work less and have more money now, but they spend it all. Nowadays, instead of only buying a cup of coffee, you gotta have snacks first, and then brandy after the coffee. Yessir, folks are soft now. Why, if they had to work hard and didn't have much money, like it used to be, they'd probably all go off and shoot themselves."

Lorenzo paused here just long enough to move away from the shadow that was creeping up on his end of the bench.

"When I was young, Cadaqués was a whole lot smaller than this. But a lot of the old families are still here. My children still live here. They take care of me now that my wife is gone. I live with one of my daughters and her family, and she cooks all my meals for me."

Lorenzo hesitated again, this time to look at his watch. It was two o'clock, time for his midday meal.

"I'll eat a big meal now; salad, lentil stew, fish, and bread and wine, and then I'll take my siesta. I'm an old man now, and my children take care of me. That's the way it is in Spain. The children care for their parents when they get old. That's the way it should be. I cared for them, now they care for me.

"Well, I've got to go now. My daughter don't like it when I'm late because the food gets cold waiting for me. Now you remember what I told you about this plaza here. You come here after five. This is the only place in Cadaqués that catches the last of the sun."

A few days later, the storm hit Cadaqués. Clouds closed in over the rooftops of the village, the temperature plummeted, and a fierce wind came powering down off the mountains and pounded so hard it forced the sea swells to break away from the shore. As soon as Larry and I set out on our morning run, we knew it was hopeless. We were no match for the wind, and the air was so cold it hurt to breathe. The village was almost deserted. Only two women had ventured outside to buy their morning bread, and the wind bounced their bundled bodies along the pathways as if they were as light as straw. We turned back to our pension, and as we came across the courtyard Señora Nadal stuck her head round her door and yelled, "It's the tramontaña. The terrible wind. Stay inside. No one goes out during the tramontaña, except to buy food."

Larry and I sprinted upstairs and curled up in front of our butane heater for the rest of the day. In the late afternoon the electricity went out. Since it was too dark to read without a light, we pulled on our down jackets and mittens and walked downstairs. As I stepped outside into the courtyard, the tramontaña swept my face with snowflakes, and again Señora Nadal called to me from across the patio. She and one of her friends were huddled in front of the heater, embroidering by the light of a kerosene lamp. Larry and I sat down in the empty chairs nearest the heater.

"The lines are blown down," the women explained. "It'll be another hour before they're fixed. And what do you think of the snow? They say there's a blanket of white on the mountains."

Information traveled by mysterious ways in Cadaqués. Neither

Señora Nadal nor her friend had left the living room all afternoon, but still they knew about the power lines and the snow on the mountains.

"Does it snow very often here?" Larry asked.

"Oh, we usually have a few flurries like this. But only twice that I can remember has the snow ever stayed on the ground for very long," answered Señora Nadal. "There was the frost of '56 that split the olive trees, and then there was *Pito helado* in '62.

"*Pito helado?*" I said. "What's 'frozen Pito' supposed to mean?" The two women winked at each other and chuckled.

"Pito," Señora Nadal explained, "was an old man here in Cadaqués. He was very senile, and when the snow started falling that evening in February of '62, well, old Pito walked out onto his balcony and sat down to watch. He sat down to watch, and he kept right on sitting there. In fact, it seems he got so engrossed in what he was seeing, he forgot to come back inside. Well, it snowed a meter or more that night, and the next morning the people found Pito still sitting out there on his balcony. He'd frozen to death watching it snow; so that's why they call the storm of '62 "frozen Pito." Yessir, that was quite a storm to see."

"Yeah. I guess Pito must have thought so too," Larry commented, and the two women chuckled in agreement.

"It was a nice way for him to go though," nodded Señora Nadal. "His time had come, and he must have enjoyed the show."

After we had finished talking with the women, Larry suggested that he and I drop in on Chico, the est painter. Chico had been raised in Hawaii and worked there as a construction engineer until several years ago, when he quit to become a full-time artist. The rocky, deserted pathways between our pension and Chico's apartment were dark and slippery, and we had a tough time keeping our footing in the wind. When we arrived, Chico was just leaving for the Marítimo. His painting had gone badly today, and he was determined to drown his sorrow in wine; so the three of us stumbled our way down to the beach.

It was immediately obvious that the Marítimo was the place to go during a *tramontaña*. Most of the inhabitants of Cadaqués, foreigners and fishermen alike, were crowded around its tables, and most everyone looked as if he or she had already consumed a fair share of alcohol. Chico promptly ordered himself a bottle of bloodred Torres wine—*Sangre de Toros* (Blood of Bulls) it said on the label—and wasted no time in catching up with the others. Twenty minutes later Brooks, the rich American writer in town, wandered in with a look of utter dejection etched into his face and confirmed the nasty rumor that his wife had indeed gone off to the South of France with Max, the smooth French photographer. By now Chico was already slurring his speech. He tried to console Brooks by expounding

117

upon the est solution to Brooks' unfortunate predicament, but Brooks was in no mood for Chico's "You've got to take control of your life and feel good about yourself and your actions" discourse.

"Dammit, fellow! Don't start in on that slop at a time like this," grumbled Brooks.

"But now's when you really need est the most," Chico objected. "I'll tell you what. I'll—"

"Chico!" Brooks screamed directly into the artist's opened mouth. "I said *no est* and that means *no est!* Now *drop* it!"

The Spaniards at the next table glanced over at Brooks for a moment, then turned back to the Marilyn Monroe movie on the television above their heads. Chico started to yell something at Brooks, but he suddenly changed his mind and moved to another table where Caroline, the Dutch prostitute, was sitting with her back to one of the windows overlooking the Mediterranean. She was busy writing a letter and didn't bother to look up when the three of us sat down across the table from her.

Caroline was a big woman. When she walked through Cadaqués, she towered over the squatty fishermen. A thick crust of powder, rouge, mascara, eye shadow, and lipstick always buried her face, and a bushy blond mass of curly hair swirled around her head and toppled onto her shoulders and down her back.

Tonight Caroline was wearing her white silk blouse that exposed a generous portion of her cleavage. She had decorated her long white neck with a red scarf and thin gold chains; rows of fat, gaudy bracelets hid her wrists and forearms; and, as usual, her fingernails were painted dark red. When Chico ordered Caroline a glass of vermouth, her favorite drink, she flashed him a wide smile, which exposed two even rows of teeth and gums darkened by too many cigarettes. As quickly as it appeared, the smile vanished, and Caroline returned to her letter and cigarette, again ignoring our presence.

"Caroline, 'member the party las' summer when we danced together all night?" queried Chico, staring intently at the top of Caroline's forehead and trying hard not to slur his words.

Caroline kept her mouth closed and her eyes on her letter.

"I know you haven't fergotten 'bout dat night, Caroline. Everbody in town was talkin' 'bout us afferwards. We danced great together dat night. Didn't we?"

Again there was no response.

"Lissen Caroline. Why don't we get together again? Les you and me go to the disco and do some hot dancin' tonight. Watcha say?"

Still, the woman did not answer, and her reticence incensed Chico.

"Damn you Caroline! Look at me and say somethin'!" he screamed at the top of his voice as he jumped to his feet. "You're not deaf, dammit, so answer me!"

Caroline ignored the outburst, but Brooks looked over at Chico from two tables away and yelled, "Say there Chico old boy, by the tone and volume of your voice, I get the distinct impression that you've just taken leave of your much celebrated est self-control. What's the matter? Here I've been thinking all this time that you 'had it all together,' to quote your slick consciousness rhetoric. Dear me, now don't tell me nothing more than an insolent woman and bit of wine is enough to make you lose 'it' after you worked so hard to finally find 'it'!"

Chico refused to acknowledge Brooks' sarcasm and continued to shout at Caroline like a man possessed

"You think you kin 'nore me woman? You think you kin perten' like I'm not here and I'll go away? Well you're wrong, woman! Dead wrong! I'll get your attention. I'll get it all right. I'll get you to look at me, and I'll wash those filthy windows back o' you all the same time!"

On that note, Chico whirled around and grabbed the pressurized bottle of tonic water sitting on the bar behind him, took his position across the table from Caroline, pointed the bottle's nozzle at her face, and squeezed the lever. The bubbly liquid shot through the air and splattered the window, missing Caroline's head by no more than an inch. Caroline, however, remained eerily unruffled. She kept right on with her letter as if nothing had happened—she never looked up, ducked, or uttered a word. And Chico went right on firing. He blasted back and forth around her shoulders and head, covering the entire window in tonic water; but somehow he managed to miss Caroline's face, which was nearly unbelievable considering his inebriated state.

When it was all over, Chico stood with the empty bottle in one hand and watched the water gurgle down the window pane behind Caroline's still downturned head, while the Spaniards and foreigners kept their eyes on Chico to find out just what he was going to do next. What Chico did next was admit defeat. He returned the tonic bottle to the bar, blew Caroline a big kiss, then staggered back outside into the wind and the snow.

"The *tramontaña*," muttered the fishermen, nodding to each other. "It makes people crazy. They have this wind in France too. It made Van Gogh chop off an ear."

Two days later the wind died, the warmth returned, and Larry and I resumed our hiking and bike rides, our afternoon reading sessions in the plazas, and our walks at sunset along the waterfront.

At the end of February, we decided it was time to move on. We loaded up our bikes and pedaled south on the inland route back to

Barcelona, through Figueras, Olot, and Vich.

The roads wound through the mountains past old rambling farmhouses, vineyards, and small villages that clung to the hilltops and cliffs. When we stopped to look north from the crests of the hills, we were afforded some spectacular views of the snowcapped Pyrenees. The air was frigid in the mountains below Olot, and often the pavement was spotted with patches of ice, which knocked us off our bikes every time we hit them.

We planned to stop in Barcelona just long enough to collect some extra spending money: Tom had drawn us a crude map directing us to the street where the blood bank was. He couldn't remember the exact address, but once we found the street we had no difficulty spotting the place—the long line of drunks standing outside was a dead giveaway.

We locked our bikes to a pole and walked inside. The entryway led downstairs into a single huge room filled with beds occupied by what looked to be the world's largest collection of seedy, only slightly sober, horizontal men. A lone nurse moved about the room, adjusting the tubes that protruded from the scores of dangling arms. Larry suggested that we "get the hell out of here," when the receptionist spotted us.

"There's nothing to worry about," the receptionist shouted across the room. "Give me your passports and have a seat. Come on now. What's the matter? Can't you move?"

"You guessed it. I can't move," I grinned nervously.

Larry asked how long it would take to draw the blood.

"About ten minutes. Now hand me your passports and fill out these forms."

We tossed our passports onto the receptionist's desk. I tried not to look at the men on the beds while I filled out the forms. Then I sat fidgeting nervously for forty-five minutes before the nurse picked up our papers.

My name was called first, and I commanded my legs to walk the twenty feet into the doctor's office at one end of the reception area. The doctor's assistant, who met me at the door of the office, continued to chew on his sandwich and gulp down his beer while he weighed me.

"Fifty-five *kilos*," he mumbled through a soggy mixture of bread, tomatoes, lettuce, and pork. He burped and motioned for me to step off the scale.

"Fifty-five *kilos*," repeated the doctor. "I'm very sorry, but you don't weigh enough to give blood. You must weigh at least sixty-five *kilos*. I'm very sorry."

"Hey, don't be," I smiled broadly, "'cause I'm sure not!"

It was Larry's turn next. The doctor gave him the OK, and the nurse led him to a vacant bed and plugged a tube into his arm. The look of terror that had crept onto his face when the nurse first called him into the office never dissolved, and he managed to pump out the half liter of blood in just over two minutes. Afterwards, the receptionist slapped one thousand six hundred *pesetas* (twenty-five dollars) into his hand, and we headed to the nearest liquor store.

The Spaniards we'd talked with on our way down from Cadaqués had assured us that a couple of sips of brandy at the beginning and end of each day would help us to cope with the frosty late-winter weather. Larry paid for a bottle of Carlos III with a portion of his blood money, and we poured the brandy into our spare cookstove fuel cannister. (In America we had used white gas and filled two cannisters at a time. Since white gas wasn't available in Europe, we were now using automobile gasoline in our cookstove, and to keep our weight down filled only one cannister at a time. There wasn't any need to carry an extra supply of gasoline, as it was never far between gas stations.)

Armed with our hefty supply of brandy, Larry and I headed south from Barcelona along the coast, through Valencia, Alicante, and Almería. The practice we developed in America of stopping at campgrounds now and then for a hot shower came to an abrupt halt. Most Spanish campgrounds were crowded and noisy, and they charged four dollars a night to pitch a tent and take a "hot" shower, which was often cold. And with an extra sizable charge for bicycles, two bicyclers with a tent paid more to camp than two people with a car and a trailer. The whole setup made us so furious that we stuck to free camping on the beaches, in olive and orange groves, and in farmers' fields. Only when we went into the cities did we stay in campgrounds.

There was almost always a lot of dirt floating in the air in Spain, and by the end of each day, our faces, arms, and legs were streaked black. When we camped on the beaches, we bathed in the sea; inland, we kept our eyes out for a river or stream. When we couldn't find water to camp next to, we washed up at a gas station. The station attendants were always happy to let us use their restrooms. Like the French, most Spaniards were bicycle fanatics, and many of the attendants were or had been amateur racers. While Larry and I washed up in the sinks in the restrooms, we could hear the attendants outside examining our bikes and our gear, puzzling over the amount we managed to pack into our panniers and attach to our rear racks, and how we'd lodged our spare tires between our spokes.

Before we left the station, we would scrub the food we'd bought for dinner (potatoes, tomatoes, zucchini, cauliflower, eggplant, brussels sprouts—whatever we had found in the marketplaces we'd passed during the day) and fill up our half-gallon plastic water bottle. We used the water for cooking and washing dishes; for drinking, we bought bottles of purified water each day at the grocery shops.

Vegetable stews were our favorite dinners in Spain. We would boil up a packet of dried soup and toss in chopped fresh vegetables. When we couldn't find vegetables, we sometimes heated canned tomatoes, tomato paste, onions, salami, and garlic, and poured it over rice. Other days, our meals consisted of potatoes, onions, tomatoes, and salami mixed with a jar of lentils or garbanzo beans.

No matter where we free-camped, a *Guardia* or two inevitably materialized in a gray-green jeep to take a look at us. The *Guardia Civil* seemed to be everywhere, watching. When they spotted our bikes, they smiled and waved, then drove away.

It was along the coast just north of Valencia that Larry and I ran into Christine and Greg, the only couple we met on our journey who were also bicycling around the world. They too were from California and had pedaled across the United States. They were headed for North Africa. The four of us had a lot in common: we were about the same age, were native Californians; loved bicycling, camping, and the sand and the sea; and Greg, like Larry, was an engineer.

"Like you guys, Greg and I hadn't done any bicycle touring before we took off across the States," Christine said. "It was rough going at first, but once we got into the groove, we were having the time of our lives, pedaling through America, seeing the country and meeting people. We didn't want it to end; so when we got to the East, we kept on going."

The following two days the four of us lounged on the beaches with our cheap wine and chunks of bread and goat cheese and bent each other's ears. Then Greg and Christine traveled with Larry and me through southeastern Spain as far as Granada; it felt great having two new companions to travel and talk with.

Southeastern Spain was much dryer than the north. Trees and grass were scarce, and a thick layer of dust hugged the tiny villages that sprouted along the narrow back roads. The villages were clusters of decaying, one- and two-story cement houses and shops. Long thin strips of plastic hung in the open doorways to keep out the flies; and women set their chairs outside on the sidewalks and sat knitting and watching the cars and trucks trickle by.

Since the people in the south were generally short in stature, dark complexioned, and dressed in black, brown, dark green, or dark blue, our arrival in their villages often proved to be a monumental event. Christine and Greg were both tall and blond, and Christine's thick, near-white hair hung down to the middle of her back. When the four of us light-haired giants, wearing our bright red, yellow, orange, or green clothes, rolled down the main street of a *pueblo* on bicycles loaded with orange and yellow panniers, people dropped what they were doing and gaped.

Whereas the Catalans always waved and shouted to Larry and me when we pedaled by their farms, and smothered us with questions about ourselves and our trip when we stopped in their towns, in the south we were greeted by silent suspicious stares. The southerners seemed poorer and less educated than their countrymen to the north, and most of them looked as though they couldn't comprehend what they were seeing when they spotted us cycling by. The store owners and the women shopping in the marketplaces never spoke to us, and nowhere, neither in the towns nor the countryside, were our *hola's* ever answered.

And then too, Christine and I were plagued by the southern macho males—we couldn't walk anywhere alone or together without being grabbed at. If I went shopping in the marketplaces by myself, they hounded me every inch of the way. Even when Larry was with me, the men leered and whistled.

People weren't our only problem down south. Between Valencia and Granada, Larry and I were hit by a series of gear and equipment failures: our aluminum rear racks cracked, the zipper on our tent door gave out, my only pair of shoes were torn apart in a fall, and my rain jacket started to leak.

The first to go—somewhere between Alicante and Almería—were the racks. When we reached Almería, we took them to an arc welder—the best in all of Spain, everyone assured us—for what we thought would be a simple five-minute fix-it job. The welder worked on my rack first. It took him fifteen minutes to sloppily repair the crack, but we were in no position to complain; besides being the best, he was also, he informed us, the only. Then he picked up Larry's rack and disappeared once again into his shop. Thirty minutes later he was still welding. Larry paced nervously around the office. After another half an hour had passed, he headed into the shop.

"I can't wait any longer," he announced. "Let's go back in there to see what's happened."

At the back of the shop, we found the welder staring down at Larry's rack with a perplexed look on his face. He had accidentally vaporized an entire section of aluminum. While we surveyed the gap, we were both thinking the same thing—Spaniards race bicycles, but they don't tour. Which means we won't be able to buy a rack anywhere in Spain. Somehow we had to salvage the rack.

It took them an hour, but Larry and the welder managed to rig up a support by attaching a round piece of steel across the missing section of aluminum with some copper wire. The support looked like hell, and Larry didn't expect it to last more than a day or two, but he couldn't think of anything else to do. As it turned out the rack held out all the way to England, where we picked up a new one.

That evening, when Larry and I set up camp along with Christine and Greg at the outskirts of Almería, the zipper pull on the front door of our tent gave out, and the nightly swarms of mosquitoes promptly invited themselves inside for an evening feast. After we discovered that one of the pulls on our day pack fit the tent zipper, we made the switch.

The following morning the four of us pulled onto the main coastal highway, which we followed west along the bottom of Spain as far as Motril, and pedaled smack dab into a bicycler's nightmare: a treacherous head wind, an unpaved road, and a brigade of heavy trucks hauling dirt. The highway had been torn up in preparation for repaving. The head winds slammed us around in the dirt, rocks, and potholes, while waves of thirty-ton trucks sprayed us with dust and gravel. As the day wore on, the gales became fiercer, and by late afternoon, it took all our skill, strength, and concentration to remain upright and pump forward over the loose, uneven surface.

At the end of the day, the road suddenly turned at an angle to the wind, and the gales broadsided us. My bike and I, being the lightest of our group, were sent sailing off the side of the road. I landed in a pile of gravel, and all seventy pounds of my bike and gear came crashing down on top of me. One of my feet was jammed in its toe clip, and the other cracked into a rock—the sole of my right shoe was torn loose, and my left shoe was a mound of shredded leather. Unfortunately, Spanish shoes didn't fit me, so for the next three months, until I bought shoes in England, I had one hell of a time slipping my mangled shoes in and out of the toe clips.

By the next morning, the winds had died down, and we turned north to begin our forty-mile climb into Granada. An hour later the temperature dropped, it started to rain, and I realized that my rain jacket no longer shed water. Not only had the seam sealer worn out, but the fabric itself was leaking. By the time we stopped for lunch, part way up the pass in the tiny *pueblo* of Beznar, I was thoroughly soaked.

In Beznar most of the houses and shops bordered the main road. Their front doors opened onto the street, and only the narrow strip of sidewalk and the houses' front walls separated the traffic from the people's living rooms. As in many of the *pueblos* in southern Spain, there were no signs to tell us where the grocery shop or bakery or even the local bar might be. The locals all knew where they were, and no tourists ever stopped in places like Beznar.

As we rode into town, a woman dressed in the traditional black sweater, blouse, and skirt emerged from one of the doorways with her plastic shopping cart on wheels. To our surprise, she smiled at us. And when we asked her where the grocery shop was, she led us there, asking questions the whole way. Her friendliness was a refreshing change from the blank stares and suspicious looks we'd become accustomed to in the south.

The local general store, which measured no more than forty by twenty feet and which sold primarily food, clothing, and kitchenware, was packed with women, all just as friendly as the woman who brought us there. Larry and I felt as though we'd suddenly been transported back to Cataluña.

"You're Americans?" a teen-aged girl asked us. "Where are you from in America?"

"California."

"California! That's wonderful! San Francisco, Hollywood, sun and beaches! I'm going to visit California someday."

The older women all laughed.

"You're a real dreamer, Lidia," one of them scolded the girl. "Women in Beznar don't go to California. They stay right here all their lives and have their babies and raise their families."

After the four of us picked out oranges, bread, cheese, and tomatoes for lunch, Larry asked if there was a sheltered plaza in Beznar where we could eat our lunch. Everyone agreed that we should go across the street to the bar, so we left our bikes out front and headed over there with the food.

Roberto, the owner of Beznar's bar-cafe, was a short, middle-aged man, who walked with a limp. He was more than happy to have us in despite the fact that we arrived with our own food. He seated us at the largest of the five tables, shut the front door to close off any draft, handed us each a plate and some silverware, and motioned for us to make ourselves at home.

The cafe was a cavernous room with a cold tile floor and stone walls, which were bare and unpainted. The unheated room felt icy and damp, and the one bulb that hung from the ceiling back behind the bar furnished the only light. It was quiet inside the cafe; there was no television or radio turned on full blast. The three middle-aged men sitting at the bar nodded to us when we entered, then went back to arguing politics in a hushed tone.

Now that we were no longer pumping up the grade or moving about, our body temperatures took a nose dive. Even the brandy we ordered, in hopes of injecting some warmth into our systems, didn't keep us from shaking. My clothes were wringing wet, and they felt like a shield of ice against my skin. Between sips of brandy I cupped my hands over my mouth and blew into them in an effort to thaw them out so that my fingers would close around my knife and spoon.

While we sat shivering and nibbling on our food, Roberto was busy grumbling about the upcoming elections with the three men at the bar. It wasn't until nearly a half hour after he had seated us at the table that he looked over to see how we were doing.

"Diós mío!" he shouted across the room. "Why didn't you tell me you were freezing to death over there? What's the matter? Don't any of you know how to talk?"

Shaking his head and muttering to himself, he disappeared into the back room. A few minutes later he emerged with a huge round brass platter piled high with hot coals.

"I should roast the bunch of you over these for not telling me you were cold. Anyone can see by looking at you you're all about to shiver your hair loose, especially that one," he said pointing to me. "Her clothes are so wet they're dripping on the floor. Now don't you be blaming me if you catch pneumonia. No sir! You can blame yourselves for not opening your mouths!"

While he bellowed at us, Roberto slid the platter of coals into its wooden holder underneath our table. Once he secured the platter, he pointed out the series of slits in our floor-length tablecloth and motioned for each of us to push our legs and hips through one of the slits. The cloth held in the heat from the coals, and the instant I slid my legs under the table, a warm, melting sensation washed through my body. I pulled off my sweat shirt and laid it on my knees. Ten minutes later my clothes were bone dry. Roberto brought us each another glass of brandy and one for himself, and the five of us drank a toast to the hot coals, the brandy, and the bar at Beznar.

From Granada Larry and I headed northwest toward Cordoba and Sevilla, while Christine and Greg turned southwest toward Algeciras to catch the ferry to Morocco. Our two friends planned to pedal across North Africa into Tunisia, cross into Italy, cycle to Greece, then fly to Egypt. Larry and I planned to stay in Spain and Portugal until the end of June, then hop the ferry to England and roam the British Isles for a couple of months before plunging across central Europe toward Greece. We talked about meeting up again in Egypt, but Greg and Christine expected to reach Cairo by August, two months before Larry and me. Maybe India, we decided. We would keep in touch by writing to each other at the American Express offices along our routes.

It was the middle of April when Larry and I rolled into Sevilla. The weather was still cold and rainy in southern Spain, and we could expect more of the same in Portugal. Our spirits were low. We had been looking

Cycling light—Larry's bike, loaded for touring.

Endless Route 212, South Dakota.

Bicycling the backroads of Spain, near Trujillo.

Barbara and Larry Savage bouncing along the cobblestones of Culross, Scotland. (Cary Holst photo)

Plastic sacks add rain protection in Sheep Haven, Ireland. Note spare tire stored in spokes of front wheel.

Crossing the Alps in the snow, near Kempten, Germany.

Light and lattice in the medina, Fès, Morocco.

Moroccan in typical hooded robe and pointed shoes, the medina, Fès.

Barbara found this alternative mode of transportation even rougher than a stiff bicycle seat. Cairo, Egypt.

These Egyptians offered to buy Barbara's bike. Valley of the Kings, Luxor, Egypt.

"So which way to Agra?" Road signs in Kanpur, India.

Tenting with the monkeys in Ayodhya, India.

Geoff Thorpe fixes one of his many flat tires, near Ayodhya, India.

Larry's tire change
draws a crowd of
Nepalese schoolchildren.
(Geoff Thorpe photo)

A Nepali "backpacker"
shares the road.

Road sign in Waitaha Valley, New Zealand.

WELCOME TO
WAITAHA VALLEY
WET WEATHER CAPITAL
OF NEW ZEALAND
Pop: 70
Ht. Above Sea Level: 30 m.
Av. Rainfall: Too Bloody Much.

Lining up to pass through a construction zone, Lindis Pass, New Zealand.

Tired cycling shoes: Barbara's are held together with duct tape while Larry's, center, are beyond repair.

forward to a few sunny weeks exploring the deserted beaches along the south coast of Portugal, yet now it looked as though we'd be camping and swimming in the drizzle and the cold. However, a few days before we planned to leave Sevilla for Portugal, Larry encountered an elderly Australian couple in the city campground, who were convinced that he and I had our itinerary all wrong.

"You'll be makin' a big mistake givin' Morocco a miss, mate," the husband said to Larry. "It's exotic there. Terribly different from anything you'll see in Spain or Portugal. Really now, you must have a go at Morocco. Anyway, you're almost there. I'd recommend the city of Fès. It's only a couple hundred miles due south of Ceuta, the city on the north coast where the ferry drops you off. Fès is absolutely remarkable. The *medina*—that's the old, decaying section of the city—is over a thousand years old! And everything about Morocco is so strange and different—the people, the food, the music, the shops—bizarre I'd say."

The Spaniards, however, had warned against bicycling in North Africa.

"Morocco is nothing but filth, poverty and sickness. The Moroccans will steal you blind. They'll steal your bicycles right out from under you! And besides, foreign women aren't safe in Morocco. You don't have much protection on those bicycles. It's not like you can lock yourselves up in your car if there's trouble."

But the Australians had sparked our curiosity.

"Maybe we should go on down there and see for ourselves," Larry suggested. "We've still got a month before we're supposed to meet your parents in Madrid. We could spend a week or so down there, then come back up and cycle through southern Portugal. It'll probably be nice and warm in Morocco now, and the extra week might give the weather up here a chance to clear up. That way we'd enjoy Portugal a lot more."

For two days we vacillated. Portugal would be safe, we reasoned. We hadn't heard rumors, as we had about the Moroccans, of Portuguese robbing or murdering young foreign travelers camped along the beaches. Yet Morocco sounded more challenging. It couldn't be too dangerous there, I figured, or the Australians would have said something.

On the morning we were to leave Sevilla, we still hadn't come to a decision. We packed our gear, pushed our bikes to the campground exit, and Larry propped his bike against a tree and pulled a *peseta* out of his front pack.

"Franco, it's Morocco. The coat of arms, it's Portugal," he said as he tossed the coin into the air.

When the *peseta* landed in the dirt, Franco's single beady eye was staring up at us.

It took us only two days to reach the Straits of Gibraltar.

MOROCCO

CHAPTER TEN

On the high cliffs along the southern tip of the Iberian Peninsula near Algeciras, Larry and I stopped in the rain to lean our bikes together and look out across the straits. Africa loomed dark and ominous in the distance. Its towering coastal mountains erupted like great monuments of rock from beneath the black stormy sea. It was an awesome sight. And as we stared long and hard at the strange new continent, we felt nervous about what might lie in store for us.

It had rained all day and was still at it when we pedaled up to the ferry terminal in Algeciras. On ship, we pulled on dry clothes and wrung out our wet ones. We were the only bicyclers on board.

Ceuta was a bustling, duty-free port city, still controlled by Spain. The Spanish dock workers directed us to the cheapest place in town to sleep—under the overhang outside the ferry terminal. We pushed our bikes along the cement, past rows of sleeping bodies—young travelers from Europe who, like us, had just arrived on the ferry from Algeciras, or who were waiting to ship out for Spain first thing in the morning. I propped my bike against a wall and draped my wet clothes over my handlebars and rear panniers to let them dry out overnight. Then we laid our mats out on the cold, damp cement and pulled our muddy, sweaty bodies down into our sleeping bags. It had been two days since we washed. Larry stuffed our valuables into the foot of his bag, and we fell asleep.

In the morning we hit the public shower facilities in the station parking lot, then changed our money and stocked up on food: rice, cauliflower, bread, eggs, and two pounds of cheese. Larry scouted around for a map of Morocco, but even the cheapest ones were selling for five dollars;

so, instead of buying one, he memorized the road to Fès. The route seemed simple enough—all we had to do was to keep to the main road south. We hoped any forks in the road would have signposts.

After spending nearly two hours filling out forms and standing in line at the border, Larry and I entered Morocco in the early afternoon of April 14. We pedaled right out of modern civilization and into the past. Feet and donkeys were the common mode of transportation, and the hilly countryside, not paved roads, was the main avenue of transit. There was no jumble of economy cars; no Toyotas, Datsuns, or Fiats cramming the road. Only wealthy Moroccans owned cars, invariably Mercedes. Occasionally a compressed collection of people, boxes, animals, and crates rumbled past us in one of the country's many moaning, dilapidated, public buses.

But while the twenty-five miles of paved road between the border and the first city due south, Tetouan, were nearly deserted, the surrounding countryside was crawling with human figures in transit. Creeping mounds of clothing—groundlength skirts, blouses, sweaters, scarves, and shawls, topped by gigantic beach towels—littered the hillsides. These mounds proved to be Moroccan women. The beach towels, which they draped over their heads and fastened under their chins, were their veils. The only exposed flesh on a peasant woman's body were her hands and a small portion of her face. These women traveled with bulky cloth sacks stuffed with most of their worldly possessions slung over their backs, and they always walked, while the men sometimes rode donkeys. The women never looked directly at me or Larry, but the men, dressed in long, hooded, heavy cloth robes and slipper-like leather shoes with pointed toes, peered out from under their floppy hoods and smiled and waved.

On one side of the road stretched empty, white sandy beaches and the clear blue Mediterranean. On the other side were grassy green hills dotted by trees and occasional rocks. There was a total absence of litter. The peasants were too poor to know the luxury of thoughtlessly tossing things away. What little was discarded, primarily orange peels, was quickly devoured by the passing donkeys.

As we entered the city of Tetouan, I prepared myself for the onslaught of whistles, shouts, and leering faces that had so often greeted me in southern Spain, expecting Moroccan males to be as obnoxious as the Spanish. But I was surprised. The men smiled and nodded to me, and the teen-aged boys all shouted a polite "Bon jour, madam! Bon jour, monsieur!" Then, jabbering away in French, they gestured that they were pleased that Larry and I were bicycling through their country.

We wanted a cheap map of Morocco, but the stores in Tetouan were closed when we pedaled through. A policeman explained that, as in

Spain, the shops in Moroccan cities closed between two and five o'clock, and he directed us through the city center and out to the road again.

Five miles outside of town, we stopped in a deserted area to eat a snack and relieve ourselves. There was no one in sight when we pulled off the road and walked back among some rocks and shrubs, but no sooner had I scouted out a circle of bushes to squat behind than the surrounding hillsides sprang to life. I could hear people shouting to each other across the narrow valleys, and within seconds they materialized around us, the men in their long hooded robes. Realizing what I was doing, they kept their distance, staring down at us from the low hilltops. But when we pedaled away, they climbed down to the spot where we had rested and searched the area for anything we might have left behind.

My knees were swollen and sore this day. Some days were like that; my knees would ache for a day or two, and then one morning I'd wake up and they'd be as good as new for the next month. Because of my knees, we began our climb through the Rif mountains, just south of Tetouan, at a slow pace—slow enough to make us ripe for attack. The mountainsides were sprinkled with groups of children tending sheep, goats, and crops, and these children were unquestionably some of the fastest and farthest-running humans on the face of the earth. The minute they spotted us grinding slowly up the inclines, they dropped everything and were off and running. Squeals of delight exploded in the air as the children pounded up and down slopes, across fields, over rocks, and onto the road, the boys running in their baggy pants and shirts and the girls in their long skirts, loose blouses, scarves, and jewelry.

Each child tried his or her damnedest to reach us first and have the initial crack at a possible cigarette. Cigarettes were what they all wanted. They never asked for anything else, never food nor money, only cigarettes. The "Cigarette! Cigarette! Cigarette!" chanting began with the first arrivals, and it amplified into a deafening roar as the others plunged onto the scene.

A number of things happened when the children found we had no cigarettes. When we were creeping uphill, they crowded around us and slapped our bikes. A stern, loud no was usually enough to send them scattering. When we were pedaling downhill and could stay out of their reach, the children either chased behind us for a half mile or so before giving up, or they heaved whatever they had or could get hold of—rocks, sticks, hoes, hatchets—at us as we whizzed by. They never aimed to hit us, everything was tossed a little to one side. But a few times someone would go too far.

Once, a boy grabbed Larry's spare water bottle off the back of his bike. Larry stopped, climbed off his bike, and walked angrily back toward the boy. The culprit's older brother, sensing a bad situation developing, grabbed the bottle out of the boy's hand, handed it back to Larry, and slapped his brother on the side of the head. The group then stood silently and meekly by as we pedaled away.

Ten minutes later we were enveloped by a crowd of teen-aged boys as we inched our way up an especially steep grade. As the gang swarmed around us, some of the boys grabbed our arms and legs, while the others tried to yank our bikes out from under us. Larry and I threw a few punches to scare them away, but they kept clawing us. Just as we were about to hit the pavement, a shiny new Mercedes rounded the top of the climb. The driver took one look at what was happening and gunned the car straight toward us. Brakes screeched, and out jumped two Moroccan men in western dress. They chased off the kids and motioned for us to make our getaway, but three miles down the road we were mobbed again.

As it turned out, the bands of children and their screams for cigarettes plagued us every day, every three or four miles, all the way to Fès. And while the mountain children wanted cigarettes, the men wanted to sell us hashish. In the Rif mountains, the Moroccans cultivate hemp, from which they produce hashish. Whenever we passed a gathering of adobe houses, men dashed out and chased after us with huge cubes of hashish in their hands.

"You want hashish?" they yelled. "You stay here. Hashish and shower." The mountain men knew just what the foreigners wanted.

"You me distributor?" asked one man. "You buy me hashish cheap, sell in you country. Much dollar."

At day's end, we were still in the mountains, pedaling along the steep slopes that dropped into deep, narrow valleys. The far slopes were speckled with clusters of adobe houses. There were no roads to these remote settlements, only an occasional footpath. We could hear people shouting across the mountains and valleys to one another. Whenever an adult walking near the road spotted us, he called the news to the people farther up the cliffs, and immediately hooded heads popped out from behind the trees, rocks, and houses. Some of these silent human forms surveyed us from afar, while others came down the slopes for a closer look. When there were adults nearby, the children never bothered us.

As darkness approached, Larry and I had no idea where to pitch our tent for the night. The mountain slopes were too steep, and we worried that the children would chuck rocks through our tent. Without a map, we didn't know whether or not we were nearing a town, although we could see what appeared to be a pass up ahead. We kept pedaling and my knees ached. I prayed that we'd find a settlement at the summit.

Small Moroccan settlements, the few that were scattered along the road between Ceuta and Fès, generally consisted of mud-brick houses with dried straw roofs; a bar-cafe, which, because consumption of alcoholic beverages is forbidden by Muslim law, served only mint tea and soft drinks; a community well or fountain; some wandering chickens; and no electricity or plumbing. Except that it boasted two cafes instead of one, the village that greeted us at the pass fit this description perfectly. It sat at the center of a narrow, marshy plateau.

This night, for the first time on our trip, we would be among people whose primary tongue—Arabic—we could not speak. As we leaned our bikes against one of the cafes, we were wondering what hand motions we should use to ask permission to pitch our tent on the wet, soggy land next to the building. We were a bit anxious about what the reaction of the townspeople would be to our arrival and request.

At the entrance to the cafe, a hunk of rotting, hairy, fly-covered meat rested on a dirty wooden table. A primitive scale, consisting of a rod and two pans and a small collection of round weights, sat beside the meat. The butcher knife was caked with a layer of hardened blood and dust.

Larry stepped past the meat and into the cafe, and I followed behind. I wasn't sure exactly what my role as a female should be in this Muslim country, where so far I'd rarely seen women and men talking together and never once saw a woman in a cafe.

The tables in the cafe were filled with men smoking hashish and sipping mint tea or soft drinks. When we entered the room, all conversation stopped, and the silent faces examining us remained totally expressionless.

"Hello. Does anyone here speak English?" Larry asked hesitantly.

No one said a word. One man, the only one in the cafe not dressed in a long robe, shook his head.

"*Habla español?*" Larry asked.

"*Sí!*" answered the man in the tattered suit, who, it turned out, worked for the Ministry of Justice and had stopped in at the cafe on his way north to Tetouan from Meknes. His name was Merouane, and he spoke Arabic, Spanish, and French. In Morocco the educated youth spoke French as a second language, and some of the older people, who were schooled when Spain controlled parts of Morocco, still remembered Spanish.

Larry explained to Merouane what we wanted to do, and he in turn explained our intentions to the men in the cafe. When Merouane finished talking, the hooded men appeared extremely pleased. Merouane motioned for us to follow him, and everyone emptied out of the cafe behind us. By now the village children had spotted our bikes resting against the cafe wall and were busy spreading the word. It wasn't long before all the men and children of the town had gathered around us. But no women ever appeared.

"Put your tent anywhere," said Merouane. "We want to watch."

Larry and I scouted out the driest area near the cafe and set about pitching the tent. As we worked, Merouane asked us questions about ourselves and our bike trip then translated our answers for the others. When the dome of our bright blue and yellow tent popped up, everyone, including Merouane, stood transfixed. A few of the children started to move in closer, but they were held back by the men, who shot us questioning looks. As soon as Larry motioned for everyone to go ahead and examine the tent, the men squatted down and peered in through the windows, then gingerly touched the nylon walls or studied the aluminum poles and stakes. After a while they asked Merouane something.

"We want to know how you get inside," Merouane explained.

Larry unzipped the door, then crawled in and looked back out at us through the windows. That impressed everyone; and when I unpacked our sleeping pads and down sleeping bags, the men took turns feeling them. Merouane wanted to know if President Carter owned a tent like ours.

Just as we finished unloading our gear, it began to sprinkle. Merouane quickly bid us farewell, then climbed into his car and drove away. The other men pulled their hoods down over their foreheads, hunched their shoulders, and hurried upon pointed slippers or bare feet to the shelter of the cafe or their nearby homes. Larry and I climbed inside the tent, while the children huddled around the windows and stared in at us. They waved and giggled.

With Merouane gone, we figured we had lost all verbal communication with our newly adopted village. But suddenly the worried face of the cafe owner appeared at one of the tent windows. In very broken Spanish and with the help of a spectrum of hand motions, he told us that the ground around the tent would flood if it rained hard tonight. He had a better place for us, and gestured for Larry to follow him. I waited inside the tent and rested my knees.

The better place turned out to be a large windowless room made of cement blocks, with a corrugated steel door. The room was newly constructed and would soon become the village's only market. The cafe owner was its proud proprietor, and a broad smile burst across his face when we told him that we greatly appreciated his offer and agreed to spend the night inside.

We collapsed our tent and moved everything into the dark room, which would shelter us from the rain and the noise and lights of passing cars and trucks. Then we walked with our stove, cookset, rice, and vegetables to the cafe, where we could cook and eat by the light of the kerosene lamps. Two young men, who spoke French and could read some English, joined us at our table. I pulled out the *Time* magazine I'd bought in Ceuta and handed it to them. They opened it, pointed to a picture of Carter, Sadat, and Begin, and smiled.

"Jimmy Carter," one of them nodded. "Good. Peace."

The other fellow pointed at a picture of an atomic bomb exploding, then wrinkled his brow and shrugged his shoulders to indicate that he didn't understand. His friend glanced at the picture and said "Hiroshima," and the other nodded that he understood.

While the two studied the magazine together, they were smoking hash and holding hands. In Muslim Morocco the young men in the country settlements had no sexual contact with women until they married, and our two new friends, like so many other young Muslim men we would encounter, shared their sexual desires with other men either because women were off limits or because they preferred male partners.

While we ate our dinner, a truck driver stopped in for his evening meal of beef shishkebab and tea. He spoke to us in Spanish, and before he left he informed the men in the cafe that we had no map. That news prompted everyone to put their heads together and draw us a map detailing the route to Fès. Afterward, someone wrote in the place names in French. It was a sketchy map, but the road had only two forks in it: the turnoffs to Chechaouen and Meknes.

After we'd finished eating, Larry and I thanked everyone for the map, told the fellows next to us to keep the magazine, and started back to our cement room. The cafe owner was worried that we might be too cold, but we assured him that we had enough bedding.

The village was quiet. The usual modern small-town sounds of televisions, radios, cars, water faucets, and flush toilets were absent. The children had all been put to bed, and only a few tall hooded figures moved about in front of their silent homes in the darkness and the light rain. They nodded to us and smiled, and a peaceful feeling permeated the crisp night air. Larry and I relieved ourselves at the edge of the village, then entered our pitch-dark room and pulled the heavy door closed behind us. While I groped for my sleeping bag, I remembered the advice of a German woman I met in Spain.

"If you're going to Morocco," she said, "be sure to always stay in a nice hotel. Get a room with a good lock on the door. You can never be too cautious with those crazy Moroccans. They're very dangerous people, all of them. They'll rob you and they'll slit your throat. They steal everything."

I smiled to myself, then I slid down into my bag and fell asleep at the complete mercy of the "crazy, dangerous" Moroccans.

The next morning, after we'd eaten breakfast inside our room, we pushed open the corrugated door and walked with our bikes to the community fountain. The men and children were heading out into the mountains to tend their animals and crops, and when they saw us at the fountain, they walked over to watch us clean our dishes. Two men kept asking us something we couldn't understand. Finally, one of the men hunched his shoulders, crossed his arms in front of his chest, clenched his hands and shivered, then pointed to the cement room.

"They want to know if we got cold during the night," Larry decided. We shook our heads and everyone smiled. Before we headed south, we stopped at the cafe and thanked the owner for his hospitality.

From the south end of the plateau, where the road dropped down off the pass, we could see snow on the tops of the high mountains to the east. The air was still damp and cool again, and I would be comfortable in my sweat pants and sweat shirt, which was good, because I wanted to keep my legs and arms covered out of respect for the Muslim dress code.

"Oops, looks like trouble up ahead," I called to Larry as we coasted to the foot of the mountain. Blocking the road stood two men with their motorcycles. Even from a distance, I could see that they were armed. Like most Moroccans, both of the men were slightly darker in complexion than southern Spaniards. They were tall and heavyset, with black hair and thick mustaches. There was a fierce look in their eyes. Larry and I rolled to a stop. There was no other traffic on the road.

"Passport!" ordered the shorter of the two. They were policemen. We fished out our passports from our handlebar bags and handed them over. The policemen eyed our bicycles curiously, then they each grabbed a passport and stared in amazement at the front covers.

"U-ni-ted States of A-mer-i-ca," one slowly read aloud.

"*Americain?*" the taller one asked increduously.

"Yep," said Larry.

"But how here with bicycle?" The shorter policeman could speak some English while his partner spoke only French.

"We flew from America to Spain with our bicycles. We've cycled here from Barcelona."

"Long, long way! Where go Morocco?"

"Fès."

"*Americain?*" the taller one was asking again. He was having a difficult time comprehending the concept of two Americans arriving in Morocco on bicycles. His partner explained.

"Americans travel only tour buses!" he said. "But you no. You bicycle. That good. Come, we help."

They led us into an isolated bar-cafe up the road and told the owner to bring us some food. The man handed us a small loaf of bread and some packets of processed cheese packaged in foil, and the policemen bargained the price.

"The last thing we need is more cheese to add to the two pounds we bought in Ceuta," Larry groaned. "But I'm sure as hell not going to argue with these guys." We smiled and thanked the owner and the policemen, then continued south.

After a few hours of pedaling through grassy mountains, the road suddenly filled with men, women, and children, moving south on foot or on donkeys with large baskets strapped to their sides. We felt uneasy. It seemed as if the entire mountain population had joined a mass exodus, and we wondered if there had been or was expected to be some major catastrophe we were unaware of. But, although the people were moving quickly, everyone appeared calm. One old man riding on a donkey led by a woman began laughing hysterically when he saw us pedal by. No one traveled by bicycle on the open road in Morocco, and there were no bicycles in the small towns. To the Moroccans, Larry and I were a queer sight.

We pedaled for nearly ten miles alongside the flood of people and donkeys before we reached its end at a large village and discovered the reason for the mass migration—it was market day in the village. A circular brick wall with one wide opening stood at the center of the village. Inside, the farmers had set out their produce for sale, and merchants were selling beach towels, clothes, and candles from makeshift wooden stalls. The market was crowded and so muddy that the people had laid down wooden planks to form dry pathways. Larry and I wanted to go inside and buy food for lunch and dinner, but that meant we would have to leave our bicycles outside, out of eyeshot.

"I don't know about you, but I've decided the rumors about the Moroccans all being a bunch of cutthroat thieves are a lot of bull," Larry said. "At least I don't think anyone's going to steal from a couple of bicyclers. I get the feeling they respect what we're doing. I think we could leave our bikes here and nobody would touch anything on them. What do you think?"

I was a little leery but thought it was worth a try. Using gestures and mime, Larry asked one of the thirty children who were crowded around us to watch our bikes while we shopped. The boy, once he realized he alone had been chosen above all the others to guard the possessions of the two newly arrived aliens, quickly assumed an air of supreme self-importance and took his position next to our bikes. I knew right then that we had nothing to worry about.

Inside the market, we plodded through the slush of mud and donkey manure and looked over the stalls and food. Some of the merchants tossed us packets of hard candies, and everyone shouted a cheerful "Bon jour, madam! Bon jour, monsieur!" One of the farmers spoke to us in Spanish and sold us two pounds of oranges, some carrots, zucchini, onions, and tomatoes. The total bill came to a whopping dollar fifty. To a couple of cheapo cyclers who loved to eat, Morocco was looking better by the minute. The man dropped a bag of candy in with our food and wished us a safe journey.

We reached Quezzane, the only city between Tetouan and Fès, by midafternoon, and we stopped to buy bottled water and bread. The man at the bakery told us that we could find bottled water at the bar in the tourist hotel up the street. Two Spanish couples from Malaga were seated on the patio of the hotel sipping soft drinks, and one of the women gasped in disbelief when she saw us ride up.

"*Diós mío!* Did you come all the way from Ceuta on those things?" she shrieked. She and her friends were returning from Fès, and they offered us their maps.

"The road forks up ahead," the woman explained. "We came by way of the main road, which is relatively flat, but it's in terrible condition. There are potholes big enough to swallow your bicycles, and there are rocks all over the road. I'd advise you to take the mountain road to Fès. It might be better than the main road; at least it couldn't be worse."

An ultramodern, air-conditioned tour bus pulled up to the hotel just as we finished talking with the Spaniards, and we decided to ask the driver about the two roads going south. We wanted a second opinion before we took off over the tiny mountain road, which was a barely visible line on the maps the Spaniards had given us. When we approached the bus, we could see that the passengers were Americans. Both of us were excited to have encountered some fellow countrymen, and we rushed toward them to strike up a conversation.

The expression of horror on the passengers' faces when they looked our way brought my forward motion to an abrupt halt. At first I couldn't understand what exactly had terrified them. But then it occurred to me that Larry and I were caked with dirt and sweat. We hadn't washed in a while. Our clothes were tattered; mud and donkey manure clung to our shoes; our hair was greasy and matted; our bicycles were dusty and battered. I froze. They're afraid of us, I said to myself. They're afraid of us because we look like filthy weirdos, and they're going to keep as far away from us as possible. I looked over at Larry. The poor soul was busy making a hopeless effort at starting a friendly conversation with the folks from back home.

"Hi everybody! Are you all Americans?"

Silence.

"Say, can someone tell me where your driver went? I'd like to get some directions from him."

There was no response to that question either, but I knew exactly what the people were thinking: *You* want to talk to *our* driver? Forget it. You're not catching a ride with us. No sir. We don't allow any degenerates on *this* bus. We're into good clean fun, and who knows what you two filthy freakos are into. Probably hashish and stealing our money. You and the Moroccans would steal us blind if you got half a chance. Rob us and use the money to buy drugs. No sir. You're not talking to *our* driver! No way, no how!

As soon as Larry walked close enough to the unloading passengers to give them a good whiff of his killer body odor and scented shoes, they fled to the bar inside the hotel—all except one man from San Jose, who was tottering his way toward me.

"Shay. Wh-what er ya two doin' 'ere? Ya studying' fer yer pos' doctorate en fereign geography?" the man asked sarcastically. His "little something to nip on" was tucked into the right-hand jacket pocket of his bright orange leisure suit. Gold medallions dangled on his hairy chest, exposed by an unbuttoned, flowered shirt. Around his bulging abdomen he wore a wide belt of shiny white plastic, which matched his equally shiny white loafers.

"Did I shay *geography* or *porn*ography?" he continued in his inebriated slur. "Shay, did ja know dat da Vatican 'as da worldses larges' collection of por-no-gra-phic art? Yep, nude statues and pitchers everwhere."

Larry and I shook our heads.

"OK. Now ya do. Name's Adams and I'm en con-struck-shun in California. Know where dat is?"

"Yep. We're from California ourselves," answered Larry.

Mr. Adams seemed perplexed by Larry's response. He rolled forward on his toes and squinted to bring us into focus.

"Ya A-mer-i-cans?" he asked suspiciously. "Ya don' look like us 'mericans. Shay, wha's dat on da seatta yer sweatpants?" he wanted to know.

I had turned to look at the donkey that was sniffing our bikes and unfortunately had given Mr. Adams a clear view of my rear end. I'd forgotten about the sheep turds. The day before, when we stopped to eat our afternoon snack just below Tetouan, I accidently sat in a pile of sheep droppings. And the warm and gooey brown pellets the size of marbles had embedded themselves into the seat of my yellow sweats. I had forgotten all about the hardened mess that decorated my rear and emanated its own rancid odor, similar to that which wafted from my shoes. I'd forgotten because the Moroccans never took any notice of it. In Morocco, peasant's clothes stayed dirty and smelly for a long time before they were washed.

"Sheep turds," I said as I turned around and shot Mr. Adams a wide, pleasant smile.

Mr. Adams had pulled out his flask by now, and was pouring the brew down his throat. When I spoke, he stopped abruptly and stuffed the flask back into his pocket. Then he gave me a long, hard, suspicious look. I continued to smile as innocently as I possibly could.

"Whad ja shay?" he slurred.

"Sheep turds."

"Sheep? Sheep? Now don' ja blame *dat* on no sheep!" Mr. Adams yelled angrily. Then after a moment's hesitation, he got his bearings and made his way to the bar to join the others. What he was about to tell them would greatly substantiate their already abysmal opinion of Larry and me.

When we climbed on our bikes to leave, the bus driver walked out of the hotel. We asked him about the two roads to Fès, and he warned us against the mountain road. "It's nonexistent in places," he explained.

The Spaniards were right about the potholes, rocks, and rough blacktop. But since there was almost no traffic on the main road, we could ride in either lane to avoid the obstacles, and we managed to keep our speed up enough to stay just ahead of the packs of children who chased us. By late afternoon we were out of the mountains and pedaling through gentle rolling hills and flat fields of wheat. We stopped in a tiny settlement to fill our reserve water bottle with water for cooking and washing dishes.

While Larry searched out the community fountain, I stayed with the bikes. Two barefoot girls about twelve years old ran toward me. Bright red and blue scarves tied back their dark hair. Each wore bead necklaces and bracelets, a blouse, and a long skirt, and both of them were holding one hand behind their backs. About six feet from me they swung their hidden hands in front of them; they were each carrying a gigantic, sharp, lethal-looking sickle. They moved their sickles back and forth through the air, and with their free hands they drew their index fingers across their throats to indicate that they were about to slit mine.

My initial thought was to drop the bikes and run like hell, but eventually I decided that the girls were only teasing. Besides, I reasoned, the old man sitting near me wouldn't let them slice me up. I called their bluff.

"*Bon jour!*" I blurted in my best attempt at French. I held out my hand but kept my eyes on the sickles and my legs ready to sprint. The girls giggled in delight. They lowered their sickles and each one took her turn shaking my hand and cautiously touching the strange blond hairs that covered my exposed forearm.

At sunset Larry and I found ourselves in a flat area devoid of trees, bushes, or roadside settlements. We pushed our bikes into a barren field and started setting up camp. As always happened whenever and wherever we stopped in the countryside, human forms materialized out of thin air. It was an eerie occurrence, which we never quite got used to. This night, the first person to approach was a rugged and crazy sheepherder, who ran around in circles uttering weird gurgling sounds. Each time we glanced in his direction or tried to talk with him, he broke into wild hysterical laughter and ran off, only to return seconds later and resume his circles and noises. Eventually he ran off for good.

Three young men, who spoke only Arabic, and their donkey were the next to wander over. Fortunately, these three fellows seemed completely sane. They sat down beside us and indicated that we should continue preparing our dinner. One fellow pulled from his robe what remotely resembled a handmade ukulele. The body of the instrument was a metal can with a hole cut in the center of the front. A flat stick protruded from the top of the can. Two metal wires were secured to the top of the stick, drawn down across the hole in the center of the can, and attached to the bottom of the can. The instrument was played with a pick.

While Larry and I cooked our meal of steamed zucchini, onions, and tomatoes over rice, the Moroccans serenaded us with melodic wailing accompanied by the *plunkity-plunk-plunkity-plunk* of the two strings. In fifteen minutes they exhausted their repertoire and were ready for a different form of entertainment—donkey riding.

"I'm not gettin' on that thing," Larry protested. "Besides, it's you they're pointing at. They want *you* to ride it, not me."

"Oh, what the heck," I said, "I've ridden horses before, this oughta be a piece of cake."

And I calmly climbed onto the donkey. Once I was on, though, I realized there were no reins, which meant that I'd be riding bareback with no means of controlling the beast's direction of movement. I thought better of the situation and started to climb off, but the Moroccans shoved me back on. One fellow gave a shrill whistle and I was off and running—*bouncing* is a better word. The little animal blasted into a fast trot, and it was all I could do to hold onto its shaggy mane. My crotch smashed into the donkey's protruding backbone several times a second as we bobbed across the fields.

"Whoa!" I screamed.

The animal kept going.

Big problem, I thought; this donkey, being Moroccan, does not understand English. I tried yanking its mane, slapping its neck, and emitting bloodcurdling screams, all to no avail; I continued bouncing farther and farther away from my beloved husband. We bounced toward a lone farmer, who looked as if he were viewing the arrival of some otherworldly apparition: a strange, light-haired female wearing peculiar yellow slacks and screaming unintelligible words, while jostling wildly atop a donkey. But before I had time to say anything to the farmer, I heard a high-pitched whistle, and he was immediately out of my field of vision. The donkey had executed a swift one-hundred-and-eighty-degree turn, and we were thundering back to its master.

Even before I'd climbed on the donkey, my rear and crotch were sore from the afternoon's rough bicycle ride. And so, when Larry pulled me off the animal's backbone, I was in excruciating pain; but I forced myself to smile at our three friends, who were anxious to know if I enjoyed my ride. They appeared pleased by my attempt at enthusiasm. It was dark now, and they headed toward the hills to their makeshift tents at the edge of the fields.

After they had gone, Larry and I pitched our tent by the light of the moon and stars overhead. The field was completely silent now. There was no traffic on the distant road. I felt uneasy and vulnerable lying inside our tent. I had my bottle of dog repellent close at hand. It was a chemical spray that could temporarily blind an animal or human. I was thinking about the farmers' warnings that wandering nomads might throw rocks at our tent if we pitched it in a field, and also about the stories I heard in Spain of foreigners being raped and murdered by Moroccan bandits. Tonight we had no cement walls around us and no village people to watch over us. Larry, however, wasn't worried in the least.

"The Moroccans have been nothing but kind and generous," he said. "The children are a problem, but they don't go wandering through fields in the middle of the night. There's nothing to worry about, Barb. Forget about the rumors."

Ten minutes later we heard people approaching. I grabbed my dog repellent. The voices stopped just as the footsteps reached our tent. Then there was a long agonizing silence, and beads of perspiration popped out all over my body. How many are there? I wondered. Why don't they move? Why don't they say something? No one stirred, and the silence seemed endless. Then came a noise—*plunkity-plunk, plunkity-plunk, plunkity-plunk.* A warm, safe sensation washed through my body. Our friends sang softly, and soon Larry and I were fast asleep.

A Moroccan and his cow joined us for breakfast in the morning. The young man first built a small fire with some twigs he was carrying to warm the animal, then he sat down with Larry and me. We offered him a piece of cheese, which he attached to the end of a long stick. He squatted next to the fire and proceeded to roast it. After a few minutes the cheese was a gruesome, hot, rubbery glob, and not even the cow knew what to do with it when the man flicked it at her in disgust. He motioned for another piece of cheese, and this one he dropped into the pocket of his robe for safekeeping.

After breakfast Larry brushed his teeth. A perplexed expression crept across the young man's face. He stuck his head directly in front of Larry's and watched incredulously as Larry moved the end of the brush around inside his mouth. All of a sudden Larry pulled the toothbrush out of his mouth, grinned a big, wide smile, and forced a flood of white frothy paste out from between his teeth. Our friend broke into hysterical laughter and trotted around his cow, slapping himself and pointing to Larry's foamy grin.

Soon after we started out, a fork appeared in the road that was not shown on our maps. The signposts were all in Arabic, and Larry and I studied them thoughtfully.

"Well, what do you think?" Larry asked. "Which looks more like Fès? The squiggles on the right or the ones on the left?" While we examined the squiggles, two boys who were tending goats in the fields nearby came running over to have a good look at us.

"Fès?" Larry asked, pointing in the direction he figured Fès was located, to the left. The two nodded. "Fès?" he asked again, this time pointing to the right. We had learned that some children answer yes to whatever they're asked; so we were careful to always double-check. The boys shook their heads no and pointed back to the left.

By noon we were within twenty miles of Fès. The terrain was dry and dusty, and the temperature had pushed into the eighties. I continued to cycle in my sweat pants until I couldn't stand it any longer.

"I've got to get these sweats off," I called to Larry. "Keep your fingers crossed. We're about to find out what happens if a woman wears shorts in a Muslim country."

I ran off the road behind some boulders and hurried to change before any curious forms began to materialize. I returned wearing a short-sleeved T-shirt and my black cycling shorts, which extended much farther down my legs than my gym shorts. I felt totally naked.

For the first few miles, I wouldn't look at anyone. I was embarrassed by my exposed skin. Convinced that everyone was staring at me in utter disgust, I couldn't bring my eyes to meet theirs. Eventually, I summoned my courage and searched the farmers' faces for disapproving scowls. There were none; the men looked at me no differently than they had when I was heavily clothed.

We saw the Atlas mountains before we saw Fès; their peaks still covered with snow. Fès sat in the plain at the base of the range. The oldest of the Sultan's four traditional capitals, Fès had been there for over twelve hundred years. In the mid-fourteenth century, it was the center of learning and commerce, and it was still the center of religion and traditional crafts. At the outskirts of the city, Larry and I stopped at a modern gas station, something we hadn't seen in days, and asked directions to the campground. The attendants sent us to the separate "new city," founded in 1916.

New Fès boasted modern shops and hotels, and nearly all the men and some of the women dressed in western clothing. It shocked us to see women wearing knee-length skirts, high-heeled shoes, and tight blouses. The majority of the women, though, wore long, hooded, tight-fitting satin robes, which covered their clothing. Some women pulled their hoods over their heads and wore veils that covered their whole faces except for their eyes. Others wore hoods or scarves but no veils, while still others wore neither, only the long robes, with the hoods resting on their shoulders.

The campground was tucked into a classy residential area of New Fès and surrounded by a high brick wall with two guards stationed in front. Inside there were showers, squat toilets, sinks to wash dishes in, and cement basins and washboards for washing clothes. The camping fee for two people was five *dirhams* a day, or a dollar ninety. The showers were ice cold, but in the heat they felt wonderful. We washed away the dirt, sweat, mud, donkey manure, and sheep turds that had attached themselves to our bodies and clothing over the last two and a half days. I bought oranges, bread, and yogurt for dinner at the shop across from the campground, and by six o'clock Larry and I had collapsed into bed.

We were up early the next morning, walking the eight kilometers to visit the *medina*, the walled, ancient city of Fès. The brilliant sunlight could barely filter through the smoke, dust, and shadows that filled its intricate maze of crowded, narrow passageways. Flies dotted the hazy strands of sunlight. The smells, sights, and sounds of the *medina* were exotic and alien. Odors came from the steaming mint tea, the hashish, and the fresh warm piles of manure left by the donkeys, which were used to carry everything into and out of the labyrinth. The dying vats in the giant open-air tannery had their own special smell, as did the decaying buildings, the spices, the dirt and dust, the freshly baked pastries, and the rotting meat at a few of the butcher shops.

Through the odors, made especially pungent by the heat, swayed a collage of white turbans, red fezzes, jeans, tailored shirts, knee-length skirts, long hooded robes, veils, scarves, beach towels, and flat leather slippers. Women tourists in scant tube-tops and shorts moved along beside Muslim women who exposed only their eyes. People were pushed awkwardly against the walls of the shops lining the pathways by the force of the crowds making room for passing donkeys laden with boxes or baskets of merchandise. The dark men leading the donkeys were continually calling out to the wall of bodies up ahead, but often the confusion in the bustling narrow passageways drowned out their pleas for more room.

Static and grating high-pitched singing blared from radios inside the tea shops, and five times a day the summons to prayer was cried out by the *muezzin* from the top of the slender, towering minarets. Below, cramped into tiny one-room stalls, which opened onto the alleyways, carpenters, leather and brass craftsmen, weavers, and tailors worked feverishly. Young boys hired as weavers' assistants stood some twelve feet up the alley from their shops, each holding three or four strands of wool fibers in his hands. The strands extended into the shop, and were woven into robes and suits by the weaver. The boys moved the fibers around as the men weaved, the children running past sometimes tripped over the strands. Old men stood nearby selling mint leaves, five cents a bunch, for tea, while small children begged goodnaturedly from the foreign tourists, and the butchers hung out the severed heads of the animals whose meat was for sale.

Rugs, hardware, footwear, fruits, vegetables, blue jeans, fabrics, furniture, lamps—nearly everything imaginable—were stocked or produced in the shops of the *medina*. The diversity of shops matched the multiformity of people, smells, and sounds. Inside the Qarawiyin mosque, the oldest mosque in North Africa and the seat of a university founded in 859, devout Muslim men knelt on exotic handwoven rugs and bowed toward Mecca in prayer to Allah. At the bus station just outside the walls of the *medina*, the blind, deformed, and destitute begged from the Muslim passengers, most of whom passed them a few coins.

Each day for part of a week, Larry and I lost ourselves in this tangled, exotic world, which at times seemed like a surrealistic dream. We watched and we listened and we breathed in its aromas, and then we pulled ourselves away and headed back to Ceuta.

Taking the bus to Ceuta seemed like a good idea for two reasons. First, we would avoid spending two days retracing the two hundred miles between Fès and Ceuta. And second, we figured the bus ride might prove to be an interesting experience.

At five thirty on the morning of April 22, we pedaled from the campground to the bus station. The sunlight had yet to brighten the dusty air, and sleeping bodies clogged the alleyways around the station. For thirty-five *dirhams* (eleven dollars), we were given two seats on the six o'clock bus. Our gear we could stuff under our feet and seats, but the bicycles had to ride on the roof, and that cost us another ten *dirhams*. The bikes joined the large packages and crates carried up a ladder at the back of the bus, placed on the roof, and secured with a net. During the eight-hour ride, whenever the bus stopped to take on more passengers and crates, Larry climbed up the ladder behind the boy doing the loading to make sure our bikes were still there and in one piece. Because of the rough road surface and the bus's apparent absence of shock absorbers, the parcels banged noisily against the roof and each other. Each time the bus plunged into and leapt out of a road-wide pothole, we half expected to see our mechanical companions come flying past the windows.

If only Mom could see me now, I kept thinking, as the bus headed out of Fès. Here we were, Larry and I, squashed into our tiny seats with hardly enough room in front of us to place our knees, legs, and feet. The two men standing in the aisle next to us each held two live chickens, one in either hand, upside down by their muddy feet. The chickens hung there motionlessly.

The bus's radio speakers were located just over my head, and the driver had the volume turned up as far as it would go. What came out of the speakers were the voices of wailing Moroccan mammas accompanied primarily by static. A few miles outside of Fès, the man in front of us banged the back of his portable radio-cassette against the back of the seat in front of him, and his electric box burst to life. He preferred wailing males, yet with the identical nerve-racking accompaniment. The bus was close and hot, and I leaned my head out the window for some dusty fresh air and wind in my ears.

Once, when the bus lunged into a pothole, one of the men in the aisle was caught off balance. He let go of the chicken in his right hand and grabbed for a seat back to balance himself. The loose chicken went beserk, and by the time someone had wrestled it down, there was hardly a feather left on her body. She was returned to her owner. The music blared on.

There were only three scheduled stops between Fès and Ceuta—Quezzane, Chechaouen, and Tetouan—but our driver stopped for anyone waiting at the side of the road who signaled for a ride. The blind rode free. At Quezzane, before anyone was able to get off the bus, a few beggars climbed on board and made their rounds. Then children selling fruit, candy, and gum streamed in. Almost every passenger got off in Quezzane to stretch and stop at the cafe. They all left their possessions unattended on their seats, which made me wonder what had happened to all the Moroccan thieves the foreign travelers warned us about.

In Tetouan the two men seated in front of us got off, and two smartly dressed Moroccans in their early twenties took their places. Both fellows could speak English, but their speech was slurred and they giggled a lot. Shortly after they sat down, one of them pulled out a half-empty bottle of gin and two glasses. This was the first time Larry and I had seen a Moroccan with alcohol. The others on the bus glared disapprovingly at the bottle, but the two ignored the hostile stares and commenced belting down whole glassfuls of straight gin. With their third glass, they each swallowed a strange looking pill. It wasn't long after that that they both started laughing uncontrollably and experiencing great difficulty in sitting upright, especially the one seated next to the aisle. The other Moroccans hissed in disgust.

Giggle, giggle, flop. The torso of one of the gin drinkers tumbled into the aisle; the armrest prevented the remainder of his body from following. The other drinker leaned over, grabbed his friend's nearest dangling shoulder, and yanked his body upright. There was more laughter, and in their drunken stupor the two offered the hooded farmer seated across the aisle from them a sample of their beverage. The farmer raged in horror and stormed off to another seat.

Giggle, giggle, flop. The fellow on the aisle fell overboard again. We were now within fifteen minutes of the border and the Spanish border police, who were internationally notorious for their exhaustive hashish searches. It was well known to anyone traveling in Morocco that getting caught bringing hash into Spain could put a human being away in some black hole of a Spanish prison for the good portion of his lifetime. Fifteen minutes from the border, and zeroing in at forty miles an hour, the two gin drinkers lit up a joint.

"Oh won-der-ful," groaned Larry. "Their number's up now. The state they're in, I won't be surprised if they offer all the customs officers a hit or two. This here ought to be one real interesting border crossing!"

The bus rumbled on and the two kept smoking. And they smoked and they smoked and they offered. "No thank you, no we don't care for any hashish right now, thank you very much," we answered. And then the border appeared and the bus stopped.

"Oh great. We smell like hash," Larry grumbled.

Sure enough, our clothes, skin, and hair reeked of hashish as we rolled our bikes up to the crossing, but no one could smell us over the aroma of donkey manure and exhaust fumes. "No customs' checks until Algeciras," the Spanish border official shouted as he waved us through.

Before we headed into Ceuta, I looked back at the bus. It was empty except for the two drinkers. They were still slouched over in their seats, smoking joints and laughing hysterically. They never made it to the ferry that night.

~ · ~

At Rota, Spain, ninety miles northwest of Algeciras on the coast near Cadiz, there was a U.S. naval base. Lee Trani, whom we had met with his wife, Sheila, at the campground in Granada, was stationed there. Lee and Sheila had masterfully bribed us to visit them at the base by handing us a giant jar of extra chunky peanut butter and intimating that there was more to be had at the commissary in Rota. After three months of the sweet, pasty, Spanish concoction ever so loosely referred to as peanut butter, our first spoonful of Yankee extra chunky was pure and simple ecstasy. And so, on April 23, when Larry and I rolled off the ferry from North Africa, we pedaled straight for Rota.

In the mere forty-eight hours it took us to travel from Morocco to Rota, a self-contained little America, we leapt from a past century into what felt like the twenty-second. While Spain, with its cars, electricity, plumbing in the villages, and heavy farm machinery in the fields, seemed modern in comparison to Morocco, Rota was a step beyond. The base had a drive-in theater, a motorcycle track, a golf course, tennis courts, and in front of the houses sat power lawn mowers and recreational vehicles the size of four or five Moroccan homes. The Tranis' home sported a stereo, a bathroom with wall-to-wall carpeting, and a queen-size mattress in what was to be our room.

We stayed in Rota for three days. It felt good to talk with someone in English again and to reminisce about America with people who had lived there. It felt good to be settled for a while and not have to scout for food and a place to camp each night. It felt good, and it stirred certain emotions that made us think of home and caused us to wonder if maybe we weren't getting tired of traveling. In the past when people had taken us into their homes, we usually felt revitalized by their friendships and eager to travel on and meet more kind, caring people. But in Rota we felt homesick.

Lee and Sheila stuffed our packs with chocolate and oatmeal cookies, peanut butter, and granola the morning we left Rota and headed north—directly into a stiff head wind. The terrain north of Rota was uninteresting, and besides, we had seen it all on our way down from Sevilla. Rows of low gnarled stumps covered the dry rolling hills, and the wind lifted the dust from the Spanish vineyards and tossed it into our eyes. The head wind and our homesickness dampened our spirits.

After three hours of battling the wind and a strong desire to hightail it back to Rota, Larry and I pulled off the road to eat lunch. We both felt drained from not having slept much the night before, and our muscles ached from fighting the head winds. The wind blew dirt and trash all over us—the roads in Spain were often littered with trash and garbage, and some of the streams were so polluted the reeking water looked black and sudsy. A passing motorist slowed down long enough to shout and whistle at me, even though I was clad in sweat pants and a baggy T-shirt. And I thought back to how the arrogant woman at the bakery had jacked up the price of her bread when we, "las turistas," walked into her shop. And soon, depression, homesickness, and physical and mental fatigue were taking their toll, and Larry and I started to argue.

"I wish you hadn't made us leave Rota. I wasn't ready to leave," I blurted. I could smell the garbage that someone had tossed out of his car, rotting nearby.

"Me! I didn't want to leave either. I thought you wanted to leave!" Larry shouted back.

"Then why didn't you tell me? Why don't you communicate what you want to do and what you don't want to do? Why didn't you tell me you didn't want to leave Rota?"

"Because we always do what you want to do, so I didn't even bother."

"Now that's a crock! We *always* do what *you* want to do, and you know it!"

The next thing we knew, the two of us were standing beside our bikes screaming about being sick of traveling, sick of the trash and dirt, sick of the Spaniards whistling at me, and sick of each other.

"When I get to Sevilla, I'm flying home! I've had it! I'm through! The end! I'm going home!" I shouted. "And I never want to see you again, ever!"

"Fine! The feeling's mutual! We're through!"

In his anger, Larry grabbed up my bike and tossed it into a ditch. I rushed over and picked it up, pushed it out to the road, jumped on, and pounded the pedals. I had no idea whether or not Larry was following behind me, and I couldn't have cared less. After ten or fifteen minutes, Larry eased up alongside me.

"Let's pull over and talk," he said in a surprisingly even tone.

"No! I've got a plane to catch!" I shot back.

"Now come on, let's calm down and talk." I pedaled on for a while without saying anything. Larry stayed behind, giving me more time to get control of myself.

"OK, let's talk," I finally agreed.

We sat side by side at the edge of the road, and Larry stretched an arm over my shoulders. This time neither of us noticed the litter, wind, dirt, or passing motorists. We both felt sorry, very sorry, for what we'd said to each other. Larry explained that he was depressed and tired of traveling, and I tried to rally our spirits.

"We're in a slump right now, that's all," I reasoned. "We've got to figure that on a two-year trip like this we're going to hit some lows every once in a while. We had a great time in Morocco. Rota just made us homesick, and we feel lonesome 'cause we're sad about leaving Lee and Sheila. And these head winds aren't helping either. But something will happen pretty soon to set us on another high. It always does.

"Look, the most important thing for us to do on this trip, especially as we head further east and the touring gets more difficult, is to support each other. If one of us gets irritated or depressed, instead of just yelling back, the other person's got to take the responsibility for calming that person down and caring for his or her feelings. We need each other's support to keep going through the rough times and the lows, and that's going to take some real effort on both our parts; because not getting upset when the other person is is tough to do sometimes, even under the most ideal circumstances.

"I love you Larry, and I'd never be able to do this alone. I'm sorry I got mad, and I'm going to be more understanding from now on. Everything will be OK. Portugal will probably turn out to be a great place, and even if it doesn't, we've got my parents' visit to look forward to. They'll be in Madrid in less than a month."

When we climbed into our sleeping bags at the end of the day, Larry and I held each other tight. We still felt homesick, but we could also sense a new closeness forming between us. The knowledge that we had only each other to share, and to struggle through, whatever our journey might throw at us was drawing us together and strengthening our relationship.

PORTUGUESE PARADISE

♦ CHAPTER ELEVEN ♦

Ah, Portugal. Thank God for beautiful, cheap, friendly, unspoiled Portugal. Too bad about the roads though.

Cobblestones, ugh! I pushed one pedal one full revolution, and my bike and I jumped and rattled forward, jolting over the jagged, uneven rock bricks. Sometimes my wheels descended into the huge spaces left by a few missing bricks or into the places where the separation between bricks was too wide. I kept a firm grasp on my handlebars, but my crotch was doing a painful jig atop my bouncing bicycle seat. Not until the bike slowed to a near stop and the bouncing subsided did I dare to push the other pedal. And when I did, I immediately braced myself for more shake, rattle, and roll. Lord! Not even Morocco was this bad!

It took us half the morning to cover ten miles of cobblestone road through and north of Lisbon. Inch-and-a-quarter bicycle tires and brick roads do not a compatible combination make. By the time we came to asphalt pavement, Larry's rear hub, a Campagnolo high flange, was cracked, and we still had another one hundred forty miles to go before we would reach the Spanish border on our way to Madrid. A good portion of those one hundred forty miles would be cobblestone or rough pavement. Portugal, we learned, was not known for smooth, modern roads.

Besides rattling our brains and teeth, pounding our butts, and cracking Larry's rear hub, the jolting vibrations of the cobblestones did something else; something that struck terror into Larry's heart. He didn't say anything when it first developed. He kept pedaling for a half hour or so, hoping that it would go away, but then when it didn't, he pulled off the road. We were in a deserted, desolate area near Evora, eighty miles east of Lisbon, and Larry sat down at the side of the road and stared off into the distance at nothing in particular. A look of horror and disbelief clouded his eyes.

"What's up?" I asked. "Looks like you've got a bad case of shell shock from too many cobblestones."

"They're dead," Larry answered.

"What's dead?"

"They're dead," he said again. The tone of his voice sounded flat.

"Look, I know they're dead. You already said that. What I need to know is what *they* are."

"My genitals."

"Oh."

"They're dead," he stated for the third time. "They're numb and they're useless and they've been that way for almost an hour now. It's all over, Barb. Everything's dead, *d e a d*, dead."

The two of us sat there together in silence at the edge of the road and waited to see what would happen next. It was a rough blow to a man of twenty-nine, loosing all feeling in his sexual organs. For thirty agonizing minutes, Larry remained motionless, lamenting his incredible loss. Then, suddenly, the faraway expression left his face. He uttered a long, reassuring "ah-h-h," and his eyes rolled skyward in an offering of thanks to the merciful heavens above. He felt a tingling sensation. After a few minutes his genitals were back to normal. We found out later, talking with other cyclers touring in central Europe, that the "dead genitals syndrome" was not uncommon to bicyclers who covered long distances over rough surfaces.

Yet bicycling hundreds of miles over brick and dirt roads and battered asphalt was well worth the effort. There weren't many Old World places left in Europe, but there was Portugal. Portugal, where peasants still transported their goods in donkey carts and herded their cows and goats through the village streets; where women washed their clothes outside in the community cement basins, then carried them home in baskets balanced on their heads; where many farmhouses lacked both electricity or running water.

On our first day in Portugal, we asked for six eggs and a bottle of drinking water at a one-room grocery store in a tiny village along the southern coast. The owner sent his daughter out behind their attached, whitewashed house to check the chicken coop. "Very sorry," he said when she returned, the daughter had found only four eggs. He shook his head. The chickens weren't laying like they used to. As for the water, he was out of bottled drinking water—but hold on a minute. The daughter was sent out back again. This time she returned with a long rope with a four-liter bucket attached. The owner handed the contraption to Larry and pointed out the window of his shop: there stood the community well.

The differences between Portugal and southern Spain were many. No one raised the prices because we were foreigners. Instead of whistling, or laughing, or leering, Portuguese men clapped when I pedaled by. There were no piles of litter or garbage along the roads. And the campgrounds were a delight; the one-dollar fee covered a hot shower and use of the cement wash basins. Every three or four days, we pulled into a campground to shower and wash our clothes.

It was late April when we pedaled the hot and sunny southern coast of Portugal on our way to Lisbon. Except for a few pockets of concentrated tourism and highrises, particularly around Albufeira and Quarteira, the coastline was nearly deserted. We made our way along dirt roads from one sandy, isolated cove to the next and spent the days sunbathing, swimming, reading, fishing, and hiking the jagged coastal cliffs.

Once each day, we cycled out to the main road and bought our provisions at the tiny grocery stores. There was never much selection in the shops, but the prices were always right. Eggs and cheese for breakfast, bread and six to eight containers of yogurt for lunch, and onions, tomatoes, smoked sausage, and rice for dinner usually ran us about three and a half dollars. In most of the stores we stopped in on our way north to Lisbon, there was so little available that we virtually cleaned out all the shelves buying a one-day's supply of food.

The road from Lisbon east to the border of Spain bounced us through the fortified, medieval towns of Evora, Estremoz, and Elva. The heat and dryness were so oppressive that we stopped at the community fountains in every village we came to and ran cold water over our sweltering bodies. People passing by always smiled and nodded their approval. At the end of the day, before we pulled off the road to free-camp in a field of olive or cork trees, we'd hit one last fountain, and bring out the soap and wash cloth and scrub the sweat and dirt off our arms, legs, faces, and necks.

It was an early Sunday afternoon when Larry and I rolled into Estremoz, twenty-five miles before the border of Spain. Nearly all the shops were closed, and most of the people had either gone home to eat their midday meal or were napping in the shaded parks and plazas. Even so, Larry found one pastry shop open where we were able to buy our usual lunch of yogurt, bread, and bottled water. Afterward, we pushed our bikes down the street a half block to where the sidewalk was shaded and sat down in front of a closed shoe store.

No sooner had we spread out our food and started to eat than a waiter emerged from the restaurant across the street and invited us inside, where it would be cooler and more comfortable. By now, after a few weeks of pedaling through Portugal, we had managed to pick up some Portuguese, which vaguely resembled a garbled form of Spanish spoken at top speed, and we quickly accepted the invitation. We gathered up our food and followed the waiter, Paulo, inside.

The restaurant had one large wooden door, which stood wide open. There were two small windows on either side of the doorway, but their shutters were closed tight. The room inside was dark and somewhat damp, and its coolness met us at the door. The walls were unpainted, the cement floor bare. On the bar at the far end of the room rested a television set, which was broadcasting the Sunday mass from Fatima. The television and the open doorway provided the only light in the room. A somber, elderly couple dressed in black sat at one of the six tables. They were eating fried fish and a salad, and they shared a large bottle of red wine. Their eyes were glued to the television.

Larry and I sat down at a table near the door and again spread out our lunch. Paulo brought us napkins, silverware, and glasses, and while we ate, he stood in the doorway and kept an eye on our bikes. It felt wonderful to be in out of the heat, but Paulo was worried about the long, hot, dry stretch that lay ahead of us, between Estremoz and the border.

"You will be very, very thirsty," he muttered, shaking his head. "In this region of Portugal, in the afternoon, it is too hot to bicycle. Those little water bottles on your bicycles will not carry you through."

Larry showed Paulo our reserve quart water bottle and assured him that we had more than enough water for the twenty-five-mile ride to the border.

"No. Not enough. Not enough," Paulo grumbled. He continued to shake his head and look preoccupied.

After a few moments, Paulo's face brightened, and he took off down the street toward the modern restaurant on the corner, where the tour buses stopped. Fifteen minutes later, Paulo came strolling back in through the front door with a gigantic, bright-yellow, plastic, five-liter jug of water in his arms and a smile that wrapped halfway around his head.

"Oh my God! That sucker must weigh fifteen pounds! And it's huge! I don't know how I'm going to strap it to my bike," Larry shuddered under his breath while he grinned at Paulo. Both of us knew there was no way out of it. We absolutely *had* to take the bottle with us, no matter how much it weighed. By the expression of supreme triumph on Paulo's face, we knew that if we refused his gift, his feelings and pride would be devastated. Paulo handed the jug to Larry.

"It's filtered ice water. Very, very good," he explained. "The restaurant did not have bottled water, but I found this bottle in their back room and cleaned it out and then I filled it with the filtered ice water."

Ice water sounded like a godsend in the Portuguese heat, but I could see by the expression on Larry's face, as he slipped one of the straps that held his sleeping bag onto his rear rack through the handle of the jug and cinched it down, that the bottle was too heavy. But Larry made no mention of the weight. We thanked Paulo enthusiastically, and pumped a hearty good-bye handshake.

At the edge of town, gypsies had set up an open-air market where they sold, among other things, clothes, towels, linens, shoes, and yardage. I decided to stop to look for a skirt to wear when we went sightseeing with my parents in Madrid. The gypsy families that ran the marketplace were a rough-looking lot. Their children dressed in rags; and the adults prided themselves on being expert bargainers.

I picked out a skirt of wrinkle-proof jersey material, which I could wad up and stash in the bottom of my packs. I offered the gypsy my Levi's in exchange. In 1979, everyone in Europe craved a pair of genuine American Levi jeans, so I was flabbergasted when the man shook his head at my offer.

"The skirt costs three hundred *escudos*. I do not want the jeans. I want the money," he said.

"But these are *genuine* Levi's. See, they're honest-to-goodness Levi's. They're worth a lot of money in Lisbon."

The gypsy cocked his head to the side and squinted his eyes. I could tell he didn't believe me.

"The Portuguese women around here do not wear jeans," he said. "Maybe American women wear jeans, but Portuguese peasants do not. I could not give those jeans away, let alone sell them."

Amazing, I said to myself, I never thought I'd see the day when a European turned down a pair of American Levi's. But that was Portugal. Modern times had yet to spoil her. The gypsy and I settled on two hundred *escudos*, about four dollars, and everyone was happy.

As it turned out, Larry and I guzzled down the entire five liters of ice water before we reached the border. Paulo was right; the ride was torture. As we pumped up a hill in the pounding sun and motionless air, we swore the heat would knock us out before we reached the top. The ice water relieved our throbbing heads and our parched mouths, which felt as it they'd been packed with cotton balls.

After we'd drunk all the water, we decided to hang onto the jug after all, and that proved to be a good idea. We kept it until we reached England. Larry carried it empty during the day, then just before we set up camp, we'd fill it so that we had plenty of water to cook and wash with. The extra supply of water came in handy for cleaning the layer of black which the gasoline we were now burning in our stove deposited on the bottoms and sides of our pans.

The one-hundred-five-degree heat chased us for two hundred fifty miles, all the way to Madrid. Returning to southern Spain was a letdown.

We crossed the border on a Sunday evening and ate dinner at a cafe in a small village east of Badajoz; we'd run out of food and all the grocery shops were closed. When the waiter tried to overcharge us for the meal, we knew we were back in Spain.

The day after we pedaled into Madrid, my parents flew in. While they slept off their jet lag, Larry and I disassembled our bikes and cleaned, greased, oiled, and readjusted them. Larry was able to buy a new rear hub.

A week later, after we'd seen the sights of Madrid, Mom and Dad rented a car, Larry and I locked our bikes to the rack on the roof, and the four of us took off for northern Portugal together. As we neared the border, I worried that the people of central and northern Portugal might not be as friendly as their countrymen to the south.

I didn't worry for long. When Mom went into the tourist information office at the border to pick up a few brochures, she returned not only with a mountain of pamphlets but also with two red roses. The woman in the tourist office had taken a shine to Mom and gave her the roses as a gift and a token of their friendship. The next day, in the mountain city of Viseu, Mom and Dad struck up a conversation with a young Portuguese secretary while they were eating breakfast in a cafe across the street from their hotel. At the end of the meal, the secretary, who spoke some English, declared that she was taking the day off from work so she could show us around the city. In every village and town we stayed, the Portuguese were immediately attracted to my parents, primarily because Mom and Dad hadn't arrived on a tour bus, they dressed simply, and they took a genuine interest in what they saw and who they met.

Pensions and restaurants in Portugal were a real bargain. While Larry and I camped, Mom and Dad stayed in pensions or hotels for seven-fifty to ten dollars for a double room and private bath. And when it came to meals, Portuguese restaurants knew exactly how to feed a big appetite. For two dollars a person, each of us would receive a huge, silver serving platter holding enough food to fill our plates twice with heaping servings of meat, french fries, rice, and salad. And for an extra twenty cents, the restaurant threw in a plateful of cooked vegetables.

"Now here's a country that knows how to eat!" Larry announced, the first time we ate in a restaurant. "I'm in heaven! It's just too bad I didn't know about these meals sooner. I could have eaten my way through southern Portugal, as well. No wonder there was never much food in the grocery shops down there, it was all in the restaurants!"

At the very northern edge of Portugal, along the Spanish border, we found the medieval village of Valença do Minho, perched on a cliff overlooking the Minho River and its lush green valley. The three towering gray rock walls that encircled Valença, and that had once protected it against attacks, stood intact. Inside these walls, the narrow cobblestone streets and gray stone buildings looked the same as they had for centuries. The countryside outside the walls was covered with the leafy vines—most were suspended more than seven feet above the ground—that bore the grapes used to make *vinho verde branco*, a tart white wine produced only in northern Portugal. Valença was a serene, picturesque place, and the four of us spent our last days in Portugal exploring its vineyards and farmland, and eating and drinking.

Larry and I pitched our tent just below the village on the grassy banks of the Minho, a wide river with a gentle flow. It was a quiet, peaceful spot; not even the noises from the distant farmhouses penetrated its hush. Only when a boat putted past in the middle of the river, or the birds landed nearby, was the silence ever broken. In the mornings we dangled our feet in the cold river water while we ate our breakfast. The temperatures were much cooler in northern Portugal, and our scrambled eggs, toast, and hot tea tasted perfect in the crisp dawn air. After breakfast, before we rejoined Mom and Dad, we would jog along the cobblestone paths that wound through the vineyards, past the farmhouses and vegetable gardens, sometimes coming upon a herd of cows or sheep.

Like the rest of Portugal, Valença do Minho was a special place. A place I could imagine staying in for a long, long time.

On June 23, 1979, at the airport in Santiago de Compostela, Spain, one hundred miles north of Valença do Minho, Larry and I said good-bye to Mom and Dad. We wouldn't see them again until we returned home to California sometime next year, and that particular moment seemed very far away right then. It loomed somewhere in the distant future, beyond Egypt, Nepal, and New Zealand, which themselves sounded remote.

The next day, Mom and Dad would be back in California—back home, back with their friends—while Larry and I would find ourselves no more than sixty miles down the road—the first sixty of the eleven thousand five hundred miles we had left to pedal before the end of our journey. A strange sensation grabbed me as I watched my parents move through the airport; I was worried that maybe I might never again lay eyes on Dad's shiny bald head or Mom's tiny five-foot frame.

I could hear Mom and Dad telling Larry how excited they were for us; telling us to be careful, to write often, and not to worry, they would be sure to wire the three thousand dollars to the main branch of Barclays Bank in London. (That amount, I had calculated, would be more than enough to see us through to the Bank of America in Kuala Lumpur,

Malaysia, our last place to pick up money.)

I could hear my parents' words, but I couldn't concentrate on what was being said. The old worries were coming back now: being struck and killed by an automobile, murdered by bandits, bit by a poisonous snake, or stricken by some incurable, fatal disease. And I worried too that something might happen to Mom and Dad while I was traveling. As I watched them disappear into the jet, I wondered if I would ever see them again, and I felt very alone.

But by the afternoon, after Larry and I had bounced along forty miles of rough pavement and potholes heading northeast from the airport toward Santander, an awful pain had taken up residence in my rear end and knees and blurred my loneliness and worries about hypothetical disasters. It was a cruel reprimand which our bodies inflicted upon us for subjecting them to four solid hours of rough treatment after a month of no cycling. They'd become accustomed to the good life, and they complained bitterly now that we'd summoned them back to work.

Unfortunately, we had only four and a half days to reach Santander, the port city on the Atlantic coast toward the French border, some three hundred forty miles from Santiago de Compostela, if we were to catch the ferry to the south coast of England before the high summer ferry rates went into effect. This meant pedaling seventy miles each day over roads that were either unpaved or cluttered with ruts and chuckholes and that wound up steep coastal grades. Our tender knees and behinds took a terrible beating for those four and a half days. I sometimes doubted that we would ever make it to Santander at all. But we stayed at it, and exactly forty-five minutes before the rates shot up, we rolled into the ferry office and purchased two tickets to Plymouth.

THE BRITISH ISLES

CHAPTER TWELVE

There was a queer tone in Cary's voice, which betrayed more than simply surprise or disgust. His words had an I-can't-believe-I'm-involved-in-this tone. It was the morning after Cary's first full day of cycle touring in Scotland, which was also his first day of cycle touring anywhere. He was seated outside of his tent in a field in Culross, near Edinburgh, and he was preparing to partake of his first breakfast on the road.

"There's this fly in ma tea. There's gnats in ma eggs. A slug's just 'bout ta ooze its way onta that there plate a' toast. And we're surrounded by cow manure and sheep droppin's!"

Twelve hours later, the three of us were in Loch Lomond, pitching our tents in the pouring rain. When it started to rain, a half hour before we reached the campground, Cary had quickly pulled to the side of the road.

"I felt a few drops, folks. It's startin' ta rain, so we'd better set up camp right soon," he said.

"Cary, it's only another five miles to the campground," Larry replied to his best friend.

"Yeah, but it's rainin'! We can't bicycle in the rain!" Cary was looking at us as if we'd taken total leave of our senses.

Poor unsuspecting Cary, I thought, as I stared back at him standing there beside the road, shivering. He had no idea what was in store for him. Sure, we'd warned him about the rain when we'd called him from Ireland to set up our final plans to meet in Scotland. But, like us, Cary was a native southern Californian; he hadn't really believed us when we told him he'd be bicycling a lot in pouring rain. I'll be there in August, the dead of summer; there won't be any rain then, he'd told himself. Cary

158

had the same approach to Scotland and the rain, that I had to Oregon and the rain.

It had been one hundred five degrees in his hometown of Paso Robles the day Cary drove to San Francisco to catch the plane to Scotland. He arrived in Edinburgh with a five-dollar plastic jacket-and-pants outfit from Woolworth's which was too small for him, and a nylon tent minus the rain fly. Little did he know that, of the eighteen days he'd be spending in Scotland, it would rain thirteen.

"Cary, it's probably going to rain a lot in Scotland. If we stop and set up camp every time it does, we'll never get anywhere. I know you've never cycled in the rain before, but you'll learn to bear it after a while. What do you say we keep on going to the campground? That way we can all get a hot shower tonight," Larry explained, hoping to coax Cary on.

Our friend started to say something, then nodded reluctantly. He pulled on his hoodless plastic jacket, which hung to within a couple inches of his waist and three-quarters of the way down his arms, covered his panniers with the plastic garbage bags we'd given him, and eased his bike back onto the road. I knew he thought Larry and I were crazy.

It was ten at night when we came into the campground at Loch Lomond. Cary was bone tired. We'd only cycled about forty miles that day—we'd spent most of the day sightseeing in Culross and Sterling. But for Cary, who was new to cycle touring, forty miles was a long way, and the last five miles had been through rain and included a hefty sixteen percent grade. Now we still had to pitch our tents, cook and eat dinner, wash the dishes, and shower.

As soon as we rolled into the campground, Larry and I scouted out a good place to set up camp, while Cary staggered along behind us. After we pitched our tent, we helped Cary put his under the shelter of some pine trees, which were to act as a substitute for his missing rain fly. Then we gathered in his tent to eat our dinner—beef stew and a salad. Cary started to laugh.

"Tough! You folks 'er real tough. I'm dyin', and ya'll 'er goin' a mile a minute. They'll never believe this back in good 'ole Paso Robles," Cary chuckled in his country drawl. "I thought the rough part o' yer undertakin' would be gettin' used ta pedalin' long distances. Heck, that's only a fraction of it! You've gotta get used ta bugs in yer food and campin' in animal manure and shoppin' fer food three times 'er more a day. An' then at the end o' the day, when yer tired and hungry, you've gotta search fer a good campin' spot and cook up yer dinner on that little stove before ya kin eat. And then you've still gotta wash the dishes before ya kin go ta bed, and lotsa times ya go ta bed dirty. And besides all that, ya hafta bicycle in the rain and git all wet and miserable. Now that's what I call tough!"

It seemed strange to hear Cary talk about the basic elements of bicycle touring as if they were great difficulties to be mastered. By now, Larry and I had long considered them routine: neither of us would have noticed the bugs in our breakfast that morning back in Culross if Cary hadn't pointed them out to us. While Cary continued talking about how we were all "really roughin' it like nobody's business here in Scotland," I thought back to when Larry and I first arrived in the British Isles.

After six months of cycling in Spain, Morocco, and Portugal, the civilized, quiet, and tidy British Isles gave us a real shock. It took us only a day or two to see that touring them would be a breeze.

The very first thing we did when we rolled off the ferry at Plymouth was to beeline it—on the left-hand side of the road—to the nearest self-service laundry and wash all our clothes in honest-to-goodness hot water for the first time in half a year. Then we went shopping for the clothes, shoes, and the spare parts for our stove that we hadn't found in Spain or Portugal. We were both in dire need of a new pair of shoes. Larry's soles had given out even before we headed south from Cadaqués, and mine had been taped together with duct tape since my spill along the south coast of Spain. We each picked up a pair of leather training shoes at an athletic shoe store in downtown Plymouth; they would last us the rest of our journey.

That night we splurged and stayed at a bed-and-breakfast home in Plymouth, where in the morning, Mrs. Grant served up conversation, corn-flakes, bacon, sausage, eggs, broiled tomatoes, toast, jelly, and an endless stream of hot tea with milk and sugar.

During the next few days, as we pedaled north through Dartmoor and east to Stonehenge, we discovered that the roads in England were completely free of rocks, giant potholes, and rough surfaces; and for the first time in months, we spent our time looking at the scenery rather than watching the road. We also found that grocery shopping in England took a quarter of the time it took in Spain or Portugal. Because British supermarkets stocked all the food we wanted, we no longer had to hit four different shops to buy fruit, vegetables, yogurt, and bread. And our daily searches for bottled drinking water were now eliminated, since the water out of any faucet in the British Isles was safe to drink. Shopping in England was also much more relaxing than in Spain, where everyone pushed and shoved his or her way through the stores. The British are great believers in the art of politely forming lines and patiently standing in them—queuing up, as they say. If two Englishmen walk up to a queue at the same time, each insists that the other go first.

Our first weeks in England, Larry and I spent hours each day devouring foods we had rarely, if ever, laid eyes on in the past six months: British chunky peanut butter, whole wheat bread, granola, and crisp New Zealand apples. Because the British Isles have no long, unpopulated stretches, unlike the western United States and Canada, we never worried about packing an extra supply of food or water. At lunchtime we'd pull into a small town, do our shopping, and eat our meal, either in the spotless town park or on one of the benches in front of the quaint shops along the main streets. After lunch, we'd take a walk past the white wattle and daub cottages with brown thatched roofs, and flower and vegetable gardens out front.

The elaborate British public toilet system helped make touring and camping in Great Britain even more of a cinch. Two signs appeared at the entrance to every town; one gave directions to the town center, and the other pointed to the public toilets. The epitome of English neatness, the restrooms even provided toilet paper—though sometimes waxed—and paper towels. We no longer had to keep an eye out for a private place off the side of the road where we could relieve ourselves. And since we could wash ourselves, our dishes, and our clothes in the sinks in the restrooms, we tossed out the cumbersome five-liter plastic water bottle.

Finding a place to camp never presented a problem in Great Britain. Farmers always offered their fields, and even the guard at Stonehenge, good ol' Fred, helped us out when we pedaled up at dusk.

"So you're keen on campin' 'ere now, are ya?" Fred smiled at us. "Well if you pitch yer tent over there in that grassy area, you'll 'ave a lovely view of sunrise over these three-thousand-five-hundred-year-old stones tomorrow mornin'. Now never mind the NO CAMPIN' sign over there. It's only there to keep away the undesirables. I'll let you two camp there as long as you promise not to 'op the fence in the middle o' the night and sniff around the stones. People try that you know. But just remember, I'll be 'ere all night and I 'ate to be disturbed. If I catch you over that fence, you'll be two un'appy Yanks on the next flight over the big pond. So behave yourselves, all right?"

"OK, Fred." Larry answered.

"Oh, and by the way," winked Fred. "When you 'ear what sounds like bullets flyin' by at ten o'clock, not to worry. Just the British military, doin' target practice. They do it every night out 'ere. That and maneuvers. Usually lasts three hours. No problem though. The tanks should give your tent a miss."

"Sure Fred," I laughed. "If you think us Americans are naive enough to believe that the British army does maneuvers and target practice around Stonehenge in the middle of the night, you're mistaken. We aren't *that* gullible."

Fred smiled mischievously and wished us luck. Later in the evening he came by our tent to give us some history of Stonehenge, and to tell us that during World War II, a U.S. Air Force official stationed in England had suggested that the British tear down the stones and use the area as a landing strip. Soon after Fred left, Larry and I climbed into our tent and fell asleep.

I'd only just exited the realm of consciousness when the night exploded in a deafening, terrifying, and disorienting barrage of noise. I bolted upright in my sleeping bag and mentally groped for my whereabouts. The sounds of artillery fire and rumbling tanks were coming from every direction.

"We're in a war!" I screamed. But where? Why? How did we get here? I mean, my God, what are we doing camping out in the middle of a battle field? Are we stark raving nuts?

"And Fred speaketh the truth!" Larry shouted over the roar of explosions and grinding gears. He fumbled with one of his packs and eventually pulled out his light and my watch.

"You know, they're late. It's ten-twenty."

From Stonehenge, we headed through Bath and Bristol into Wales, where we found the kindest people in the Isles, the prettiest countryside, and the neatest and quaintest towns—although we did have difficulty pronouncing the names of a few of the villages, such as Llanfairpwllggyngyll on the Isle of Anglesey. We pedaled through the center of Wales from Newport, north through Brecon Beacons, Snowdonia, and onto the Isle of Anglesey.

It was on Anglesey, in a pub, that we were treated to an example of the Welsh dry humor. Larry and I had just dropped in at the pub for a hot meal, some beer, and a bit of gossip, when two burly Welshmen lumbered through the front door carrying a complete exhaust system for an automobile. They bumped and jostled their way past the dart game and the tables and stools, yet no one except Larry and I paid them the slightest bit of attention. A few seconds before they disappeared behind the door to the women's restroom, one of the men noticed the look of bewilderment on my face. "Plumbing difficulties," he winked; then closed the door behind himself.

The grades in Wales were incredibly steep. Twenty-five percent grades were common, and we made good use of our lowest gears. We cycled alongside rivers, streams, and lakes, and past medieval castles and hilly fields the color of emeralds, dotted with the ever-present flocks of white sheep and checkered by gray stone fences. The Welsh towns had narrow streets lined by attached stone buildings with colorful awnings and flower boxes, and as in England, the villages were spotless and quiet.

The farmers in Wales were quick to invite us to camp next to their farmhouses. Many of them had relatives who had emigrated to the United States, and they loved to hear stories about America. As soon as we'd pitched our tent in their front yards, they would bring us in out of the cold and the drizzle, which seemed to follow us everywhere in Wales, and seat us in the overstuffed chairs in the living room in front of the fireplace. Then someone would put cups of hot tea in our hands, and everyone in the family would gather around to listen to our tales and to take turns firing questions at us. Is everyone rich in America? they all wanted to know. Does everyone drive big cars? Is everthing modern? Does the Mafia control the politicians? Is it always hot and sunny in California? How could a peanut farmer be elected president? We answered their questions about America, and they told us about farming on the steep Welsh slopes and about raising sheep and cattle.

It wasn't only the farmers who took us into their homes in Wales, the city folk were just as friendly. In Caerphilly, a city in southern Wales, we pulled up to Larry's favorite haunt in any town, the local grocery store. A middle-aged couple stopped to look our bikes over and talk with us. When we asked them for directions to the nearest campground where we could get a hot shower—our sense of smell had informed us it was getting to be that time of the week—Fred and Grace Bull promptly invited us to their house in the village of Machen, a few miles down the road, for a lunch of salmon and cucumber sandwiches and a hot bath—a long, blissful and soothing soak.

There are certain people I've felt I could talk with forever and never run short of things to say, and Fred and Grace were just that type of people. When we rode up to their house, we expected to visit with them for a couple of hours and then head on toward Brecon Beacons' National Park. But five hours after we arrived, the four of us were still sitting comfortably in the living room discussing politics, our backgrounds, our travels, and a host of other topics. When someone noticed the time, Fred and Grace immediately let it be known that Larry and I were going nowhere until after breakfast the next morning. Grace sent the rest of us to the butcher shop for meat for dinner, and after the meal and more conversation, we all climbed into their car and headed out into the country, down a narrow road edged by gray stone fences, to the Bull's favorite pub for a few ales.

It was almost noon before Larry and I got on the road the next day. The Bull's neighbors probably found our departure a strange sight: two couples, who only twenty-four hours earlier were total strangers, hugging and kissing like life-long friends. The day after we left Machen, Grace did an amazing thing. She called California to assure my parents that Larry and I were doing just fine; to tell them how much she and Fred enjoyed becoming our friends; and to invite them to come and stay in Machen whenever they pleased.

The weather was the only drawback to cycling in Wales. The summer days were cold and wet. Almost every day a bothersome drizzle fell, and when we crossed the Irish Sea to Ireland, the weather got worse. We found ourselves pumping through heavy rains. Unfortunately, the Goretex rain jacket that my parents had brought me leaked in the hard rain. The waterproof material was supposed to breathe: to push my perspiration out from the inside, but not allow rain water to penetrate in from the outside. The breathing principle worked fine in a light rain, especially when we were pedaling up hills where I sweated a lot. Those times the jacket did breathe the sweat out, unlike my old nylon jacket. But in an Irish downpour, the Goretex couldn't stop the pounding water, and by the end of the day, I was just as saturated as Larry in his leaky, aging nylon jacket.

To avoid cooking and setting up and taking down camp in these downpours, and to have dry space to hang our sopping clothes, we took to seeking shelter for the night in partially constructed houses along the roads. We always made sure we were packed and on the road each morning before the construction workers arrived. During the days, we spent a good portion of our time inside the dry, warm Irish taverns downing warm Guinness and joking with the locals. The only problem with taking refuge in taverns was that the friendly Irish bought us too much beer, and we'd spend the first hour or two after we left a tavern pedaling in a state of semi or total intoxication. Cycling drunk, however, rendered us oblivious to the nagging cold and wet.

We expected the rain in Ireland. What we didn't expect were the high food prices, which made Ireland the most expensive country in Europe we traveled through. We found ourselves spending over ten dollars a day on food alone.

From Ireland we crossed into Northern Ireland, where we encountered our only uneasy cycling in the British Isles. We were met at the border by an impressive roadblock, complete with barbed wire, machine gun nests, and British soldiers dressed in camouflage outfits and bulletproof vests. One of the soldiers was taking snapshots of the drivers and passengers crossing the border. He waved us through, but we had to carry our bikes over the wires, with nails attached, that were stretched across the road. (If someone tried to run the roadblock, the soldiers would yank up the wires, and the nails would shred the car's tires.)

After the roadblock, as we pedaled into Londonderry, we managed to lose our way near the bridge over the Foyle River, and the next thing we knew we'd cycled into what resembled a war zone. Whole neighborhoods had been blown to pieces or gutted by fire. Here and there a few buildings, surrounded by charred rubble, still stood intact. On the front porches, men and women sat with unsmiling faces, which spoke of hate and revenge. We thought better of stopping to ask directions; instead, we kept pedaling until we found our way onto the bridge.

Across the river, in the downtown shopping district of Londonderry, armed British soldiers stood at each street corner, while trucks loaded with more soldiers patrolled the streets. With all the guns around, the quiet that clung to the city on this warm Sunday afternoon seemed like the calm before the storm. Pedaling through the patrolled, deserted streets, I felt vulnerable and exposed, and at times I imagined I heard the machine guns go off and felt the bullets plow through my back.

From the city center we climbed upward, alongside the sloping banks of the river, into a plush residential area. The residents had barricaded themselves into their stately homes. Every house we passed had rolls of barbed wire strung along the tops of their protective walls and fences. Jagged pieces of broken glass were cemented into the tops of the walls, and Dobermans snarled in the yards.

It took us two days to wind across Northern Ireland from Londonderry to Larne, the port city just north of Belfast. Many of the towns along the way were scarred with graffiti; inscriptions of hatred splashed in paint across the streets and buildings; BRITS GO HOME or TAIGS WILL BE SHOT. We saw only a few tourists driving across Northern Ireland; all of them, like us, on their way to or from the Scotland ferry at Larne.

On the last day of July the ferry dropped us off at Strangraer, in southern Scotland, and three days later we rolled into Edinburgh to meet Cary, who had flown in from America.

While the rain pounded Loch Lomond, Cary talked all through dinner about the cold and the wet, his tired aching muscles, and about how we were all living the rough life. Larry and I tried to explain to our friend that cycling in the British Isles was easy: no endless miles of bumpy or unsurfaced roads, everyone speaking English, plentiful food, drinkable water, and toilets and sinks with running water. But Cary was too overwhelmed by his first two days on the road to pay us much attention.

Cary Holst was born and raised in Paso Robles, California, a small country town of twelve thousand people, where most everyone drives a pickup truck with a gun rack mounted in the rear window. The year before Larry and I left on our trip, Cary moved a hundred miles south, to Santa Barbara, and hired on as an engineer with the same company Larry was working for. Larry liked Cary's simple, honest, country ways, and the two of them became fast friends. Not long after we started our trip, Cary decided that Santa Barbara was too "big city" for him—"too much traffic, and folks talk and move too fast"—and he moved back to Paso Robles. Four months later, this country boy who had never traveled much, had never been outside of the United States, and had never toured on a bicycle, struck upon the idea of joining us in Scotland to do some touring himself.

During his first three days in Scotland, Cary functioned in a daze, while he grappled with the trials of pedaling forty miles or more a day, cycling in the rain, setting up and taking down camp, and organizing his gear. But on the afternoon of his fourth day on the road, Cary came alive.

We were grinding at a snail's pace up a long steep climb just before the village of Killin, northeast of Loch Lomond, and the clouds were dumping torrents of water over us. Cary was cycling in front, to set the pace, and I felt sorry for him. This was a truly miserable predicament we were in. The water had saturated every ounce of my clothing, and my feet and hands felt frostbitten. I knew Cary was no better off. He's probably up there wondering how he can move up the departure date on his plane ticket home, I thought to myself. I'll bet he's up there cussing at himself and us and Scotland, and he'll be calling it quits any minute now. But my thoughts were interrupted by Cary's voice cutting through the roar of the downpour.

"How's it goin' troo-pers?" A tone of pure delight sizzled in his throat. Larry and I were so shocked that we both fell speechless.

"Hey ya'll back there! I said, 'How's it goin' troo-pers?' " he called again.

"What do you mean, 'How's it going?' It's pouring rain and I'm pumping water out my shoes. That's how it's going. What about you?" Larry yelled back.

"Hey listen, this is great, troopers! If the folks back home could see me now! I'm actshuly plowin' up this here hill on ma bicycle in this pourin' rain, no sweat. Yup, here's ol' Cary bicyclin' through Scotland. I mean, I'm gonna pull this bicyclin' Scotland thing off after all. I mean, I'm gonna make it! I can hardly believe it maself. It's great!"

Then Cary began to sing—soaked and cold and happy as could be. When a tour bus passed us, he started talking again.

"Look at all those folks cooped up in that bus. Now that's the way the folks in Paso Robles thought I shoulda traveled through Scotland. Man oh man, if they could see me now! They'd think I was some dim bulb all right. But hey, puttin' up with the rain and the steep climbs is worth it. I mean, I feel like I'm 'complishin' somethin'. I'm provin' to maself I'm tougher 'n I thought. And besides, who wants to be stuck inna tour bus gettin' all car sick along with thirty other folks? Not me! I'm fer bikin'. This here's great!

"I mean look at these here beautiful green mountains and the rivers and lakes. Just think, if I was back in Paso Robles right now, I'd be stuck inside ma office at work. But here I am off work and outside in all this fantastic scenery. Who cares 'bout the rain! I'm feelin' great!"

And so, after just three and a half days, Cary was already over the hump. His muscles had stopped screaming, his stamina had picked up, and even in the rain, things had begun to look much brighter to him.

That evening the three of us stayed in a bed-and-breakfast home in Killin to dry out, take a hot bath, and gorge ourselves on a gigantic Scottish breakfast in the morning. The house was a Scottish country cottage right out of a picture book: a white, wooden, two-story gingerbread structure with bright-yellow shutters and eaves, surrounded by a manicured lawn and flower gardens. After we soaked the warmth back into our bodies and scrubbed away the layers of mud, we joined Mrs. Jones, a widow, in front of the fireplace in her cozy living room, chock full of antique furniture. The frail Scottish woman brought out a huge tray of cookies and a pot of tea, and the four of us sat together watching the firelight flicker on the walls and listening to raindrops tap on the roof.

"Boy, this here's the life," Cary grinned.

From that day on, Cary's enthusiasm never waned. And his passion for experiencing the out-of-doors, exercising and strengthening his body, and building his endurance rekindled our own zeal for our undertaking and renewed our appreciation for things we had come to take for granted.

Cary adapted remarkably well to his new experience and especially to the small rivers of water in his tent when it rained at night. His remedy for the flooding was quite simple—one small bottle of Scotch whiskey at bedtime to render himself totally immune to the sensations of wet and cold. It worked every time. No matter how much water flowed through his tent, Cary would always sleep straight through the night. There was, however, one aspect of cycle touring, the lack of shower facilities, that Cary initially did not handle well. After a while, it made cycling next to him a sobering experience.

"Say, Holst," Larry commented one day, when the problem had become overpowering. "You know you've really begun to smell. Didn't you take a shower last night at the campground?"

"Nope."

"You're kidding. Why not? We hadn't had one in three days, and who knows when we'll get another one."

"I know, but all ma clothes were dirty, so I figured why shower if I'm only gonna put those same dirty, stinky clothes back on."

"Well, why are all your clothes dirty?" Larry asked. "Didn't you wash any out back at the other campground?"

"Nope."

Larry quickly set our friend straight. "One easy lesson in keeping BO under control while bicycle touring by Larry Savage," he began. "If you have two pairs of shorts and T-shirts, you wear one set every day until you shower. Then you put on the clean set and wash out the dirty one. In the morning, you hang the clothes you washed on the back of your bike to dry out while you cycle, and when they're all dry, you pack them away until you shower again. It's a simple routine, and it makes sure you always have something clean to put on after you shower."

The day we told Cary he smelled, he bought himself a bottle of deodorant and a huge container of liquid after-bath freshener, large amounts of which he poured over himself each morning from then on.

For almost three weeks, we pedaled past the lochs and rivers and streams of Scotland, through its rolling, green mountains, tiny, well-kept towns, and picturesque fishing villages that dotted the jagged, stormy coastline. We explored castles and attended sheep-dog trials. We weathered rain and hail storms, head winds, flat tires, broken spokes and brake and shifter cables, and swarms of bloodthirsty no-see-ums. And when the sun occasionally shone, we warmed ourselves together.

Then, one day, it was time for Cary to leave; and for the umpteenth time on our trip, the gnawing ache of loneliness was back. The ache ground deeper than usual this time, because now Larry and I were on our own until the end of our journey. Neither our parents nor any of our friends would be joining us on this last and most difficult leg of our journey. While we watched Cary's familiar figure grow small as it pedaled away from us down the road, once again we could feel ourselves drawing closer together.

We headed toward London through north Yorkshire and the Yorkshire dales, the prettiest area we cycled through in the Isles outside of Wales. The old stone fences, farmhouses, and villages made quilts of the rolling farmland, and the streams glistened in the sunlight. We were two days outside of London and twenty miles south of the city of Lincoln, in the spot on the map called Silk-by-Willowby, when the strangest coincidence of our trip occurred.

It was dark when we came into Silk-by-Willowby, and everyone in town seemed to be in bed. After taking a quick look around, we decided to spend the night in the foyer of a thirteenth-century church. We rolled our mats out on the stone floor and fell asleep. In the morning, an elderly man, who opened and closed the church each day and set the church clock, showed up just as we were finishing our dishes. He invited us inside. Larry surveyed the plaques decorating one long wall.

"Barb, come over here and look at these," he said. "This you are *not* going to believe. Look at these plaques. Look at 'em. They're full of the names of your relatives—the Mitchells and the Holdens—and it says here that the church bells were donated by the Mitchells."

Mitchell was my maiden name, and according to the family history I'd read at Uncle Clarence's, a Mitchell had married a Holden somewhere near Yorkshire. I found my own maiden name, Barbara Jean Mitchell, listed three times in the church register, along with a Clarence Mitchell and a John Mitchell, the name of my grandfather. It was eerie that the only church we slept in on our entire trip had my name and the names of my relatives in its register and on its walls, bells, and gravestones.

On September 1, 1979, we pedaled into London and headed to the Crystal Palace campground, fifteen miles south of the city. We were anxious to finish our business in London and head toward Austria, to cross the Alps before the weather turned foul.

It took us nine days in London to prepare for our push to the East. There was the three thousand dollars to pick up at Barclays Bank and change into travelers' checks, and there were cholera shots, tetanus and polio boosters, and a supply of malaria pills to get. Our applications for visas to Egypt took two days to process, and we spent another two days checking with the Nepali, Indian, Thai, and Malaysian embassies. The Indians and Malaysians assured us that we would be issued visas when we arrived in their countries, and we were advised to apply for our visas to Nepal in New Delhi and our Thai visas in Kathmandu. The official at the Nepali embassy handed us a pamphlet on his country, which showed that the two roads in Nepal were paved, as was the road running between Kathmandu and Pokhara.

Next, after we'd bought spare gaskets and jets for our stove, washed and dried our down sleeping bags and jackets, and cleaned up our rain gear, we set out on a campaign to reduce the weight and bulk of our packs. Our bath towel was replaced by a hand towel, and we tossed out our forks and knives—we could use our spoon handles to spread peanut butter and cut soft food, and we could eat everything with a spoon. We kept our Swiss army knife for chopping and cutting. All extra or nearly worn-out socks and underwear were tossed out. And we boxed and mailed home my journals and all the maps and pamphlets we had collected in the last eight months. I took on more of the overall weight—a larger share of the tools and spare parts—because the bottoms of Larry's rear panniers were ripping apart.

Another of our projects was to repair and modify our rear panniers to make sure they would hold together through the rest of our journey. Larry taped the bottoms of his panniers with duct tape; and to more securely attach the rack mounting clips to our panniers, we added some nuts and screws. Our rear racks were in bad shape. The two nuts that fastened them to our bike frames were stripped, and the Almería weld jobs were cracking. We took the racks into Blackburn's London distributor and we were given new racks free of charge.

Just before we left London, we cleaned and adjusted our bikes and replaced their worn-out and faulty parts. Since this would be our last major overhaul of the trip, we put on new clusters and chains and tires, repacked the wheel and pedal bearings, adjusted the spokes to realign the wheels, lubricated the derailleurs and brakes, and bought spare spokes and brake and derailleur cables.

London was also a major mail stop for us, and we checked for letters every day at the American Express office. We were especially anxious to get a card from Greg and Christine, the Americans we'd cycled with in Spain. They had written to us in Edinburgh, saying that they were in Italy and planned to slow down their pace so that we possibly could meet in India.

The day before we left London, Larry and I walked into the American Express office to check one last time for mail. As I moved toward the counter, I heard someone next to me gasp in surprise. There stood Christine.

"What in the world are you doing here?!" I screamed, as we threw our arms around each other. "You're supposed to be in Egypt. And where's Greg?"

"Greg's not here."

"Well, where is he? Back at the hostel? Is that where you guys are staying?"

"No. Actually Greg's not here at all. He's in Egypt."

"Oh. Well, then why are you here?"

"We split up in Greece. I caught a flight here from Athens, and I'm going back to California." Christine shook her head and shrugged.

"It all came to a head a couple weeks ago in Greece, just before we were going to fly to Egypt. We'd been cycling together for a year by then, and for most of that year it was just the two of us. Well, you know, after twelve months of being together nonstop for twenty-four hours a day, I finally reached the point where I knew exactly what Greg was going to do and say in any given situation, and it was driving me right up a wall.

"For most of last year, I got up every morning and looked at that same face of Greg's, and I kept right on looking at it all day long. And we kept having the same arguments over and over. Anyway, I guess it all boiled down to the fact that I got sick and tired of seeing and hearing the same person all the time with no break.

"And what about you two? Aren't you a little tired of each other by now, too?"

Christine didn't give us time to answer, but her words made me uneasy, as I thought about the times Larry and I had ridden as far away from each other as possible when we'd gotten tired of looking at or arguing with one another.

"There was another reason too," Christine continued. "But first I should say that I'll always appreciate the experience of bicycling across North Africa. I wouldn't trade it for anything. The people were wonderful to us. We came out of Algeria with more money than we went in with, because the truck drivers stopped and gave us candy and money, and the farmers took us in and fed us every night. And I'll never forget the day we took a taxi into the desert and watched the sunrise turn the endless miles of sand every color you could imagine. But—well—being dirty, being the center of attention, and looking at poor, nasty living conditions all the time got me down after a while. I was ready to leave North Africa when we did. A couple of times when we were there, we stayed in a hotel just to get cleaned up and away from all those staring faces. But the hotel rooms were always dirty, and that depressed us. We never could get away from the dirt.

"So anyway, I got to thinking in Greece about what cycling in Egypt and Kenya would really be like. Greg wanted to get to Mombasa and try and get a boat out of there to India. Well, you know, the more I thought about it, the more I realized that I didn't want to go on. In North Africa it was only for a couple weeks, but if I went on I'd be spending *months* being dirty, being stared at by noisy masses of people, and being surrounded by poverty and filth. And there was the heat too. Greg loves to bicycle in the heat but I hate it.

"It took me two weeks to make my decision to head back home. But anyway, Greg and I parted as friends. And that's good. I mean, I figure if I'd kept on going, the extra tensions of traveling in the Third World countries probably would have demolished our relationship altogether."

While Christine talked, Larry and I were both wondering whether the same thing would happen to us. We knew that physically we were strong enough to finish the rest of our journey. But were we mentally? Would we stick together when things got really tough in Egypt and on through Southeast Asia? I was a lot more certain we would stay together than I had been when we started our trip, but listening to Christine made me edgy. We'll have to work at it, I told myself. And with a little luck, we'll make it.

BROKEN FRAME

♦   CHAPTER THIRTEEN   ♦

From London it took us fifteen days to reach the Alps at the German-Austrian border. In those two weeks, we had two near disasters.

The day we rode into Paris, we had roared over one hundred miles of rolling hills. The final forty miles we covered at a steady, nonstop pace of seventeen miles an hour. Once we reached the city limits, we bounced and rattled over ten miles of brick streets to the city campground in the Bois de Boulogne. It was nine o'clock when we stumbled into the campground, and every inch of our bodies ached.

Before we fell asleep I mentioned the wobble again. I couldn't see Larry's face, but I knew he was rolling his eyes in disgust. He rolled them whenever I talked about the mysterious wobble and its grinding noise. For almost a month now I'd felt something peculiar in the way my bike was handling. The front end seemed to vibrate all the time, and it made a strange grinding sound. Every day I commented on the wobble, and every day Larry told me it was all in my head. His reaction never varied.

"Look," he'd grumble, "you're either imagining the wobble or you're causing it by the way you steer and pump your pedals. There's nothing wrong with your bike frame. We've checked it out. And there's absolutely nothing wrong with your front forks. Ignore it."

But I was convinced there *was* a problem with my frame and frustrated that I could never find its source. Today the unsteadiness had made me especially nervous, particularly while I was pounding down the hills at forty miles an hour.

"You know," I said softly after we'd been in bed only a few minutes. "I felt the wobble again today and I think it's getting worse."

Larry faked a few long, grumbling snores and I took the hint and dropped the subject.

In the morning, we hopped on our bikes, minus our gear, and cycled into downtown Paris to do some sightseeing. It didn't take us long to discover that in Paris, the finish point for the Tour de France, a bicycler is God. Seated on a sleek racing frame and clad in a multicolored cycling jersey, a racer can shoot through stop signs and red lights, and motorists and pedestrians will carefully and graciously make room. Larry and I, dressed in our faded shorts and T-shirts, most certainly did not look like racers, but we were on bicycles, and that proved to be good enough. Everyone gave us the right-of-way, even at the celebrated *Arc de Triomphe*, where an incredible twelve lanes of traffic fed into and out of one roundabout, with cars shooting every which way like sprays of fireworks.

We managed to survive the roundabout, but just after we shot out of it and turned down a wide brick boulevard, my bike swerved to the left and I nearly collided with the car next to me. I jerked my handlebars to the right, but the bike failed to respond. It moved straight ahead. I looked down at the awful sight of my handlebars pointing one way and my front wheel another. I slammed on my brakes and jumped off the bike. Larry followed me onto the sidewalk.

"What's wrong?" he asked.

"It's the front end, it—"

"Oh no! Not *this* again! Of *course* the front end is going to wobble, Mitchell. We're riding on a brick surface. Even *my* bike vibrates on this surface." Larry only called me Mitchell when he thought I was acting especially lame, and he preferred not to be too closely associated with me.

"I *know* we're on bricks. I'm not talking about a mere vibration. I'm talking about turning the handlebars to the right and having the front wheel turn left! Now that's serious! Bricks don't cause that. I think the front forks are broken."

For a moment I thought that possibly Larry's eyes would never again roll back down into their natural position. All I could see were the very bottoms of his irises and a lot of white. His lips were pursed together so tightly that his mouth completely disappeared behind his moustache and beard. I was looking at one real exasperated human being.

"Front forks do not break! Here, give me the bike and I'll settle this argument once and for all! I'll show you there's nothing—I repeat, nothing —wrong with this bike; it's just your technique."

Larry grabbed the bike, jumped on, and pushed one of its pedals. But before he had time to push the other one, the bike was already swerving across the crowded sidewalk. Not more than fifteen feet from the point where he climbed on it, the frame collapsed and sent him tumbling through the wall of passing pedestrians.

His crash landing into the cement pavement scraped some large chunks of skin off his hands, arms, and legs, but there were no broken bones. Larry gingerly picked himself up, then lifted my bike off the pavement. The front wheel and forks dangled separately from the rest of the bike, connected to the frame by only a brake cable. The steering column had broken where it entered the head tube, and Larry was staring in astonishment at the severed edge. I couldn't resist the temptation.

"Say, that there's sure some sweet cyclin' technique you've got there, handsome. You did great!"

We laughed, but it was a nervous laughter. Both of us knew how narrowly I'd escaped tragedy. If the forks had broken just minutes earlier in the roundabout, or yesterday on the downhills, the outcome would have been extremely grim. Watching the wheel dangling like a yoyo at the end of its string made my stomach queasy.

"Well, if it was going to break, we're lucky it broke in Paris," Larry said. "There must be a dozen bike shops on the Champs Elyses. We shouldn't have any trouble finding forks, since it's a French frame. I'll cycle over to the shops, and you can carry your bike over to American Express and pick up the mail and wait for me there."

For two and a half hours I sat outside the American Express office with my broken frame and waited for Larry. While I waited, two separate American tourists offered to buy my bike. They each had rented a car to travel around Europe in and were quickly going broke paying the exorbitant gas prices. After those two, a couple of meter maids came over to take a look at my crumpled frame. One of the women spoke Italian; so, trying to recall what little Italian I'd learned in college, I explained my problem to her as best I could. When I finished, she walked out into the street and stopped the next policeman that drove by. They talked for a while, then she came back and gave the name of a bicycle shop, Cycles C.N.C., located a mile and a half away. I thanked her and continued waiting. An hour later, Larry finally returned. He had some surprising news.

"I didn't get the forks because there wasn't a soul in any of those shops who'd give me the time of day, let alone new forks. I'd walk into a shop, and the minute I started speaking English everybody'd walk away. They'd flat out refuse to acknowledge my existence. Then, finally, at the seventh or eighth shop I went to, I got this fellow to listen to me, but that was a waste of time 'cause he kept telling me that forks never break.

"I know, I know—*imagine* someone saying that forks don't break. Well anyway, then the man in the last shop I went to refused to believe that your frame could possibly be French. And you know why? Because I was speaking English! I speak English, so the frame is English. Real simple.

Yes indeed, that was a refreshing two and a half hours! Now what do we do? It'll take us half the night to drag the bike back to the campground."

"Well, the police gave me the name and address of another shop not far from here. Let's give it a try," I suggested. "Maybe since it's not on the snooty Champs Elyses, the people there won't be so arrogant. And this time we'll take the bike along with us as evidence that the frame *is* French and the forks *are* broken."

I set out at a jog through the rush hour traffic, pushing my bike along on its rear wheel with the dangling forks and wheel thrown over my shoulders. We arrived at C.N.C. only fifteen minutes before it closed, and we were in luck. There was a man there who not only spoke English but who was also willing to talk to us. He brought out two sets of forks from the basement. The first ones were made of the same lightweight Reynolds 531 tubing as my frame and sold for ninety dollars. The others were steel, weighed nearly as much as my entire frame, and looked like hell because they'd never been painted; but the price was right—twelve dollars. Since we were trying to cut our expenses to compensate for the big outlays we'd made in the last two months for ferry tickets, new bicycle parts, shoes and clothes, and visas and shots, we opted for the cheaper forks. I wasn't excited about the prospect of increasing the weight of my frame, but I liked the idea of descending the Alpine grades up ahead with a sturdy set of steel forks.

Before the new forks would fit properly into the head tube of my frame, a length of the forks' steering column needed to be sawed off, but the man informed us that the shop couldn't get at it until next Friday, a week and a half away. We had planned on leaving Paris in four days. We were cutting our crossing of the Alps too close as it was, and an extra week's delay would probably guarantee a miserable crossing in the snow.

By now it was six o'clock, and the owner of C.N.C., who spoke only French, showed up to close the shop. The man who was helping us talked with the owner for a few minutes, and the next thing we knew, the owner grabbed up my frame and the new forks and disappeared into the back room with them.

"He fix zee forks and put on zee bicycle for you now," his assistant explained to us. "If you like, you walk, come back one hour. He need zat hour to do zee work. We close now. When you come back, knock and I be here and let you in."

Now that it looked as though the forks might be fixed after all, we both heaved a mental sigh of relief. Larry suddenly realized that he hadn't eaten anything since breakfast and that he was nearing his state of "acute starvation," which commonly set in whenever he went longer than three or four hours without food.

"You wait here in case there's some problem and they need your advice," Larry said to me. "I'll run out and get us a snack. I'll be right back."

Fifty minutes later my frame was repaired, and the shop owner handed me a bill for twenty *francs* for the labor. Five dollars for an hour's worth of labor done after closing time. It was a gift, and I pumped the owner's hands in thanks. He shrugged his shoulders, grinned a broad smile, and wished me a *bon voyage*.

Another twenty minutes went by before Larry finally came back to the shop. There was a peculiar look on his face.

"What happened to you?" I asked. "I was really getting worried."

"What happened?" he mumbled. "Well you see, I got a little tied up— and, well, I guess I even forgot about the food."

"*You* forgot about the food?"

"Well, you see, I was walking down this street here looking for a food store, and when I got about a quarter mile on down that way, I ran smack dab into this full-fledged red-light district that kept right on going for blocks and blocks. There were women standing in all the doorways and the alleyways and on all the corners, and the sidewalks were all jammed with men checking out the women and trying to strike up a bargain.

"So anyway, I got to thinking I should take a picture or two of the area to spice up our slide collection; so I pulled the camera out of my day pack as inconspicuously as I could, and I tried to snap a quick shot before anyone noticed. But one of the women spotted me, and she started screaming and running toward me. Then some of the other women took up the chase, and the next thing I knew one of 'em had me by the arm and was trying to wrestle my camera loose. Fortunately, I kept ahold of the camera and got away from her before the others caught up.

"I took off running like the blazes in the opposite direction from here, and I ran a long way before I finally stopped and decided I'd better turn back. But I had to swing way out around the red-light district on my way back, and that took me forever!"

And for the first time in his life, Larry had forgotten to buy food for his starving stomach.

∽∾∾

On September 16, we left Paris and cycled directly east to the German border at Strasbourg. We took four days to reach the border. Each day was hot and sunny. Our only mishap occurred when Larry's cluster came loose and most of the ball bearings spilled onto the edge of the road. We spent an hour and half outside of Nancy sifting through a three-foot-square patch of dirt and gravel, collecting the scattered bearings, repacking the cluster, and hammering it back onto the bicycle.

On the morning we crossed the border into Germany the skies clouded over, and by six o'clock that evening, after we'd pumped over the mountains in the Black Forest, an icy rain began to fall. For the next three days, until we reached the town of Füssen, at the Austrian border, we pedaled through a nearly continuous freezing downpour. These were three of the most miserable days of our journey, and they hit us one right after the other like shots from a rapid-fire rifle.

Our first evening in southern Germany we set up camp in a pine forest near Haigerloch. It was dark and rainy, but we managed to coax our cookstove to life and fry some grilled cheese and bratwurst sandwiches on thick slabs of heavy, dark, German bread. That day we'd discovered that, contrary to what we had expected, the prices of food in Germany were very reasonable. Based on our first shopping spree, we figured our daily food bill would run us only seven dollars, and possibly less if we made good use of the huge, seventy-five-cent cans of lentils all the German grocery stores stocked.

It rained hard throughout the night. In the morning it was still raining, and there were a couple of small puddles in our tent where the water-proofing had begun to peel off the moldy floor of the tent. We pulled on our sweat shirts and rain jackets and crawled outside to cook and eat breakfast in the frigid downpour.

Our rain jackets, booties, and gloves never had a chance. In less than an hour from the time we started pedaling, the water, which poured down as if someone had thrown open the sky's floodgates, had soaked every layer of our clothing. Water came not only from the clouds, but also from under the passing trucks. Commercial truck traffic was impossible to escape in Germany, even on the most obscure back roads, and every truck that sped past us bathed our bodies with sweeping blasts of mud and water.

We did a lot of coasting downhill that day, and the cold wind turned our soaked feet and hands to ice. When lunchtime came around, we spread out our plastic ground cover underneath the shelter of some pines, sat on the dry plastic, and hunched our heads and shoulders over our food to keep it dry while we ate. Neither of us ate much of the apples, bread, and cheese we pulled out of our packs; we were too cold to have an appetite.

By late afternoon, after six hours of pedaling in the deluge, my nerves were shot. My feet and hands stung so badly from the wet, icy cold that I wanted to scream. I felt nauseated from breathing the foul-tasting diesel exhaust that the trucks belched into my nostrils and mouth, and the sound of grinding truck gears pounded in my ears. My nose was gushing a river of mucus, I was wringing wet and shivering uncontrollably, and to all this, with two hours of pedaling still left to go, my body somehow found it possible to add the ultimate insult—diarrhea.

"Oh no. You poor kid," sighed Larry, when I jumped off my bike three-quarters of the way up a long climb and made for the nearest clump of bushes. This was one case of the runs I couldn't hold back no matter what, and each time I stopped pedaling and squatted to relieve myself, my body temperature dropped lower and the cold ate deeper into my body. Soon I was stopping every fifteen minutes, when the cramps got so bad that my bowels felt like they were about to explode. The wad of toilet paper I carried in the pocket of my rain jacket was so sopping wet it had nearly dissolved.

I started to cry, and I cried for the rest of the afternoon. Crying, I found, worked as a release valve for my frustration and misery. I cried, but I continued to push on; I was determined to beat the elements and the pain.

It was a stroke of luck that the forest path Larry chose to turn down in search of a flat, not-too-saturated, area on which to pitch our tent led to a deserted, one-room cement block structure. A pile of hay covered part of the floor. There was no glass in the windows, but there were wooden shutters, which we closed tight. A covered porch with one rickety wooden table extended out from the only door in the room. To Larry and me, the place was a Hilton International.

We ducked inside the frigid room and peeled off our wet clothes, toweled ourselves dry, then jumped into our sweat pants, long-sleeved shirts, our only dry pairs of wool socks, and our down jackets. Even buried beneath these layers of warm dry clothing, our skin still felt frost-bitten, and we couldn't stop trembling while we cooked and ate dinner. It wasn't until I climbed into my down sleeping bag, which I laid on top of the hay mattress, that my body gradually began to thaw. An hour later, after the stinging cold lost its grip on my feet, I drifted off to sleep.

When morning came around, I forced myself to do something that took every ounce of willpower I could muster: I pulled on the same clothes I'd ridden in the day before even though they were still wringing wet. I did have some dry clothes—my sweat pants and a long-sleeved blouse—but I wanted to save them so that I'd have something warm to put on at the end of the day. The rain was still pounding down outside and whatever I started out in this morning would be saturated anyway in less than an hour.

Just as I began to struggle into my soggy clothing, Larry stood up and peeked outside.

"Trouble!" he yelled. "The ground's buried under water. Looks like our room's about to be flooded. We'd better get moving fast!"

On that note, we dove into our wet clothes, tossed everything into our panniers, hefted our bikes onto our shoulders, and took off on foot, splashing our way through the water and mud to the paved road. After hanging in the cold air all night, my wool socks, long knit cycling shorts, sweat shirt and two T-shirts I wore in layers, felt like ice against my body. I was shivering even before I climbed onto my bike and pedaled off through the rain and the icy wind. It took no time at all for the torturous cold to needle its way through my feet and hands, causing an agonizing sensation, similar to having all one's toenails and fingernails ripped out at once.

The day before, I'd been determined to keep pedaling, and to help myself along, I'd kept my mind's eye on the prospect of bicycling through the spectacular beauty of the Austrian Alps. But that morning, the frustration of facing yet another miserable day obscured any sense of determination or anticipation. I was too cold to daydream about more pleasant times. And now I was worried that the storm might never let up, and we'd be forced to climb the Alps in it. I felt defeated. I cried all morning, but I kept pedaling.

When we stopped for lunch, I was again too cold to be hungry; yet I knew how important it was that I stuff my body with food. Bicycling on an empty stomach always brought on a solid case of depression and the shakes, and things were going bad enough as it was.

"What the heck's gotten into you?" Larry asked, watching me out of the corner of his eye while he sat on a log, slicing off hunks of bread and cheese. The rain had stopped just before we pulled off the road in a wooded area east of the city of Bad Weldsee. The fact that it was no longer pouring should have made eating a less difficult task, but, unfortunately, when the rain stopped, the temperature tumbled even lower than before.

"I'm just trying to warm myself up so I can eat," I answered.

"Oh. I see. Well, you had me going there. I mean, I figured you were trying to get warm when you pulled on your sweats and down jacket and started jumping up and down, but you threw me off there when you started kicking the tree."

I *was* kicking trees, all right—kicking them just as hard as I possibly could without permanently damaging my feet. It was a peculiar remedy for frozen feet, but it helped. The way I figured it, as long as my feet felt like two blocks of ice, the rest of my body would never warm up, and I wouldn't be able to eat anything. So here I was, jumping up and down smashing my feet into hard surfaces. I kept at it until I could feel the blood circulating at the base of my legs once again, and then I sat down and ate my meal.

After lunch, we continued pedaling southeast through more forests and farmland to the village of Isney. By the time we reached Isney and started up the grade between it and the city of Kempten, fifteen miles away, the clouds had descended so low that we couldn't see the mountains surrounding us. It was five o'clock and bitter cold. A mile outside of Isney the clouds enveloped us, and it began to snow. Within ten minutes, the ground had completely disappeared under a fluffy layer of white; it frosted the boughs of the dark, towering pines and filled the air. We could barely see more than twenty feet in any direction. The road was narrow and slippery, and there was no shoulder.

"It's too dangerous to stay on the road!" Larry hollered at me. "The trucks can't see us 'til they're practically on top of us. Let's stop at the next farmhouse and ask if we can spend the night in the barn."

In less than a mile we spotted a chalet farmhouse and pedaled up to the front door. A rugged Bavarian man in his late forties came around the side of the attached barn to meet us. In his minimal German, Larry explained our situation and asked if we could sleep in the barn or pitch our tent under an overhang that might shield us from the snowstorm. The man was quick to shake his head no and walk away. We climbed back onto our bikes and cautiously made our way on up the mountain.

At the next farmhouse we went through the same explanation and received the same answer. In the sixteen months and almost sixteen thousand miles we'd cycled thus far, no farmer had ever denied us a place to camp or sleep on his land. But now, for the first time on our journey, we'd been turned down—twice within ten minutes and in a snowstorm to boot. It was an unsettling experience, and we decided not to inquire at any more farmhouses. Instead, we kept on pedaling. The cars and trucks managed to miss us as they shot through the white blindness.

Our refuge for the night was in a house not yet completely constructed, which I spotted at the side of the road. The house had a roof, cement-block walls, and a cement floor, but the windows had no glass or shutters. We set up camp in the smallest room and hung our plastic ground cover over its one window. The room felt like an icebox, but it sheltered us from the snow, and we were glad to be in off the road. After we'd settled in for the night, Larry looked over his map and found that we were only thirty miles from Austria.

"I can't imagine tackling the Alps in this blizzard," he whispered. "I sure hope the weather clears up tomorrow."

By morning, it had quit snowing, but the ground was still buried. I decided to pedal in my sweat pants, since it wasn't raining either. It was so cold, I pulled on two pairs of socks.

It had been a week since I'd taken a shower, and all my clothes were filthy and smelled sour from having been damp for so long. I looked down at my T-shirt. I'd worn it nearly every day in France, and every day in Germany. I tried to think when I washed it last—over two weeks ago in

London, I remembered; and last night I'd slept in it.

Our hands and feet stung from the cold, and the clouds hovered so low, we couldn't see the Alps to the south of us. It was a hilly ride to Füssen, through tiny Bavarian villages, whose stores and houses were chalets decorated with colorful flower boxes. A few miles before Füssen, the rain started again and soaked the very last of our dry clothing.

We splashed up to the front gate of one of Füssen's campgrounds, glanced at the fees posted at the entrance to the campground, and frowned. Seven dollars for a hot shower and a piece of ground to pitch a tent on seemed awfully steep.

"Zwei person, ein tent, thirteen marks," announced the gruff Bavarian campground owner. But after a short pause he cracked a slight grin and said, "But fir zwei person what bicycle Bavaria en dis bat veder, pay only four marks. Yah, courage you hab."

"Well, it's either courage or plain stupidity," groaned my drenched and shivering mate. "Tomorrow we're headed through Austria. Do you know the weather forecast?"

"Austria no gudt. Much snow und much colt in der Alps. Tomorrow ist bat too. Vait fir clear veder, den bicycle Alps. Den ist beau-ti-ful."

When we set up our tent, Larry noticed a series of cracks in two of the aluminum poles. The rain was pounding down now, and we decided to take the campground owner's advice and hole up in our leaking tent until the storm passed. For two days we huddled inside and listened to the water batter the rain fly.

But on the morning of the third day, we awoke for the first time in almost a week to partially clear skies, and our spirits soared. I crawled out of our tent and looked up—way up—at the Alps, draped with snow and towering only five miles away. There was blue in the sky, and the miles of green countryside that spread along the base of the Alps held lakes, farms, chalets, and snow-covered hills. It was an awesome sight. For the last week the clouds, the rain, and the snow had limited our field of vision to a gray, contained world, which extended no higher than the treetops and no farther than a mile in any direction. It took a long while to absorb all the color, brightness, expanse, and height that now confronted us. We broke up camp and pedaled into Austria through a deep green valley.

The neatness of the Austrian countryside was nearly perfect. It seemed all the grass in Austria had been cut to one uniform height, and on top of this smooth carpet sat tidy chalet farmhouses surrounded by gardens. The carpet extended upward along the sloping bases of the mountains. Higher up, the timber began; then it gave way to the rugged snowcapped peaks, which were a startling contrast to the sharp blue sky. Because of the blizzards, the snow level was down into the timbered areas.

We pedaled through a series of long narrow valleys toward our first alpine pass, south of the town of Lemoos. At the end of the last valley, the road shot skyward into a maze of switchbacks along the side of a mountain. We cycled up into the snow, rounded the summit, then descended and started up the next pass. At the top of the second pass, we stopped. We stood together, dwarfed by timber and majestic peaks, and a glorious sensation poured into our souls that made the misery and frustration of the last week more than worthwhile. I was glad I'd kept pedaling in Bavaria; that I'd fought off the sometimes almost irresistible desire to jump on a train to Italy and warm, dry weather.

We set up camp on the summit. The sky was perfectly clear now, and there was a full moon. The ice and snow on the peaks overhead glowed in the moonlight. We'd made it. These were the Alps. We were here at last. We hugged each other and savored every moment of the evening.

Curled up inside my sleeping bag that evening, I stared out the window by my head at our bikes, leaning together against the base of a fat pine tree. Their frames were badly scratched, and my unpainted front forks had rusted over. Mud still clung to the wheels, rims, fenders, pedals, and cranks. I rolled over onto my back and followed the trunk of the tree to the top. Up there past the treetop glistened the pointed edges of an alpine summit encased in ice. It's late September, I thought—a frigid, crystal clear night in the Austrian Alps. I rolled back around and looked again at my tired, worn bike. In less than a month, it would be carrying me over the hot, desert roads of Egypt.

Up until the day we pedaled east from Foligno across the mountains to the coast near Civitanova our ride through Italy had been an easy, pleasant one. We'd crossed into Italy at the Brenner Pass below Innsbruck, Austria, and headed south through the dry rocky Dolomites (an extension of the Alps in northeastern Italy), into Venice, then on to Florence. In Venice and Florence we had joined the droves of tourists taking in the museums, churches, palaces, and concerts. From Florence we'd pedaled southwest through Arezzo, Perugia, and Assisi, to Foligno.

We'd enjoyed the ride down from Austria. Food was relatively cheap and plentiful, and the people, though generally poorer than the Austrians, Germans, French, and British, had that special Latin warmth and generosity. Although Italian drivers live with one hand on the horn, they waved to us and gave us a wide berth.

North of Venice, on our third night in Italy, still smarting from our bad experience with the two Bavarian farmers, we reluctantly rode up to a house surrounded by vineyards and asked permission to pitch our tent under the grape vines. It took Signore Tonon and his wrinkled mother, who were standing in the front yard, a few minutes to decipher my Italian. They leaned forward and put their faces close to mine in order to carefully study each word that dropped out of my mouth. Once they figured out what I was asking, their faces exploded into smiles so big their skin was pulled tight across their cheeks. And they shook our hands and slapped our backs with all the animation of two truly excited Italians.

No sooner had Larry and I pitched our tent under the labyrinth of vines and bloodred grapes, than the entire Tonon family came out to meet us and invite us to dinner. Bruno explained that he worked at a factory in Treviso that made gas stoves, while Maria, his wife, did varnishing for a furniture company, and Vitoria, the grandmother, stayed home and tended the cows, chickens, and children. His two children, Teodoro and Sabrina, were in their early teens and had just begun studying English in school. Maria could speak some English and Spanish, which she'd picked up while working in Switzerland as a waitress before she was married. But even so, Larry and I communicated with everyone primarily in Italian.

The Tonons hurried us into their house and directly into the dining room. The room was small, just large enough to hold a long rectangular table, seven chairs, and a cupboard full of knickknacks. There was one picture hanging in the room; it was a photo of the pope.

Grandma gestured for Larry to sit next to her, then she leaned over, gave him a bear hug, and flashed him a broad, mischievous, and toothless grin. Grandma was a polished charmer. She loved to giggle, and she loved her *vino*.

Maria was a short, dark, pretty and pudgy woman. She wore lots of religious jewelry and jumped around the dining room making sure that everyone had what they wanted. For dinner she'd prepared minestrone soup, a green salad, and a plate of tuna, salami, cheeses, and fruit. It was Bruno's responsibility to see to it that no one's glass was ever less than three-quarters full of the family's deep-red wine.

For three hours we drank, ate, talked, laughed, and shouted, and threw our arms in the air and stomped our feet in true Italian style. And then we drank some more when Bruno brought out his homemade *grappa*.

"You two should stay on longer with us. You can move into Teodoro's room and stay on for a month or so," shouted Bruno. After a few glasses of Bruno's *grappa*, everyone was talking in a shout.

Grandma liked the idea of our staying on; she clapped and giggled and threw her head up and down. And besides, Granddad had been killed in a bicycle accident years ago, so she wasn't too keen on the idea of us bicycling in Italy. It would be much, much better, Grandma explained, if we stayed with her family and helped harvest the grapes and tend the chickens and cows.

Larry and I thanked Bruno for his offer and proposed another toast to our newly acquired family; but we knew we'd be leaving in the morning. We needed to keep moving or we would arrive in the Himalaya after the clear months of November and December, would hit the monsoons in Thailand, and would end up in New Zealand in the winter instead of summer.

When Larry and I pedaled down the Tonon's driveway the next morning, we could hardly steer our bikes. Maria and Grandma had tied two plastic sacks to each bike, each containing a one-liter bottle of wine from their vineyards.

"Some of the wine is very bad the closer you get to Venice," Maria explained. "This ought to see you through the next few days."

Actually, it saw us all the way through to Greece and eased most of our aches and pains along the way.

All of the Italians we met between the Austrian border and Foligno were like the Tonons. Whenever we free-camped alongside a lake or in a field, the people working and living nearby would bring us a bucket of tomatoes or a jug of drinking water or a cardboard mat to pitch our tent on if the ground was too rocky. When we stopped in the villages, people hurried over to us to ask where we were from and where we were going, and they stood along the road and cheered us on as we pedaled out of town. This had happened everywhere, every day, except in the farming community eight miles east of the coast city of Civitanova. Here we ran into trouble.

It was evening when we stopped in the farming community to ask for water. First, the attendant at the gas station refused to give us any water or allow us to use the restroom. Then we were turned away by an equally unfriendly woman in a farmhouse up the road. But at the second farmhouse a typically generous Italian family filled our bottles with ice water. Darkness was just setting in by the time we got our water, and it looked like rain. Since there wasn't enough light left to cycle on to the campground at Civitanova, and because all the land nearby had crops growing on it, we rode back up the road to a partially constructed house halfway between the gas station and the farmhouse where the woman lived who had refused us water.

The house had two stories, and we carried our bikes upstairs to the second floor. I spread our mats and food out on the floor, and Larry fired up the cookstove. It felt good to relax and smell the aroma of a meal cooking after a strenuous day climbing over steep mountain grades. I stretched out on my mat and began writing in my journal while Larry steamed the rice and vegetables. We felt warm and comfortable and protected, and the police would have taken us completely by surprise if it hadn't been for the car crash. It was the sound of colliding cars that sent us stumbling for the window.

The first thing I saw were two police cars, their emergency lights flashing, parked in front of the house. The two policemen, who were half-way between the road and the house, were walking back toward the road to where the Fiats had just smacked into each other. Each of the police-men carried a submachine gun and a huge flashlight. The traffic on the road was moving slowly, and all the drivers were staring at the crash and at the house.

"Oh wonderful," groaned Larry. "Somebody called the police on us, and I'll bet it was the lady down the road."

It was easy to tell what had just transpired. The police had pulled up to the house and left their cars parked out front with their blue lights flashing. They had been sneaking up on the house and us with their guns held ready, when a couple of gawkers watching them instead of the road piled into each other.

"As soon as they get that accident cleared—and it doesn't look like there's much to it—they'll be in here looking for us," said Larry. "You'd think someone told them a couple members of the Red Brigade were holed up inside here by the looks of those submachine guns. Look, we don't have time to pack up everything and sneak out the back. Maybe if we turn off the stove and pull all our stuff over to one corner, they won't find us."

We knew they'd find us. But since neither of us wanted to pack up and leave, we decided to give the idea a try.

Within ten minutes two beams of light were scanning the wall directly behind us. I held my breath. The lights bounced around on the cement just above my head for a while, and then a brilliant whiteness struck my eyes, and we were had.

The policemen ordered us downstairs, and they waited at the foot of the steps with their guns aimed upward. Both men were tall, with dark hair and complexions, and they looked especially mean in their military uniforms. I started down the steps first. When the two men saw my cycling shorts and my blond hair, a perplexed expression spread across their faces.

"What are you doing here?" one of them asked in Italian.

"Bicycling," I answered in Italian. My answer obviously puzzled them, so I pointed upstairs.

While one of the policemen kept his gun leveled at us, the other climbed to the second story to have a look around. When he came back down, he told his partner what he'd found—two bicycles, two sleeping mats, and a cookstove—and the partner immediately slapped himself on the side of the head and uttered an exasperated "Mamma Mia!" as if to say: A car accident and all this sneaking around with submachine guns for two harmless foreigners on bicycles. After that, the men lowered their guns.

They checked our passports and listened while we explained our reasons for setting up camp in the house. Then one of them trudged off to the neighboring farmhouse to tell the occupant that we were causing no harm and should be allowed to spend the night where we were, because it was too dangerous for us to cycle eight miles in the dark to the next campground. We were told not to worry; that we'd be able to stay in the house. But Larry and I knew better. The woman in the farmhouse was the one who had denied us water and scowled at our appearance. We knew she'd never go for having us camp up the road from her. And she didn't.

Even though fifty yards separated the farmhouse and us, we could hear each and every word with distinct clarity. Only a couple of genuine hot-blooded Italians could have gone at it the way they did. She screamed at him, and he screamed at her, and both of them were tossing their arms every which way and pounding the air with their fists.

"No!" she thundered. "I don't want those two bicycling weirdos around these parts. They look strange, and I want them *out, out, out!!*"

The officer raged back at the woman. He waved his submachine gun at her and called her an idiot. But it was a hopeless situation. The woman finally stormed back into her farmhouse and slammed the door. "*Out! Out! Out!*" she kept screaming from inside her home.

The policeman stomped his way back to us, and he continued to slap the side of his head while he and his partner discussed what to do next.

"The gas station!" one of them finally shouted in a tone that indicated he'd made a momentous discovery. "That's it, the gas station! They can pitch their tent behind the station up the road."

"Oh Lord," I groaned. "Here we go again. That's the station that wouldn't give us any water. Here we go again."

And there we went again.

"Pack up your gear. We're going to the gas station," the officers announced victoriously.

"I'm sorry sirs, but we can't bicycle on this road at night. It's too busy. We don't have any lights," I explained.

"Don't worry about that. Pack up. Here, we'll help you."

They rolled up our mats and crammed our sleeping bags into the stuff bags, while I dumped our half-cooked dinner into a plastic bag and Larry carried our bikes downstairs.

"*Bene;* now the gas station is about a half a kilometer up the road. You two start pedaling and we'll follow behind," one of them explained as they switched on their sirens and their flashing blue emergency lights. And off we went. Passing motorists swerved off the road when they neared us and stared in disbelief at the sight of two ragged-looking foreign bicyclers pedaling along in the dark with their very own Italian police escort following behind.

I was right about the attendant. He wanted nothing to do with us, our bicycles, or our tent. But by now the policemen had had just about enough of the American bicyclers' problem, and they started to rant and rave at the attendant who, being of equally excitable Latin blood, raved and ranted right back.

"Here we go again," I groaned—again. "This could go on all night."

But we were in luck this time. A truck driver who left his semi parked at the station each night came to our rescue. He'd just parked his truck, and he hurried over to see what the commotion was all about.

"They can sleep in my cab tonight," he said after he'd caught the gist of the argument. The policemen and the attendant, however, were too possessed by their tirade to take any notice of the trucker's words.

"I said they can sleep in my cab tonight," the driver explained again, and this time he shouted it at the top of his voice.

Arms froze in midair, words were left unfinished, and all eyes turned toward the truck driver. Minutes later, Larry and I and our packs were crammed so quickly into the cab of the truck that we barely had time to lock our bikes to the truck's front fender. There was a narrow mattress behind the seat in the cab, and it was determined that one of us could sleep on the mattress and the other on the front seat. The policemen, who were so relieved to have finally deposited us *somewhere*, wished us a safe journey; the attendant shut down the station early, and it began to rain.

Larry and I sat cross legged on the cab's long seat with our packs jammed into the space beneath and directly in front of us. I lit our candle lantern and pulled out our soggy, sticky, half-cooked meal. Neither of us had eaten a thing in the last eight hours.

"I feel like I'm getting bit," Larry commented, as he started in on our mess of a meal.

"So do I. Turn on the overhead light, and I'll hold my arm up in front of it so we can see if anything lands on it."

I examined my illuminated arm. "Fleas," I groaned. "The cab's crawling with fleas."

It was raining hard out now, and the empty furrows in the field next to the truck had turned to muddy troughs. We set aside our dinner and climbed outside into the mud and the rain and began pitching our tent.

EXHAUSTION

CHAPTER FOURTEEN

It was mid October when we rode into the smoggy, busy metropolis of Athens. We had spent a week pedaling down the east coast of Italy to the port city of Brindisi, where we caught the ferry to Patras, Greece. In Athens we made our final preparations for our departure from western civilization. In all Europe, the capital of Greece boasted the cheapest air fares and the most up-to-date information on travel to the East, and its bike shops sold parts and tools for English, French, and Italian ten- and fifteen-speeds. Between Athens and Bangkok, parts for our bikes and even tire-patch kits would be impossible to find. We stocked up on ball bearings, spokes, nipples, and patch kits, and bought four spare inner tubes, six spare tires, and an extra tire pump, with an attachment for both Shrader and Presta valves, just in case we lost our one and only pump along the way.

By now, the routes through Afghanistan and Iran were too dangerous to travel because of political chaos and anti-American demonstrations. The student travel agencies that lined the streets near Athen's Syntagma Square advised us to fly over the disastrous Mideast and resume pedaling in India. Each agency offered an almost daily cheap flight to New Delhi.

"What about a flight from Cairo to New Delhi?" Larry asked one of the travel agents. "We're headed to Egypt, so we might as well fly to India from Cairo instead of from here."

"There aren't any flights between Egypt and India right now," the woman explained. "The two countries aren't getting along with each other, and that means their air-traffic controllers won't land each other's planes. You'll have to come back to get to India. For one hundred forty dollars I can get you two round-trip plane tickets to Cairo. That's cheaper than the boat. And then I can get you two tickets on Biman Airlines from here to New Delhi for six hundred forty-eight dollars. For the tickets to Cairo, though, you'll both need an International Student ID card."

"Looks like we're out of luck then on those tickets. Neither of us is a student, and besides, Larry's over the age limit," I said. "Guess we'll have to pay full price."

"Pay full price? Are you kidding? Where you're headed, no foreigner ever pays full price for an airplane ticket. In the East everybody travels on bogus student ID cards. You can buy the cards on the streets in India for next to nothing. As soon as you start walking down the streets in New Delhi or Calcutta, sure enough, some shady-looking character will come along and offer to sell you a cheap plane ticket back to Europe or on to Thailand or the Far East, and he'll sell you the ID card to go along with it. It happens all the time. You can get some terrific deals that way!

"So look, for let's say, oh say two dollars each, I'll set you two up with ID cards, and Larry's will say he's twenty-nine instead of thirty. No problem. All right?"

Both Larry and I stared at the agent suspiciously. She giggled and flashed us a wide, knowing smile. "Welcome to the East, or at least to the gateway to the East. Don't worry. You'll learn the ropes soon enough."

We bought the tickets and ID cards, and as we were leaving Larry thought to ask what country operated Biman Airlines.

"Bangladesh," smiled the agent.

Bangladesh? My heart pounded. Wasn't Bangladesh the country where everyone was starving to death? I hated to fly. Flying scared me to death; and the horrible thought of climbing into an airplane operated by one of the poorest countries in the world made me panic. My mind flashed up a picture of an ancient prop job complete with battered propellers, two flat tires, and barely discernible through the peeling paint on the side of the plane, a foreign scribble saying BIMAN AIRLINES. In the cockpit sat a malnourished pilot wearing a turban.

"Biman is a world-famous airline," the agent smiled again.

Famous for what, I wondered, but I didn't dare ask since I half expected the woman's answer might be, "It's famous because its wings fall off all the time." And then she would turn on that same sweet, hollow smile, and I'd die a thousand deaths. No, I didn't ask. Instead, I chose to toss the thought of Biman Airlines completely out of my mind—after all, the flight wasn't for another month.

Before we left Athens, we picked up a two-quart spare water bottle and four rolls of film to see us through to Bangkok. Film, we were told, was selling for twenty dollars a roll in Kathmandu. We mailed home a package of maps, journals, and the film we had already shot. The day before our flight to Egypt, we swallowed our first antimalaria tablets. Beginning with our arrival in Cairo, we would be spending the next one hundred ten days in areas where we could contract malaria.

Olympic Airlines agreed to take our bicycles unboxed, after Larry explained that the baggage clerks would have an easier time handling them if they could be rolled from place to place. We removed our panniers and gear from the bikes before we checked in. Everything—panniers, tent, sleeping bags, sleeping mats, and bikes—was all checked through as luggage at no extra cost.

On October 20 at eleven at night, Larry and I landed at Cairo International Airport. Security at the airport exemplified the high level of tension that existed in the Mideast and Egypt in particular. For months now, the other Arab nations had been hurling threats against Egypt because of Sadat's peace talks with Israel, and Cairo's airport was crawling with hundreds of armed soldiers, who scrutinized everyone's each and every move.

After spending nearly an hour waiting in line to be processed through customs and immigrations, Larry and I walked over to the baggage conveyor belt. We arrived there just in time to watch the front wheel of Larry's bicycle come tumbling out the chute. There was no bicycle attached to it.

Larry grabbed up the wheel and ran with it to the door of the baggage room, which was guarded by four soldiers holding rifles with bayonets. None of the soldiers spoke English, so Larry went into a mime routine until one of the men caught on. Gesturing for Larry to follow, the soldier charged into the baggage room with his bayonet poised for attack. The baggage clerks fled out the back door, and the soldier found our bikes lying one on top of the other on the floor next to the chute. Except for Larry's missing front wheel, both bikes were in one piece. Apparently the quick-release lever had been jarred, and the wheel had fallen loose.

While we loaded up our bikes, a crowd of airport employees wandered over to take a close look at our bikes, our gear, and us. Everyone wanted to know if we planned on bicycling in Egypt, and when we answered yes, they stared at us in horror and disbelief. And as I surveyed the rows of strained facial expressions before me, it occurred to me that I had never met anyone or heard of anyone who had bicycled through Egypt.

As we approached the exit of the airport, two men stopped us. They appeared to be in their late twenties and were neatly dressed in slacks and tight-fitting shirts. One of the men spoke directly to me. His English was excellent.

"Excuse me, but we understand that you are going to bicycle through Egypt," he smiled.

I nodded.

"Yes. You see word of your arrival spread rather quickly, because no one here has ever seen a woman ride a bicycle. Egyptian women do not bicycle. Therefore, a group of people has gathered outside to watch you ride. For this reason, we should like to ask that you bicycle out first. Shall I give a push to help you get started?"

A push? They really *don't* believe a woman can ride a bicycle, I thought to myself. I started to answer no, but it was already too late the man was propelling me forward, while his friend threw open the double doors of the exit. Larry scrambled to stay in behind me.

I shot through the doors, and there they were. Hundreds of them. Hundreds of silent, staring Egyptian men, bedecked in everything from white turbans and floor-length *galabias*—cotton caftans with long, loose-fitting sleeves—to three-piece suits. There was not a single woman in the crowd, and no one uttered a word. The men had left a narrow path through their midst, and as I pedaled along it, scores of intense, penetrating eyes inspected my bike, my gear, and my clothing—my blue jeans rolled to my calves and a short-sleeved T-shirt. Their eyes bore deep into mine, as if they expected to find there an explanation for what I was all about.

While I pedaled, I stared back in amazement at the dark, eerie figures that engulfed me. No one breathed a word. Then, just as I reached the end of the crowd, a loud shout sliced through the hush.

"I love Jimmy Carter!"

My head swung around, and I looked back at the mob. The men were smiling now, and they all cheered in unison, "Welcome to Egypt! I love Jimmy Carter!"

Now what to do. It was one o'clock in the morning, and here we were at Cairo International Airport with no place to go. There was no campground nearby. Downtown Cairo and the cheap hotels were twenty miles away, and we didn't have a map of the city.

"Let's head over to that gas station across the parking lot and see if we can camp in that field behind it," suggested Larry. "I'm too tired to tackle the ride into Cairo. We'll get some sleep and do it in the morning."

Camping beside an international airport, especially with hordes of armed soldiers milling around the area, would not normally sound like a particularly bright idea, but right now I was all for escaping into the privacy of our tent and falling asleep. The station attendant nodded his approval, and we set up camp in a section of the field out of the path of the airport's sweeping searchlights.

Five minutes after we climbed into our tent, someone grabbed one of its sides and began shaking it so violently that he nearly ripped it apart. The man was hysterically screaming, "Police! Guns! No! No! No!," over and over.

I bolted out the door and came face to face with a frantic, toothless man wearing a filthy *galabia* and no shoes. Speaking Arabic with a smattering of English sprinkled in here and there, the Egyptian made Larry and I understand that he wanted us out of the field. We couldn't make out his explanations, but it was obvious that arguing would be futile. If we tried to stay he would tear our tent to shreds. Bone tired, we packed up and headed into Cairo.

By now it was two o'clock, but the air in Cairo was still hot and dry. The roads were dark or only dimly lit; full of potholes, debris, cars, trucks, bicycles, and donkeys; and devoid of any street signs. We made slow progress and had to stop and ask directions every ten minutes. Toward the center of Cairo, the city was full of activity. Construction workers were busy working on the new highrises, food stands were open, and pedestrians crammed the sidewalks.

It took us two hours to make our way to the "celebrated" Golden Hotel in downtown Cairo, near the Nile and the Egyptian Museum. The Golden Hotel was one of the cheapest places to stay in Cairo. For five dollars and forty cents, the night watchman led us to a room with an attached restroom and shower. He sprayed the air with some lethal-smelling DDT to kill any bugs, then waved us in. We deposited our weary, dusty bodies onto the bed and passed out.

Cairo proved to be exactly what a number of newspaper articles I'd read before we started our trip said it would be: filthy, decaying, and choked by smog and poverty. Every surface in Cairo supported its own layer of dirt and rubble. Even the floors on the second story of a government department store were buried beneath a half-inch of dirt. And our fifth-story hotel window overlooked rooftops piled high with scraps of plaster, wood, glass, and cement. Amid the debris, scores of families had set up housekeeping.

Except for the snazzy five-star hotels, everything in Cairo—the buildings, museums, cars, trucks, buses and parks—was in a state of extreme disrepair. Sections of the city had been declared unfit for human habitation because they lacked sewer maintenance and their water lines were polluted. At the edge of the city, the newly constructed housing that lined the road to the pyramids was already falling apart.

Most of the city buses looked as if they had seen plenty of action at the front lines in the last war with Israel. Huge sections of their crumpled bodies had been ripped apart or completely torn off. Glass was missing from their windows, which made it easier for passengers to hang their torsos outside when the buses were crammed past full, and for men to enter or exit the bus when bodies clogged the doorways. When their engines blew, the buses were promptly abandoned by their drivers and passengers and left to block traffic on the avenues for a week or so, until someone finally hauled them away.

By day and early evening, Cairo became a giant, deafening traffic jam and most of the city disappeared behind a dark cloak of smog. And the fact that the telephones in Cairo almost never worked only added to the congestion—people were always jumping into their cars and driving around town to drop off messages or talk with friends. No one paid any attention to the few traffic lights and signs. Sideswiping one's way through cracks in the traffic and driving with one or two hands on the horn at all times was common practice. The buses, belching out plumes of black exhaust, proved especially adept at ramming through the cracks.

In most areas of Cairo the exhaust and dirt in the air was so thick that it looked like smoke; it had a metallic taste and a burnt smell, and passing through it at a rate faster than a walk drove the pollution into our eyes. On our one and only try at cycling, we had to squint, and even then our eyes filled up with so much debris we could barely see. After an hour our eyes were bright red and stung, our faces and arms were black, and our hair a dusty gray. We could hardly recognize ourselves when we peered into the mirror in our hotel room. We decided that walking was the only way to get around.

The poor in Cairo were incredibly poor. A family with thirteen members would squeeze into a filthy, decaying, rat-infested, nine-foot-by-twelve-foot room and struggle to get by on the forty-seven cents father earned each day as a porter at the train station. Food was dirt cheap—a loaf of bread cost one and a half cents, a *felafel* six cents, yogurt fourteen cents, and a glass of fresh-squeezed lemonade fifteen cents—but not cheap enough for the masses of poor, and many families supplemented their earnings by begging from the tourists. Even the guards inside the Egyptian Museum, which housed the King Tut exhibition, begged for alms—*baksheesh*.

Larry and I were fortunate to have been put in contact with a young Egyptian couple living in Cairo, Mohsen and Samira, who spoke

English. They were friends of an Italian fellow we'd met traveling in Scotland, and they took a day off work to give us a tour of their city—the pyramids, the Citadel, and the Mohammed Ali mosque. Samira and Mohsen lived in Maadi, the exclusive residential area at the edge of Cairo. After they took us around Cairo, they invited us to dinner in a restaurant in Maadi, along the Nile, where we sat and watched the ancient *feluccas* ply the palm-lined river. During dinner, Samira explained that most of the American Embassy officials lived in Maadi, and that many of their wives never ventured into downtown Cairo because they considered it too dirty. Yet even Maadi was dusted with sand and dirt.

While Mohsen and Samira knew the history of their city, Fares was the person who prepared us for bicycling in Egypt. At eighty, Fares Sarofim owned and managed the Golden Hotel. He had graduated from Oxford and the Sorbonne, and he spoke a handful of languages, knew all the travel tips, loved bicycling, and possessed one of the kindest souls on the face of the earth. Fares considered himself a father to all the foreign travelers who stayed in his hotel. He helped straighten out visas, passports, and plane tickets, and he tracked down lost luggage. He directed everybody to the cheapest shopping spots in Cairo, supplied the names of the cheap hotels in other cities in Egypt, and charged us all less than we had expected to pay for our lodging, because he never added the tax, service, and registration surcharges onto the price of his rooms.

Before we set out for Luxor, the site of King Tut's tomb and the ancient city of Thebes, some four hundred fifty miles south of Cairo along the Nile, Fares sat down with Larry and me and imparted his words of wisdom on bicycling in Egypt.

"Any water that comes from a faucet in Egypt is safe to drink. But never drink water in the small villages. There it comes from wells or canals.

"As you found out your first night in Egypt, camping out, except in certain tourist areas, has been forbidden for foreigners ever since the last war with Israel. Therefore, on your way to Luxor, you must stay in hotels or *lokandas*, which are the boardinghouses for Egyptian laborers. I'll mark on your map the towns between here and Luxor that have lodging.

"You, Barbara, must keep your shoulders covered at all times and your legs covered to your knees. This is very important. This summer in Al Minya, one of the cities you'll be staying overnight in, a busload of tourists was stoned by a group of devout Muslims because the women in the tour were wearing sleeveless dresses. Once you reach Luxor, you may wear shorts and sleeveless tops. There are so many tourists in Luxor that the people there are accustomed to seeing foreigners dressed that way. I know Samira told you she wasn't sure how the people in the small villages in Upper Egypt will react to a woman on a bicycle. I should think you'll be safe as long as you keep your shoulders and legs covered.

"I'll jot down some basic vocabulary you will need to know in Arabic: the numbers from one to ten, and words like water, bread, fruit, and lodging.

"You won't find any shops that sell parts for your bicycles. Egyptians ride only old one-speeds, so I hope you are carrying a good supply of spare parts. The road to Luxor is very rough in sections. Your bikes will be taking quite a beating.

"Remember, foreign tourists never venture into the tiny villages in Upper Egypt, so be prepared for the masses of curious peasants. Two foreigners—and especially a foreign woman—on bicycles with huge packs will be one of the strangest sights those people have ever seen. As a matter of fact, in some of the settlements, this year will quite probably be referred to in the future as the year when the fair-skinned aliens appeared riding their bizarre bicycles.

"I hope you two can cope with bicycling in extremely hot dry weather. The farther south you go, the hotter it gets. As you near Luxor, the temperature will stay over one hundred degrees Fahrenheit all day long.

"And now for one last bit of advice: remember to take your malaria pills."

Since shorts were out of the question in Egypt, and sweat pants or rolled up blue jeans too hot and uncomfortable to cycle in, I spent our last day in Cairo searching the clothing bazaars for the perfect pair of "Egyptian pedal pushers." I spotted them hanging from the roof of a wooden kiosk that was so tiny it barely contained its owner and his stacks of dusty galabias. They were a pair of white cotton pants. A good color to wear in hot weather, I figured. And they had two bright-blue competition stripes down the side of each leg. Actually, they looked more like bloomers than pants. They were so baggy that the crotch hung halfway to the bottoms of the legs which were gathered by elastic at the ankles.

I snapped up my find for two Egyptian pounds—two dollars and seventy cents—and back at the hotel I chopped the legs off just below the knees to make them cooler. Next, I stole one of Larry's short-sleeved T-shirts. Its loose fit would allow more air to circulate around my torso while I cycled than would my snugger-fitting T-shirts. The T-shirt hung down to within a few inches of my knees.

"You look simply smashing, my dear Barbara. A genuine heartthrob, I should say," giggled Fares when we set out the next morning.

My billowy bloomers filled up with air while I pedaled through Cairo, making me look like a one-hundred-ten-pound woman with the world's largest thighs. I wore my new cycling uniform every day on our way to Luxor, and the bloomers saw me through to Nepal. Larry, being a male, was fortunate to get by in Egypt wearing only his cycling shorts.

It took us five and a half days of pedaling to reach Luxor. It was a tough ride; the toughest of our journey. Egypt tested our stamina and our ability to cope with trying situations. She threw a massive and unexpected spectrum of obstacles at us, and she prepared us for cycle touring in the East—in India, Nepal and Southeast Asia—where all our senses were constantly challenged and there was little or no opportunity to relax.

The road south from Cairo followed along the Nile through a narrow strip of cultivated river valley (palm trees, wheat, cotton, and sugar cane), bordered on either side by seemingly endless miles of sand. From the road we could almost always see the edge of the desert and the camel caravans in the distance. Because there was only one road south, traffic was heavy, which meant we listened to honking horns all day every day. The dusty shoulder of the road was also crammed with traffic—people on foot or riding their donkeys, bicycles, or camels.

Tiny villages of small, mud-brick houses with roofs of dried cane sprang up about every five miles. Narrow, uneven dirt paths, filled with people, animals, flies, and excrement, wound their way through the jumble of mud and cane. The men in the villages wore *galabias*, walked barefoot or in plastic sandals, and often wrapped long narrow strips of white cloth around their heads as shields against the sun's pounding rays. The boys dressed in *galabias* or in cotton pajamas. Women and girls wore long-sleeved blouses with plunging necklines and layers of full skirts that hung to the ground. They dressed mainly in black and wore mounds of necklaces and thick silver anklets. Like the vast majority of Muslim women in Egypt, the women of Upper Egypt never wore veils.

A wide irrigation canal paralleled the road. The water in the canal was filthy, and sometimes we saw dead, bloated water buffalo floating in it. But even so, it was the local watering place, laundry, kitchen sink, and bathtub—where women washed clothes and their legs up to their knees, rinsed their dishes after scouring them with clumps of dirt, and nude men and boys swam and bathed, even while dead animals floated past.

All that we saw our first day cycling south mesmerized us. We watched camels pull crude wooden plows through the fields. We stared back at the eyes, wide and blank, of freshly severed cows' heads, which boys tied to the handlebars of their bicycles and transported to neighboring villages. We witnessed the Egyptian method of using a shovel, which called for four men per shovel: a rope was tied to the place that the handle meets the blade, and three men pulled the rope while the fourth guided the shovel. And then there were the roadside butcher shops that turned out to be car engine tripods with meat-hooks attached. Butchers slapped chunks of an animal, still covered with tufts of wiry black hair and encased in a quilt of flies, to the hooks. Passing trucks laced the suspended flesh with blasts of dirt and exhaust.

Our first encounter with the curious crowds Fares spoke of occurred in a town thirty miles south of Cairo. We stopped to buy oranges and a couple of cold drinks to go with the chicken and olives Samira's mother had packed for our lunch. After we pulled off the road, Larry walked toward the center of town, and I stayed with the bikes. Two seconds later, at least a hundred men had gathered around me. Some smiled and nodded, others stared suspiciously, but no one said anything. Eventually, I broke the ice by telling everyone where Larry and I were headed.

"Luxor," I blurted.

"Ah, Luxor," they all nodded knowingly.

"Bani Suef?" asked one of the men, as he placed both his hands under the side of his tilted head.

Yes, I nodded, we would sleep in Bani Suef tonight. Then I named off the other towns we planned on spending the night in on our way to Luxor: "Al Minya, Asyut, Suhag, Qena."

The men nodded and grinned their approval. I couldn't think of anything else to say after that, so I stood there and studied all the robes and turbans and the smiling faces whose eyes were in turn examining me. After spending four days in Cairo, where not ten minutes ever went by without someone pleading for baksheesh, I was surprised that no one in the group begged. I was also surprised to find that I felt relatively at ease standing in the middle of so many strange looking men. When Larry returned with the oranges, my bike and I were completely hidden by the mob.

"Barb, where are you?!" he hollered from outside of the crowd.

"I'm over here," I yelled back. We continued calling back and forth to each other until Larry made his way through the ring of bodies to where I was standing.

"That about scared me to death, coming back here and finding you gone! I couldn't see you over all these men! Listen, I'm not real excited about eating lunch right here with a couple hundred eyes staring at us. Let's pedal on out of town and stop in a field someplace where there aren't so many people."

I motioned to the men nearest us that we wanted to get back out to the road. They jumped back, turned and shouted to the others, and the sea parted. As we pedaled off, everyone waved and yelled what seemed to be the one and only phrase that nearly every Egyptian knew in English: "Welcome to Egypt!" Even Egyptians who claimed they spoke English answered our every question—How far it is to Bani Suef? How much are the oranges? Is there someone else who speaks English?—with a cheery and inevitable "Welcome to Egypt!"

A half mile south of the town, we spotted a group of palm trees down a slope beside the road and decided to eat there in the shade and the dirt. Even in the Nile River valley there was never any grass to sit on, only dirt or sand. I pulled out an orange and stretched out on the ground. But as I started to peel the orange, something, a sudden movement, caught my eye. I looked up. My eyes scanned the opposite bank of the canal: it was crawling with rats. They were big rats, about the size of squirrels. I glanced around us; everywhere I looked there were rats, dozens of them. Fortunately, they seemed to be afraid of us, and they kept their distance. Not one ventured any closer than five feet from where we were sitting.

I'd heard a lot about the rats in Egypt. When the Egyptians abandoned the towns along the Suez during their war with Israel, a breed of giant rats moved in and multiplied. From the Suez, these rats had fanned out across the delta area in Lower Egypt, north of Cairo. Many grew to be as large as small cats, and every year the delta farmers lost a good portion of their crops to them. According to the reports I'd read in Cairo, the giant rats often killed the cats the farmers sent after them, and there was at least one confirmed report of two rats attacking and killing a farmer's newborn baby. Fortunately, the giant rats had yet to move as far south as Cairo. Although Upper Egypt was overrun by rats, they were smaller, like those darting through the dirt and bushes surrounding us.

Once I'd decided that the rats wouldn't bother us, I turned my attention to the flies. By now a battalion of them had formed a black crust over our food, and they swarmed into our mouths, nostrils, and eyes. We tried to brush them off, but they came back as soon as we pulled our hands away. It was a hopeless battle, and we soon resigned ourselves to eating our lunch in the dirt, the rats scurrying around us and the flies nibbling at our faces and food. Just as we finished our meal, a truck turned off the road near us. The driver jumped out, yelled "Welcome to Egypt!," and tossed us two handfuls of sugar cane, then, without pausing, climbed back in his truck and drove away.

***

When it was there, the asphalt road between Cairo and Bani Suef was generally smooth. But there were a number of unpaved sections where we pedaled through loose dirt, rocks, and thick clouds of dust kicked up by the cars, buses, and trucks. Even where the road was paved, the air was always choked with dust. By the end of the day, after cycling in the dusty haze for ten hours, our vision had blurred, our throats stung, and gobs of black mucus streamed out our nostrils. We'd sweated hard, and a thick coating of dirt clung to our sticky bodies. At dusk, clouds of tiny gnat-like bugs filled the air and stuck to our skin and hair.

By the time we rolled into Bani Suef, eighty miles from Cairo, both of us wore a black, gummy suit of dirt, sweat, and bugs. Our ears rang with the echos of blasting truck horns, and our stomachs were empty. It had been six hours and long miles since we'd last eaten. We were two beat cyclers when we reached Bani Suef, just as darkness fell, and were in no shape for the two-hour registration that the local police had in store for us.

Standing at the turnoff into the city was a ragged-looking policeman. When we stopped and asked him for directions to the nearest hotel, he hailed a twelve-year-old boy cycling past and told him to guide us. The boy hustled us through a maze of dirty, narrow, winding streets to the hotel across from the train station. While we pedaled through the city, men in *galabias* walking along the sidewalks offered to help our young guide find his way to the hotel, and small children who started to chase after us were slapped and scolded by their fathers.

"No room. Police stamp passport," was all the man in the dingy hotel could say to us. We shrugged our shoulders to indicate that we didn't know what to do. What we wanted to do was to fall asleep right then and there. We waited while the man talked with our guide. At the end of their conversation, the boy motioned for us to follow him. We walked back outside again, climbed back onto our bikes, and followed him to the police station. After our escort talked with the guards at the entrance to the station, he waited at the gate with our bikes while Larry and I were led inside. A guard took us to a room near the entrance to the compound and left us there alone.

The room was completely bare except for a battered wooden desk and three chairs. The desk top was empty. There were no papers, telephone, or typewriter. The walls in the room had never been painted and the floor was bare cement. A naked light bulb hung at the end of a long cord that fell from the ceiling, but it gave off very little light. Larry and I sat down in the chairs and waited. For what, we weren't exactly sure. Something strange, I figured. Everything about today had been strange. We waited for twenty minutes before a group of police and soldiers, five in all, walked into the room. One of the policemen spoke English.

"Where are you from?" he demanded.

"The United States."

"Ah, Americans—Welcome to Egypt!"

"Thanks."

"My name is Helmy. Passports, please."

Helmy took my passport first and sat down with it at the desk. It was then that I realized the desk was facing the wrong way—the drawers were facing Larry and me instead of Helmy. Helmy held my passport upside down and flipped through the pages until he came to my picture, then he turned it right side up. He studied my picture and he looked me over.

A nearby *muezzin* cut loose with his wailing call to evening prayers, and one of the soldiers jumped to a corner of the room, grabbed a rolled-up prayer rug, and placed it on the only remaining piece of empty floor in the tiny, crowded room—at my feet. He then knelt down beside me and bowed up and down in prayer to Allah. Helmy and the other men ignored the soldier and kept their eyes riveted on Larry and me. Every other second, when the praying soldier's body bobbed up between us, Helmy's view of me was obscured.

"You register with police before you stay in hotel," explained Helmy, now that he'd finished studying our passports. "That is rule in Egypt. In tourist cities like Cairo, Luxor, and Aswan, hotels register passports with police. In small cities like Bani Suef where tourists do not come, you come to police station and register. The reason of registration is check people travel in Egypt. We look for criminals and Palestinian and Israeli spies. Now I take passports to boss. Boss must see passports. You wait here."

We waited all right. We waited for over an hour. I was hungry enough by now to commence chewing on my chair legs, but instead I spent my time flicking the bugs and clumps of dirt off my skin and clothes. While we waited, a steady stream of police flowed through the room. Everybody wanted to have a look at the two aliens who had just rolled into town. As tired and hungry as we were, Larry and I tried our best to smile and answer their questions about America. But since most of the police could speak no English and our Arabic was limited to numbers and the few words Fares had taught us, we did more smiling and nodding than anything else. When Helmy finally returned, he too asked us questions about America, and it was another half hour before he finally handed over our passports.

Helmy sent two policemen back to the hotel with us to tell the manager that we had been processed. The young boy followed us to the hotel and stood guard over our bikes once again while we plodded through yet another long delay—filling out the lengthy hotel registration form. It was written in Arabic, and the two policemen, neither of whom spoke much English, had a difficult time telling us what to put in the blanks. When we finally finished, the boy helped us carry our bikes and gear upstairs to our room. I handed him a couple of coins as a thank-you for his help. A shocked look came over his face as he eyed the *piastras* I held out to him. He swayed his head as if to say I helped you because I wanted to, not because I wanted your money. He pushed the money aside, shook our hands and smiled proudly, then ran off.

Our room was large but dirty and noisy. Most of the paint had long ago peeled off the walls. The wooden floor was rough and unvarnished. Light from the bare ceiling bulb filtered down through the dusty air and illuminated the mosquitoes and flies dancing about the room. A loud, shrill singing blasted from the radios in the cafes nearby.

It was nearly midnight before we finished shopping for groceries at the fly-infested open-air food stands, cooking and eating dinner, and cleaning our bodies under a faucet that protruded from one of the four blackened walls in the dark, slimy hall restroom. To prevent ourselves from becoming a feast for the mosquitoes, we slept inside our tent, which we set up in the middle of the room after we'd pushed the two soiled mattresses into a corner.

After a four-hour break, the cafe radios fired up again. It was six o'clock, and I awoke to a bad case of stomach cramps and nausea. I felt too sick to eat breakfast; the smell alone was enough to make me want to vomit. It wasn't long after I'd gotten up that the diarrhea hit. I spent the next hour charging once every ten minutes into the restroom to the squat toilet—a hole in the floor surrounded by porcelain.

As I set out on my seventh run to the toilet, I knew I was too sick to bicycle that day. I dashed out of our room, raced down the hall, grabbed hold of the door, and gave it a quick jerk. It held tight. I panicked—there was someone inside.

Try the next floor up, I thought; it must have a toilet too. I shot up the stairs, yanked open the door, took one step in, and froze. By now I'd encountered a lot of filthy, reeking, squat toilets splattered with excrement in Europe, Morocco, and Cairo. But this one was different. This one was alive. Roaches, lizards, and giant hairy spiders were wiggling about in the overflow of damp human waste.

I jumped back out of the cubicle and closed the door. The sight of the crawling toilet demolished any compelling urge I had to move my bowels. My sphincter muscles had slammed shut. I walked back downstairs, packed up my bike, and rolled it out to the street.

As sick as I was, the fact that I set out for and reached Al Minya that day, pumping a seventy-pound bike in the sweltering sun for seventy-five miles over a rough, jarring road, said a lot about how the last seventeen months had toughened and seasoned me. I stopped once every hour or so to sit and rest. I was weak and shaky, always on the verge of defecating, and my stomach felt as if someone had plunged a butcher knife into it. For lunch I forced down two pieces of bread smeared with some of the peanut butter we bought in Athens. Every time we stopped, crowds of humans or rats gathered to watch us, and the flies bit our bodies and food.

There were more strange sights that day. Just south of Bani Suef, the Cairo to Aswan third-class train passed by us. Its compartments were near solid masses of bodies and packages. The excess passengers rode on the outside, sitting on the roof or clinging to the front end or the sides of the train. These people actually had the better deal, I figured. And I wondered how it was that the poor souls sandwiched together inside the hot, stifling train didn't die of heatstroke or suffocation.

Not long after the train passed us, we encountered our first baby camel. Larry spotted the little fellow standing with his mother next to a small gathering of mud huts and decided to get a close-up shot of the two-some.

"Maybe you shouldn't get too close," I suggested, as he took off across the sand toward the camels. "Mothers can be super protective of their newborns, you know." I stayed by the side of the road balancing Larry's bike against mine.

"Don't worry," Larry called back. "There are some children over there near her, so she must be used to people."

"She's used to Egyptians," I corrected him.

I'd noticed that even the animals in Egypt seemed to sense we were foreigners. The easy-going water buffalo that plodded along unconcerned among the Egyptian people sometimes bolted away when they saw us approaching—especially if Larry was holding his camera. It was a peculiar phenomenon.

"See. She's pretty mellow," shouted Larry. He was squatting down in front of the two camels. The baby was nursing, and Larry hurried to focus his camera. Just as he started to snap the picture, Mom attacked. She lowered her head, straightened out her long neck, and rollered her lips back exposing an especially sinister set of enormous, protruding incisors and canines, which she mashed together to produce a loud grating noise. Mom meant business, but Larry was hypnotized by the teeth.

"Get moving!" I screamed.

Larry responded by stumbling awkwardly backward in the deep sand. He kept his eyes glued to the camel's mouth. When Mom closed in, he grabbed up a handful of sand and threw it in her face. She kept coming. Larry heaved another handful.

"Help! Get help quick!" Larry shrieked. Running backward, he couldn't get his footing in the sand, but he refused to turn his back on the attacker's vicious mouth.

There were no adults to be seen anywhere. The men must all be in the fields, and the women are probably off doing their washing in the canal, I reasoned. Only small children were around, but they were all laughing at Larry's predicament.

Just as I started to drop the bikes, a woman emerged from the door of one of the huts and looked toward the screaming. I could tell by the expression on her face that Larry was in real trouble. The woman leapt to the side of her hut and grabbed up a thick, three-foot-long stick. She moved amazingly fast and sure-footed in the deep sand. When she reached mother camel, the woman grasped the stick in both hands, brought it back behind her shoulders, then swung it down onto the camel's skull—*ka splat*. I could hear the impact from the road. It sounded like a watermelon hitting cement after a ten-foot drop. Mom stopped her attack, uncurled her lips, and hung her head dejectedly while Larry turned and ran. The baby camel wobbled after him for a few yards, nipping at his feet, then sprinted back to his mother, who was catching hell from the woman with the stick.

"Telephoto lens," was all that Larry said as he climbed back onto his bicycle and pedaled away.

It was dark when we dragged into Al Minya that evening. A college student who spoke English led us to the City Hotel.

"The room is five pounds—six dollars and fifty cents—for each of you, and that includes dinner and breakfast," explained the hotel manager. Thirteen dollars sounded astronomical, since the night before we paid only a dollar forty for our room. But the City Hotel was spotless, and Larry thought that staying in a clean place might make my stomach feel better. And best of all, the manager agreed to take care of the police registration for us.

"Do not worry about the food. It is very safe," he added. "Tour groups stop in here on their way from Cairo to Luxor. We have plenty of experience preparing food that foreigners like and that does not make them sick."

We spent an hour scrubbing our blackened bodies, then wandered into the dining room. My stomach still felt queasy, but the food they brought us was like nothing I had set eyes on in a long time. A lettuce, tomato, and cucumber salad was followed by fried rice with chicken livers, moussaka, roast beef with potatoes and carrots, and dates and cheese for dessert. It was a far cry from our cookstove meals.

By morning, I was feeling better. We stuffed down an omelette, bread, and a couple pots of hot tea, then hit the road.

Our third day out of Cairo marked the beginning of a transformation in the behavior of the Egyptians we met. The two previous days, people had been orderly when they crowded around us, and the ones closest to us had been careful to leave a small pocket for us to move around in. But when we stopped to buy a snack in a village two hours south of Al Minya, things changed. Men and boys came at us as if their very lives depended on becoming one of the privileged few with a position right next to the newly arrived foreigners. As they shoved and clawed at one another, they drove their bodies up against us. Everyone was in a frenzy to reach us.

While the old woman in the fruit stand yelled at the mob to back away so that she could sell us her oranges, I watched six bare feet come plowing through the back of the flimsy wooden shelves stacked behind her. Then a rush of bodies trampled through, and the entire stand, awning and all, collapsed. The woman screamed and grabbed her scattered boxes of fruit. Bodies kept charging, and about the time Larry and I were on the verge of being trampled, a commanding voice stopped the surge.

The voice belonged to the lone policeman in town. He was a chubby man, getting on in years, and his official brown shirt and pants were threadbare. He pawed his way through the hysteria, and everyone froze as the sound of his booming voice reached their ears. When he reached us, he motioned for everyone to back off. He had come armed with a narrow, two-foot-long stick, which had three pieces of white styrofoam attached to the end of it. When he swatted at people with it, they cowered and slinked away.

Larry and I grabbed our oranges, paid the wailing woman, and shrugged our apologies. Then, with the policeman and his three tiers of styrofoam clearing a path to the road, we squeezed ourselves and our bikes through the wall of humanity and fled down the highway.

The road was rough and bumpy all day, which aggravated my stomach pains. But even so, we managed to reach Asyut, a city eighty-five miles south of Al Minya, well before dark; after our experience at the fruit stand, we hadn't stopped again to buy snacks. We ate a quick lunch of oranges, tomatoes, and peanut butter sandwiches in a field of dirt, with our usual company of rats and flies and wandering camels. Just before we pulled into Asyut, we ran out of drinking water.

A group of young boys playing at the edge of the city led us to the Omar Khayyam Hotel. We were given a tiny room with no mosquitoes for three dollars. The hotel owner took our passports and agreed to register us with the local police, and since we'd stocked up on rice and zucchini in Al Minya, we didn't have to shop for food for dinner. By eliminating the police registration and grocery shopping, we were able to get to bed by nine thirty. Unfortunately though, at one o'clock in the morning the male maids began cleaning the empty rooms on our floor. They turned on their portable radios full blast, clanged their buckets, and snapped their cloths at tables covered with dirt.

In the morning, carrying our bikes on our shoulders, we carefully stepped around the bodies of the hotel workers, fast asleep on the floor of the small lobby. Larry awakened the man nearest the front desk and asked him for our passports.

"Pass-port?" the man mumbled blankly.

"Yes, passports. We are leaving now. We'd like our passports. Do you have them?" Larry asked again.

"Pass-port? Pass-port?" came the same hollow response.

Larry and I combed through all the desk drawers in the lobby, but there were no passports anywhere. My heart sunk. Our passports were gone, vanished, and that left us stranded in Asyut. It would take the police forever to figure out what to do with a couple of foreign bicyclers with no passports. The man repeated our search, but he too found nothing. Next, he woke the other sleeping hotel workers, one at a time, and asked each one if he knew where our passports were. The seventh man reached into the pocket of his *galabia* and pulled out two blue American passports. He handed them to the man, eased a smirk across his face, then laid down on the floor again and fell asleep.

The transformation in the people went a step further that day. The mood of the people turned ugly. The men and boys quit smiling at us from the side of the road. No one yelled "Welcome to Egypt!" The kind words and broad smiles that greeted us our first two days out of Cairo were now replaced by stern glares and screams for *baksheesh*. Everybody in the towns and the mud villages, even the women, begged from us when we pedaled by. Occasionally a teenager threw a rock at us. We heard nothing but honking horns and loud, hysterical pleas for *baksheesh*.

When Larry got a flat tire twenty miles outside of Asyut, near a small gathering of mud houses, the village people poured around us and started yanking at anything they could get their hands on—our panniers, water bottles, brake cables, derailleurs, and spokes. While I repaired the flat, Larry shoved the villagers away to keep them from destroying our bicycles.

By noon the temperature had reached one hundred five degrees and a head wind came up soon after. The people screamed, the cars, buses, and trucks honked, dirt clogged our noses and eyes, and for the first time, we saw bodies of dead animals, mostly donkeys, lying beside the road. Starving dogs hurried to devour their carcasses. It was a gruesome sight. Sometimes animals staggering at the edge of the road keeled over just as we pedaled by, dead from starvation or disease. And we also noticed an increase in the number of diseased children—emaciated children, with their eyes full of pus.

By midafternoon the heat, head winds, noise, and dirt had taken their toll on our nerves and stamina, but we didn't dare stop at any of the rare roadside stands to rest or to quench our craving for something cold to pour down our parched throats. Battling the crowds would be worse than bicycling nonstop in the relentless sun; we forced ourselves to keep pedaling.

It was four o'clock when we reached the city of Suhag. Our skin was fried, the heat had sapped our strength, and our throats felt like sandpaper when we tried to swallow. Someone directed us to a *lokanda*, a boarding-house, and the owner lead us to our room. There was nothing in it but two beds. The sheets had been tossed into a corner, and piles of dirt covered the floor and both mattresses. The owner explained that the price of the room was two dollars, but that we were each to pay him four dollars above and beyond that figure before he would tell us where the police station was located so that we could register. When we refused to pay the extra eight dollars, he shrugged his shoulders.

While Larry argued with the man, I walked outside and tried to ask the people in the streets for directions to the police station. No one responded. Finally, Larry and I decided to pedal on to Girga, another twenty miles south. There was still an hour and a half of daylight left, and that would be just enough.

But those last twenty miles supplied a disastrous ending to an already bad day. Five miles outside of Suhag, the pavement disappeared and the road turned to dirt and rocks. Trucks crowded us into ditches; people in the nearby huts screamed for *baksheesh* and heaved rocks at us. When darkness set in, we had no idea how many miles we had left to pedal. My nose was bleeding now from sucking in the hot, dry, dusty air all day, and the gnats had come out in full force. Occasionally we had to stop and dig the tiny bugs out from under our eyelids to stop the stinging. To keep myself going, I chanted: "Gotta getta Girga. Gotta getta Girga. Gotta getta Girga."

It was a terrible place, Girga. It sat a kilometer off the road, and the people reacted to our arrival by chasing after us in a mindless, screaming frenzy. The driver of a horse-and-buggy taxi agreed to lead us to the police station, and when the crowds in the narrow, crammed streets tried to mob us, pulling at our clothes, hair, bikes, and gear, he snapped them with his horsewhip.

At seven o'clock we stumbled into the office of the chief of police, Larry in nothing put a pair of shorts and me in my bloomers and king-sized T-shirt. Both of us were caked with dirt, sweat, and bugs from head to toe, and my nose was gushing blood.

"Welcome to Egypt!"

"Yeah," sighed Larry.

"Any service?"

"You bet. We want to go to a hotel. We're very, very tired. We pedaled from Asyut today."

"Please have tea and we shall talk. Sit."

Neither of us wanted to douse our scorched throats with pots of scalding tea, but we were in no position to argue. We forced ourselves to drink the tea and smile and chat with the policeman in the room. Each policeman worked hard at impressing us with his status within the force, and we worked at acting as impressed as possible. Even though my appearance was repulsive, the looks the men gave me were long and leering, and I felt like a prostitute on display. I wanted to walk out, but I continued to smile dumbly while I cursed our predicament under my breath.

Registration lasted two and a half hours. We answered a long list of questions about our trip and about America. Larry did most of the talking, while I kept wads of toilet paper jammed up both my bleeding nostrils. When the police were through with us, they sent us to what they described as "the good *lokanda* in Girga, but not so good." Two policemen escorted us to the *lokanda* and prevented the people in the streets from mobbing us and smashing our bikes.

Our room at the *lokanda* was a nine-by-eight-foot unpainted compartment, bare except for two twin beds, which nearly filled it. The cement floor was lost beneath a deep carpeting of dirt. There was a small window up near the ceiling. It was closed, and the room felt like an oven.

We pushed the beds together and stuffed our gear under them. Then we wedged our bikes into the room. With the bikes inside, there was no empty floor space, so we crawled around on top of the beds. Larry closed the door to our room to keep out the mosquitoes that were swarming in the hallway and left the window shut for the same reason. Our cell was suffocating, and its temperature put our bodies on slow bake.

I lay down on one of the beds, sweat pouring from my skin.

While I nursed my bleeding nostrils and rinsed my throat and eyes with water to sooth the stinging and clean away the dirt and bugs, I took a good look at the walls of the room. They were splattered with little red splotches. I sat up and examined one of the splotches. It was a squished mosquito. Between the splotches rested the tiny bodies of living mosquitoes. Each wall supported fifty or so living bloodsuckers and as many red splotches.

For half an hour, Larry and I labored at increasing the splotch count, then we took a break and headed to the restroom down the hall to clean our bodies. The room consisted of a filthy, fetid squat toilet, a sink that emptied directly onto the floor, and a faucet two feet directly above the floor-level toilet. Greasy black grime clung to every surface, and the air hummed with mosquitoes. To shower, Larry and I took turns squatting under the faucet, which was so close to the toilet that when I put my head under it my face was no more than a foot from the reeking hole. Mosquitoes punctured my bare skin, and in the closeness of the cubicle I was sweating even while the cold water poured over me. After our wash, we

resumed the mosquito massacre, then went shopping for supplies for dinner and breakfast.

We had to fight our way through the streets. The throngs of people,
and especially the children, who clogged the tiny alleyways turned wild
when they saw us coming. Everyone wanted to get at us, and those who
did shoved and clawed us. Some screamed "What your name?" over and
over with such hysteria that they never expected or paused for an answer.
We shielded our faces from the clawing hands and groped from one alley
to the next hunting for bread and fruit. By now it was eleven o'clock.
Hunger, fatigue, and exhaustion were grinding away at our nerves. Noises
and bodies pounded us from all sides. But the sight of food kept us fighting, even when some of the fruit vendors waved us away, fearing that the
crowds might trample their stands. The mob pawed and yanked at our
bodies until we reached the door of the *lokanda*, and the manager came
outside with a long pole and beat the people away.

Once inside, we sat naked on the beds in our filthy, depressing, hot
box and devoured the bread and cheese and oranges and tomatoes we'd
managed to buy. The dirt from the mattresses now stuck to our bodies,
which we'd made even stickier by smearing on layers of mosquito repellent. Occasionally one of us moved to squash a mosquito. By now the
walls were almost completely covered by mosquito bodies. Music and
voices from the cafes down the street blared into our room, and I could
hardly hear myself thinking: Just one and a half more days to go, kiddo. Just
one more night of this. Hang in there. You'll make it.

At five thirty, the *muezzin's* call to morning prayers shot through
our room as if there were no walls. I felt tired, very tired. I took my time
eating breakfast; I was in no hurry to step outside into the mobs again.

The crush of humanity was waiting for us when we rolled our bikes
out the front door of the *lokanda*. We pedaled for a hundred yards, then
Larry stopped to snap a picture of the sea of bodies that engulfed us. He
pulled the camera from its foam-rubber sack and held it up to his eyes, but
as soon as he looked through the lens he knew he'd never get the picture.
The lens was covered with dirt—in Egypt, dirt makes its way into everything—and with people grabbing at our bodies, bikes, and the camera
itself, there was no way to clean the lens. When someone kicked my right
pannier, Larry promptly plopped the camera back into its pack, and we
pedaled and pawed our way out of town.

Conditions deteriorated even further that day, and so did our
humor and patience. Added to the screams for *baksheesh*, the bumpy
roads, honking horns, dead animals, sick children, dirt, and a midday high
of one hundred six degrees, we had something new to contend with—a
menacing barrage of low-flying objects. It seemed that every human we

passed between Girga and Qena hurled something at us. As soon as they spotted us coming up the road, people rushed to pick up a rock or a stick to toss at our faces. Why? We never found out. We were too busy dodging airborne objects to stop and ask for an explanation.

In addition, there were the "heavy breathers"—the men and teenaged boys who chased me on their bicycles. Their usual approach was to pedal up alongside me, move in as close as possible, and whistle, make lewd gestures, and pant. Some preferred to pull directly in front of me, maneuver their bicycles to keep me from passing, then, looking over their shoulders, whistle, gesture, and pant. How anyone could find me attractive in my bloomers and T-shirt was beyond me; yet there was no getting rid of the "breathers." No matter how much we yelled or how hard we swatted at them, they continued to pant and drool. Finally, Larry hit upon an idea, and the first time he tried it out it worked beautifully.

Our first victim was a tall man in plastic sandals and a ragged *galabia* whose lascivious smile exposed a mouth missing most of its teeth. As soon as the fellow pulled beside me, Larry went to work. First he squeezed his bike between the "breather" and me; next he began slowly edging his victim away from me and toward the opposite side of the road. Rather than look where he was headed, the "breather" kept his eyes glued to my body while he pushed his pedals. Larry continued edging, and the man continued leering. Our victim was like putty in Larry's hands. Within a few minutes Larry had succeeded in edging him clear off the road and sending him crashing into the dirt and bushes.

The method worked perfectly every time. Once, just as Larry was about to give one of his catches the final nudge off the side of the pavement, a second "breather" came charging up from behind, his eyes focused on me, and collided with the first at full speed. Two screaming bodies flew into the air and splashed down into the canal, while pedals and other bike parts came flying past us.

By late morning, the small plastic bottle attached to my bike frame was empty. As I stopped to fill it with the water from my reserve container, which I carried in my rear pack, three men on a motorcycle pulled up behind us. They were dressed in slacks and shirts instead of the traditional *galabias*. They climbed off the motorcycle and stood close to me. Larry and I nodded hello, and they smiled back. Then one of the men motioned for me to go into the bushes with him; but before the man's words and gestures had time to register in my brain, Larry's fist had exploded into the side of the man's face. The strike was a reflex reaction on Larry's part, and it surprised us both.

"Now we're in for it!" I screamed. "There's three of them and two of us! And those guys are big!"

I grabbed my bicycle pump. It had a mean metal lever at one end, which, if used properly, could inflict a great deal of pain. I figured that I could take on one of the men, and Larry was stuck with the other two. Larry reached for his spray bottle of dog repellent.

By now the man Larry had hit was grabbing his face and slowly stumbling backward. He looked stunned, as if it never occurred to him that Larry's reaction to his proposal might be so drastic. The other two men took off running, shaking their arms in the air to show they wanted no part of a fight. When the stunned man gathered his wits about him, he too shook his arms in the air. Then he jumped on his motorcycle and roared off in the direction he'd come from, with his two friends chasing behind him on foot.

Larry and I stood at the side of the road for a few minutes until we regained some semblance of calm, then we went back to our pedaling, dodging whatever people threw at us, eliminating "heavy breathers," and lunching with the rats and flies. Again, we didn't stop to buy food or even to rest for fear of what the people might have in store for us. The ride from Girga to Qena proved to be a long hot ordeal.

After Girga, the city of Qena, thirty-six miles north of Luxor, at the edge of the desert, was a relief. People jammed its streets, but they left us alone, and we had no problem getting directions to the police station. The police sent us directly to a small hotel and assured us that the hotel manager would bring them our passports for registration later in the evening. "There is no need for you to wait here to be registered," explained the officer. And that suited us just fine.

The hotel was rundown, but our room was large enough for us to set up our tent in to escape the mosquitoes. The room next door housed a goat, which bleated all night.

It was a religious holiday in Egypt, and most of the food stands in Qena were closed. After searching for an hour for something to eat for dinner, we returned to our room with nothing more than two small loaves of bread and a package of spaghetti noodles. We had found nothing to put over the noodles, not even margarine.

At ten o'clock, just as we sat down to eat and were looking forward to getting to bed early for once, someone knocked at our door. Larry flung it open, and in the hallway stood the young hotel manager in his green-and-white-striped *galabia* and worn-out leather shoes. He was holding our passports in his hands, and there was a tone of urgency in his voice.

"You come police station now!"

"No. We've been to the station already," Larry answered. "They said that you could take over our passports. I don't need to go."

"No! I go and you go!" the man shouted. People had been shouting at us all day, and for Larry, this man's screaming was the last straw.

"Wrong! I'm not going!" Larry thundered right back. "I'm hungry and I want to eat. I'm tired and I want to sleep. I am *not* going! That registration bullshit is a waste of time! Listen, I want to eat and I want to sleep. Now won't this country allow me that after all I put up with today?"

For the first time on our journey, Larry was near tears.

"No! No! You come! You come!"

Larry slammed the door, but the man kept screaming. Larry opened the door and hollered, "All right. You win. Let's go.

"I'll be *right back*," he muttered as he stomped out the door. "When I get through at the station, those guys'll be praying they never meet another American for as long as they live!"

The young man took Larry to a different station from the one we had gone to earlier. The guards at the front gate motioned for him to wait, but Larry pushed his way in and yelled that he wanted to "see the chief of police and see him now!"

"I take you there," one of the policemen answered from inside the compound, and Larry followed the man into the main building and down a long hall to a closed door. The policeman opened the door. Inside was a tiny cubicle with a squat toilet. The policeman stepped over the porcelain, spotted with excrement, opened the door at the other side of the cubicle, and stepped into what proved to be the office of the chief of police. Larry followed, and the policeman tossed our passports onto a desk and left. Then the chief walked into the room, but before he had time to welcome Larry to Egypt, Larry's mouth was off and running.

"Now what's the problem here? My wife and I already checked in with the other station, and they said we didn't need to register in person; that the hotel could do it for us."

"Please have a seat and some tea. I only want to talk," the chief smiled.

"Well I only want to finish my dinner and get some sleep. Look at me. Do I look like a Palestinian or Israeli? No. I'm American and so is my wife, and we're obviously not spies. I mean, come on. Do you honestly think that the CIA has taken to sending out their spies on bicycles? No, of course not. So as you can see, a personal two-hour interview with me would be a total waste of everybody's time. Right?"

The chief smiled and stood to shake Larry's hand. "I hope this can be the beginning of a meaningful relationship."

"A what??"

211

"Please be seated. Are you enjoying your visit in Egypt?"

"Enjoying Egypt?" Larry grabbed the passports off the top of the desk. "Since six o'clock this morning I have eaten exactly two oranges and one very tiny loaf of bread. On that and few hours sleep, I managed to bicycle the fifty or sixty miles between Girga and here in the blazing sun and incredible heat, while everyone tossed stones and assorted other crap at me and screamed for *baksheesh*, and the men propositioned my wife, and we couldn't stop for food or water because the people would mob us and probably pull our bikes apart. No, I am *not* enjoying Egypt. Obviously I am very, very tired and hungry right now. I'm going back to my hotel room to eat and sleep. Good night!"

Larry opened the door, stepped over the porcelain, opened the next door, walked down the hallway, through the compound, out the gate and back to the hotel. He then inhaled his share of the spaghetti noodles and bread, and climbed into our tent.

It was especially hot, and the air hung stagnant in our room. We both had trouble falling asleep, even though we were physically and mentally exhausted. All night long our bodies poured sweat, the mosquitoes bounced against the tent walls, and the goat bleated.

When I woke up the next morning, I was greeted by a strange sensation. That pocket of reserve energy, from which in the past I'd always been able to summon my last bit of umph, had dried up. I felt depleted, sapped, and withered.

"Barb?" whispered Larry.

"Yeah?"

"I feel weird."

"Me too."

I searched my mind and soul for some hidden spurt of energy, but came away empty-handed. I hadn't slept or eaten much in the last few days, and the day before I'd burned up a lot of nervous energy worrying about being clobbered by rocks. My empty stomach lay flat against my body this morning. I was hungry, but I tried not to think about that. For breakfast we would each have one hard-boiled egg; two eggs were all we could find last night in the few stores that had stayed open. The egg, and a lot of water, would have to carry me the thirty-six miles to Luxor.

"Thirty-six miles. Only a few more hours and we're in Luxor. If I can just keep thinking about that, somehow I'll muster up enough energy to make it there," Larry muttered as he strained to sit upright.

But those last thirty-six miles packed a real wallop. The mood in the villages between Qena and Luxor was ugly, even brutal. Instead of grabbing for a single rock or stick when we approached, the villagers gathered mounds of debris to hurl at us. A group of boys would run into the street to slow us down, while the others launched their arsenals and clawed at our bikes and bodies. Some of the villagers came at us brandishing tree branches. The branches were a new development and a terrifying one. We made sure to keep away from them at all costs and paid less attention to the flying rocks that ricocheted off us and our bikes.

Fortunately, none of the stones hit either of us in the face, and it wasn't until a man nearly eliminated the top of Larry's head with a masterful swing of his tree branch that we decided the time had arrived for some self-defense. Before we reached the next settlement, we each scouted out a branch of our own. After that, we charged through the villages swinging branches at our attackers and driving them back from the road.

For nearly three hours, we literally fought our way to Luxor, stopping only that one time to arm ourselves. Our fear of being struck or mobbed and beaten pumped a continuous rush of adrenaline through our systems and kept us pounding our pedals. When we finally rolled into Luxor, we were shaking from exhaustion and from not having eaten enough, and we were bruised where the rocks had struck us.

I figured a clean hotel room, a meal, and about twelve hours of sleep would bolster our spirits and help restore some strength and stamina to our bodies. But Luxor was a tourist city, and its hotels catered to tour groups of well-scrubbed Americans, Australians, and Europeans. The hotels wanted nothing to do with a couple of tattered, smelly bicyclers. Each time we pedaled up to a hotel, the desk clerk came running outside and waved us away. Even when we hid our bikes around a corner and walked up to the hotels, after a quick glance at my dusty bloomers, our blackened skin and teeth, and greasy, matted hair, the clerks always assured us that their hotels were full and would remain so for the rest of the week. Every time a hotel turned us away, I felt myself sinking further into the clasp of exhaustion and despair. And I harbored a real desire to punch one of those pompous, I-don't-give-a-damn-about-you hotel clerks right in the ol' kisser.

It took over an hour, but we eventually found a hotel that agreed to take us in—the Horus Hotel across from the Temple of Luxor. We were given the last room. It was hot and dingy and on the second floor just above the noisy main street, but that was the best we could do in Luxor, given our appearance.

There was a restaurant in the hotel, which served a lunch of salad, rice, potatoes, green beans, pot roast, and oranges for two dollars a person. As soon as we checked in, we each devoured two complete meals, then collapsed on our beds for the rest of the afternoon and most of the next day. Larry had found a fan in the storage room on our floor, and that allowed us to sleep in our room, which would otherwise have been un-bearable in the sweltering desert heat.

Before he fell asleep, Larry put into words what we were both think-ing: "I'm not fighting my way back up to Cairo. I vote we take the train."

Luxor was an awe-inspiring place, with temples and tombs over three thousand years old. We spent part of a week there, wandering through Karnak, the ancient city of Thebes, Luxor Temple, and the tombs of King Tut and other pharaohs, and of queens and nobles. The magnifi-cence and grandeur of the ruins of ancient Egypt set a sharp contrast to the squalor and primitiveness of present-day Egypt.

The day before we left Luxor, we sent our bikes back to Cairo on the baggage train and prayed that they wouldn't be smashed or stolen along the way. We figured the chances of the bikes not being stolen were slim, although the hotel clerk felt differently: "Egyptians beg, but they do not steal. Your bikes will be safe."

With our student ID cards, we paid half price for a sleeping compart-ment on the night train to Cairo. We traveled on the night of November 4, the day the Iranian students took over the American Embassy in Teheran. The next morning, when the train eased into Cairo station past tracks cluttered with sections of disabled trains, dusty rubble, and debris, we ran straight to the baggage office. Our bikes were there, and the clerk had locked them safely inside a small room separate from the baggage area. For this added touch of attention, the man demanded a hefty tip before he would hand them over to us.

From the station we headed out to a residential area of highrise apartments near the airport. Jim Pett, a member of the religious group my brother belonged to, had invited us to stay with him when we returned from Luxor. Jim was a British citizen who had spent a good portion of his life in Egypt, and he was now teaching education at the university in Cairo. His apartment was immaculate; so different from the *lokandas* and cheap hotels we'd slept in each night since our arrival in Egypt. We stayed with Jim for three days before flying back to Athens, and each moment of those three days I struggled with my "almost" decision to go home.

While Jim was away during the day, Larry and I stayed in the apart-ment, an oasis safe from the surrounding filth, noise, and poverty. We spent our time writing letters and listening to Jim's John Denver tapes. Denver's nostalgic, bitter-sweet songs about the Rockies, about green grass, trees, and mountain streams, and about "goin' home" made me so home-sick that I lost the battle to fight back my tears. I cried a lot during those three days, and only twice did I venture out into the streets of Cairo—on two quick trips for rice and bread. For those three days, Larry and I talked mostly about our ride to Luxor: about the rats, the flies, the filth, and the exhaustion, and the people—those who had smiled, those who had stared, those who had begged, those who had spit on us and hit us with rocks and sticks.

And I did a lot of thinking about Egypt. In Egypt I had come face to face for the first time in my life with acute poverty, squalor, and disease. These were no longer things I only read about, saw in magazines or on television, or heard about on the radio. They had been my environment. I had eaten, slept, and moved through them. I had learned their sounds and smells. I had touched them and they had touched me. In the villages, I'd touched and talked with people who were nothing more than flesh-covered skeletons, and sometimes the bread and fruit that I ate for dinner had been handed to me by jaundiced victims of schistosomiasis, a disease the people in Upper Egypt pick up by touching the canal snails or the infested water.

The poor had reached out and pulled at my dirty clothing, which to them looked clean and new, and begged for money to buy a piece of precious rotting meat to fill their empty bellies. I'd often wondered whether they guessed that in our dusty packs Larry and I were carrying more money than they would earn in a lifetime, simply because by chance or fate we had been born into middle-class America, while they had begun their lives among the poor of the Third World. How, I asked myself over and over again, could I rationalize why these people should be condemned to such a terrible existence while most Americans—for no other reason than the fact that they had been born in the United States—lived like royalty by comparison? I couldn't. I felt guilty for spending so much money to fulfill my whim of pedaling around the world, while the mass of Egyptians were barely scraping together enough food to sustain themselves from one day to the next.

On our second day at Jim's, Larry bought an English magazine to read. Its feature article talked about the mass starvation in Cambodia. I read the article and my guilt turned to despair. The more I thought about our ride through Egypt, the more I worried abut India. India was famous for its starving masses, filth, diseases, chronic overpopulation, and the dead in the gutters of Calcutta. And now that I'd seen how harsh life could be, India loomed in my mind like a vision of hell. I didn't want to pedal through a country worse than Egypt. I'd come a long way since Santa Barbara, but even so I doubted that I could cope with India.

I wanted to go home, and yet I worried about that too. How could I go back to America and ignore or forget all that I'd seen and learned in Egypt? How could I be happy living in America knowing what the people in much of the rest of the world were living like? How could I raise a family and clothe my kids in the latest Nikes, buy them toys and games and all the trimmings, knowing that for the cost of the Nikes alone I could have fed a starving Third World family for nearly a year?

I worried about going home, but even more, I dreaded the prospect of going on to India. Yet Larry wanted to continue on.

"Barb, I feel the despair too. Egypt was the first country where I couldn't sing while I was cycling. In other countries, I sang when I was happy, or when I was bored, depressed, or in pain, to help boost my spirits. I sang happy songs and songs to take my mind off things. But Egypt didn't have a song. I didn't sing our first two days out of Cairo because I was too enthralled by all the weird sights. And later, when just making it through the days and nights became a real struggle, I couldn't sing because I was too depressed and too hassled. I never really knew what being exhausted, hassled, and depressed was like until we got to Egypt.

"But somehow, in a peculiar sort of way, I appreciated the challenge of cycling in Egypt. Egypt demonstrated how much tougher we've become. I mean, if we'd started out our trip cycling in this country, we wouldn't have lasted more than a day or two. But you know, all that we'd been through up until Egypt helped prepare us for that ride to Luxor, and I think that Egypt has prepared us for India.

"I figure the longer we stay immersed in the poverty and all of the Third World, the less it'll sadden us and the more we'll come to accept it. Sure, India scares me, but I still want to go there. I still see an adventure in bicycling there, and I want to prove to myself that I can make it through all the hardships it throws at me. And there's another reason I want to go on. To me, seeing Karnak, the tombs, and the Temple of Luxor was well worth everything I went through to get there. I think the same will be true of India and the Himalaya. No matter how rough India might be, I know when I finally pedal into Nepal and set my eyes on Mount Everest at long last, it's going to be one awesome, priceless feeling.

"Yeah, I want to go on, but I won't go if you don't. Mentally, I couldn't make it without you. You're my constant friend, confidante, and supporter, and we've shared so much together that going it alone now would be impossible for me. I'd miss you too much. I'd feel empty, and I just wouldn't feel like doing or seeing things. I want to go on, but I can appreciate why you want to go back. You're a lot more sensitive to things than I am. I don't feel personally responsible for or guilty about the living conditions here. I accept them. They're what they are for a multitude of reasons—the distribution of the world's natural resources, the country's geographic location, climate, politics, birth rate—you name it.

"Listen, I've got an idea. Let's talk with Jim tonight about this. Maybe he'll have some advice for us."

Although he'd never been there, Jim reassured us that India

wouldn't be as tough as Egypt.

"In Upper Egypt, there's only one paved road running north-south. There aren't any alternates, so that's where all the traffic is, and you were stuck in it the whole time. Also, practically the entire population of Upper Egypt is clumped along that road in a string of villages, towns, and cities, and that made it impossible for you to get away from the crowds. But in India you'll be able to take back roads and escape the traffic and the crowds. I think you should go on."

At the end of our stay at Jim's, Larry and I came to a decision. We would go to India unless our airplane tickets, which we were to pick up at the student travel agency in Athens only four hours before our departure time, had fallen through.

"If we can't get on that flight, then I figure that's a sign for us to turn back," reasoned Larry.

When we flew back to Greece on November 8, I was ambivalent about what might happen next. I was terrified of India. But I knew if we flew home then I'd feel like a quitter.

On our second time around, Athens looked like a very different place. After Egypt, the smoggy, dusty, decaying Greek capital appeared spick-and-span. I'd forgotten all about flowers, shiny green leaves, and thick green lawns. I suppose the shrubs and palm trees in Egypt were green too, but their greenness had long been buried beneath the brown and gray of sand, dust, and dirt.

We stayed at a campground near the airport. Our campsite was surrounded by pine trees and a thick green hedge, and the birds sang all day long. It felt wonderful to camp out again, even if it was in a campground. After we pitched our tent, we hit the well-stocked grocery store up the block and came away with two whole barbecued chickens, peanut butter, crisp green apples, thick creamy yogurt, lettuce, salad dressing, and—sin of all sins—a package of chocolate chip cookies. Larry had called an official pork-out in anticipation of our impending starvation in India.

At noon on November 9, the day after we flew into Athens, the travel agency came through with our tickets for that day's four o'clock Biman Airlines flight to India. The clerk at the airport check-in counter agreed to take our bikes on as regular luggage at no extra charge. He informed us that our flight was fully booked, yet fifteen minutes before we were to board the plane, there were only twenty-three other passengers seated in the waiting room.

"I don't like the looks of this one bit," I commented as I surveyed the near-empty waiting room. "Both the travel agency and the check-in clerk said the flight was full. Does this mean the plane only holds twenty-five people?"

I could feel myself panicking. I never was very good at remaining calm while I waited to get on an airplane. I always figured *this* was the one destined to fall out of the sky.

"Oh Lord, don't tell me we're flying from Greece to India on a Cessna!" I gasped.

"Now Barb, don't get all hysterical about this. I know you hate to fly but—"

"Hysterical? Look, I'm talking logic. Count 'em," I almost shouted pointing to the others in the room. "There are twenty-three plus you and me, that's twenty-five. Simple arithmetic. Now if the plane is supposed to be full, and there are only twenty-five people going into it, then we're talking about one real small plane, aren't we? Well? Aren't we? You watch. They're going to put us on Bangladesh's answer to the 747—a Super Cessna Stretch!"

"Now Barb try to calm down. I—"

"And another thing," I shouted. "Look at the people in this room! There's that girl over there with those weird, wooly, combat boots, and a jacket that looks like an entire polar bear, and it's hot in here and probably even hotter in India. And there's the guy with her that's shaved his head and eyebrows and he's wearing a black leather vest, no shirt, and khaki shorts. And both of them have a picture of their favorite fanatical Indian guru in a pendant hanging from their wooden necklaces.

"OK, now look at the rest of the people. They're all just as strange as those two. There's the German girl over there dressed all in black and those two Frenchmen who've been strung out on drugs for so long that their eyes are on permanent hold. And there's that silent guy wearing the white blouse, tight jeans, and scarves around his head, neck and waist, who hasn't done a thing for the last hour except stare at his groin and make funny chirping noises!

"Freakos! Weirdos! Dropped-out druggies and two crackpot bikers! We haven't got a chance! I'm a firm believer that the chances of a plane staying up depends a lot on the type of passengers it carries. That's why I always like to see a few nuns or a pregnant woman on the same flight with me. Their presence makes me feel more secure. God wouldn't let a plane go down that's full of good, wholesome folks. Nope. But He's not going to pay one iota of attention to this flight. There isn't a single semi-normal human being in this room. You and I are probably the straightest-looking souls of the bunch, and that means real trouble. We don't have a chance! The plane's going to crash! I know it! I know it! I just know it!"

"For Petessake Barb, *calm down!*" Larry pleaded. A voice boomed over the loudspeaker: "Biman Airlines flight 714 to Dacca with stopovers in Dubai and Bombay now boarding at gate five."

"Dubai?! Where's Dubai?" I shouted back at the loudspeaker.

"I don't know," answered Larry matter of factly.

"*Wonderful!* I, Barbara Savage, am about to board a plane that shall land in a place I have never heard of! I don't even know what *country* it's in! That cinches it! We're going to crash! We're—"

"Look, here comes our plane now," Larry interrupted. "The one taxiing around the side of the terminal. See, it's not a Cessna, it's a 707. Not too bad looking, either. New paint job. Looks fine."

"Twenty-five people are going to fill a 707?" I muttered as I made my way to the gate. "I don't like the looks of this *at all.*"

A young Bengali stewardess met us at the door of the plane. She had wrapped herself in a bright yellow and orange sari. Her skin was very dark, darker than the Egyptians'. Her long black hair was pulled back into a huge bun. I stepped past her and glanced nervously inside the cockpit. The two Bengali pilots looked healthy enough, and I was extremely relieved to see that they were both wearing pilot's suits and caps instead of turbans and *dhotis*.

I looked back into the plane. It was already almost full—European hippies, students, mountain climbers on their way to the Himalaya, and Bengalis, Indians, and Pakistanis who probably lived in Europe and were returning to their homeland to visit relatives. The stewardess informed us that the flight had originated in Amsterdam.

"Cheap seats to the East," I said aloud. Biman obviously catered to the weirdo squads.

It was an eight-hour flight to Bombay, including the refueling stopover in Dubai. Not knowing what to expect from Biman Airlines, Larry and I had packed some yogurt, fruit, and bread in case no meals were served during the flight. As it turned out, we were each given one tiny paper cup of orange juice after takeoff and nothing more for the next three hours. Just before we landed in Dubai, the flight crew served dinner: a few spoonfuls of especially hot curried chicken over rice, a roll, and nothing to wash it down with. The meal fueled Larry's fear that his stomach would be traveling on empty in India and Nepal. He was sorry he hadn't eaten more chicken the day before.

When the plane eased down into Dubai International Airport, I asked the French fellow sitting behind me what country Dubai was in. He said Saudi Arabia, and the men in the modern airport did indeed look like Saudis, in their long white robes. It wasn't until the next day when we talked with an English traveler at the campground in New Delhi that we found out we had in fact landed in the United Arab Emirates, and not Saudi Arabia.

When we landed in Bombay, Larry and I were given a thirty-day visitors visa and transferred onto an Indian Airlines flight to New Delhi. The instant I stepped out onto the runway in New Delhi, I felt immeasurably far from home. It was a gripping feeling. I felt as if I'd lost all my bearings.

LUG NUTS

CHAPTER FIFTEEN

The Indian baggage handlers paid special attention to our bikes, which were transported from the plane to the terminal in their own cart, separate from the luggage wagon. While we loaded on our gear under the watchful eyes of the friendly handlers, an American businessman approached us. His name was Barry Crocker, and he was from South Carolina. Mr. Crocker had come to New Delhi for an international textile fair and to visit a missionary friend in northeastern India. He asked us about our bikes and frowned when we explained our plans. I could tell that the idea of a young American woman bicycling through India troubled him. He reached into his carrying case, pulled out a pocket-sized New Testament, and tucked it carefully into my hands.

"Keep this with you always in India. You'll need it. This is a bizarre and dangerous country," he said softly in a tone that indicated great concern for my well-being.

I thanked him for the gift and he walked away, then returned suddenly and cast a worried look at Larry and me.

"Are you sure this is what you want to do? Bicycle in India?" he asked hesitantly. Then, as if to answer his own question, he said, "Good luck and may God be with you always." And again he walked away.

As I watched Mr. Crocker disappear through the throngs of dark faces, *saris*, *dhotis*, turbans, and tunics, a clump of nerve endings tingled in my stomach. I was afraid.

Standing in the airport with a Bible in my hand, petrified by Mr. Crocker's unsettling words, I had no idea that India was about to take Larry and me almost completely by surprise. I say almost because on one point, yet only one, India lived up to her reputation: she *was* crammed with people. But in her other aspects, she was not what we had expected, not at all. The first thing we noticed about her were the colors. After the browns and grays of Egypt, India shocked us with a kaleidoscope of brilliant hues. Women wore *saris* splashed with bright oranges, yellows, reds, blues, greens and turquoises, and sparkling gold and silver jewelry. Hindu temples were painted in pastels and were surrounded by deep green lawns and flowers of every color. Even the fruit and vegetable stands with tomatoes, zucchini, tangerines, cauliflower, apples, and bananas arranged in high, neat rows, added sprays of color to the cities and towns.

Pedaling the six hundred miles from New Delhi to the Nepali border, we encountered exactly two beggars out of the millions of people we passed. We saw no dead bodies, no dead animals. In fact, the people, though thin, appeared and acted both strong and healthy. Each day, skinny young men on their heavy, black, one-speed Hero bicycles rode along with us, keeping up with our fifteen-miles-per-hour pace for as long as an hour, oftentimes with the added weight of a buddy riding on the rear rack. And they smiled, laughed, and chattered the whole way. The Indians were strong, tough, and curious people. And too, we found no shortage of food in northern India, much to Larry's relief. Stands chock full of fruits and vegetables lined the streets of every town we pedaled through.

Before we left the airport, the man at the information desk handed us a free map of the capital and pointed out the city campground near Connaught Square, at the center of New Delhi. He also warned us to always be sure to boil the water in India.

From the terminal, remembering to keep to the left-hand side of the road, we rolled out onto a four-lane highway and into a realm of total chaos. It took us forty minutes to reach the campground from the airport, and in that short time, we made the disturbing yet unavoidable observation that our chances of reaching Nepal alive were extremely slim indeed. Mixed together on the highway and flowing in all possible directions were sacred cows, trucks, pedestrians, camels, buses, carts drawn by bullocks or water buffalo, bicycle-drawn rickshaws, motorscooters, a smattering of private cars, and a sea of bicycles and three-wheeled motorscooter taxis.

No person and no animal paid the slightest bit of attention to the movements of anyone or anything else until the split second before they were about to collide with one another, at which time one gave way to the other. Who or what retained the right-of-way depended on some vague Indian pecking order. Private cars, trucks, and buses reigned supreme and pulled onto the highway from side streets without so much as a glance at approaching traffic, causing mad scatters and more than a few fallen cyclists and bumped pedestrians. I rear-ended a cow and a kamikaze rickshaw driver slammed into us sideways. But Larry and I managed the miraculous feat of remaining upright the whole six miles to Connaught Square.

The campground, surrounded by a high brick wall, was a gathering of bungalows, tents, vans, and overland tour buses. We pedaled in expecting to find a crowded, filthy place but instead were greeted by spotless restrooms, perfectly manicured lawns, birds singing and flitting about the trees and lawns, and a restaurant that served tea with milk and sugar at the very door of one's tent.

New Delhi was an important watering hole for European, Australian, New Zealand, Canadian, and American travelers. It was the eastern destination of the overland buses from the west and a departure point for those returning to Europe. Every Tuesday a doctor came to the campground to rid newly arrived foreigners of whatever parasites or amoebas they had picked up in their journeys through Pakistan, India, Nepal, or Indonesia. A "medicine box" sat at the campground's exit, and departing foreigners dropped in it medicines they no longer needed. The contents of the box was then dispensed to the ailing who remained.

Hashish (*ganja*) and magic mushrooms were in great supply and demand in the campground. Both could be had for next to nothing, and many foreigners came to India for the express purpose of submerging in a cheap drug daze for a few months or years. The lawns in the campground were littered with mellow, strung out hash heads, who occasionally fell into loud, extended coughing fits or stirred long enough to summon the roving waiter-groundskeeper for more tea. When they ran short of funds, the druggies would pack up their belongings and wander off to their respective embassies to plea for mercy. Depending on the humor of the embassy officials, they were either turned away or given a ticket home, the price of which they were expected to repay at some future date, when they were settled and employed back home. Rumor had it that the French Embassy never took pity on its wayward citizens, and that because of this, there was a number of French panhandling through India with expired passports and no way home.

Rumors and assorted tales were told and spun at this crossroads campground. There was the story of the Dutch traveler who died after swallowing the dysentery medicine given him by the camp doctor, and talk of *dacoits*, Indian bandits who roamed the highways at dusk and robbed motorists. There were stories about overland bus drivers who smuggled arms and drugs on the side, and about Raj Neesh, the popular Indian guru in Poona, who preached mind control and promoted group sex encounters, and who, some feared, might be the next James Jones. Still other rumors claimed that Americans had been dragged from their hotels in Teheran by the militant Iranian students, and that an overland bus run by the Magic Bus Company of England had disappeared in Afghanistan.

It was late afternoon by the time Larry and I paid our fourteen-*rupee* camping fee (equivalent to a dollar seventy-five), pitched our tent on the grass amid the other tents and the groupings of drooling *ganja* freaks, and crawled inside to sleep off our jet lag. Periodically, someone's gasping cough awakened us, and we would listen for a while to travelers' hushed conversations before falling back to sleep.

In the evening, we ate dinner at the campground restaurant where everyone congregated at night to swap stories, news, and travel tips, and down hot curry dishes. The Indian waiters wore long white tunics over lengths of cotton fabric wrapped around themselves like a skirt; the front portion of the skirt they pulled between their legs and tucked under their waistband above their buttocks.

We sat down at one of the long wooden picnic tables beside Howard and Yan, an English couple in their mid twenties. Yan and Howard had been in India for nearly two months, most of it at a hill station in the mountains north of New Delhi. The British, while they ruled India, had built mountain retreats, which they called hill stations. They would escape to them when the heat, dust, snakes, and insects in the flatlands became intolerable, or when the monsoons failed bringing famines and epidemics.

"Some of the foreigners working in India nowadays still travel up to the hill stations. Everything's clean and fresh and beautiful and uncrowded up there, compared to the rest of India. And the Indians there cater to the foreigners. They sell pies and cakes and biscuits in the bakeries, and one Indian woman in the village we stayed in made peanut butter and sold it door-to-door," Yan explained. "And there are sure a lot of missionaries up at the stations. The churches own these big houses there, where the missionaries can go to get away from the poor and sick every once in a while. You wouldn't believe how modern those places are. Some of 'em have everything; washers and dryers, and you name it.

"We got dreadfully lazy, living in the tidy little house we took for next to nothing. The bread and vegetable vendors came to our door every day, so we rarely bothered to go out shopping. Spent most of our time resting and reading and taking a lot of short treks in the mountains. And I have to admit, we sorely needed that after our bus ride from England."

"You came overland?" I asked.

"Right-o," answered Howard. "Magic Bus from London."

"Magic Bus, huh? Say, there was this rumor going around Europe back about the time you would have been crossing the Mideast, back in September, that a Magic Bus went into Afghanistan and never came out. I even heard somebody today say that none of the overlands are going through Afghanistan anymore, because of the Magic Bus incident; that now the only way through to here from Turkey is by way of Iran and Pakistan. You don't know anything about that bus rumor do you?" I asked.

Howard glanced uneasily at Yan.

"Yes we do," he said with a strained calm in his voice. "Yan and I were on that bus."

He continued looking at Yan and the two of them were silent. From the look in their eyes, I could tell they were back on the bus, back in Afghanistan somewhere.

"You never think something like that's going to happen to you," Howard blurted suddenly. "But when it does, well, afterwards you leave off worrying about a good many things in life. You're just pleased to be alive."

Howard's eyes became clear and focused again, and he began his story.

"We got on the bus in London, and it took us through to Istanbul; no problems. A lot of the people put off in Istanbul, and we took on other travelers there—Europeans, Australians, and Canadians. And we changed onto a Turkish bus with two Turk drivers who'd subcontracted the Istanbul to New Delhi run. We were supposed to take the route through the desert in southern Iran, but when we got to Teheran, the drivers told us the bus couldn't make it through the desert. They said the bus's wheel base was too long and the tires were too narrow to make it over the desert roads. They told us we would keep north and cross Afghanistan.

"Well, no one fancied going through Afghanistan; so we all checked with our embassies in Teheran, and all of 'em told us not to go through there under any circumstances. The British Embassy told me and Yan that the place was a total madhouse; that the rebels were ambushing anything that moved.

"But the drivers insisted on going through Afghanistan, and they wouldn't refund any money to us folks who wanted out in Teheran. They kept telling us that everything would be all right; that Afghanistan really wasn't as awful as everyone was making it out to be; that we would shoot through, no problem. 'Why would the rebels ambush a tour bus? They're after the government forces, not tourists,' one of the drivers kept saying.

"Well, so anyway, most of us did want to get the hell out of Teheran. We never saw very many other foreigners there, and the Iranians were always coming up to us and asking us what we thought of Khomeini; so after a while we all decided to take the chance and stick with the bus. I think deep down inside none of us really believed that the Afghans would shoot tourists. We all adopted this ignorant it-couldn't-happen-to-me attitude.

"I should tell you now, before I go any further, that up until Teheran, Yan and I always sat in the front two seats behind the driver.

But when we set out from Teheran, a couple of chaps, a Canadian and a Swiss, who'd been sitting in the back of the bus the whole way from Europe, asked if they could switch with us for the rest of the trip. So you know, that sounded fair enough to Yan and me, and we said all right.

"When we got to the Afghan border, we sat there for three days waiting for permission to get in. In those three days, we were the only bus or automobile waiting there. And once we did get in, we only traveled in convoys, groups of buses and lorries and a few automobiles with military escorts. Well, that was fine until this one night when our drivers decided the convoy we were in was going too slow, and they talked some soldiers into riding on the bus with us, and we struck out alone.

"And you know, it wasn't more than an hour after we got rolling that we heard gunshots. The soldiers were riding in the front of the bus, and they returned the fire. They really did it up big too. Later that night I counted forty shells on the floor of the bus. Anyway, as soon as the soldiers started firing, the ambushers poured a flood of bullets through the bus. Most went into the front, up there where the soldiers were, and all us passengers got down on the floor and prayed. We were all bloody-well cursing ourselves for having a go at Afghanistan. I'll tell you, it was the most terrifying moment of my life. Lord, was I scared! The shooting prob-ably lasted only a minute, but it seemed like half the night.

"When the soldiers finally jumped out of the bus and chased after the rebels, the gunfire went away. But you know, none of us moved for a long time after the bullets stopped whizzing past our bodies.

"When it was all over, there were two dead bodies in the front of the bus. And you know who they were? The Canadian and the Swiss who traded seats with Yan and me in Teheran. I looked at their bloody bodies, and you know, I felt spared and I felt a terrible remorse both at the same time. Lord, it was awful, seeing 'em dead there where we'd always sat.

"Anyway, six of the passengers were wounded, and one of the Turks was shot in the leg—the other driver deserted us during the ambush. We needed to get to a hospital quick because this one Aussie was a bloody mess. Lucky for us, this Swede knew how to drive the bus, and he sped us back to the nearest city, which was thirty kilometers away. The place had a hospital, all right, and when we helped our wounded inside, there sat the other driver. You know, we took one look at him and we all wanted to kill that bloody bastard right then and there; kill him for what he'd gotten us into and to avenge the two dead chaps. But in the end we de-cided against it. It wouldn't have accomplished anything, we all reckoned.

"While we waited there in the city for a few days for the people who were hurt to heal enough so we could all charter a plane to Kabul, all us British on the bus tried to get a British reporter to come out from Kabul and write up a story on what had happened and publish it in England and Europe, so other people traveling overland would know to keep away from the Magic Bus lines. But the only reporter who came out was an American—from a Chicago paper, I think it was. He told us that the Afghan government kept a close watch on reporters and what they wrote. And he said if a reporter published something derogatory, that the government didn't want in print, the reporter'd be shot and the government would say the rebels did it.

"Well, we got a flight out to Kabul all right, and waited there for a week for a flight to India. The first thing we did when we got to Kabul was contact the Canadian and Swiss embassies so they could send word of the two blokes' deaths to their families.

"You know, every day, the whole time we were in Kabul, the rebels set off bombs all over the capital; but the people in Kabul had learned to ignore the explosions 'cause they'd become commonplace. I'll tell you, it felt grand indeed to get the hell out of Afghanistan! But you know, there were four people in our group who didn't have enough money to pay for the plane flight out. And you know, I'm always wondering what happened to 'em."

Howard stopped here as the vacant look crept back into his eyes.

"I wonder about those four too," added Yan. "And I wonder about the families of our two dead friends. And every day, there are moments when that same horror that gripped me when the bullets were ripping apart the bus, while I was lying there helpless on the floor, comes over me, and I have to take hold of something to steady myself."

In the morning of our second day in New Delhi, Larry and I walked the mile or so to Connaught Square to change money, apply for our visas to Nepal, pick up mail and a map of India, and have a look around the city. The moment we stepped out of the campground compound onto the narrow, dusty sidewalk and began our walk into town, we were struck by the dizzying sight of human bodies everywhere. A solid, flowing mass of humanity gushed its way along the sidewalks, across the parks and through the streets. Vacant lots were packed with families, which had set up housekeeping in them. They slept in the open or beneath suspended tarps and cooked over tiny kerosene stoves.

The sweepers and dryers of New Delhi wove their way through this clog of people. Women street sweepers cleared the city's grass, pavement, and dirt of litter and manure. Their constant sweeping filled the air with a fine dust, and when an occasional sprinkle fell, the dust clung to everyone's clothing. Men and women dryers tended laundry scattered across any unoccupied surface they could find. White tunics, loose pants, and yards of cotton fabric, which the *Sikhs* wrapped into turbans, hung from bushes and fences and covered sections of playing fields, lawns, and yards. The piercing Indian sun soon baked the dampness from the clothes, and the driers gathered and folded them with lightning speed to make room for the next batch.

People hurried along quickly in New Delhi, and no one, not even those who lived or sat in the parks, seemed to notice the two fair-skinned foreigners passing by. Only one woman took any notice of us. She ran up to Larry and thrust out a hand for money. When Larry shook his head, she shrugged and walked away.

Connaught Square, with its rows of one- and two-story storefront buildings, resembled the downtown of many American midwestern towns. Even though its sidewalks were crawling with people, downtown New Delhi was clean and quiet compared to Cairo. And we were relieved to find that no mobs of beggars materialized to harass us. In fact, we didn't see any beggars at all that day in or around Connaught Square.

We spent most of the day lost amid the shops and stands selling exotic batiks, silver and gold jewelry, brass, ivory, flower garlands, and all type of foods, meals, and spices. Larry's favorite food, bananas, sold for twenty-four cents a dozen. The only Indians who approached us were the slick-looking *Sikhs* selling cheap airplane tickets and International Student ID cards made to order, just as the agent in Athens had said they would. The *Sikhs* also offered to change our money and pay us U.S. dollars for our camera, books, and clothing. One man, when he found out we were cycling through India, offered to buy both our bikes for two thousand dollars. "I know rich man who pay me much money for fifteen-speeds. He no can find in India," he explained.

The *Sikhs* and most of the educated Indians in New Delhi spoke some English. And since there were so many Indian dialects, we relied entirely on English. In the small towns and villages in the countryside where no one spoke English, we used hand motions.

By late evening, Larry and I had finished our errands. The next day we would try being genuine tourists. The tourist office in New Delhi offered a bus tour of the city, with an English-speaking guide, for only six *rupees*. And now that we'd discovered that the city was not the bastion of beggars and diseased and starving masses most American tourists told us it would be, we were anxious to explore the capital. As it turned out, taking the city tour was important because it supplied us with the simple answer to why tourists who travel through India in group tours and stay in nice tourist hotels return home with a completely different opinion of India than Larry's and mine. Had we skipped the tour, we would never have known what sights greet foreign tourists in India each time their bus pulls up to a hotel or into a tour bus parking lot.

Our city tour began in the early afternoon and lasted three hours. It took us to the mosque in Old Delhi, the Red Fort, and the Mahatma Gandhi Memorial. At each stop, the beggars and lepers of New Delhi congregated in the parking lots, waiting for the tour buses to arrive. They were wretched looking souls. The beggars were emaciated and dressed in rags. Some were missing a limb or two.

As soon as our bus unloaded, each beggar chose a foreigner to cling to and follow. Their pleading eyes, their deformities, and their upturned hands, bony and grasping, penetrated the soul of every middle-class American tourist in our group and pierced that pocket of guilt in all of us, which becomes so vulnerable in the face of such overwhelming poverty and disfigurement.

The little children made the best beggars. The beggar girls, their hair and ragged clothes gray tangles of dust and dirt, each carried a starving infant brother or sister in their arms. They thrust the tiny, pitiful bodies into our faces and pleaded hysterically for money to buy food for their dying siblings. The infants' bloated stomachs, bulging eyes, cavernous faces, and limbs that were nothing more than bones sheathed by a thin layer of skin, made guilt-wrenching sights. The professional beggars, our tour guide told us, maimed or starved themselves and their children on purpose in order to look as pitiful as possible.

It was in the parking lot of the Red Fort that I came face to face with the only leper I would encounter in India. The sight of him was horrifying. His fingers were gone, and his nose and lips had been eaten away. He moved what was left of his face up against the window next to my seat on the bus and banged with his palms against the glass. I looked away trying hard not to cry, and when I stepped off the bus in Connaught Square at the end of our tour, I promised myself that I would never again set foot on another tour bus in India.

The next day, Larry and I returned by ourselves to Old Delhi, one of the most densely populated areas in all of India. Its narrow, dark, and dusty streets were so jammed with people that no motor vehicles attempted to enter them. We pressed our way through the solid gush of human bodies, and although our light hair and complexions and my T-shirt and knee-length skirt made us stand out sharply, neither beggars nor lepers came to prey upon us. They were all waiting at the mosque and the Red Fort for the tour buses to arrive.

On November 14, two nights before we started out across northern India, Geoff Thorpe, who had arrived in the capital two weeks earlier aboard an overland bus from Istanbul, spotted our bikes locked behind our tent. Geoff had taken a year off from college in New Zealand, flown into London six months ago, and bicycled to Turkey. He originally had planned on pedaling from New Delhi to Nepal, but now he'd all but abandoned that idea.

We were sound asleep when he began shaking the tent poles, too excited to wait until morning to meet the fellow bicyclers inside. Geoff's enthusiasm and kind, gentle nature won us over instantly, and the three of us stayed up most of the night, talking.

"I've been in New Delhi for two weeks now, tryin' to get me strength back up," began Geoff. "That bus ride from Istanbul 'bout did me in. When I first got 'ere I was too bloody weak to bicycle. Lost two stones since Istanbul. There wasn't much to eat in the villages in Iran. Rice and a pinch o' mutton, that's it. Then I picked up dysentery in Pakistan, and I've still got it, I have. Brushed me teeth with the water in this town near Lahore. Well, some of the chaps on our bus boiled it for drinking, and afterwards they noticed a bunch o' tiny worms floating on the top, so I reckon scrubbing me teeth in that water's what gave me the trots.

"For the last two weeks now I've been eatin' well and gettin' lots o' rest. Reckon I feel strong enough to give bicyclin' a go, but I'm not too keen on gettin' out on an Indian road with me bike. Can't believe the way people drive in this country. You couldn't imagine the accidents I saw on the bus ride between Lahore and 'ere! Watched this one Indian bus rear-end a cart bein' pulled by two water buffalo. Everything—the cart, the driver, the water buffalo—flew into the air on impact, and the bus just kept right on goin'. I saw buses and lorries and cars and motorcycles run into each other and into cars and rickshaws and bicycles. And you know what else? 'Alf the lorries on the road at night don't 'ave any lights. Our driver couldn't see 'em 'til he'd almost smacked into 'em. Can you believe that?

"Anyway, by the time our bus arrived in New Delhi, I'd decided it was too dangerous to bicycle in India. At least I'd reckoned I'd never go it alone. But now that I've come upon you two, think I'd like to give it a go. I reckon I've got a better chance o' survivin' cyclin' with two other people than if I pedaled by meself; bein' as 'ow that way there'd be three of us watchin' out for the traffic rather than only one. And besides, I git real lonely pedalin' by meself. I'd sure appreciate the company if you wouldn't mind me taggin' 'long. And if you decide you can't stand me, well then you tell me to git lost and I will, no problem there."

Both of us were happy to have Geoff's company. We had no idea how the Indians in the mud-hut villages along the back roads of northern India might react to foreigners, and Mr. Crocker's words of warning still burned in our minds. And too, after our experiences in Egypt, the prospect of adding another male to our ranks made me feel more comfortable. Possibly I wouldn't be hassled as much if I was accompanied by two men instead of one. If dangers were awaiting us in India, better face them with as many able bodies as possible, I figured.

I was too nervous to sleep our last night at the campground; I kept thinking about Geoff's stories of the reckless Indian drivers. It was almost morning before I finally dozed off, and I dreamt that a truck ran over Larry and me, and the driver left our broken lifeless bodies lying in the dirt at the side of the road. The Indians from the nearby fields gathered to stare at our corpses; eventually they cremated us, but no one bothered to report our deaths to the authorities.

Probably I had never really expected to reach India, and as the three of us pedaled out of the campground with most of the foreign campers lined at the exit waiting to watch us be swallowed by the waves of bicycles, a rush of anticipation came over me and buried my apprehension. The Taj Mahal and Mount Everest felt very close. We're on our way, and we're gonna make it after all! I shouted to myself. But my excitement was short-lived.

It took us only two minutes to reach the main highway south to Agra, and there at the intersection we were met by a tangled mass of sheet metal. Two commercial trucks had just plowed into each other, spraying the asphalt with shattered glass and truck parts.

"What'd I tell you folks," yelled Geoff. "Let's keep alert!"

In the next ten miles, we watched a bus, unevenly crammed full of people, topple over on its side, two motorscooters collide head on, and a dozen bicycle accidents in which the riders either crashed into other cyclers or fell over trying to avoid a reckless truck driver. One cycler plunged headlong onto the paved highway when his bike hit a giant tortoise lying in the road.

We pedaled full speed through wide packs of bicycles, keeping our eyes out for manure piles, ambling wooden carts, stray cows, and the rickshaws and motor vehicles that periodically swerved into the bulging flow of bicycles at the edge of the highway. I was glad I still had Mr. Crocker's Bible stashed in my handlebar pack.

Twenty miles south of New Delhi, we escaped the busy commercial area that encircled the capital, and the traffic dropped to a trickle. There were very few private cars on the road. In a country where a schoolteacher makes twenty-five dollars a month, not many people could afford the price of a car or, at two and a half dollars a gallon, the cost of gasoline.

For the rest of the day, we had a relatively quiet and peaceful ride over a smooth asphalt surface. Periodically, a *Sikh* riding a motorscooter pulled up alongside us and greeted us in English. And sometimes we rode with farmers on bicycles and men riding camels or elephants. The dirt shoulder was traveled by people on foot; local farmers, groups of wandering nomads, and skinny, barefoot, bearded and long-haired holy men, who wore nothing but their white *dhotis*. One young boy walking south was accompanied by a full-grown sloth bear on the end of a long chain. Footsteps and hoofs stirred the dirt at the edge of the road and caused a brown haze to rise over the highway.

None of us said much to one another; we were busy assimilating all that confronted us. We studied the houses in the tiny villages—clay structures with clean-swept earthen floors. Compared to those in Egypt, the homes and paths in these villages were neat and well kept. Women cleared the highway, fields, and villages of the perennial manure piles, which, after baking in the sun, were burned as fuel. Even in the poorest villages, women and girls wore bright *saris* and gold and silver jewelry. And they hurried through the dirt streets with their shiny brass water jugs balanced on their covered heads. Men and boys dressed in loose cotton trousers and tunics, or in western-style shirts and pants. I was surprised to see that often the men did the family's laundry.

The times we stopped to rest, repair a flat, relieve ourselves, or snack on bananas and tangerines, the people alongside the road and in the villages and fields always stopped to stare. As we would learn in the days ahead, being stared at is what bicycling in India is all about. We would know no privacy in India. There would never be a time when we could look down the road or across a field and not see human forms.

Every day, everywhere we looked, there were people watching us, surveying our each and every move. In Egypt, between the villages, there had been some deserted areas, where we could pull off the road and not be seen or where we could look down the road and not see anyone coming. Such was never the case in India.

When we stopped on the open road, anywhere from two to ten people would group around us. Whether they were in the fields, or walking along the shoulder, or bicycling by, when they spotted us they would drop what they were doing and rush toward us. Then they would stand close, staring curiously, often in disbelief, at our bikes and gear. When we stopped in towns to buy food, word of our arrival spread instantly, and within seconds we were surrounded by hundreds of dark, anxious, staring faces. The faces belonged to men, girls, and boys; in the towns, women never joined the crowds.

The constant presence of people in India made it nearly impossible for me to relieve myself during the day without being seen. Larry and Geoff had no problem; it was common practice for men to urinate and defecate by the side of the road in full view of passersby—but not for women. Unfortunately, the terrain between New Delhi and the Nepali border was generally flat, cultivated farmland, with only a few trees or shrubs to hide behind—and those shrubs inevitably had an Indian or two standing nearby. I took to walking to a spot as far away from the road and people as possible; then I'd wrap a towel around my waist and squat. Sometimes the people still watched, but I learned to ignore them.

The Indians proved to be quite different from the people of Upper Egypt, which was a genuine relief considering their numbers. Cycling through a country crammed with humanity is draining in itself, but had the thousands of Indians we encountered been hostile, we'd have met our match. On the whole, they were kind, polite people. With one exception, no one ever yelled, shoved, screamed for *baksheesh*, propositioned me, or threw rocks or sticks at us. When we stopped to eat lunch in their fields, the farmers sat with us and smiled and offered their drinking water. In the towns, in most cases, people were careful not to jostle us as they pushed each other aside in their struggle to get as close to us as possible.

At Mathura, the birthplace of Lord Krishna, some eighty miles south of New Delhi, we turned off the main highway and took a back road to the bird sanctuary at Bharatpur, near Agra. Geoff did not have a tent, so we spent our first night on the road in Bharatpur at the government tourist camp—a spartan hotel that catered to the foreigners and Indians who came to visit the sanctuary. For ten *rupees*, Geoff was given a bed in the dormitory, while Larry and I paid five *rupees* to pitch our tent on the lawn.

The young manager of the camp, Rakesh, made sure that the three of us were well cared for. When we pedaled up the road a mile in the dark to shop at the fruit stands, Rakesh sent his assistant to accompany us on his bicycle and to carry a lantern to light the way. The assistant sang for us while he pedaled, and he helped us bargain the price of the fruits. And in the morning, before we set out for Agra, the city of the Taj Mahal, he prepared a breakfast of omelettes, *chapatis*, and hot tea.

We arrived in Agra in the early afternoon. The city's narrow streets were so clogged with pedestrians, bicycles, rickshaws, cows, bullock carts, fruit, vegetable, incense and spice shops, grimy hot-meal stalls, bicycle-repair areas, and men and boys urinating or moving their bowels in the gutters, that we could barely keep track of one another. The scents of flowers, excrement, incense, curry, and animal and human sweat mingled in the hot dusty air and burned in our nostrils. And over the clang of bicycle bells, the roar of human voices and the screech of unoiled rickshaw wheels floated the melody of *sitars* and flutes.

I spied a camping sign printed across a high brick wall. We followed the wall around to an entrance and looked inside at a plush hotel, with a fancy, uniformed doorman standing at the entrance. Manicured lawns and flower gardens surrounded the hotel, its swimming pool, and bathhouse.

"Can't be any camping here," I commented. "It's too classy a place."

"Augh, what the 'ell. Let's give it a go," grunted Geoff.

Geoff pushed his bike toward the lobby, but Larry and I hesitated. Geoff was a mess, and he stunk; and we knew we were no better off. It had sprinkled in the morning, and Geoff's dusty body was spotted with droplets of mud. His bare legs and arms were smeared with chain grease, and his hair was matted in sweat and dirt. His bike and panniers were filthy, and the wheels reeked from rolling through manure. Today, as every day, Geoff was wearing his shiny-blue running shorts and his tan tennis shoes—they were probably white underneath the layers of grease and dirt—and nothing else. Larry had on his khaki shorts, and I had donned a sleeveless T-shirt riddled with holes and my Egyptian pedal pushers. To the average westerner, we were a disgusting looking threesome.

First Geoff, then Larry, then I sheepishly stepped inside the Hotel Laurie and peered self-consciously around the lobby decorated with antiques and Persian rugs. On one wall hung the framed photographs of Queen Elizabeth and President Eisenhower, both of whom had stayed at the hotel.

All conversation stopped when we entered the room. The middle-aged and well-dressed American and European tourists who filled the lobby glared at us disapprovingly. I held my breath and waited to be thrown out; the doorman had already gone to summon someone. After several long, agonizing moments of cold silence, the manager burst into the lobby.

"Welcome, welcome, welcome my friends. You wish to camp?" boomed the man's voice. He grabbed our hands and shook them.

"Yessir, we do," answered Larry.

"Fine. Pitch your tents anywhere you please. Better to stay on the grass that is freshly cut. There are snakes—cobras—in the higher grass at the far end of the lawns. There are toilets and showers in the bathhouse for you to use, and help yourselves to the swimming pool. We are very pleased to have you. You are bicycling through our country?"

"Yes, from New Delhi to Nepal."

"Wonderful. And where are you from?"

"We're Americans and Geoff here's from New Zealand."

"Ah, Americans." The tone of the manager's voice went flat. The Indians were not pleased with America's friendliness toward Pakistan, their archenemy.

"'Ow much for a room 'ere?" asked Geoff.

"Usually they are eighty *rupees*, but I could give you one for sixty-five *rupees* for all three of you. That is a very good price. In American currency, that is eight dollars."

"And how much to camp?" asked Larry.

"Five *rupees* each person."

"We'll camp," said Geoff. And to us he whispered, "I'll sleep in the bathhouse. They'll never know."

We chose a flat, grassy area next to the pool, and the doorman set up a table, three chairs, and three chaise longues. Next, we pulled out our stoves and prepared a feast of vegetable stew. Geoff ran up the street to a meal stall and returned with a dozen hot *chapatis*, and the waiter from the hotel's restaurant brought out a huge bottle of beer. While we ate, a man came in from the street and offered to wash our clothes for next to nothing; so Geoff bundled up his dusty threads and sent them off. Then came the hotel's hairdresser, a thin man with greasy hair, carrying an old briefcase filled with shampoos and hair oils.

"I wash hair good," he explained to me.

"Oh, no thank you. I wash my own hair," I smiled.

"'Nah-shun-al-la-tee?" he asked, carefully enunciating the difficult word.

"I'm an American."

"Humm, A-may-ri-cun. Yes, A-may-ri-cun I have. I have!" he exclaimed as he fumbled through the pouch of ancient yellowed papers in his briefcase. He pulled out a letter addressed to him, dated 1968, and handed it to me. It was from a woman in Omaha. She'd written to compliment the man on what a great job he had done washing her hair while she stayed at the Hotel Laurie during her visit to the Taj Mahal. I skimmed the letter, then looked up at the man. He was beaming with an air of self-importance, and he tapped the letter with his long, dark index finger.

"O-ma-ah, A-may-ri-ca. Beeg impotant seetee. Laydee say so. She like varee much my work. Now I wash you hair. You like varee much."

"Thank you, but my hair is clean now. I just washed it."

"Maybee tomarow I come wash hair." He bowed and moved quickly away.

At six the next morning, the three of us rode to the other side of Agra to watch the sunrise over the Taj Mahal. Geoff was groggy from too little sleep.

"Bloody full o' mosquitoes and rats, that bath'ouse is," he grumbled. "Barely slept a wink."

The city was just waking. There was no traffic, and the shops were all closed. Men sang as they crawled out of their beds inside the shops and along the sidewalks, and the aroma of hot tea and *chapatis* penetrated everywhere. The few people who had risen early waved and smiled to us. And even though the streets were splattered with dirt, trash, and manure, and the people were poor, I felt good about Agra and India and its people that morning. As I watched the sun's rays strike the Taj Mahal and turn its massive ivory marble a gentle pink, I was glad I'd come to India.

The following day Geoff was sick.

"Can't stop crappin', and I've got dreadful stomach cramps, but I'm ridin' today anyway. Won't spend all me time in India settin' around bein' sick," he announced in the morning. The hotel manager prescribed yogurt and a massage; so Geoff downed a bowl of hot curd from the stand across the street while the doorman called a masseur. After the massage, Geoff packed up his gear, and we said good-bye to the staff at the hotel and thanked everyone for their hospitality.

The fifty-mile ride from Agra to Mainpuri was a rough one for Geoff. He stopped several times and sat beside the road holding his stomach and grimacing in pain. Each time he stopped, the Indian farmers came running off their fields to have a look at us. People don't like to be stared at when they're sick, and Geoff was no exception. By the late afternoon, he'd had his fill of being watched.

"Can't do anything in this bloody country without bein' stared at!" he shouted at the curious faces. "Can't even be sick in private. You chaps are goin' to stand right there and watch me die aren't you? Probably don't even care if I do die, as long as you can watch!"

That night in Mainpuri, after my encounter with the ape on the rooftop of the boardinghouse, Geoff collapsed onto his cot and fell asleep moaning in pain. By morning his cramps had stopped but not the diarrhea; and unfortunately, all three of us now had the runs.

Larry was the first to bolt out the door and run for the bucket upstairs. Geoff woke up, yelled, "Oh my God, hold on a minute *please!*" to his bellowing bowels, and dashed out just behind Larry. By now I, too, was wide awake, and I had to go worse than bad. No way was I waiting for Geoff and Larry to finish up on the roof.

I jumped out of the room and made for the shower stall down the hall. There wasn't really a shower in the tiny room, just a three-foot-high metal barrel filled with water. Floating in the barrel was a bowl to scoop out the water and pour it over oneself. There was a small hole at floor level in one wall of the stall, out of which the water was supposed to drain. Because of the layer of scum and dead bugs that spread across the top of the brown water in the barrel, none of us had bothered to shower the previous night.

I plowed into the shower room, slammed and locked the door behind me, and squatted down near the drain hole just as my lower tract exploded. After I finished, I lowered the bowl into the barrel until it filled with water, then tossed the liquid onto the floor to wash what I'd done out the drain hole. But instead of splashing toward the drain, the water flowed away from my pile and out the bottom of the door at the other side of the stall. I looked closely at the floor: it was slanted in the opposite direction of the drain. Oh now you've *really* gone and done it this time Barb, I scolded myself. I glared in disgust at the floor and at what I'd deposited there, which was going nowhere. Cover it up, I thought. Cover it up, and we'll be out of the boardinghouse before anyone discovers what you've done. I grabbed a handful of rags from the chair next to the barrel and laid them over the evidence; then I hurried back to our room and began to pack as rapidly as possible.

We were only five minutes short of being ready to go when someone pounded on our door. Larry threw open the door, but I kept my back to the Indian standing in the hallway. I couldn't bear to see the expression on his face.

"Hello," Larry said. "Is there a problem?"

"You come," the man demanded.

The boardinghouse owner led Larry to the end of the hall, and Geoff and I listened to the man's words echo back down the bare corridor.

"Shawar. No toilet. I tell you yessirday. Toilet, roof. Why do this?"

"Now what the heck's that all about?" wondered Geoff out loud.

I shrugged a "who knows" and kept my back to the door. Two minutes later, Larry and the Indian came back to our room.

"OK," said Larry. "Who shit in the shower?"

"Yes, who shit shawar?" the owner repeated Larry's question.

"Shit in the shower? What in 'ell you on about, mate? Why would— Oh." Geoff turned slowly and looked over at me. "So that's why you didn't 'ave to go up on the roof this morning. I couldn't figure that out; why you were the only one that didn't 'ave to go this morning. But you did! But why the shower of all places?"

"I couldn't wait. You two were already upstairs, and I couldn't wait," I whispered in a tone that pleaded for understanding. "Now quit laughing. It's not funny. I'm really embarrassed about it. I tried to wash it out the drain but the floor's slanted all wrong."

"You shat in the shower?" Geoff was howling. "Man, I can't believe it. Little Barb took a dump in the shower! Ten minutes and this'll be all over town. Mainpuri's special news release of the day: AMERICAN WOMEN SHIT IN SHOWERS. I love it."

Geoff threw open the shutters and hung his head out the window.

"Now let's get this clear," he yelled to the masses below, none of whom could understand a word of English. "Kiwis no shit showers. Yanks, yes. Kiwis, no. I'm a Kiwi, so I didn't do it. Me, no. Them—" he pointed back into the room, "yes. You got that everybody? Watch out for the Yanks. Yankees no go home—Yankees shit showers!"

The people in the streets were looking up at Geoff as if he were some sort of alien raging idot, and by now the owner had figured out which of us was the guilty party, and he stared at me with a look of horrified incredulity. To him the deed itself was repulsive enough, but the fact that it had been performed by a woman made it especially bizarre.

"Why laydee shit shawar?" he asked.

I couldn't force myself to face the man; Geoff continued to roar, and Larry sat shaking his head. When the owner realized that no one was going to answer him, he left the room and hurried out into the streets to hire an untouchable to clean the shower stall.

"It's a good thing you couldn't wash it out that drain," chuckled Larry. "It opens out onto the front steps of the boardinghouse!"

From Mainpuri, it was one hundred twenty miles over a narrow back road to the next city with lodging, Kanpur. Although the terrain was flat the whole way, it was slow cycling because of potholes and bumps in the road. And when the road went through towns, it was blocked by human bodies. Whereas the crowds moved aside to let the trucks and buses and Indian bicyclers pass through, when they spotted us approaching, they froze in place. Most of the people in these towns had never before seen a light-skinned person, and the sight of us riding our strange-looking bicycles stunned them. They stared long and hard at Geoff's nearly white hair. No one moved. They couldn't; they were transfixed in a state of shock. To make our way down the road, we were forced to physically push people aside.

Geoff had two flat tires from faulty inner tubes. And in one village a pothole swallowed my front wheel and hurled me off my bike. The fall scraped up my hands and legs, and the bleeding gashes immediately collected castles of dirt and biting flies. I had heard rumors about how in India cuts always become infected and never heal; so with a hundred or so curious eyes looking on, I washed my wounds with our boiled drinking water, then smeared them with an antibacterial ointment to prevent infection. Dad had given me the tube when he and Mom met us in Spain. The flies stuck to the gooey ointment, but they couldn't bite through it.

Geoff felt much better that day, and he kept us entertained telling stories about his bike ride from England to Turkey and the overland bus ride from Istanbul to New Delhi. Geoff was glad to have someone besides himself to talk to, and Larry and I enjoyed his company. Listening to Geoff helped make the day's long mileage less tedious.

"There were two Americans on our overland bus; two women in their mid-twenties," Geoff explained. "The rest o' the passengers were mostly British or French. We went through Iran just before the American Embassy was taken over, and the anti-American sentiment was sky 'igh. And all of us were bloody nervous 'bout 'avin' a couple Yanks on the bus with us.

"Anyway, when we got down into the desert in southern Iran, we got stopped by a roadblock one night, and these two soldiers came on board and started checkin' over all our passports. Well, everybody gits all quiet as the chaps git closer and closer to the Americans, and you could 'ave 'eard a pin drop when the two women 'anded over their passports. We're all lookin' at the soldiers' faces waitin' to see what's goin' to happen next.

"So anyway, the two blokes open the passports, and one of 'em says, 'Ah, Americans,' and the women nod, and I'm scared to death and so is everybody else. The soldiers don't say anything straight away. They go on lookin' at the women's passports, and I'm feelin' really sick now, and then all of a sudden the two snap to attention and they salute the Americans. The chaps 'ave got these big smiles on their faces, and they 'and back the passports and git off the bus and away we go!

"I liked the American women all right, but were they gullible! You think I'm gullible, you should 'ave seen these two. You wouldn't believe the way they got taken by this man in Quetta our second day in Pakistan.

"We come rolling into Quetta in the late afternoon, and we're all pretty zonked from all that desert in eastern Iran and western Pakistan. So when this Pakistani runs up to us and offers to clean our ears, everyone ignores 'im—everybody that is except for the two Yanks. Those two think it's a good idea, and the Pakistani says 'e'll clean their ears for fifty cents; but if 'e finds any stones, it's a dollar a stone. Well who's ever 'eard of 'aving stones in your ears, right? So the women decide it's a good deal for fifty cents and say OK.

"So this bloke starts to work cleanin' the wax out o' one o' the women's ears with this funny little spoon. And 'e just gits started and out drops a tiny piece of gravel, and 'e shakes 'is 'ead like that's really bad. Now the woman takes a look at the stone and gits all nervous and wants to know 'ow the 'ell the gravel got in 'er ears; so the Pakistani tells 'er she picked it up in the desert. 'In desert all peoples get stones in ears. Stones varee bad,' he says, and then he proceeds to dig out one piece of gravel after another.

"About now some of the Pakastanis standing around the sidewalks come over and take a look at the gravel and smile. I mean, they know this chap's takin' the foreigners for a ride. And the bloke pops out some eight or nine pieces o' gravel out o' *each ear* before 'e's finished with 'er.

"Now you tell me, can you imagine anyone believin' that they're runnin' around with all that gravel in their ears and it doesn't bother 'em?

Well this lady did. She believed it, and she 'anded over almost twenty dollars. Twenty dollars! That's more than most Pakistanis see in a month if they've got a good-paying job! Now you know the man 'ad a stash o' gravel 'idden somewhere on 'imself, and 'e made it look like 'e was pulling the pieces out o' the woman's ears. Anybody could 'ave figured that out. But not these two. I couldn't believe it when the other one wanted to 'ave 'er ears cleaned out too! And you guessed it—'e scooped a mound of gravel out of 'ers just like the first one. And I thought us folks from Down Under were supposed to be gullible!"

Geoff's stories filled up most of the day as we bumped our way through the heat and dust, dodging people, bicycles, trucks, water buffalo, cows, camels, and elephants. By sunset we had six miles left to bicycle, and we pounded our pedals as fast as we could to beat the darkness. The road was crammed with bicyclers who worked in the outlying factories and were cycling home to Kanpur, but they made room for us to pass.

Just when it looked like we might reach Kanpur before dark, one of the bicycles rammed Larry from the side. Since no Indian had ever shown any aggression toward us before, the action took him completely by surprise. The man seemed to have materialized out of nowhere. He pulled up alongside Larry, turned his bike into Larry's rear panniers, and pushed him over. When Larry threw out his arm to catch himself, the impact of the fall broke his wrist. Then his bike crashed down on top of his chest and cracked a few ribs.

Before the dirt had time to settle, Larry's temper was out of control, and he was on his feet chasing down the assailant. He grabbed the man, who was feverishly trying to escape, by the neck of his white cotton tunic and yanked him off his bike. The man fell onto the pavement and rolled to the edge of the road. Larry then picked up the fellow's gigantic one-speed and heaved it into a ditch. While Larry was tossing the bike, the man quickly grabbed a brick lying nearby and moved in to clobber the back of Larry's head. But before he got his chance, Geoff started after him. The short, thin Indian took one look at Geoff's six-foot-two-inch frame and dropped the brick.

By now a crowd of some fifty men from a nearby factory was zeroing in on us. I yelled to Larry and Geoff, and they raced to their bikes. We had no idea who the mob would side with; so we sped off before it reached us, and roared on toward Kanpur.

A half mile down the road, after his anger had subsided, Larry noticed the pain in his wrist and ribs for the first time. His right brake lever had snapped during the fall and was dangling from the handlebars. Fortunately it was his right wrist that had broken and not his left, which he now needed full use of to work his one and only brake.

"It hurts to steer and shift with my right hand, but I'll manage," he commented as we pumped out the last two miles into Kanpur. "I'll have to do something about this broken brake lever, though, before we reach Nepal. I'm not going through the Himalayas with only one functioning brake, that's for sure."

"What about your ribs?" asked Geoff.

"Guess they'll hurt for a few weeks or a month. There's nothing you can do about broken ribs. Let 'em hurt, and grin and bear it. Yessir folks, I'm gonna be in great shape for those mountains up ahead!"

Kanpur was a big city, and the endless city streets crammed with bodies, vehicles, and animals only fueled our exhaustion. After bouncing over one hundred twenty miles of rugged roads, we wanted to collapse in to some sanctuary of peace and quiet, but we still had hours of work ahead of us. We needed to find a hotel or boardinghouse; shop for food and cook our meal, and spend our final waking hour boiling water. Each night in India we prepared the next day's supply of drinking water. The Indians could never figure out why we spent so much time boiling water that we never made tea with. They'd watch us in total amazement as we boiled pot after pot of tap water, only to pour it all into a plastic water bottle and leave it to get cold again.

While we stood at the edge of Kanpur resting and summoning the last bit of energy to see us through the evening, a college student on a motorscooter stopped and offered to help us.

"My name is Pradeep," he smiled. "I will lead you to boardinghouse. We must go only a kilometer from here."

The boardinghouse was a square, three-story building with a cement courtyard in the center into which all the rooms opened. It looked like a prison—dark and filthy, with rats scurrying across the floors. There was no electricity. Everyone had their doors open because the heat was stifling. When we entered, the people in the upper stories hung over the railings to stare at us. Those on the ground floors stood in front of their doorways. They were ragged and dusty, and no one smiled. The owner of the boardinghouse told Pradeep that all his rooms were full and that we should try the hotel on the other side of the city.

"How far away is that?" Larry asked.

"Eight kilometers," Pradeep answered.

Five miles. The three of us cringed. That sounded impossible right now. We were too beat to put in another five miles, especially through city streets.

"Isn't there anything closer? We're pretty tired," groaned Geoff.

"No. Nothing closer that is cheap. You rest here a little, then we go on."

Pradeep spoke to the owner, who called to a young boy standing nearby. The boy ran over to a bucket and brought it back to us. It had a scoop floating in it, and he motioned for us to rinse off our hands and faces. After pedaling for two days without washing, our skin was caked black. While we cleaned up, the owner brought out three wooden beds with rope bottoms for us to rest on. He placed them in the center of the courtyard.

Pradeep stood guard over our bikes and talked with the owner while we rested. The boardinghouse was noisy with the sounds of small children playing in the courtyard. There was a faint scent of sandalwood incense in the air. We rested for a half hour, then Pradeep called us to follow him to the hotel. My muscles tightened up while I was resting, and they protested painfully when I climbed back on my bike. Larry must have been in agony, but he never said anything, and neither did Geoff, who was holding his stomach.

The three of us managed to keep Pradeep and each other in sight for the entire five miles, which was a real feat considering how crowded the smoky, dimly lit streets were. The hotel Pradeep took us to had big clean rooms with ceiling fans, and after we rolled our bikes inside our room, Pradeep took Geoff and Larry to the market area near the hotel so they could buy food for dinner and supplies for tomorrow.

"You stay here," Pradeep said to me. "It is not good that a woman go out at night in this part of the city. You stay here and always lock the doors."

After they left, I scrubbed my body under the faucet in the restroom and washed out my bloomers and T-shirt. The men who ran the hotel knocked on the restroom door while I was washing and tried to jar it open; I was glad Pradeep had warned me to keep the doors locked. I yelled at the men to go away, and eventually they did. When Larry and Geoff returned an hour later with the food, Pradeep was no longer with them.

"He went home from the market. We thanked him for all his help, and he said he'd come back here tomorrow before we left. We're sure lucky he stopped to help us," said Larry.

Geoff nodded and stretched out on his bed.

"Man, it sure is nice to git away from the crowds," he sighed. "People, people, people. That's all you see out there. By the end o' the day in this country, I'm real tired of people, and I'm keen to git away from all those faces and eyes and git meself some quiet and privacy. Git somewhere where people aren't starin' at me all the time, and where they're not ringin' their bicycle bells at me. Lord, I git so sick o' 'earin' those bells ringin' at us all day long. I know people are ringin' to say 'allo, but do they 'ave to keep it up for the whole time they ride with us? In the mornings, I'm in good spirits 'cause I'm rested and I've just eaten a nice breakfast; so I can 'andle everybody crowdin' me and starin' at me and ringin' their bells at me. But by nighttime I'm tired and 'ungry and irritable, and I'm in real need o' some privacy.

"Look at that," Geoff pointed around the room. "That's what I need. Nothing but four blank walls lookin' back at me. No faces, no eyes, no shiny white teeth."

Geoff pulled out his journal, and I fired up the stove and started chopping up the cauliflower and zucchini. It *was* nice to be inside away from people, I was thinking to myself, when suddenly someone knocked on the door.

"Yes?" Geoff called back making no effort to move from his bed.

"Hello, darling. Open door please, darling."

It was the hotel manager. Larry opened the door and in walked two men, the manager and his assistant.

"Good evening, darling," said the manager to Geoff. "Good evening, sir," he said turning to me.

"I'm not darling," Geoff snapped, irritated that his peace and privacy had been invaded. Geoff was especially short-tempered right now because his stomach cramps were raising hell.

"Thank you, darling," smiled the manager. The man's knowledge of English, we soon found out, was limited to approximately fifteen words. He and his assistant invited themselves in and jumped around our room examining our bikes and gear and our clothes hanging out to dry. The manager watched me cook, while his assistant lifted the journal off Geoff's lap and flipped through the pages.

After they surveyed all our belongings, the men sat down on the two chairs in the room and nodded and grinned. Larry tried talking with them, but they couldn't understand a thing he said. They turned down the food we offered them. They were content to watch us prepare and eat our meal and listen to our conversation. While we talked, they followed every movement of our mouths with their own; they chuckled and slapped themselves when we laughed and frowned and shook their heads when we sounded upset. The two sat through dinner and the water-boiling session, then Geoff asked them to leave so that we could get some sleep. Unfortunately, they were having the time of their lives and had no intention of leaving.

"I reckon these two'll stay 'ere the night if we don't boot them out," Geoff reasoned. Larry agreed, and he and Geoff each took one of the men by the arm and hauled him out the door. Once outside, the two Indians protested loudly and banged on the locked door.

"Open please, darling!"

"No. We're going to sleep now," Geoff called back.

"Open please, darling!"

"Go away!"

"Open please, darling!"

"Aw shuddup."

"Open please, darling!"

We quit answering, but they kept hammering and hollering at us to let them back in. Larry lit a mosquito coil, and he and I jammed our earplugs, which we had bought in Athens after Egypt, into our heads to block out the noise.

When Larry and I awoke in the morning, Geoff was sitting upright in bed. His face was pale and contorted in pain. It frightened me to look at him.

"Couldn't sleep last night," he whispered weakly.

"The stomach cramps and diarrhea again?" I asked.

"That. And now me lungs and back really 'urt. And I feel like I've got meself an appendicitis. Don't reckon I can ride today. You two go on, and I'll 'op the train to Calcutta. If I still feel poorly when I get there, I'll fly 'ome. If I git better, I'll take a bus to Kathmandu."

"Listen Geoff," said Larry. "I'll fix you up some breakfast and maybe that'll make you feel better."

Pradeep came in just as we were finishing breakfast and insisted on taking Geoff to the doctor.

"Trains in India are not good," he explained. "They are very crowded, and there are many delays. Once it took a train two weeks to reach Calcutta from here. It should only take a few days. It is better for you that you bicycle and that you stay with your friends. I take you to the doctor now, and he shall tell us what to do."

Geoff agreed to go. While he was gone Larry repaired his right brake as best he could. The clamp that held the brake lever to the handlebars had broken off. He bent the lever back into shape, then strapped it onto his handlebars with a spare length of brake cable.

Forty minutes later, Geoff returned looking paler and shakier than ever.

"Bloody rickshaw ride 'bout did me in! Bumpiest ride you ever knew. Thought I'd die. Took all me willpower to keep from messin' me shorts!" he sputtered. "Won't be complainin' 'bout bicyclin' ever again, that's for sure."

Geoff and Pradeep accepted the cups of hot tea Larry offered them, and Geoff stretched out on the bed. He'd bought some *chapatis* on the way back from the doctor's and nibbled on one while he sipped his tea.

"So tell us about your doctor's visit," said Larry.

Geoff tossed a small, plain manila packet filled with pills onto the table.

"Doctor said to take three pills, one pill of each color, once a day for the next three days."

"What are they?" I asked.

"Don't know. Don't even know what's wrong with me. Doctor never said," he shrugged. "I walked in and told 'im what me symptoms were and 'e pulled those pills out o' some bottles and dropped them into the packet. He took me blood pressure first, but that was it."

I examined the pills. There was nothing written on them or the packet.

"I don't imagine it's too safe taking these. You don't have any idea what's in them," I said.

"Already took the first three, I did."

"Oh. Well, let's see. You're not allergic to any kind of medication are you?" I asked.

"Well no, not that I know of."

Geoff stared at the packet for a while, then shook his head.

"Decided after the rickshaw ride that if the trains in India are any-where near as bumpy as the rickshaws, I'd never make it to Calcutta. I took the pills, and I'm 'opin' they'll make me feel better so I can bike today."

"OK. Then you lie there and rest, and Larry and I'll pack up every-thing. Then we'll see how you feel."

Geoff slept soundly for an hour. Even the manager's banging on the door and the "Open please, darling!" didn't rouse him. When he awoke, he felt well enough to try to pedal on to Lucknow, fifty miles away.

We each thanked Pradeep for all his help, then cycled to the main government bank in Kanpur, where Geoff changed some travelers' checks. No one in the bank knew exactly how to go about cashing the checks, and it took the tellers the rest of the morning to figure it all out. Mean-while, the bank guard, who had agreed to protect our bikes from the crowds that followed us into the bank compound and from the bank employees who piled out of the building the minute they saw us ride up, decided to play with our shifters and broke Geoff's cables.

It was afternoon before we finally pedaled out of Kanpur. At the edge of the city, we crossed over the Ganges. Near its banks, standing knee deep in the muddy water, the washers of Kanpur were hard at work scrubbing tunics, *dhotis*, and turbans, and swinging them against the rocks that protruded from the river.

The road to Lucknow was relatively smooth, and the *shisham* trees lining it protected us from the blistering sun. As usual, we were joined by ambling bullock carts, elephants, and camels; sometimes bicyclers and rick-shaw drivers followed us from the one village to the next. The cyclers smiled and clanged their bells while they pedaled beside us, and if we stopped to relieve ourselves, they stopped too and waited patiently for us to finish and continue on. Twenty miles outside of Lucknow, the sun disappeared behind a shield of clouds, and a light rain began to fall. The cool raindrops felt good in the afternoon heat.

Soon after the rain started, we came up behind a bus blocking the road. It had blown its engine. We approached it in single file: I first, Geoff right behind me, and Larry following some twenty feet back.

As I started to pull out around the disabled vehicle, I realized I couldn't see past it well enough to spot oncoming traffic. I tapped my brakes to slow myself. Little did I know the road surface was coated with a slick mixture of mud, water-buffalo manure, and oil that had spilled from the engine of the bus. The moment my brakes took hold, my wheels skidded across the pavement as if it were covered with ice, and my bike shot out from under me. I was flung sprawling across the road. When I slid across the manure, mud, and oil, I looked back to see Geoff's body come sailing toward me. He too had tried to use his brakes.

Before I coasted to a stop, I remembered having seen a truck right behind Larry just before I started to pass the bus. I turned my head to look for him. If he puts on his brakes, I said to myself, he'll fall, and with the truck so close—. I didn't have time to finish my thought. I spotted Larry just as his head was being crushed beneath the truck's right front wheel. My eyes slammed shut, but I could hear myself screaming.

There was a loud crash behind me. I spun around and opened my eyes. The truck, its tires locked into a skid, had rolled over my bike, which was now caught in the undercarriage. I stood up and watched helplessly as it dragged my bike and gear twenty feet down the road, then smashed into the bus.

"Get your bike!" a voice hollered at me from the side of the road near where Larry had been killed. I figured it was Geoff's voice. I didn't want to look back. I didn't want to see Larry's lifeless body lying in a pool of blood. I didn't want to see him gone forever. And yet, what if he's still alive? I wondered. Could Geoff and I save him? None of the hundreds of Indians that had rushed to the scene would know what to do, and there were no ambulances in the countryside, no telephones. I forced myself to look back. Larry was stumbling to his feet; his head looked fine.

"Get your bike! There's more traffic coming!" he yelled again as he and Geoff pulled theirs off the road. I dove under the truck and yanked my bike loose from the undercarriage. The packs and the bike were scraped up and embedded with the gooey road coating, but nothing was broken. My handlebar bag had been jarred loose and tossed across the road. I grabbed it and my bike and ran for the shoulder of the road before any more trucks came by.

A mass of people—farmers, villagers, passing bicyclers, and passengers from the bus—were crowding around Larry and Geoff. I pushed my way through to the center. Geoff was crying.

"Man! I thought you were dead!" he was sobbing. "I thought you were dead!"

I pressed up against Larry. He seemed dumbfounded by what Geoff was saying. I threw my arms around him and tears gushed down my face.

"Your head! The truck ran over your head," I moaned. "I saw it run you over when I looked back, and so did Geoff. I thought you were killed! Oh God, I thought I'd lost you forever!"

The Indians who surrounded us, not knowing how to react to the arrival of three foreigners, the near-fatal encounter between Larry and the truck, and the astonishing sight of a woman throwing herself around a man, ignoring completely the Indian taboo against any public display of affection between opposite sexes, were all laughing nervously while they poked at us and our bikes and gear.

"Oh yeah," Larry said softly, "the truck." He paused for a moment to hug me tight against his chest. "That was such a scary thing, I guess my mind erased it for a while there.

"When I saw you two fall, I hit my brakes, and down I went. The road was like ice. I skidded a ways, and when I finally came to a stop, I had this real peculiar feeling. It was like I sensed a presence behind me. My head was turned toward you guys and the bus, so I couldn't see behind me. But I sensed there was something there; so before I tried to get up off my back, I turned my head. When I looked back, I was looking straight into the tread of a truck's front tire. I jerked my head up off the ground and felt the tire and lug nuts brush by the side of my face. Damn, that was close! That was *way* too close! Scared me out of my wits!"

Geoff threw an arm around Larry's shoulders, and the three of us stood hugging each other and crying.

"Let's get out o' 'ere," Geoff said finally. "I can't bear havin' these people all laughin' at us. I know they don't find it funny that you were almost killed. They're only laughin' because they're nervous about what they saw and about us 'aving our arms around each other, but I can't stand to 'ear people laughin' right now. Not after what just 'appened. Let's push on."

We squeezed through the crowd and ever so slowly and reluctantly climbed onto our bikes. At first we rode on the dirt shoulder, because none of us had the courage to get back out onto the road right away. But some of the boys from the crowd followed us on their bicycles. They rang their bells and laughed at us, and after ten or fifteen minutes of that, we rode on the pavement again so we could pick up our pace and outdistance them. Every time a truck or bus passed us, we hugged the edge of the road and cringed in fear.

The last twelve miles into Lucknow seemed like an eternity, especially to Larry and Geoff. Because he'd jarred his broken wrist and cracked ribs, Larry was in a great deal of physical pain on top of being in a mild state of shock after having nearly lost his life. Geoff's stomach, lungs, and back still ached, and he was feeling the effects of not sleeping the night before.

Unfortunately, Lucknow, the capital of the state of Uttar Pradesh, was a huge city, and it was after dark when we arrived. Pradeep had advised us to stay at the YMCA, but we had no idea where it was located. We stopped at the train station to ask directions. The man at the information desk explained that the Y was on the other side of the city, and he asked a little old man standing nearby with his bicycle to take us there.

For an hour and a half, we followed the little man through streets so crowded with people, animals, bicycles, rickshaws, and motor vehicles that there was barely enough room to put our feet down when we came to a stop. Once I set my right foot down too far from my pedal, and a rickshaw wheel ran over it. The bicycles and rickshaws engulfed what few cars and motorscooters there were and forced them to move along at a pedaler's pace. At intersections, there were always some two hundred bicycles spread across the lanes of traffic waiting for the lights to change.

Bicycling through Lucknow was like a bad dream. The little man kept losing his way, and he stopped every five minutes to ask directions. The dim street lights did little to dispel the darkness or the smoke and dust that choked the air. Wherever I looked, silent, dark, male faces stared back at me through the brown haze. Everywhere, there were too many people, and it made me sad to think that this nightmarish setting was life for millions of Indians.

We each breathed a long sigh of relief when we finally pedaled through the gates of the YMCA and peered in at the lawns and gardens and neat, white, two-story building. We walked slowly and stiffly into the office and collapsed in the rattan chairs. Mud, manure, dust, and oil still clung to our clothes and bodies. Geoff sat clenching his stomach and rocking back and forth, and Larry held his ribs. We were all shaken from the accident, and nervous exhaustion had sapped all our energy.

Five minutes later, the assistant director came into the small, cluttered office and informed us that there were no rooms available and that we should pedal back across the city to the government tourist bungalows. Because of the snakes in the lawn and gardens, he thought it would be too dangerous for us to pitch our tent within the compound.

"We can't make it back across the city," breathed Geoff. "We can't do it. I'm quite sick, and my friend 'ere 'as some cracked ribs and a broken wrist, and 'e was nearly killed a few hours ago."

Geoff explained about the accident.

"I am sorry to hear about your mishap, but you cannot stay here. There is no room. All our rooms are filled with Christian students from India and Nepal," answered the assistant director. "But I will call the tourist bungalows to see if they have room for you."

He tried for ten minutes to reach the bungalows. While he phoned, he kept an eye on Geoff, who was rocking and gasping in pain. Geoff went off to the toilet four times during those ten minutes.

"I cannot reach the bungalows," the man finally announced. "But I have been watching this young fellow here," he said, pointing to Geoff, "and he looks to be in very poor health. Therefore, I have decided to allow you all to sleep in the dining room. You may pay us a small fee tomorrow. Do you have food for your meal?"

"Not much. A few bananas and some peanut butter."

"Then you should tell me what you need, and I shall send one of the two orphan boys who live here to buy it for you."

By the time we washed our hands and faces, unpacked our eating utensils, and laid out our mats and sleeping bags in one corner of the dining room, an orphan boy, who looked about eight years old, had returned with our eggs, cheese, tomatoes, bread, and margarine. Keeping his head bowed, he handed Larry our change. Larry thanked him and shook his hand, but the boy was too shy to look up. He ran from the room just as the director and his son walked in.

Like the assistant director, the director was a pudgy man. Both he and his teen-aged son spoke perfect English and dressed in western-style shirts and slacks. They sat down in the dining room and talked with us while we downed our peanut butter sandwiches. None of us had the energy to cook a meal or to boil drinking water for the next day.

Our short stay at the YMCA was to be our only contact with Christians in India, and it proved to be a disappointing one. The director and his son spoke contemptuously of their Hindu countrymen, and told us that they considered Hinduism to be a hopeless and worthless religion. While he spoke, the son ordered the orphan boys to bring him this and that. He shouted at them, called them "stupid people," and never once did he thank them or say a kind word to them. I hated to think what opinion the Hindus might form of Christianity if their only exposure to it was through people like the director and his son.

After dinner, since I was in the best shape of the three of us, I washed out everyone's cycling clothes, cleaned up our utensils, and packed away our gear. Geoff plopped down onto his mat and fell asleep; he was too exhausted to be bothered by the pains in his body. I set up our tent inside the dining room to protect Larry and me from the swarms of mosquitoes that would collect once the temperature dropped.

Tonight I held Larry especially close and thanked God that he'd survived the accident. For eighteen months he and I had struggled and laughed and shared together in the face of all types of experiences, and a bond had been forged between us that I then knew would never be broken.

"Larry?" I whispered.

"Yeah?"

"Know what day today is?"

"Today? Oh, I don't really know. Let's see now. Thursday, I guess."

"I mean the date."

"The date? Let's see, I guess it's the twenty-second. November twenty-second."

"Know what that means?"

"What?"

"It's Thanksgiving."

There was a long silence.

"Thanksgiving. It is, isn't it," he said after a while. And then he was quiet again.

"Barb?"

"Yeah?"

"I love you. I love you very, very much."

"I know. Happy Thanksgiving, trooper."

―❧―

A grating, nerve piercing noise woke me in the morning. It sounded like someone running his fingernails down a chalk board. It was still dark, and there were no lights on. The electricity must be off, I thought. It's being directed to the countryside again, because of the drought. The noise came again. It sounded very close. I rolled over and looked at Larry. He was sitting upright with our metal file in his hand. Whenever we needed a special tool we weren't carrying, we used the file to fashion it out of a piece of metal. But right now Larry was working the file back and forth inside his mouth.

"Whatcha doin'?" I asked sleepily.

"Filing my tooth," he answered, stopping for a moment. "I chipped it yesterday. Must have done it when I fell."

Larry opened his mouth to show me the jagged edge on one of his molars.

"Makes my skin crawl to file it, but I've got to or that sharp edge'll tear up my tongue."

After Larry had finished his filing, we hurried to pack up our gear and clear out of the dining room. The director had asked us to be gone by eight o'clock so that the students could eat their breakfast in the room. Since the director and his son were still asleep when we left, Larry placed a thank-you note and our lodging fee on the dining room table. We filled our water bottles with tap water and poured a couple of drops of foul-tasting iodine into each bottle to purify the water. As I rolled my bike across the front porch, I pulled the Bible out of my handlebar bag and left it on one of the porch chairs for the director. I was sure Mr. Crocker would have approved.

Larry's chest and wrist were stiff, but Geoff's stomach had greatly improved, and after our solid night's sleep, we all felt rejuvenated. The ride that day went smoothly—no flat tires or broken spokes. And we were able to hide in a clump of trees and eat our lunch in relative privacy; the men in the fields nearby either didn't notice us or chose to ignore us. It was the first time since Greece that Larry and I had eaten lunch alongside a road without being watched by a group of humans or rats. I realized that I could not remember or even imagine what it was like to look down a road and not see people. I closed my eyes and still I saw people. I tried picturing a deserted road, one of the hundreds we'd pedaled along in North America, but I couldn't. The three of us found ourselves talking about the quiet peaceful wilderness areas in New Zealand and North America as we wove our way through towns jammed with bodies, followed by bell-ringing bicyclers and watched by farmers, wandering holy men, and village people.

By evening we reached Ayodhya—one of the seven sacred Hindu centers in India—on the banks of the Ghaghara River. Its streets were so crowded we had to walk our bikes to make our way to the tourist camp. It was enclosed by a high brick wall. The scores of monkeys climbing about on it specialized in lifting food the guests left unattended. Larry and I pitched our tent on the lawn, and Geoff moved into the dormitory. The manager of the camp, who spoke English, brought us a newspaper printed in English. The headlines were about the wave of anti-American activities in the Muslim world. The Pakistanis had stormed the American Embassy in Islamabad, leaving two Americans dead, and they'd set fire to the American cultural centers in Kawalpindi and Lahore. The Iranian students were still holding the hostages at the American Embassy, and the Ayatollah Khomeini was now claiming that the seizure of the Grand Mosque in Mecca had been orchestrated by the Americans.

"Much danger in Middle East," the manager said. "Here in India there is some danger too—the *dacoits*, you know. You must never bicycle when dark. *Dacoits* take from you all your money. You must be varee careful.

"Now I go to city to buy food. My assistant serve supper soon. If you need food for tomorrow, you tell me and I buy in the city."

A half hour later, the two Indian assistants, who spoke almost no English, set a table and three rattan chairs on the lawn and brought us dishes of curried rice and vegetables, *chapatis*, and cold, bottled lemon drinks. The smell of curry burned our nostrils.

"Curry hot?" I asked, pointing to the plate of rice and vegetables.

The two Indians were quick to shake their heads.

"No hot! No hot!" they answered excitedly.

I eyed the Indians and the food suspiciously; then I put a small amount of the curried mixture into my mouth. For the umpteenth time since I arrived in India, I had to wonder just what exactly an Indian might define as hot. Every time an Indian served us curry, he said "No hot!" And each time, the curry was so hot that my mouth felt as if I had bitten into a platter of hot coals, my face and hands broke into a sweat, and my heart pounded out of control. I'd come to the conclusion that anything an Indian considered to be hot would probably strike me dead with its fumes alone.

While we attempted to force down the mouth-blistering curry, the two Indians stood near us holding long bamboo poles, which they swatted the monkeys with whenever they jumped off the wall and tried to steal our food.

After dinner, an Indian businessman staying in one of the bunga-lows near the dormitory joined us on the lawn. He too warned us about the *dacoits*, and he talked about the corruption and graft in his country.

"There is so much graft in India because there are too many people here," he explained. "Take the government employees who sell train tickets, for example. For every ticket that is for sale, there are dozens of people begging for the opportunity to buy it. So what does the employee do? He sells it to the highest bidder, and pockets the amount he receives over the set price of the ticket. These things happen all the time in India because there are too many people."

The next morning before Larry and I awoke, a baby monkey climbed down off the wall surrounding the camp and busied himself yanking at our tent stakes. The sunlight had just pierced the darkness, and no one was up yet. Lying on our mats, we put our faces to one of the tent win-dows and watched the monkeys play on the lawn. The chatter of the monkeys and the chirping of the small, green, parrot-like birds that hopped along the tree limbs were the only sounds. There were no human voices, no clanging bicycle bells, no blaring truck horns. And there were no crowds of staring faces. It was one of those special Indian mornings that made me anxious to start another day.

I looked forward to watching the women in their *saris* and gold and silver jewelry carrying their brass water jugs on their heads; to pedaling alongside the elephants, camels, water buffalo, and monkeys; to bartering for food with the good-natured vendors; to smiling back at the curious, grinning faces; even to filling my nostrils with the pungent odors of incense and fresh manure baking in the hot sun.

I was anxious to begin the day, and yet I knew that by evening I would be just as anxious to end it, to escape the pressing jumble of human forms. Like many foreigners who travel in India, I'd found that India both lured and repelled me. She invited her visitors to love her, but she made it a challenge for them to do so. And somehow that made me love her all the more.

We spent half the morning in Ayodhya, meandering through ancient Hindu temples and along the Ghaghara, which was lined with emaciated holy men. By the time we finished exploring the city, it was eleven o'clock. We had only eight hours of daylight to pedal the ninety miles to Gorakhpur, and to buy food supplies, eat lunch, and fix any flat tires along the way. We considered staying another day in Ayodhya and getting an early start the next morning. But winter was rapidly approaching in the Himalaya, and we needed to keep moving.

At lunchtime, part way between Ayodhya and Gorakhpur, we stopped near a gathering of eight mud houses at the edge of a sugar-cane field. The children, women, and men who lived in the houses hurried over to have a look at us. Our appearance confused them at first, but when we smiled they grinned back and motioned for us to make ourselves at home. The men's broad smiles exposed teeth and gums stained orange by the betel flowers and nuts they chewed. We offered a portion of our food to everyone, but they all shook their heads.

I was surprised to see women crowd around us. Always before, they had kept their distance. One woman and her young daughter stood close to me the whole time I was eating, pointing at me and nodding their heads approvingly. Their lack of shyness pleased me, and after I finished my meal, I stepped up to the woman and held out my hand. She clasped it tightly and held on for a long time while we looked into each other's eyes. This was my only real contact with an Indian peasant woman. With only a grasp of my hand, I tried to convey to the bold, beautiful woman how much I valued our brief encounter.

By the time we finished our lunch, we had only two and a half hours of daylight to cycle forty-four miles. We pedaled feverishly for two solid hours. With eight miles left to go and darkness already setting in, Geoff's rear inner tube exploded. It was his second flat of the day—he was averaging nearly two a day since New Delhi—and it tossed him into a raging fit of frustration.

"*A flat! Another bloody flat!*" he screamed. "These bloody Michelin tubes are a lot o' rot they are! Keep givin' out at the valve. Every time, every day, it's an 'ole right next to the valve! Well *this* time these tubes just might bloody well get us killed! The *dacoits*'ll be out any minute now, and 'ere we'll be, fixin' another rotten tube. Sittin' ducks, we'll be, all right. Sittin' ducks!"

Geoff pulled out all of his spare inner tubes, picked out the one with the least patches on it, and jammed it inside his tire.

"If the *dacoits* git us tonight, it's all Michelin's fault!" he raged on. "Then I'll write them a letter, I will. 'Dear Michelin,' it'll say, 'Because of your bloody rotten tubes I bought in England, me two American friends and meself were robbed of all our possessions by *dacoits*, and we are now wanderin' through India 'opeless, broke, and bicycleless. Yours truly, Geoff Thorpe, The 'Apless Wanderer.'"

Whether he actually was a *dacoit*, we'll never know for sure. But Geoff still swears he was. He materialized after the flat was repaired and we had pedaled a few more miles up the road. None of us said a word when he pulled up on his motorcycle alongside Geoff. He was dressed in slacks and a shirt; he'd slung a rifle over one of his shoulders. Two large saddle bags straddled the rear wheel of his motorcycle.

The man eyed Geoff and his bike very carefully for about five minutes, and then he pulled ahead to examine Larry and me. He never spoke while he looked us over, and in our nervousness we found ourselves pedaling as fast as possible, keeping one eye out for potholes and the other on the man. We could hear voices off in the fields, and we could see the fires inside the mud houses a way off the road. But now that darkness had fallen, there was no traffic on the road. The highway would remain deserted for another three or four miles, until we reached the outskirts of Gorakhpur. We felt defenseless, and we were keenly aware of the cameras, cash, travelers' checks, and passports riding in our panniers.

It was Larry who finally broke the incredibly tense silence.

"Hello," he said abruptly.

The man did not answer. Geoff, who was last in line, groaned to himself. Why, he wondered, had that crazy Yank up front suddenly decided to strike up a conversation with an armed *dacoit* preparing to rob and probably shoot the lot of us?

"Gorakhpur," said Larry.

The man remained silent and continued surveying our gear. Larry had nothing else to say, and we pedaled along in silence once more. It was so dark, we could see no farther than fifteen feet ahead.

"Hey!"

My heart shot into my throat. The man was shouting at us.

"Hey!" he shouted again.

"Oh God," whispered Geoff behind me.

I felt like I was going to be sick.

"Yes?" Larry answered. There was a crackling of terror in his voice.

I tightened my grasp on my handlebars and stared straight ahead. I wanted to scream.

"Yaur speed twenty-seven kilometers."

It took a while for the words to sink in. I had expected something more along the lines of "Stop and hand over all your *rupees* and valuables or you die."

"We're going twenty-seven kilometers an hour? Thank you for telling us. Thank you very much," squeaked Larry.

The man nodded and continued to ride beside us for a few minutes. Then he pulled across the road and sped off in the opposite direction.

The final five miles into Gorakhpur were hell. The road was blocked by trucks and buses waiting for the police to clear up an accident at the turnoff to the city. We were forced to ride on the dirt shoulder the whole way. We spent almost an hour inching our way through the swelling of rickshaws, motorscooters, bullock carts, people on foot, and other bicyclers on the shoulder. The dirt kicked up by those using the shoulder and the fumes from the line of idling engines choked our lungs and burned our eyes.

When we finally reached Gorakhpur, the city itself was lost in a shroud of smoke and dusty darkness. Its electricity had already been transferred to the countryside, and only a handful of kerosene lamps dotted the streets. It took another forty minutes to battle the masses of humanity streaming blindly through the streets and to find the city center and a hotel.

We dragged our bikes and gear upstairs to our room on the second floor of the first hotel we came to and collapsed. We were starved, our drinking water had run out hours ago, and exhaustion had claimed our bodies and minds. There was no food left in our packs; even the supply of peanut butter Larry and I had picked up in Athens was gone. All the food stands in Gorakhpur had closed early because of the absence of street lights, so we headed into the restaurant at the hotel. Candles provided the only lighting.

I dug into the plate of "no hot" curried chicken the waiter placed in front of me. The first swallow singed my mouth. My throat was already sore from breathing in too much dirt and too many fumes and from coughing nonstop for the last two hours; so when the waiter returned ten minutes later with a cold lemon soda, I was too thirsty and my throat too scorched to worry about the half-melted ice cubes in the glass. I knew they were made from tap water, but I desperately needed something to pour down my throat to squelch the flames. While I gulped down my watery soda, I tried not to worry too much about the amoebas and parasites it probably contained. If I'm real lucky, I might not get sick after all, I reasoned. Tomorrow I'd know for sure.

ROOFTOP OF THE WORLD

CHAPTER SIXTEEN

The mountains were steep and terraced. A wispy veil of fog whispered through the deep valley and floated skyward, lending an ethereal softness to the sharp cliffs. Huge white birds glided by, disappearing then reappearing through an occasional thickening in the fog. The white birds and the reddish huts of mud and straw nestled in the mountains set sharp contrasts to the lush, dark green foliage.

It was dawn in the Himalaya. Geoff and Larry and I were lying on wooden beds with rope bottoms in a mud house, which, like all the buildings in the tiny village of Walling-Station, Nepal, clung to the side of a cliff. The windows in our room had no glass, and the damp coolness of the misty air and the smell of flowers filled our nostrils. The view was awesome, and the village was hushed and peaceful. We had reached Shangri-la: I could imagine never leaving. Downstairs, Mom and Dad Pandey were cooking rice and yogurt for their family's breakfast and boiling eggs for the three of us.

When we pedaled into Walling-Station the night before, at the end of our second day in Nepal, the oldest boy of the Pandey family had run into the street to greet us and offer us lodging in his home. He spoke to us in English, which he was studying in high school.

Walling-Station consisted of ten houses and a handful of shops, which sold soap, scarves, plastic bracelets, tea, crackers, and bread. The houses and shops were lined wall to wall along each side of the road. A gutter, three feet deep and two feet wide, paralleled the road on one side; parts of it were filled with human excrement.

The Pandey's home was the nicest of all the houses in Walling-

257

Station. Inside, its red mud walls were painted white and its earthen floors were covered with woven grass mats. The house had two stories and a thatched roof. The ground floor was the eating area, lit by kerosene lanterns—there was no electricity in Nepal outside of the few cities. The room had two large tables with long benches, and a cabinet, which held the gigantic stainless-steel plates that all Nepali villagers ate from. The plates were all the same size and had three sections: a large one for rice and too small ones for *dal*, a watery lentil soup, and for a mixture of spicy potatoes and tomatoes. In the more remote villages of Nepal, rice and *dal* were nearly all the people had to eat.

Attached to the ground floor of the house was a covered kitchen area with an open fire and an earthen oven. The dishes were washed with the water from a metal barrel, which sat outside in the dirt, halfway between the house and the road. Soap was a luxury, so the Pandey children scrubbed the dishes with dirt or rice husks.

Two bedrooms made up the second floor of the house; one had four beds and the other ten. The three of us were given the smaller room. The larger one was used by Nepali truck drivers, who spent the night in Walling-Station during their runs between Gorakhpur and Pokhara, a city forty miles to the north of Walling-Station. Each driver paid the family the usual six *rupees* (fifty cents) for his bed and a rice and *dal* dinner.

After we carried our gear to our room, Mom Pandey offered to fix us dinner, too. But I had learned my lesson about Nepali cooking two nights before, at the border between India and Nepal, after our ride north from Gorakhpur. I'd failed to heed the advice of nearly every American we had talked with who had traveled in Nepal: "Cook your own food: The Nepali know nothing about hygiene."

It had taken us most of the day to pedal from Gorakhpur to the border, and by the time we'd gone through immigrations and customs, it was too dark to cover the seventeen miles to Butwal, the first town in Nepal. We stayed at the hotel on the Nepali side of the border. It was a miserable place, but we had no other choice. For twenty-one *rupees*, we moved into a dingy room, bare except for three wooden beds draped with tattered mosquito netting. Since we'd expected to reach Butwal and buy food there for dinner, we had nothing to eat. And there were no food stands nearby.

"I've got to eat *something*," Larry complained, once we settled in. "I talked with this British guy staying here. He's taking the bus into India tomorrow. Anyway, he says he ate lunch here, and the food seemed all right."

My stomach was feeling a little queasy—probably from the ice cubes in Gorakhpur—but I was too hungry to skip the meal a young man at the hotel offered to cook for us. An hour later he strolled through our door cradling platefuls of hot food. The two-inch-thick egg rolls were delicious, but the noodles and vegetables tasted peculiar, and the Tibetan bread turned out to be greasy pieces of deep-fried batter. Larry was the only one with enough sense to stay away from the bread.

By midnight I was sick with stomach cramps and the runs. Every half hour for the rest of the night, I stumbled outside to the squat toilets (which wouldn't flush, because the water quit running when the electricity went off). I didn't sleep much; not only was I sick, but mice kept climbing up my mosquito netting. They'd tumble through the holes in the netting and land on my face, and I'd have to bat them off and back onto the floor.

By morning I was worse. While Larry and Geoff packed our bikes, I trotted off to the toilet once every fifteen minutes to deposit a stream of yellowish liquid there was nothing solid left in me. The family that owned the hotel shot worried glances my way each time I made one of my hurried pilgrimages. In between visits I collapsed on my bed, weak and nauseated. When it appeared there was no end in sight, I downed the last of the prescribed medicine for diarrhea I'd brought with me from America. A half hour went by, and still there was no improvement in my condition. About the time I decided I wouldn't be bicycling today, Larry and Geoff announced their verdict.

"We've got to get out of here, Barb," said Larry. "This place is the pits. Geoff just asked if they had any drinking water, and one of the women pointed to a bucket of water full of big worms. And she was using the water to wash the dishes!"

"And this you're not goin' to believe," Geoff interrupted. "But we stood right there and watched, so we know it's a fact. We watched the family fixin' breakfast for the guests 'ere, and you know 'ow they fixed it? They carried the bread dough and the vegetables over to the steps o' the front porch; then they scraped a bit o' the dirt and manure off to one side, and they plopped everything down on the steps. And right there in the filth, they rolled out the bread and chopped up the vegies! And the whole bloody time they were doing that, these mice were there nibblin' on it all!"

"Look, Barb," Larry continued. "We've got to go on to Butwal. There we can buy our own food to cook for ourselves. And we'll find a place where there aren't any mice running all over you at night, so you can sleep. We'll find a nice, clean, quiet place where you can rest, and we'll feed you safe food. How about it? Can you make it seventeen miles? It shouldn't take us more than an hour to get there. They say the terrain stays flat the whole way."

I knew Larry was right; we had to go on. He and Geoff had already packed my mat and sleeping bag onto my bike; so all that was expected of me was to climb on and pedal a mere seventeen miles. I had all day to do it, and that sounded simple enough.

I made one last journey to the toilet, then picked up my bike and started to carry it down the four steps of the porch outside our room. It was then that I found out just how weak I really was. My body folded under the weight of my bike, both my legs buckled and my arms went limp. I felt the teeth of the bike's chain ring dig into the back of my right leg as I hit the ground.

Larry pulled the bike off me, and he and Geoff and the Nepali family and a number of the guests stared at my leg. Four deep gashes filled with black, gummy, chain grease were spurting blood. Larry grabbed me by the waist and dragged me back into our room.

"There's nothing to wash your leg with," he said. "We're out of boiled water."

"Then we'll use spit," I reasoned. We spit and scrubbed. But without soap and hot water the grease was going nowhere. I pushed a few gobs of antibacterial ointment down into the holes; the blood continued to trickle out.

Larry carried my bike out to the road, and I climbed on and wobbled off down the street. The bike felt like it weighed two hundred pounds, and I was too weak to steer it around all the potholes and rocks in the road.

Not more than a half mile from the hotel, I hit a rock head on, and my front tire went flat. Unfortunately, this happened directly in front of the local elementary school, and within a matter of seconds some seventy kids and a handful of teachers came bounding out of the schoolhouse, swarmed over our bikes, and attempted to pull off our packs and gear. I sat in the dirt, doubled over in pain, trying desperately to control my bowels, while Larry fixed the flat and Geoff kept the kids pushed away. Besides repairing the punctured inner tube, Larry put on a new front tire. The rubber was worn down on the old tire, and the cord was exposed. This was the fourth front tire I'd gone through since the start of our trip; I'd worn through seven rear tires.

"Geoff, you'd better go on," Larry shouted over the squeals of the school children. "Barb's pretty sick and weak. There's no telling how long we'll have to stay in Butwal before she's feeling strong enough to tackle the mountains. No reason for you to waste time waiting for us. You go on ahead. We'll probably meet up again anyway in Pohkara or Kathmandu."

"Won't do that, mate!" Geoff yelled back. "Can't leave me buddies. Not after what all we've gone through together. You two looked after me all those times I was sick—shoppin' and makin' tea for me. No sir, we're lifelong buddies now, and we're stickin' together. I'm not leavin' you two. Besides, I'm not feelin' too fit meself. I could use a rest in Butwal. Got some catchin' up to do in me journal, too."

Butwal, like the rest of the Nepali towns we would pedal through, was much poorer and dirtier than the towns in India. Food, manure, human excrement, and dead mice lay rotting on its uneven dirt streets. The meal stalls looked dark and dingy, and their dishes were scrubbed out back in the dirt and rinsed with foul-smelling water. Women and children sat in the doorways picking lice from each other's hair.

We found a small hotel in Butwal with quiet rooms and a dormitory. By then, the pills I'd swallowed began to take effect, and I spent the afternoon napping and eating fruit and crackers. By morning I was still weak, but the cramps and diarrhea had subsided, and I was ready to take on the Himalaya.

Contrary to the rumors we'd heard before we started our trip, the road through Nepal, which extended from the Indian border north to Pokhara, then east on to Kathmandu and China (formerly Tibet), was paved. Potholes, rocks and landslides covered the section between the Indian border and Pokhara, which had been built by the Indians. But, with the exception of the pass, which was torn up for resurfacing just before Kathmandu, a smooth surface, well maintained by the Chinese, ran from Pokhara to China.

The day we left Butwal I was well enough to notice my new surroundings and the strange-looking people. The land stayed flat for three miles past Butwal, then the mountains began, straight up through the dusty haze of the lowlands. At first glance we thought they were clouds. These were not the snow-covered, towering peaks we would glimpse later in the day. These were only foothills. But after the flat lands of India and Egypt, they looked colossal. Once we entered the mountains, we ground up and down fifty-five miles of sheer cliffs before we reached Walling Station.

It surprised us how tropical the mountains were. Banana trees, ferns, flowers, waterfalls, streams, and rice paddies crept along their cliffs and through their valleys. Even the steepest mountains were terraced, providing level spaces for growing rice. By then, late November, the rice had been harvested, and the farmers were turning the soil with their crude wooden plows drawn by water buffalo. It seemed impossible to believe that these fat lumbering beasts could negotiate the near vertical climbs from one terrace to the next.

The mountains between Butwal and Walling-Station were sprinkled with human forms, but there were no large towns choked with people. We'd finally escaped the crowds of India. Villages were tiny—only eight or ten mud houses. The people had Mongoloid features: slanting eyes, short stature, black hair, and olive skin. The Nepali women wore *saris* or long skirts, with short blouses or sweaters and wide sash belts. They were different from any women we'd encountered in a long, long time. They smoked cigarettes and guzzled *channg* (Tibetan beer), and they shouted and whistled boisterously when we pedaled past them. They were tough cookies, these women, and after months of seeing nothing but silent, subservient females, I had a great time watching and listening to them. I couldn't remember the last time I'd heard a woman cut loose with a roaring, uninhibited laugh like these women did.

Most of the Nepali men wore khaki shorts, and their legs bulged with knotted muscles developed from hiking in the mountains. Men, women, and children, carrying huge wicker baskets stuffed with bundles of cane and wheat, dotted the mountainsides and the valleys. The baskets rested on the carriers' backs and hung by thick woven straps from their foreheads. Although they wore no shoes, the carriers moved swiftly over the rocky paths. Periodically, they stopped and massaged their foreheads and necks.

We stopped for lunch at the top of a long pass at the turnoff to the village of Tensen, partway between Butwal and Walling-Station. Our legs ached. Larry and I hadn't used our mountain-climbing muscles since Italy, and they had protested the whole way up. In the grimy meal stands, which catered to truck drivers, we managed to find crackers, tangerines, hard-boiled eggs, and bread.

No one stared at us. The people in the stands looked us over with only a faint curiosity, and the women and children outside continued to pick the lice off one another. It was nice not to be the center of attention. The handful of Nepali who walked past us while we ate our lunch outside one of the food stands stopped only long enough to smile and say hello—*namaste*—before they continued on about their business.

We hadn't pedaled far after lunch when, just as we topped a long climb and started down the other side, Geoff slammed to a stop, pulled over to the side of the road, and stared intently at a spot nearly straight up in the sky.

"What's the problem?" Larry asked.

"Those clouds. Those white clouds. I don't believe all o' them are clouds. Look up there. Way up there in the clouds. What do you reckon?" Geoff's voice quivered with excitement.

Larry and I carefully surveyed the overcast sky; two of the white clouds were actually snow-covered peaks.

"Good God, you're right!" shouted Larry. "There they are. Hell, we're looking at the Himalaya! We've made it! I can't believe it, folks! We're here at last!"

The three of us stood transfixed by the incredible sight of the two peaks suspended in the air. They looked as high as the stars. After a few seconds, they vanished behind a new stream of clouds. Geoff immediately set about celebrating; he grabbed Larry and me and shook us, he jumped up, down, and sideways, then he threw his arms around an unsuspecting Nepali boy who was walking past. When Geoff let him loose, the terrified youngster fled down one of the rocky trails along the side of the cliff, screaming hysterically. And I was so excited about having at long last glimpsed the Himalaya that my diarrhea came back. I had to hightail it back to the last clump of banana trees we'd passed.

Darkness caught us an hour before we reached Walling-Station. The batteries in our lights had given out weeks ago, so we made our way over the final ten miles almost blind. We couldn't spot the potholes, mud slides, or boulders until it was too late; but they weren't what worried us the most. The prospect of pedaling off the left-hand side of the road was what really terrified us. There was no shoulder on that side, only a perpendicu-lar, several-hundred-foot drop to the rocks and valley below. Fortunately, there was almost no traffic. We bounced our way through the darkness toward Walling-Station, the stars and the fireflies our only lights.

There were eight members in the Pandey family. The eldest son escorted us into the house and introduced us to Mom. It was immediately evident that Mom was head of the roost. She sounded the orders, and everyone obeyed her, including Dad. It was Mom who sat us down and asked all the whys and what fors. She could speak a few words of English but mainly relied on her son to act as her interpreter. Mom wanted to know where we were from, where we were headed, what our countries were like, how we liked Nepal, and how long we would stay in Walling-Station.

"Mother wants you to stay Walling-Station," her son explained. "Very nice here. Kathmandu big, many people. You no like Kathmandu. You come back, stay here. Stay our house."

Mom wore lots of jewelry and scarves, and, like the Indian women, she had pierced one of her nostrils and in it she'd placed a round, gold stud. From holes pierced in the top ridge of her ears dangled a neat row of earrings. Their weight made the ridges flap down over the openings in her ears.

Mom puffed away on her cigarettes while she talked. When we ex-plained that we wanted to prepare our own dinner because we weren't ac-customed to Nepali food and that I was still feeling sick from my meal at the border, she took no offense. Instead, she directed Dad to find enough rice, tomatoes, onions, and *loca*—a vegetable that looked and tasted like a cross between zucchini and eggplant—for us to make dinner with. We of-fered to pay for the food; for six *rupees*, Dad gave us double what we needed. Then Mom threw in a bottle of *channg*.

A couple of Mom's women friends came over while we were eating to have a good look at us. They sat down on the floor mats and gossiped, smoked, and downed *channg*. Dad played cards with the truck drivers at the other table, and the older children studied their school books.

After dinner, when I asked where the toilet was, Mom took me outside and pointed up the street past the houses. It was too dark to see what she was pointing at. But at the edge of town, I found three men squatted at the side of the road relieving themselves. They were each holding a rock in one hand, which they used as toilet paper. I went back to the house and picked up my towel, then walked back to just beyond where the men had squatted.

On my way back to the house, a vehicle passed me, and for a moment I had to think hard to remember where I was. Its massive array of bright lights made the thing look like a comet bouncing down the pitted road. It was a thirty-foot recreational vehicle with German license plates. Man's ultimate gas guzzler had penetrated the Himalaya!

The view from our bedroom window at sunrise the next morning tempted us to consider staying in Walling-Station forever. But the prospect of again setting our eyes on the world's tallest peaks by late that afternoon coaxed us on.

Mom Pandey and I hugged each other good-bye after breakfast.

"She like you," said her oldest son. "She wish you come back stay with us."

"Maybe someday I'll come back," I answered. "You never know."

As I pedaled out of Walling-Station, I looked back at the family. Dad was standing by the fire cooking more yogurt, the small children were washing the dishes, and Mom sat separating rice. As usual, Mom was joking about something, and her high-pitched giggle followed me down the road.

The thirty-two miles between Walling-Station and Pokhara wound down into deep, tropical, river valleys and shot up over a dozen or more knee-torturing passes dotted with muddy landslides. Women, naked from the waist up, took their morning baths in the streams and waterfalls. People carrying baskets on their backs hurried along the footpaths, and farmers were plowing their paddies and herding their water buffalo up and down the terraces.

It was Geoff's turn to feel sick, and he cursed each and every pass we ground over. Then, late in the morning, I started my period. I hated bicycling even on level ground when I had menstrual cramps; so pumping over the mountains was tough work. And to make matters worse, I was out of tampons. I'd forgotten to buy a supply of them in Athens, and now it was too late—I wouldn't find any in any of the Nepali villages. I had to settle for stuffing my underwear with toilet paper. I would buy a box of what the Nepali said were tampons in Pokhara. They did remotely resemble the real thing, I guess, but I never quite figured out how to use them.

It was midafternoon when we crested the last pass and began our descent into Pokhara Valley. A light rain was falling, and the low gray clouds obscured any view of the valley and the soaring Himalaya behind it.

Pokhara was a sprawling town of over ten thousand people. Its dirt streets were crowded by Nepali, Sherpas, Tibetans, and Indians. Near Phew Lake, at one edge of town, was a large community of cheap hotels, where the foreign drug freaks, hikers, and mountain climbers stayed. Larry picked out one of the nicest of these cheapies and went inside to ask about a room.

"Sixty *rupees* for the three of us. That's five bucks. I told 'em we'd take it," he said when he came back out.

"Sixty *rupees!* Are you crazy? That's a fortune in this country!" Geoff and I protested in unison.

"Yeah, it's a lot of money for Nepal, but before you go and decide to take off and look for some place cheaper, first go in and have a look around," Larry countered.

When the hotel owner led Geoff and me into one of the rooms, we could hardly believe what we saw. One by one the features of the room registered in my mind: wall-to-wall carpeting, three beds with mattresses, clean sheets, and blankets, and connected to the room, a tiled private bathroom with a sit toilet and a shower. All this, I marveled, for just a dollar sixty-seven a person. The three of us promptly moved in and stayed for a week and a half.

Larry and I were up before sunrise our first morning in Pokhara. We pulled on a few layers of warm clothing and pedaled back up the pass we'd come over the day before to the lookout near the top. As we started our climb, the first glimmer of daybreak unveiled a low-lying fog creeping unevenly along the dark curves of the valley floor, and a few scattered clouds floating across an otherwise clear sky. Families in the mud houses that pocked Pokhara Valley were busy cooking breakfast, and the brown smoke from their fires swirled up through the white mist.

It wasn't until we reached the lookout that we could see to the north, beyond the dark cliffs that surrounded the valley. This was our first long, hard look at the tallest mountains on earth, the rooftop of the world. From our grassy vantage point among ferns and banana trees, the 26,500-foot and 22,950-foot summits of Annapurna and Machhapuchre looked as if they were no more than ten miles away. Their white peaks towered over the dark-green ridges of the mountains edging Pokhara Valley and pierced the sharp, even blueness of the unpolluted heavens. Winds scraped waves of snow off the summits of the Himalaya and shot them skyward in soft billowing spirals.

For two hours, until the clouds moved in and hid the peaks, we sat on the stone bench at the lookout and hugged each other and watched the mountains we'd pedaled nearly eighteen thousand miles to see. They were gigantic, majestic, and overwhelming. We stayed in the quiet of the lookout for a long time after they'd disappeared and thought about how far we'd come and about all we'd been through to get here. Then we climbed on our bikes and coasted back down the mountain.

Larry and I spent the week and a half in Pokhara hiking, resting, reading, cycling up to the lookout on clear mornings and catching up on our letter writing. Plagued once again by diarrhea and cramps, Geoff lay flat on his back for the first two days and fasted. On the third day, he ventured into the tiny restaurant at the hotel and returned with some interesting news.

"Guess what! I've found out what's me problem. I've got meself a tapeworm," he proclaimed matter-of-factly.

"How'd you find that out?" I asked.

"Just talked to an American woman in the restaurant, and she said she met a chap travelin' in Pakistan that 'ad the same symptoms I've got, includin' losin' weight, and it turned out 'e 'ad a tapeworm. So I've decided I shan't fast anymore, because if I don't eat then Jingus won't have any food to eat, and if that 'appens 'e might start chewin' on me intestines instead, which would make me condition even worse."

"Jingus?" I asked.

"Right. Decided I should name me tapeworm, and the name Jingus popped into me 'ead. Geoff and Jingus, Not bad, ay? I reckon me and Jingus been travelin' together since Pakistan; or maybe I picked 'im up in Iran. Who knows? Anyway, tomorrow I start me cure. The woman told me that you can buy anything you want from the chemists 'ere. You don't need a prescription. Just go in and tell 'em what you fancy, and they sell it to you—no questions asked. So tomorrow I buy the pills to finish off dear old Jingus."

Geoff took his "dewormer" pills for a few days with no results. The cramps continued. And even though he ate three big meals a day, he kept losing weight.

"That bloody Jingus," he sighed. "'E's beatin' me digestive system to everything. No matter what I swallow, 'e gobbles it up."

Eventually Geoff decided to hit the local medical clinic before he got any weaker. There, his condition was diagnosed as common dysentery, and he was given a bottle of tetracycline tablets and instructed to take one or two tablets daily. After a couple of days of the tetracycline, he started to improve. By December 4, he felt well enough to pedal again, and we agreed to leave the next day for Kathmandu, one hundred and twenty-five miles due east. But Larry awoke that morning with stomach cramps and the runs; so we stayed another day, and left on the sixth instead.

Our first day out of Pokhara we pedaled fifty-six miles to the settlement of Mugling. Six miles outside of Pokhara the cement bridge that spanned the river was out. We slung our bikes, with all our gear attached, over our shoulders and plunged the fifty yards through water up to our knees. The banks of the river were covered with peepul trees packed with gigantic black bats hanging upside down from the limbs.

The sky was perfectly clear, and the crests of every rise we pedaled over on our way to Mugling treated us to a spectacular view of the Himalayan peaks. The road followed a river gorge the whole way. At times, the gorge was deep and narrow, laced with waterfalls that hung like long ribbons down the sides of its rocky cliffs; other times it widened into gentle sloping valleys of rice paddies and sugar-cane fields. When the gorge was narrow, the road clung to the cliffs on one side of the river and the villages hung onto those on the other side. Suspended bridges made of cables and wooden planks were strung across the gorge, some three hundred feet above the river, connecting the villages to the road. A number of the bridges had broken cables, and sections of their walking surface hung at a precarious forty-five-degree angle.

Just before we reached Mugling, we passed a wedding procession strolling at a leisurely pace down the center of the road. A handful of musicians playing drums, cymbals, tambourines, and horns marched in front, and behind them came the groom, family members, and guests. At the rear of the procession, carried in a huge basket on the shoulders of four men, sat the bride; her face was hidden by her velvet jacket. When the musicians saw us coming, they struck up the music, and the others showered us with flowers.

Mugling proved to be nothing more than a short string of two-story wooden houses, nearly all of which were restaurants and hotels for truck drivers. The ground floor of each house was the restaurant, while the second floor provided the sleeping quarters. If the drivers filled all the beds on the second floor, the family that owned the house slept downstairs on the floor of the dining room.

We picked out the hotel with the fewest planks missing from its wooden walls, and each of us was assigned a bed on the second floor—one big room jammed with a continuous row of wooden, mattressless beds. After we'd polished off our three *rupees* worth of rice and *dal*—there were no fruit or vegetable stands in Mugling—we joined the Nepali and Indian truckers upstairs.

Sleep was hard to come by that night. The truckers stayed up talking most of the night, and they were up again by four in the morning. Downstairs, a battery-operated radio blared at full volume, and smoke from the wood-burning oven snaked up through the two-inch spaces between the wooden floor planks and attacked our nostrils and eyes. The family dog spent the whole night jumping in and out of bed with us and barking at night sounds.

By morning, Larry felt the sickest he'd felt on the trip, but he wanted to go on. The road between Mugling and the foot of the pass before Kathmandu was full of short, steep climbs that tore at Larry's ailing innards. At the top of each rise, Geoff and I would stop and wait for Larry to come crawling up the grade.

By early afternoon we had passed a number of villages and one town, but none of them had any extra food they could sell us. Even in the town, there wasn't so much as a hard-boiled egg or a banana to be had. So we pulled out our sack of rice and the last of the granola we'd picked up in Pokhara. When I poured the rice into our pot of boiling water, dozens of tiny, leggy bug bodies floated up to the surface. We watched the bodies bubble in the water for a moment, and then we looked inside the sack of rice. It was crawling with bugs.

"I'm eatin' it anyway," announced Geoff, breaking the long silence that followed our discovery. "If we toss it out, there's nothin' else to eat except for a few bites of granola, and I'm not too keen on cyclin' these mountains on empty."

Geoff steamed the rice and bugs, and we ignored the brown splotches while we ate. Fortunately, Larry's stomach managed to tolerate the boiled insects. In the late afternoon, the road took us through a long valley filled with sugar-cane fields, and we snacked on the cane the farmers offered us.

By the end of the day, Larry was having a difficult time keeping up with Geoff and me. Every fifteen minutes, he slammed to a stop, tossed down his bike, and headed for the bushes. With only two and a half miles of pedaling ahead of us, Geoff and I were once again waiting for Larry to catch up. We watched him round the curve and struggle against his pedals to push himself ever so slowly up the road toward us. It worried me to see Larry, the one who had always bounded along with a seemingly endless supply of energy, look so weak and work so hard just to guide himself and his bike over flat ground. When he reached us, he pulled off the road and curled up on the grass.

"I need a few minutes to rest before I can go on," he said in a soft, tired voice.

"Take your time and rest all you want. There's only four more kilometers left to the intersection, then we're all through for the day," I said.

"Look, you guys don't have to stay here and wait for me. I don't know how long it's gonna be before I'll be feeling up to climbing back on that bike again and pedaling; so you two go on ahead. You can take care of getting some food and a place for us to stay tonight. And by the time you get that done, I'll be on up."

"You sure you'll be OK here by yourself?" I asked.

"Yeah, I'll be fine. I just need to rest. I'm feeling really weak and nauseated right now. Every time I pedal up a hill, my stomach feels like someone's tying it in knots."

"Well, it should be pretty flat the rest of the way. You rest as long as you want, and we'll have everything ready and waiting for you up ahead."

The road stayed level for only about a kilometer, and then it took a skyward bend. While we ground our pedals against the grade, Geoff and I were wondering how Larry would fare when he hit the climb. Both of us were exhausted by the time we reached the intersection of our road with the east-bound road from India.

At the intersection, both roads merged into one and headed up over the pass into Kathmandu. The collection of ramshackle lean-tos that huddled together at the intersection presented a sorry sight. The community had three hotels. Two were wooden structures missing large portions of their walls, and the third was a two-story clay building with five tiny rooms upstairs and no beds. The man who ran the clay hotel squeezed three ragged quilts onto the clay floor of one of the rooms and motioned for us to move in. Our room was divided from the next room by four wooden planks running from the floor to the ceiling and spaced an inch apart.

Across the road from the hotel, at the string of lean-tos, I bought enough of the four items I found for sale besides the rice and *dal* meals—lemon soda, hard-boiled eggs, bread, and tangerines—to see us through dinner and the next day's breakfast and lunch. We expected to reach Kathmandu by midafternoon the following day.

Geoff and I sat outside the hotel at a table surrounded by huge baskets of manure, and snacked—and watched and waited for Larry to arrive. We could see one kilometer down the climb. It was nearly dark by then, and Larry was nowhere in sight. Just when we'd decided to go after him, his outline came into view. His pedaling appeared labored and shaky, and I ran to the edge of the settlement to meet him.

I led Larry upstairs to our clay room, and we sat down together on the quilts. I tried not to look too concerned while I watched his quivering hands fumble with the food and lemon sodas I'd set in front of him. Flat gray was the only color in his face. His skin felt cool, but beads of perspiration kept forming on his forehead, and his hands were damp. I noticed too now how thin he looked. He'd been gradually losing weight since New Delhi; but in the last three days at least seven pounds had dropped off his frame. When he began talking, his voice was uneven, as though he was out of breath.

"After you and Geoff left, I slept in the grass next to my bike for, oh, I don't know for sure, fifteen or twenty minutes, I guess, before I started pedaling again. I was OK right at first, and then I hit that gawdawful grade. As soon as I started up it, my stomach knotted up, and my head got dizzy and nauseated. I don't know how long I pedaled like that. I guess for a kilometer or so. Anyway, the next thing I can remember after thinking I was feeling really sick, is waking up in a ditch alongside the road.

"I opened my eyes, and there was this man shaking me conscious. He looked real worried. There was a little boy standing next to him and when the kid saw me come to he started yelling, 'Hello! Hello! Hello!' It took me a long time to figure out where the hell I was. I felt so weak I could barely sit up. And you know, even though I was freezing, I was sweating like nobody's business. The boy kept yelling hello, and the man kept shaking me, and finally I put it all together: I'd passed out while I was pedaling, and I'd fallen into the ditch! Can you believe it? I actually passed out! Guess I was a lot sicker today than I thought. It was getting pretty dark by the time I came to, so I must have been out a long time. Good thing that man came by!

"He and the boy helped me stand up, and they motioned that it wasn't much further on to the intersection ahead. But I'll tell you one thing—I was scared shitless I'd pass out again before I got here. I started pedaling, and my body felt cold and clammy and weaker than ever. It's a miracle I made it here. I kept singing real loud hoping that would help keep me conscious, and I tried to concentrate real hard on the fact that I only had a kilometer or two left to go. What a nightmare! Praise the Lord and pass the tangerines! Thought I'd never get here!"

Larry tried to eat a bit more food, then he pushed in his earplugs to block out Grandpa's gasping, tubercular cough in the next room, and fell asleep for ten hours. By morning his hands had steadied, but his face was still gray, and a bunch of tiny red dots that itched like heck speckled his body. I had them too; bed-bug bites. The quilts were full of bed bugs, and they'd feasted all night on our warm, innocent bodies.

Grandpa's cough sounded worse in the morning. While his family, Geoff, Larry, and I sat eating breakfast at the table outside, he made his way downstairs bundled in a blanket and out to the vegetable garden, where he moved his bowels. Because most of the vegetables in Nepal were nurtured with human fertilizer, Larry and I made sure to cook all the vegetables we bought and to stay away from lettuce.

After breakfast, the three of us started up the pass road, a narrow path of dirt and rocks with a sheer drop of a few hundred feet on one side. In some sections, the road was blocked by construction crews: men and boys clearing away the rocks one at a time by hand and stashing them into straw baskets at the edge of the road. The road surface and the steepness of the grade made for slow, tedious cycling, and it took us nearly two hours to cover the six miles to the top of the pass. For the first two miles we battled a series of muddy, rocky switchbacks, which etched the face of a vertical cliff.

In the middle of the switchbacks, we came upon a Dutch fellow standing at the side of the road. He was carefully examining his heavy, black, one-speed Hero, a giant Indian clunker he'd bought in Kathmandu and which he planned to pedal all the way to Sri Lanka. A large tin box bolted to the bike's rear rack held his possessions, and three aluminum canteens hung from the cross bar.

"Mechanical problems?" Geoff asked.

"Something's wrong with the steering," the fellow answered. Like most Dutch travelers, he spoke fluent English. "I'm having a helluva time with these turns."

Larry got off his bike and twisted the fellow's front forks.

"Damn! It doesn't feel like you've got any bearings in there," he exclaimed.

The Dutchman shrugged his shoulders. "That's what I thought," he said. "But the Nepali who sold me the bike said he'd checked out the bearings and they were fine. But I'll tell you this, it's been murder gettin' this far in these turns. Every time I hit a bump—and that's like all the time on this road—the bike changes directions, the brakes grab, and the front end wobbles all over the place. I'm scaring myself to death trying to get down this mountain. I've almost gone over the edge I don't know how many times. And hell, if you fall over the edge in *these* mountains it's curtains, sayonara and so long!"

"Look, I'm real sorry, but we can't fix the steering for you," apologized Larry.

"Hey, that's OK. Hell, I don't know why I went ahead and bought this thing when I knew all along there was something wrong with it. But the way I figure it is, if I can make it to India, I'll be OK. It's supposed to be flat down there, and there's supposed to be lots of paved roads. And anyway, I'm hoping some Indian repair shop will have some bearings and fix my forks for me. In the meantime, I've got one helluva ride outta here!"

He also had the dead body to get around once he reached the bridge at the foot of the switchbacks. When Geoff and Larry and I had approached the bridge as we started up the pass, the traffic was backed up for a half a kilometer. We'd squeezed our way past the trucks and buses to the head of the line, and found that an empty bus was inching its way along the bridge. All the passengers had gotten off the bus before it started across, and they were waiting at the edge of the bridge. There was a nervous look on everyone's face. A group of men was guiding the bus away from the left-hand side of the bridge.

"Left edge o' the bridge must be out," Geoff reasoned, after he'd surveyed the situation. He couldn't tell for sure, because the crowd standing in front of us blocked our view of that section of the bridge.

When the bus did finally come off the bridge, the men who had guided it waved for the passengers to cross, and the three of us pulled in behind them. I went first. As I rolled onto the bridge, I glanced down at the spot the bus had so carefully avoided, expecting to see some sort of structural damage. A human head was lying in a pool of its own blood. There was too much blood—I knew the man was dead. I stopped, too terrified to move past the body. A stampede of thoughts raced through my mind. Why hasn't someone moved him off the bridge? How was he killed? Maybe he'd been riding up on the roof of a bus and forgot to duck when the bus drove onto the bridge, and one of the support beams had crashed his head. But why hasn't someone rushed him to the hospital in Kathmandu?

Larry yelled at me to keep going, and I looked away from the body. I pedaled past it and on up the pass. It wasn't until two days later that we found out why no one had moved the man's body. A Nepali businessman we met in a cafe in Kathmandu explained it to us.

"They did not want to pollute the man's soul. We believe that if you die, and someone who is not a doctor or part of your family touches your body, your soul is then polluted," he said. "That is why the people were careful not to touch the man. It used to be also in the past that Hindu women in Nepal performed *suttee*. That is, when a woman's husband died, she had herself cremated along with him to show her devotion to him."

By the time the three of us had reached the top of the pass into Kathmandu, Larry was so sick he looked as if he might keel over. Geoff on the other hand was flying high.

"I'll tell you, this is the bloody best I've felt since I can't remember when!" he shouted. "That tetracycline's a miracle drug, it is. Yessir, I'm feelin' pretty good! 'Ere we are; we've climbed the pass; we've got a grand view of the 'imalayas—all those snow-covered peaks settin' out there over the top o' the ridges. There's a mountain o' letters from 'ome waitin' for me at the post office in Kathmandu; and best of all, thanks to tetracycline, now I can look forward to eatin' all that carrot cake, enchiladas, and filet mignon!"

"*Filet mignon?* What the hell are you talking about?" Larry wanted to know. "I mean, carrot cake and enchiladas? Come on, Geoff, where do you think you are anyway? This is Nepal. Remember? Rice and *dal* Nepal. If you think you're going to find all that stuff out here in the middle of nowhere, then you're flat out hallucinatin'."

"Say, Geoff. How is it you'd even know what enchiladas are?" I asked. "They don't have them in New Zealand, do they?"

"Truth is, I've never seen one. 'Aven't a clue what they are. But as soon as we get to Kathmandu, I plan on 'avin' meself a go at one. That and a lot of other foods like pies and cakes and pizza!"

"Yeah? Well, I may be sick but you're one crazy Kiwi," grumbled Larry on his way to another visit behind the bushes. "Cakes and steak!! The guy's lost his marbles!"

"All right then, if you two think I'm wacko, 'ave a look at this."

Geoff dug through his handlebar bag and picked out a thin paperback travel guide of Nepal. He flipped through the pages until he found what he wanted, then handed the book to me.

"Read," he said.

I read, and the words that popped out at me caused an immediate overflow of gastric juices in my stomach: vegetarian pizza with cauliflower, peas, tomatoes, onions, and cheese; apple crunch pie; walnut cakes; sizzling steaks with mushroom sauce; hashbrowns; chocolate pudding; and, oh yes, carrot cake, enchiladas, and filet mignon.

According to the book, Kathmandu, the capital city of one of the poorest and most backward countries in the world, where the general population lives almost exclusively on rice and *dal*, boasts one of the greatest collections of cake and pie shops and restaurants. The book listed Indian, Tibetan, Chinese, American, Mexican, Italian, and French restaurants. There was K.C.'s Bambooze Bar, Mom's Health Food Restaurant, and the Mellow Pie Shop.

"Says that a lot o' the restaurants and pie and cake places were started by American Peace Corps volunteers who stayed in Nepal after they'd finished with the corps," explained Geoff. "Between all the foreigners 'angin' out in Kathmandu enjoyin' the cheap *ganja* and mushrooms, and the foreign trekkers and mountain climbers that fly into Kathmandu and stay in the city a while to organize their climbs, there's a big demand for 'back home' food. Guess after weeks o' trekkin' and eatin' nothin' but rice and *dal*, a person could pack in a bloody lot o' pies and cakes and steaks and pizzas and all that. The book says that the cheapest pie and cake shops are on Pig Alley—there, and around Freak Street. Freak Street's where the *ganja* 'eads 'ang out. Lots o' cheap places to stay around there and plenty o' 'ash."

The day we rolled into Kathmandu, December 7, we headed straight for the post office. Nepal was a major mail stop for Geoff, who hadn't received any letters from home since Europe, and he came away with a pile of letters two inches thick. Larry and I hadn't told anyone to send mail to Kathmandu; our next mail stop wouldn't be until New Zealand.

The sight of Geoff's stack of letters and the knowledge that we'd be spending Christmastime in Nepal and Thailand, alone, in strange Hindu and Buddhist surroundings, far from our traditional family gatherings, with no word from family or friends, brought on a good case of the old familiar homesickness. Standing outside the Kathmandu post office, both of us felt a sudden longing to return home—especially Larry.

Just as the three of us walked out of the building, I ran back in and asked the clerk if by chance he had any mail for Larry and me. The short, dark Nepali man, dressed in slacks, a pullover sweater, and the colorful cap that many Nepali government employees wear, shuffled through the stack of S's, then smiled and handed me a letter. It was from Christine. In London, when we'd last seen her, Christine had talked anxiously about escaping the hassles of bicycle touring and getting back to the comforts of living in America.

"It should be somewhere around Christmastime when and if you get this letter," she wrote. "And I know you'll be feeling homesick, so I think it's important that you know that I've changed my mind about my decision to come home. I want you to know that now I wish I'd kept going. It seems like all anyone here thinks about is acquiring things—houses, cars, hot tubs, stereo systems. Everybody talks about their jobs and how much they're making and what all they've bought lately, and that's it. And what really gets me is when they complain about things like the price of gas; and yet EVERYONE DRIVES EVERYWHERE. No one would *ever* consider biking places to save gas, even when it's only a matter of blocks. After bicycling in Algeria and seeing how little most of the people have there, it's hard for me to feel much sympathy for people here who complain because they can't seem to save enough to buy that super-deluxe color television or microwave they saw in the store window a month or so back.

"So what I'm saying is, I miss the simple life on the road and I envy you both. I can't believe I gave up a chance to pedal through the Himalayas just because I was tired of being hot and dirty. Boy, a lot of us Americans are really spoiled, huh? Keep going, you two. Believe me, you'll be glad you did!"

Christine's letter helped ease our homesickness and buoy our determination. I tucked the letter into my handlebar bag, and from the post office the three of us pedaled to a hotel someone in Pokhara had recommended, the Hotel Shakti. There was only one room left, a double for thirty-two *rupees*; Larry and I took it, and Geoff found a room in a hotel up the street.

"Bet you're glad to be rid of me and 'ave a place all to yourselves for a while," grinned Geoff. "I'll be spendin' the next couple hours readin' all me letters over about a hundred times. Then I'll come back 'ere afterwards and get you two, and we'll unleash those gigantic appetites of ours on un-wittin' Kathmandu!'"

Geoff and his guidebook proved to be exactly right about the restau-rants in Kathmandu. In the scores of restaurants throughout the city, the foreigners gathered to stuff their mouths and to talk about their treks and climbs and illnesses; about the mushrooms and the *ganja*; and about the hostage crisis in Iran. Surprisingly enough, even the European hippie-types, who generally detested all that the U.S. Government and America's materialistic and consumer-oriented society stood for, sided against the Iranian captors.

The foreigners who frequented K.C.'s Bambooze Bar were the more affluent of the cheapo travelers; most were Americans, Australians, Kiwis, or British. The more down and out—the residing and drifting druggies of Kathmandu—kept to the places on the other side of town, around Freak Street and Pig Alley. Food prices there were rock bottom, but the restau-rants were also great places to pick up the hepatitis and amoebic dysentery that ran rampant among the foreigners in Nepal. Pig Alley, a dirt alleyway littered with manure, human excrement, and dead rats, catered to those who didn't mind eating off a plate or drinking from a glass rinsed in Kath-mandu's contaminated tap water after being used by someone who most probably had some nasty and highly communicable disease.

With food being his foremost concern and joy in life, Larry made a phenomenal recovery after a few days of vegetarian pizzas, steak, hashbrowns, chocolate cakes, Scotch whiskey, and a lot of rest and not much cycling. K.C.'s Bambooze Bar sat only a couple of blocks from our hotel, and Larry dropped in there at least once a day to polish off a hefty plate of filet mignon, potatoes, and steamed vegetables, for which he paid twenty-five rupees.

I didn't fare as well as Larry when it came to eating in restaurants. I knew that, with my touchy stomach, I should have stayed away from them, but they were hard to resist. For the first four days we were in Kathmandu I ate almost everything in sight, and I felt fine. Then one morning I woke up with a bloated stomach, piercing abdominal pains, and the runs. This condition continued to plague me for the rest of our stay in Nepal, which lasted another week, and it flared up now and again throughout the rest of the trip. It wasn't until a year later that I was fi-nally rid of it.

It was the filth that hit us first in Kathmandu—dead rats floating in the gutters and manure, excrement, and urine left by sacred cows and children splattering the streets and alleys. One had to be careful walking through the city in the early morning, when the Nepali performed their morning ritual of coughing up the mucus in their lungs and spitting it out the windows of their second-story bedrooms onto the sidewalks below or when they hung out the windows and blew their noses through their fingers. Occasionally there fell a stream of vomit to dodge.

But behind the filth of Kathmandu was an exotic and captivating city in slow decay. Lining its streets crowded with Nepali, Indians, Tibetans, Sherpas, Chinese, fair-skinned westerners, and bicycles and rickshaws, were ancient wooden buildings with intricate designs carved into their leaning balconies. Doorframes and window cornices were decorated with deities, foliage, and arabesque designs. Narrow gaps between the buildings opened into tiny dark courtyards housing ornate Hindu and Buddhist temples draped with flower garlands. Temples and *stupas* and hanging banners filled the streets, intersections, courtyards, and main squares. And at the top of a hill only a few kilometers from the city center, the all-seeing eyes of Swayambu Temple, the monkey temple, kept vigil over the city, its people, and the valley below.

In the center of Kathmandu, colorful, open-air fruit and vegetable markets filled whole streets. The shops edging the road were crammed with handcrafted silver jewelry, silk and rice-paper prints, handwoven Tibetan rugs, Nepali *khukuri* knives, silver Tibetan prayer wheels, and clothing made to order.

During our first couple of days in Kathmandu, Larry and I applied for our visas to Thailand and bought our plane tickets to Bangkok. With Burma and the eastern Indian states closed to overland travelers, we were forced to fly from Nepal to Thailand. We spent our remaining days exploring Kathmandu and the area between it and the Chinese border.

Nearly every cloudless morning, we would cycle some twenty or thirty miles toward China, leave our bikes in a village, and hike to the top of a nearby ridge. If the clouds didn't move in, the views from the ridges were spectacular. From the top of one of the ridges we could take in a one-hundred-fifty-mile stretch of the Himalaya, including the awesome Sagarmatha—Mount Everest.

A couple of days before we planned to leave Nepal, I was feeling too sick from something I'd eaten at K.C.'s to pedal, hike, or even take a short walk through the city. I spent the morning sitting in the hotel's grassy courtyard. It was there I met Sally, a British woman staying at the hotel. Sally looked to be in her early forties; her brown hair hung down to her shoulders, her eyes were set far apart, and she was wearing a pair of slacks and a long-sleeved sweater.

Up until a year before, Sally had lived in Bangkok with her husband, Dixie, who was working there. Then, in her search for a religious community that would fulfill her spiritual needs, she traveled to India to check out various *ashrams*. Apparently she found what she was looking for in an *ashram* in southern India run by a Benedictine priest, Bede Griffins, who blended Catholicism and Hinduism in his teachings. For the last several months Sally had lived at Griffins' *ashram*. She'd come to Nepal to meet her husband, who was flying in from Bangkok in a few days, and they planned to trek in the Himalaya for three weeks and return together to Thailand.

A Dutch girl, Titsen, was seated next to Sally in the courtyard when I walked in. Titsen, it turned out, was headed for India to visit the same *ashrams* Sally had been to.

"I know you're headed to Poona," Sally shrugged. "But I've got to tell you, Titsen, I found the man to be both insane and quite terribly dangerous. He calls himself Bhagwan, which in English means Sir God, and he rides around in a Rolls Royce, and everyone must bow when he passes."

I knew Sally was referring to Raj Neesh. Her description of him matched some of the rumors I'd heard at the campground in New Delhi.

"Oh yes," she continued. "I too went to Poona, along with the tens of thousands of other westerners, in search of the perfect *guru*. After all, I'd heard so much about him, I wanted to see for myself.

"Well, I dare say, straight away I didn't much care for the place. There's lots of free sex and intimidation going on there, and that put me off. But I decided to stay on through the first day so I could attend the next day's morning meeting, as Raj Neesh was to lead it, you see.

"He arrived at the morning gathering in his Rolls, and everyone bowed. And straight away he began talking about Mother Teresa. He was quite disgusted that they had awarded her the Nobel Peace Prize, and he stood right there and he called her a sexual pervert who gets her sexual satisfaction from touching lepers.

"Now mind you, *that*, my dear Titsen, was much more than I was prepared to take from anyone, and especially from someone who considered himself to be so holy. I was appalled by the man's words, and appalled and stunned even more to see that no one was going to take any exception to what this man was saying. It all made me so mad, I jumped up to protest. But the moment I started to open my mouth, one of Neesh's strong men grabbed me and literally threw me back down on the floor. After that, I was too frightened to move.

"I sat there and watched and listened to the man rave on, and I was suddenly overwhelmed by a great sense of evil. I mean that. I truly felt as if I was surrounded by this massive evil force. I tell you, Raj Neesh was emanating evil. I was terrified beyond words. When the meeting was over, I fled. I went back to my hotel room in the city and picked up my belongings and caught the first train south. I wanted to get far away from Raj

Neesh and his evil as quickly as possible. It was the most horrifying experience of my life, and I sobbed for days afterwards."

Titsen seemed surprised and confused by what Sally was saying.

"But so many people from Holland who have visited Poona tell me the man is wonderful," she said.

"I know. I know. I'd heard great things about him too. So you go see for yourself. But I had to warn you," Sally answered.

Sally went on to advise Titsen about a few more of the *ashrams*, then she turned her attention to me. When she found out Larry and I were headed to Bangkok, Sally insisted that we stay at her home there. Dixie would have left by the time we arrived, and we could have the place all to ourselves.

"Our housekeeper, Ubon, lives in back of the house, and she'll be there to let you in. I'll write you a letter of introduction to the landlord. He lives in the next house over," Sally explained.

I accepted the invitation. For Christmas, it would be nice to stay in a real home in Bangkok instead of a sterile, lonely hotel room.

The day before Larry and I were to leave Kathmandu, Geoff bought a ticket to Rangoon and picked up a two-week tourist visa at the Burmese Embassy. According to the travelers' grapevine, a person could buy a duty-free bottle of fine Scotch whiskey during the flight, sell it in the black market in Rangoon, and make enough profit to finance at least a week's stay in Burma. Geoff was eager to give it a try.

"They told me at the embassy that I won't be allowed to bicycle in Burma. They'll impound me bike at the airport when I fly in and keep it there the whole time I'm in the country. So I'll be gittin' around by public transportation.

"I reckon by the time I fly from Rangoon on into Bangkok, you two'll already be 'eadin' south. But who knows, maybe we'll meet up again somewhere in southern Thailand or Malaysia. I reckon on makin' a big push from Bangkok to Singapore, so that I can fly 'ome by the middle of January. But even if we don't 'itch up in Southeast Asia, I'll be waitin' for you in New Zealand. And that, my dear friends, shall be one truly great reunion!"

That night the three of us sat in our room at the Shakti and reminisced about the ride from New Delhi. We'd survived the Indian roads and the Nepali stomach ailments, and together we'd reached the Himalaya. Geoff had been a great companion and traveling partner, and Larry and I were very sad to lose him. It would be strange bicycling by ourselves again.

At six the next morning, December 17, Geoff rode with us to the airport. The sky was a clear blue, and the towering white Himalayan peaks glistened above the dark mountain ridges at the end of the valley.

Near the tiny airstrip a man wearing shorts and a blanket draped over his shoulders to shield himself against the cold morning air walked barefoot with his plodding bullock. While I watched the two, I thought about Mom Pandey back in Walling-Station, and I wondered for a moment if I would someday return to this mountain kingdom.

The jolting sound of an airplane engine brought a prompt end to my musing. Here we go again, I said to myself; another dreaded plane flight. As always when I entered an airport, my palms went clammy and my heart pounded. I stood nervously in line and waited to have my baggage checked by the security clerk. When he came to me, the clerk reached into my handlebar bag and pulled out a silver gasoline cannister. He unscrewed the cap and smelled the contents, then turned a suspicious look at me.

"It's gas for our cookstove," I explained. "I forgot to drain the bottle."

"Gasoline not allowed. I drain it," he said curtly.

I was too busy with my worries about our plane crashing to pay much attention to what the man did with the gasoline. Larry, however, reacted just in time.

"Wait! Don't pour that in there!" I heard Larry shouting behind me.

The clerk had walked into the lobby and was holding the tilted cannister in one hand and its cap in the other, about to pour the gasoline into an ashtray filled with sand. When he heard Larry, he righted the cannister, a bewildered look on his face.

"If you pour the gasoline in there and someone tosses in a lighted cigarette, it'll explode," Larry explained in a hurry.

"Yes?" answered the clerk blankly. Then a glimmer of understanding crept into his eyes. He walked outside, dumped the gasoline onto the ground, came back into the terminal, handed me the canister, and called out our flight number. Larry and I were on our way to Southeast Asia.

A LOVE-HATE RELATIONSHIP

CHAPTER SEVENTEEN

I landed in Thailand dead drunk. In a desperate attempt to dull my fear of airplanes, I'd taken full advantage of Thai Airlines' complimentary and unlimited beer, wine, and cognac. And by the time I stepped up to the sinister-looking immigration official at the airport in Bangkok, I was so inebriated that my thinking capabilities failed me completely when he demanded to know what hotel I would be staying at in town. I could do nothing more than rock back and forth on the heels of my feet and flash a foolish grin at the scowl behind the counter.

"Tell him you're staying at the Hotel Malaysia," whispered the nicely dressed young British traveler standing behind me.

"Otal Malissa," I slurred.

The official nodded and stamped my passport. An hour later, a taxi deposited two slowly sobering cyclers, their bikes, and gear at Sally's—the home of the woman I'd met at our hotel in Kathmandu.

We had returned to the twentieth century. After Egypt, India, and Nepal, the shocking sight of freeway overpasses, Mercedes and BMWs, modern buildings, computerized gas stations, swank hotels and restaurants, stores jammed with consumer items, and people dressed in the latest western fashions hit us like a sledgehammer. We spent our first few days in Bangkok feeling bewildered and disoriented. There were no warm, familiar manure piles sitting on the sidewalks, and the streets were free of cows, water buffalo, rickshaws, and men and boys urinating. Even Sally's house, located in one of the classier districts of Bangkok, was modern and roomy. The air-conditioned master bedroom contained a queen-sized bed with pillows, a mattress and box springs. And off it was a bathroom with a bathtub and a sit toilet.

Doing anything more than sit or take short walks those first days in Bangkok proved to be a real chore. The humidity, which was ninety percent or more each day, seemed unbearable. Breathing felt uncomfortable, because the stagnant air was saturated. The temperature stayed in the nineties throughout the day, and swarms of unmerciful mosquitoes gathered in any unscreened rooms. I had no idea how we'd survive bicycling in the heat and humidity of Southeast Asia, since they sapped our energy even while we were sitting still. I figured we'd probably sweat to death pedaling south.

Each morning at Sally's, the *Bangkok Post*, an English-language newspaper, was delivered to our doorstep, and after reading it for three days running, it became evident that if the weather didn't get us, the bandits in southern Thailand probably would. Every day, an article or two told how a group of bandits armed with automatic rifles, hand grenades, and, in some cases, grenade launchers, had stopped a tour bus, or a few trucks, cars and motorcycles, and robbed the drivers and passengers.

When I asked Ubon, Sally's housekeeper, what she thought about us bicycling in southern Thailand, she shook her head and waved her right hand in front of my face to convey her disapproval.

"No, no. Sout' bery bad. Many robber. No good bicycle. Many robber," she said. On that note, Larry and I decided to pay a visit to the American Embassy and find out more about the bandit situation.

At the end of November, someone had lobbed a grenade into the embassy compound, so security there was especially tight. After the Thai guards and an American marine checked us over at the entrance, a clerk directed us to the consular office. Larry explained to the Thai secretary that we wanted to register with the embassy and talk with someone about bicycling to Malaysia.

"You are going to *bicycle* through southern Thailand?" she exclaimed. "But it is unsafe to travel through there even in a car. I mean very dangerous. It would be worse on a bicycle. You wait over there. I will have someone talk with you about this right away."

A few minutes later, Marsha, a young embassy official, ushered us into her office.

"I understand you're bicycling down to Malaysia," she said.

Larry and I nodded.

"If you've read the papers lately," she frowned, "you already know about the daily holdups in southern Thailand and about the Thai pirates down there who rob the fishing trawlers. But that's the least of it. There are also a lot of murders and rapes in the south. It's a very dangerous place to be. The Thai bandits are cruel, sick people. Look at the pirates who board the Vietnamese refugee boats. They rob the refugees of everything, even their gold fillings, and they gang-rape the women and girls. We had a report from some of the foreign relief workers who work down south picking up the boat people—and the story was even published in the newspapers here—that one group of Thai pirates boarded a refugee boat and clubbed all the men to death, and then put all the women and girls on this tiny, deserted, jungle island and proceeded to hunt and rape them.

"No, I'll have to advise you against bicycling through the south," she ended emphatically.

Larry and I glanced nervously at one another, then I turned to Marsha and asked if maybe the bandits wouldn't bother to waste their time robbing a couple of ragged-looking bicyclers.

"Look, they'll stop *anyone*," she answered. "And I sure wouldn't want to be a woman bicycling down there."

The chilled tone of her voice and the look in her eyes caused a hollow sensation inside my stomach.

"Look, I know since you've come this far already that you're probably going to bike on down to Malaysia no matter what I tell you. So I'm going to give you three very important pieces of advice, and I want you to follow them to the letter. Number one: stick to the main roads; don't ever take a back road anywhere for any reason. Number two: do not under any circumstances *whatsoever* camp out. Always stay in a hotel. And number three: when you get to Malaysia, mail me a postcard telling me that you arrived there safely. Today's December 21. If I haven't heard from you by, say, late January, then I'll be contacting the Thai authorities, and, quite frankly, your next of kin."

So we *were* going to die on this trip after all, just as I'd suspected at the very beginning. We thanked Marsha for her advice, and after we left the embassy, I spent the rest of the day conjuring up horrible visions of my body splattered across the Asian highway in southern Thailand.

Another week passed before we left Bangkok. It took us part of that week to prepare for the next leg of our journey. We'd run out of tire patches in Nepal, and by now, most of our T-shirts and shorts had disintegrated. After wandering around Bangkok's Chinatown for a few hours one day, we located a handful of bike shops and bought a tire for a dollar fifty, two patch kits and some inner tubes. Another day we shopped for clothing, and the next we applied for our visas to Australia. In Athens, at the same agency that sold us our tickets to Egypt and India, we'd bought two airplane tickets on a flight from Kuala Lumpur, Malaysia, to Sydney, Australia, on the twenty-third of January. The agency had advised us that once we got to Australia, we could pick up a pair of cheap tickets to the United States, by way of New Zealand and Tahiti, at their office in Sydney.

Just as we had done when we applied for our visas to Egypt, Nepal, and Thailand, Larry and I dressed up for our interview with the Australian Embassy. I donned my skirt and best T-shirt, and Larry put on his only pair of long pants. Unfortunately, our presentable appearance did not win the approval of the Australian official who took our application. I knew we were in for it when the man refused to shake our hands as we walked into his office. Instead, he growled at us to sit down.

"It's a waste of my time and yours my talking with you," he barked. "As the receptionist told you, it takes at least a month to process a visa to our country. There are no exceptions. And besides, you have no plane ticket out of Australia; therefore we cannot issue you visas."

"If I may, I'd like to explain our problem," said Larry. "First of all, we have tickets on a flight into Australia on the twenty-third of next month, and the plane leaves from Kuala Lumpur; so we can't wait here for a month for our visas. We wouldn't have enough time to bicycle from here through Malaysia. And second of all, we can't buy our tickets out of Australia and back home until we get to Sydney, because they don't sell the ones we want here in Thailand. We have to buy them from a travel office in Sydney. So you see, it's a Catch-22 situation—we can't get a visa into your country without a ticket out, but we can't get that ticket out until we get into your country."

"You're exactly correct," sneered the official. "So why bother? As far as I'm concerned, given your ages, appearances, and the fact that you two have been traveling for over a year and a half now, I would consider it a very high probability that you are headed to Australia not only to bicycle, but also to work to get together some more money for the rest of your trip. Or maybe you're actually considering settling down in Australia. So as you can see, we would want to check you both over very thoroughly before we issued you visas. Expect a month's wait, especially right now with the Christmas and New Year's holidays. Now if you'll leave, I have work to do."

"So much for biking Australia!" I grumbled as we left the embassy.

"Now what?" Larry shrugged. "If we stick around here for a month or so waiting for our visas—and who knows if that guy will grant them to us anyway—by the time we get to New Zealand it'll be winter there. I think maybe we should forget Australia and work on getting into New Zealand instead. Let's hit the New Zealand Embassy first thing in the morning."

That afternoon, on our way back to Sally's, the curse of the Himalaya grabbed me, and I made a mad dash for the nearest restroom. After I'd finished, I gave the toilet bowl a quick glance before I flushed it. By then I'd learned to always check my bowel movements for blood or mucus, the telltale signs of dysentery.

Oh My God! I thought, as I stared into the toilet bowl, I *am* going to die, and it won't be from sweating to death or being riddled by bullets. What I saw in the toilet made my whole body feel weak. I flushed it and hurried outside.

At first I didn't say anything to Larry, because I couldn't bring myself to accept what I'd just seen. But the mental picture of it kept flashing in my head. If my days were limited, and that seemed to be the obvious though dreaded conclusion, I should tell him right away. I knew he probably wouldn't believe me right off; but later, when it happened again, he'd see for himself, and then we would rush to the hospital. But from what I'd just seen in the toilet, it was already too late.

"Barb, how come you're so quiet?" Larry asked as we continued walking back to Sally's. "You looked kind of pale when you came out of the restroom. Everything OK?"

"Well no...No, not really," I stammered.

"What's the problem?"

"Well, see...I went to the bathroom and..."

"Yes?"

"And I think I'm going to die!" I shouted.

"So what's new? You always think you're going to die," Larry answered calmly.

"Yeah, well this time it's the real thing!"

"Why *this* time?"

"Because I looked after I went to the toilet and there were these giant worms in it! Giant, huge, clear worms! Do you understand what that means?"

"Yeah, you're seein' things."

"To hell with that. I am *not* seeing things! They were there. Big, giant worms. I saw them as clear as day. And that means my intestines are full of them, and as big as they are, that means I'm doomed with a capital *D!*"

Larry didn't respond right away. He kept walking, staring at me with an I-can't-believe-you're-really-that-dumb expression on his face.

"Barb, it's impossible for a bunch of giant worms to live inside a person's intestines," he said matter-of-factly.

"But I saw them," I shot back.

Neither of us said much after that, and the subject didn't come up again until we were back at Sally's. We fixed a spaghetti dinner that evening, and just as the first bites hit bottom, the urge struck me again. I ran for the bathroom and prayed that Larry was right—that I hadn't actually seen the worms this afternoon, that this time everything would look normal.

I looked into the bowl after I'd finished, and again my body fell limp. There they were, just like before—the worms. Larry came into the bathroom and I stood back and waited for him to take a look. He seemed unconcerned when he walked in, and that calmed me. Larry will have a logical explanation for this, I said to myself, and everything's going to be all right.

"OK, let's have a look at those so-called giant worms," he muttered. There was a hint of exasperation in his voice.

I pointed into the bowl, and for a long, uncomfortable moment, Larry said nothing.

"Can't be," he finally whispered.

My hopes took a nose dive.

"This just can't be! Those worms are huge! An inch long and a quarter inch thick, each one. Man, you should be dead by now! Nobody can live with things like that in their stomach. I can't believe what I'm seeing. But look, there they are and lots of 'em. Get your passport quick! We're going to the hospital *right now!*"

The idea of entering a hospital in a strange country terrified me as much as the worms did. I thought about how the Australian fellow staying in the hotel room next to ours in Kathmandu had gone into the city hospital to be checked for dysentery and had come away with severely damaged intestines. The doctors had given him the wrong medicine. After that episode, I swore I'd never set foot in a foreign hospital.

"Barb?"

"Yeah?" I answered hesitantly.

"Barb, come here for a minute."

I walked back into the bathroom. Larry had scooped a worm and stool sample into a jar to take with us to the hospital. He stood holding the jar up to the light, studying the worms.

"Tell me what you had for breakfast this morning," he said.

"Tea, toast, and that weird grapefruit Ubon gave me."

"What was weird about it?"

"Well, it's hard to describe. Each section was made up of a bunch of these long, clear strands and—"

"And I bet they looked a lot like these worms," Larry sighed, and both of us burst out laughing.

"You're saved kiddo!" Larry chuckled in relief. "Hey, imagine if we'd gone to the hospital with this stuff. They'd be laughing for months about the weirdo Yank with the grapefruit worms in her turds!"

The next day we hit the bargain-rate travel agencies for which Bangkok was famous, and came away with a solution to our ticket dilemma: the Singapore to Los Angeles flight on a French airline. The ticket was good for a year and included stopovers in New Zealand and Tahiti. Most of the agencies listed its price at seven hundred dollars, but since everyone bargained for absolutely everything in Southeast Asia, what we would actually pay for the ticket would depend entirely on our finesse at haggling. We decided to wait until we reached Kuala Lumpur, where we were to sell back the Sydney tickets, to buy our Singapore to Los Angeles tickets from the French airline office there.

We headed to the New Zealand Embassy to see about visas. There, an extremely good-natured official informed us that, as Americans, we did not need a visa to enter New Zealand—only a ticket out of the country. When we flew into Auckland, immigrations would automatically issue us a thirty-day visa, and we could apply for an extension at the end of that month.

"I should say you shan't have any problems at all. And do have a good stay in our country," smiled the official, as he stood to shake our hands and walk us to the door.

We spent the rest of the week sightseeing in and around Bangkok. The pagodas and temples crowded with Buddhist monks in saffron robes, the colossal, gilded Reclining Buddha, the Grand Palace with its Chapel of the Emerald Buddha, and the exotic Siamese architecture were a startling contrast to the city's modern buildings and scores of massage parlors and nightclubs.

The night before we started pedaling south, Larry and I had a look at Bangkok's notorious Patpong street. We joined the flow of tourists moving along its sidewalks and peeking into the countless nightclubs, go-go bars, and massage parlors. One of the dozens of nightclub hustlers talked us into giving his club a try. He led us to a building at the back of a supermarket parking lot and rapped on the unmarked door. A panel in the door slid open, and a pair of dark, Asian eyes looked us over; then the panel slammed shut and the door opened. The hustler pushed us inside.

The large room inside contained a bar and a "show" floor surrounded by tables and couches filled with tourists. This nightclub, it turned out, specialized in lewd sex shows, but when Larry and I turned to leave, our hustler grabbed me by the arms and pleaded with me to stay and have at least one drink so he could receive his commission from the club. I pulled my arms away, and as we headed for the door, I heard someone at the bar comment, "I'll tell you, if I was married, this is one place I'd never bring me wife. Wonder 'ow long they're goin' to keep us 'ere."

There was something very familiar about the fellow's voice, but I couldn't place it, so I kept walking toward the door. Then it struck me, and I whirled around and looked back at the bar. There sat Geoff. He and Larry and I made such a racket screaming our surprise and delight at meeting up again that the club manager anxiously shooed us out the door. And the four of us—Geoff, Ken, from Toronto, and Larry and I—headed off to a coffee shop just off Patpong street.

"Well it's a bloody good thing you two came along to rescue us when you did!" explained Geoff. "We were beginnin' to think we'd never git out o' that place alive!

"Ken and I flew into Bangkok day before yesterday on the same flight from Rangoon. And everyone's been telling us to check out Patpong street, so we decided to give it a go. Anyway, we git 'ere, and some 'ustler talks us into lettin' 'im take us to 'is 'exclusive' club, and it turns out to be that place back there. Two seconds after we walk in, all these 'nice young ladies' start crowdin' around us, and they all want us to buy them drinks and so forth. So we make the big mistake of telling them straight away that we're broke and not interested.

"And the next thing we know, a couple o' these 'eavy-duty Thai thugs are standing next to us, and they tell us we've got to pay the girls for their service. When we start to argue with them and say we're leaving, they grab us by the arms and tell us they want to talk with us in the back room. Well, I may be naive, but I'm not a total blitherin' idiot, and there was no way I'd be goin' into some back room with those two karate experts. So Ken and I agree to sit at the bar and 'ave a couple drinks. After we finished the first one, we 'ad another go at leavin', but they wouldn't let us, so we started in on a second drink. And that's when you two came in. If you 'adn't a' come in tonight, we might 'ave still been in there come the mornin'.

"I'll tell you something, all right; I've decided this country is one tough place. 'Ave you two 'eard the stories 'bout the bandits down south? Can't understand 'ow it was we never 'eard 'bout the bandits through the grapevine before we got 'ere. Anyway, what I've decided I'll do is take off me 'andlebars and stuff me money down inside me bike frame. I'm not takin' any chances, no sir. As long as the bandits don't take me 'ole bike, they'll only git what little money I'll be carryin' in me 'andlebar bag."

Geoff and Ken went on to tell us about Burma, and Geoff talked about meeting up with us again farther south. He planned to sightsee for a day or two more in Bangkok, then hop a train to a town a hundred miles south and start pedaling from there. That way he would avoid all the truck traffic that bottlenecked around Bangkok. It looked as if there was a possibility he might catch up with us again in a few days.

By the time Larry and I left Bangkok, we'd become more acclimated to the heat and humidity; but even so, bicycling in Thailand was rough going, especially the farther south we got, and particularly between eleven in the morning and four in the afternoon. We never bothered to cook a morning meal; we wanted to hit the road every morning as early as possible, while the air was still cool. Our breakfasts usually consisted of a few of the sweet rice-and-coconut balls wrapped in banana leaves we'd pick up from the food stands as we headed out of town.

Finding food never presented a problem in Thailand, since nonstop snacking was the national pastime. Food stands, wedged flush against each other, lined entire streets in the towns and cities. And on the open road, every gas station we passed had an attached open-air restaurant. Meals at these food stands were so clean, delicious, and dirt cheap that we soon quit cooking for ourselves altogether. For five *baht* (twenty-five cents), we could pick out any combination of fresh vegetables, and chopped chicken, pork, beef, or duck on display, and a good-natured Thai would toss in a selection of spices and herbs and cook the mixture in a wok. A huge mound of steamed rice was always included at no extra charge. And for another three *baht*, we were given an ice cold soft drink.

Thirst was a special problem. Often it was overwhelming. The sun's rays and the clinging humidity drew rivers of sweat from our bodies all day long. Around two in the afternoon, I would feel as if I'd been thirsty all my life. The inside of my mouth would turn to cotton, and my craving for cold liquids easily edged out all other thoughts. Only ice-cold carbonated drinks provided any relief; yet five minutes after I downed one and was back on the road again, the thirst came back just as strong as before.

We followed Marsha's advice and stayed in hotels. The hotels were cheap, about fifty *baht* a night, and spotless, and there was always a fan in the room to drive away the mosquitoes and the heat and humidity. Before we left Bangkok, Larry had picked up some pamphlets from the tourist office, and we'd taught ourselves enough Thai words and phrases to bargain for hotel rooms and meals and carry on small talk with the people in the countryside.

Our first day out of Bangkok, we pedaled southwest for fifty miles, over a flat, marshy terrain, to the old jungle village of Dammoen Saduck. A compact network of narrow rivers served as its streets. The waterways were jammed with long, narrow wooden boats selling every type of fruit, vegetable, fish, meat, poultry, and prepared meal imaginable. The village residents would stand along the water's edge and hail those boats selling what they wanted to buy. The owner of one boat, a woman wearing the traditional long, wraparound cotton skirt, short-sleeved blouse, and wide, round, bamboo hat, sold only popcorn, which she popped over a kerosene burner mounted in the center of her boat.

From Dammoen Saduck, we pedaled south along the Gulf of Thailand for three days to the city of Chumphon at the edge of southern Thailand. The ride to Chumphon went smoothly, and we were able to put our worries about being robbed or murdered in the back of our minds. Truck drivers always honked and waved at us, and the people alongside the road yelled, waved, and gave us the thumbs-up sign. Even the women called out to us, and they always giggled when we waved back. Everyone in the towns and villages was friendly and cheerful and eager to help us find whatever we needed. Those who spoke some English inevitably told us that no one in their village had ever before seen a foreigner travel by bicycle.

We celebrated New Year's, 1980, in the town of Prachuap Khiri Khan, two days south of Dammoen Saduck. The town lay along a wide sandy beach edged by towering palms and jungle on one side and the clear turquoise waters of the gulf dotted with green mountain islands on the other. The local children opened coconuts for us to eat, and when we helped them tie their swing between two palm trees, they ran home and returned with a lounge chair and a cold drink for each of us. Later in the day, when they came in from the gulf, the fishermen invited us to join them in welcoming in the New Year by helping them polish off their enormous supply of Mekong whiskey.

The next day, accompanied by slight hangovers, we covered the entire one hundred twenty miles between Prachuap Khiri Khan and Chumphon, because there were no hotels along the way. It was a grueling ride. The normally flat terrain turned hilly during the hottest part of the day, and there was no breeze to take away the sweat that gushed out of us when we ground up the inclines. Our only moment of relief in the hills came when a man, who was washing his car alongside the road, tossed a bucket of cold water over us. Twenty miles before Chumphon, as the sun was setting, we collapsed at a food stand for an hour to rest our aching muscles and down eight bottles of cold carbonation before plugging on. It was pitch black out as we struggled through the final few miles of jungle and rice paddies into Chumphon, but we were too beat to worry about any nighttime bandits.

We intended to stay in a hotel in Chumphon, but when we stopped at the edge of the city and asked a gas station attendant for directions, he informed us that we could pitch our tent at the police station free. The Thai police were as pleased as could be to have a couple of American bicyclers camp inside their compound.

The compound was enclosed by a seven-foot-high barbed-wire fence; yet the police were worried about thieves getting to us at night. After we'd set up our tent on a level grassy area at the center of the compound, between the headquarters building and the barracks, an officer came from headquarters to tell us we wouldn't be safe there.

"Why not?" asked Larry.

"Because of thieves. You in south Thailand now. From Chumphon south much danger because of thieves. Very dark here. No light. Come. I show you where put tent."

We followed the officer to a small patch of grass directly in front of the main entrance to the headquarters building.

"Put tent here," he said. And then he pointed up at the floodlights on the roof of the building.

"Lights good. Thieves no like. But thieves come. I get more help."

The man disappeared into the barracks as Larry and I moved our tent to the front of the headquarters in plain view of everyone inside. I surveyed our situation. It seemed incredible to believe that we needed more protection than the barbed-wire fence, the floodlights, and the watchful eyes of the policemen in the building. But the officer soon returned with an armed guard.

"Now you safe. Guard watch tent and bicycles all night. He shoot thieves. Tomorrow you go west coast. East coast south of Chumphon no good. Many, many thieves. Thieves in mountain road and west coast yes, but less."

Larry and I smiled and shook hands with the guard, who smiled back from underneath his metal helmet, and then we crawled inside our tent and zipped the door shut. At two o'clock I was awakened from my fitful sleep for the third or fourth time. Because of the overhead floodlights, it was like broad daylight inside our tent. I looked out the window nearest my head. He was still there, our personal guard with his submachine gun and the two grenades fastened to his belt by a rubber band. I rolled over and tried to fall asleep again, and I prayed that the rubber band wouldn't snap. I'd been sweating in my sleep and my clothes were saturated. The air inside the tent was almost too moist to breathe and it was another hour before I finally nodded off.

In the morning we headed for the west coast. We hadn't gone more than about fifteen miles due west of Chumphon, however, when we blew up at each other. I don't know for sure what brought on the outburst of emotions. Probably it had something to do with the previous day's torturous one-hundred-twenty-mile ride, coupled with lack of sleep, which left us tired, irritable, and sore. And it probably also had something to do with our dread of pumping over the upcoming mountains in the humidity and sweltering heat. In addition, our nerves were edgy. Now that we'd entered southern Thailand, we rarely watched the road; we were too busy staring into the seemingly impenetrable jungle searching for any sudden movements that might indicate the presence of bandits. Our ears strained to catch human voices. We kept thinking about what the clerk at the bank in Chumphon had said to us that morning when we changed some travelers' checks: "You haven't been robbed yet? Oh, you will be."

Whatever the reason for the blowup, my few sharp words about how sick and tired I was of the heat and humidity and of doing nothing but push pedals every day were enough to set off one hell of an explosion.

Larry slammed to a stop and cut loose.

"Damn it, Barb! All you've been doing lately is bitch, bitch, bitch! Yesterday you bitched about how it was too hot to pedal the hills. And back in Bangkok, all you talked about was how sick you still felt from Nepal, and how being sick made you tired of traveling and want to quit and go home. Well, I'm sick and tired of your complaining. If you want to go home, then *go home!* I'm sick of traveling with you anyway, and I'm not doing it anymore. I've had it! This is it! We're through traveling together, so let's split up the money right now, and you give me the stove and the tools and the spare parts you're carrying. I'm going on by myself, and you can just pedal yourself right back to Chumphon, and catch the train back to Bangkok, and hop one of those cheap flights back to the States!"

Larry grabbed my bike from me, flung open my panniers and yanked out the gear he wanted to take with him. Then he threw some money and travelers' checks at me, climbed on his bike, and rode off. I watched him until he disappeared around a turn before I sat down next to my bike and cried out of frustration. We'd done it again—we'd blown up at each other when we were both feeling irritable. It was just too difficult, when we were both down at the same time, for one to remain calm while the other flew off the handle.

I could hear the monkeys scattering through the trees behind me now. I sat and cried, and after a while I looked around. The mountains were covered with dense green jungle, and a shallow stream flowed nearby. There was a gathering of houses up the hill a way—wooden structures on short stilts, with thatched roofs and no glass or screens in the windows. The houses were raised off the ground to keep them from flooding during the monsoons. Near the settlement stood a small *wat*, a Buddhist temple, and one of the monks in his saffron robes was moving down the hill toward me. Two elephants, the first I'd seen in Thailand, plodded by. The teen-aged boys riding them waved and shouted. The monk walked to within ten feet of me, then squatted down and stared curiously. We didn't say anything to each other.

I felt incredibly and totally alone. My surroundings—the jungle, the elephants and monkeys, and the staring monk—were strange and alien, and I felt as if I were miles and miles from nowhere. I felt almost hollow inside. A good part of me had just packed up and pedaled off down the road, and I wanted the monk to stop staring at me.

Eventually the monk got to his feet, grunted something and pointed down the road. Larry was coming back.

I don't remember that we said much to each other. Larry had cooled down a lot—but not completely—when he reached me, and we headed toward the west coast in silence. Sometime in the early afternoon we reconciled.

⚬⚬⚬

It was well before sunset when we reached the town of Ranong. We pulled into the first cheap hotel we came to—and there sat Geoff: "Gudday, troopers," he grinned. "Welcome to Ranong!"

Being back with Geoff again immediately buoyed our spirits. The three of us cycled to the island of Phuket. The ride took us two days, and the whole way we joked, told stories, and cursed the heat and humidity and the west coast truck drivers, who found it particularly entertaining to barrel at us head on, then swerve out of the way at the very last second.

Geoff hated the heat even more than I did, and in the late afternoon of our second day together, after we had pedaled for over two hours without passing a village, Geoff looked nearly ready to expire. The water he carried was almost too hot to drink and did nothing to quench his thirst. When we finally came to a roadside stand, its shelves stacked full of soft drinks, Geoff didn't even bother to stop and climb off his bike. He coasted inside and grabbed the bottle nearest the door. But he held onto it for only a second before he dropped it back onto the shelf.

"Now, that's the bloody 'ottest bottle I've ever 'ad occasion to take 'old of," he muttered. "I 'ope they've got some ice around 'ere, 'cause I'm at the point right now where I've absolutely got to 'ave something cold to drink or I can't push on."

He walked back outside and asked the two short, fat Thai women lounging beneath their sun and heat shield (a square thatched roof supported by four poles) if there was any ice for the drinks. When they both shook their heads and made no effort to get up, Geoff slouched down between them, groaned, and stared off into the distance. One of the women grunted, then returned to her nap. After a few minutes, the other eased herself to a standing position, sauntered ever so slowly across the street to a cluster of dilapidated huts, and disappeared.

"We might as well head off, Geoff. There aren't any power lines around here. No electricity means no ice, and that means no cold drinks," said Larry.

"Yeah, all right, just let me git meself under control 'ere. I'll take a minute to rest and collect me saliva, and then we'll go."

Geoff sat with a glazed look in his eyes for another ten minutes and started to his feet just as the woman reappeared from between the huts across the street. In her left hand she was carrying what looked like a teapot. As she came closer, we could see that it was a aluminum bowl containing two big slabs of ice.

Geoff leaped at her and grabbed for the ice, but the woman turned away and ambled over to a filthy, truck inner tube lying in the dirt. She picked up the inner tube, which had been sliced and stapled shut at one opening, and dropped the ice down inside. Then, holding the open end, she swung the tube over her head and brought it crashing into the side of one of the shack's three tin walls. The glass bottles on the other side of the wall came flying off their shelves and landed with dull thuds on the dirt floor. The woman swung the tube into the wall three times, then she tossed it back into the dirt and picked up a hatchet. With the back of the hatchet blade, she proceeded to clobber each and every inch of the tube. When she finished, she left the tube lying in the dirt while she set three glasses and three soft drinks on the wooden table in front of the shack. Then she brought the tube over to the table and emptied out a mixture of crushed ice and dirt into each glass.

"Ice," she announced.

The tube dropped to the ground, and the woman waddled back to the shade of the thatched roof. After she nodded a sluggish you're welcome to our rambunctious thank-yous, she eased herself back to a horizontal position and a deep sleep.

That evening we pedaled onto Phuket Island. It was too late to cycle out to any of the beach bungalows before dark, so we spent the night at a hotel in town. Phuket was a large tourist town, and the prices at its food stands and restaurants were higher than those in the countryside. After we checked into a hotel, we ordered our usual mixture of pea pods, bean sprouts, cabbage, watercress, and pork over rice at a nearby restaurant. We bargained the price down to the usual six *baht* per serving—or so we thought. When we finished our dinner, the owner of the restaurant wanted fifteen *baht* from each of us.

"But we already settled the price with the waiter, and we're only supposed to pay six *baht*," protested Larry.

"No, fifteen *baht*," the owner said firmly.

Larry called over the waiter and asked him to explain our six-*baht* agreement to his boss. The waiter talked with the owner for a few moments, then he turned to us and said, "It's fifteen *baht*. I made a mistake. The rice is extra and the vegetables are eleven *baht*." With that, he disappeared into a back room.

"Fifteen *baht*. You pay now." The owner had begun to look slightly agitated, which surprised us, since it was considered extremely bad manners for a Thai to lose his temper in public. We haggled with the man for another five or ten minutes, and in the end we all agreed on eleven *baht*. But by now, the man was visibly upset, even though the three of us had made sure to keep a cheerful attitude while we bargained, something Sally had cautioned Larry and me to always be sure to do in Thailand.

"I think we better be real careful right now," said Geoff. "The man looks upset, and that's quite bad from what I've 'eard. I was talking with this Dutch fellow in Bangkok, and 'e told me about what 'appens when a Thai gets mad. Yeah, 'e told me about this Thai that got mad at an American. 'E said the Thai was driving the little local bus on Ko Samui, an island over on the east coast, and when 'e pulled into this beach community where a lot o' foreign travelers were stayin', there was a big group o' foreigners and locals waitin' to catch 'is bus back to the ferry station on the other side o' the island.

"Well, everybody managed to squeeze into the bus except for this one American who, according to the Dutch bloke, was a big Rugby type. So anyway, the American decides to ride up on the roof o' the bus with 'is backpack; but the driver tells 'im 'e can't ride up there. So the big American starts arguin' with the little Thai and says 'e's goin' to ride up on the roof because 'e 'as to catch the ferry that morning. Well, the next thing anybody knows, the American is lying face down in the dirt with 'is pack tossed into the bushes. The Thai quick-like climbs back into the bus, and off everyone goes. That Thai got that American with some slick karate, 'e did. Accordin' to the Dutch fellow, the Thais are lethal with their hands. Said they don't often lose their tempers, but when they do— watch out!

"Anyway, somehow the word got around the island 'bout the American, and no one would give 'im a ride; so 'e 'ad to walk the whole twelve miles to the ferry station. So anyway, what do you say let's pay this fellow 'ere and git the 'ell out o' 'ere. I don't like 'im bein' mad."

On that note, Larry and I quickly gave the owner eleven *baht* in exact change. But Geoff handed him a twenty-*baht* bill, and only got back five *baht*.

"Four more *baht* please," Geoff smiled to the owner after he'd counted his change.

The owner's face grew tight and contorted. His eyes began blinking with rage, and I knew we were in real trouble. The man walked to a desk at the back of the restaurant. From where we were seated, I was the only one who could see him pull the knife out of the drawer. I wanted to run, but my body wouldn't respond. I remained seated, and I watched the knife. The Thai people eating in the restaurant weren't paying any attention to the owner or the blade in his hand, and for a split second I wondered if, when it came right down to it, he would in fact stab us; kill three tourists in his own restaurant over exactly twenty cents. But then I thought, this is Thailand kiddo, of course he'll stab ya.

"He's got a knife," I muttered under my breath.

"What'd you say? Couldn't make you out," said Geoff.

"I said he's got a knife. A big knife with a long blade," I answered, speaking clearly this time.

At first neither Geoff nor Larry said a word. Their eyes got big, and they stared deep into mine. Geoff, who had his back to the owner, jerked forward in his chair and gripped the tabletop so tightly his fingers went white. After a few seconds, carefully enunciating each and every syllable of each and every word, Geoff was the first to speak.

"What-is-he-doing-with-the-knife?"

"Holding it. He's holding it in his right hand."

"Is-he-coming-toward-us?"

"No. He's just standing there. But you wouldn't believe the look on his face. This guy is *really* mad. I mean, his hands are shaking."

"You think 'e's goin' to kill us? Murder us over a trifling four *baht*?" Geoff asked, speaking faster now.

"It's not the money," said Larry. "He must have lost face in the bargaining. Maybe we bargained him too low. Maybe the meal really is supposed to be fifteen *baht*. Damn! He'll kill us if he's lost face!"

"What's 'e doin' now?" Geoff demanded to know.

"Still standing there. Look, let's get outta here. Let's get out before he makes his move," I breathed.

I stood up very slowly and turned my back on the knife and the man who held it. I harnessed my feet into a walk and moved past three tables to the street. I was the first one to reach the street, then came Larry, then Geoff.

"I'm goin' back to our room, and I'm lockin' meself inside," Geoff whispered just before he disappeared down an alley.

Larry still wanted to look around the town, and I went with him. But while we walked, I kept glancing nervously behind me half expecting the twitching eyes of the restaurant owner to appear in the crowd. When we returned to the hotel, Geoff had bolted all four locks on the door of our room and was sitting on his bed with a knife he'd bought in Burma at his side. Its blade was eight inches long.

"Here. Take these," I said, tossing him a handful of hard sugar candies. "That's your dessert."

"Where'd you get these?"

"Some children stopped us out on the street and stuffed a bunch of candy in our hands, and then they started giggling and ran off. And you know what else happened? A woman in one of the shops gave me this sun visor for free. Imagine that!"

Geoff shook his head.

"Can't figure Thailand out," he sighed. "One minute somebody's pulling a knife on you and the next they're 'andin' you candy and a sun visor. It's a weird love-hate relationship I've got goin' with this place. I love the food and the beaches and the cheap prices and the Siamese architecture and *wats* and all; but I 'ate worryin' about the bandits and the people turnin' on me, and the 'eat and 'umidity, and those crazy, reckless truck drivers. Well anyway, I'm still sleepin' with me knife under me pillow tonight, that's for sure."

In the morning, on January 5, we pedaled through the island's rubber-tree plantations to Karon beach. Two days later, Geoff took off for Malaysia and Singapore. Larry and I stayed at the beach for another two weeks, and if it hadn't been for the refund on our tickets to Australia, which we were to pick up in Kuala Lumpur by the twenty-first, we would have stayed longer.

Karon was paradise. Its half-moon, white sand beach curved for a mile and a half along the transparent turquoise waters of the Andaman Sea. Where the sand ended, the palms, the lush green jungle, and swaying rice paddies began. At one end of the beach, tucked amid the palm trees, was a gathering of thatched bungalows. Along the sand stood a few open-air restaurants—nothing more than tiny kitchens and a cluster of wooden tables and chairs—but they served everything from rice and vegetables, to fish caught that day, to pineapple milkshakes and french fries.

We rented one of the bungalows for fifty-five *baht* (two dollars and twenty-five cents) a day. Its wide wooden porch looked off into the jungle, and inside was a double bed and a bathroom with a shower, squat toilet, and faucet. The bungalow's only drawback was the gigantic hairy spiders—each one measured eight inches in diameter including its legs—that materialized on the ceiling at night. But once we discoverd that a blast from our can of dog repellent was enough to send them scattering back outside, they no longer presented any problem.

Larry and I spent our first glorious afternoon in Karon body surfing and snorkeling over beds of brilliant coral. The gentle swells that rolled in against the beach were made for body surfing, and for five *baht*, one of the food huts rented us snorkels and masks for the entire day. Swimming in the cool water beat the hell out of grinding bike pedals in the heat and humidity all day. We floated in the sea until sunset. In the evening, we sat in one of the restaurants and listened to the waves, watched the moonlight dance across the water, and devoured coconut milkshakes and fresh fish cooked in a sweet and sour sauce.

The mornings in Karon were special. They were lazy mornings, perfect for lovemaking and soothing tired minds and muscles. Each morning we stayed in bed as long as we wanted after the first rays of sunlight had filtered through the woven walls of our bungalow and coaxed us awake. Karon was the resting place where we allowed our bodies and innards to rebuild after the rough treatment they'd received in Egypt, India, and Nepal, and where we were afforded a much-needed break from cycling and traveling. On a long bike journey, it's nice to sometimes step away from the flat tires, the broken spokes and brake cables, the travel preparations and sightseeing, and the hours of pedaling. For two solid weeks, we never once worried about fixing breakdowns, finding spare parts or a place to stay at night, or getting sick on the food or water.

On our second day in Karon, we walked to the opposite end of the beach and discovered a small group of bungalows perched on the side of a hill overlooking the beach, a lagoon, and a tiny island covered with palm trees. Each bungalow had a table and two chairs and a tiled bathroom. The price was steep for Thailand, one hundred and fifty *baht* a night, but we decided to splurge for two nights, then return to the cheaper bungalows for the rest of our stay.

In the morning, we loaded up our bikes and pedaled out to the hillside bungalows. The dirt road wound through the jungle, past rice paddies and raised wooden houses. The people we passed were already dousing their bodies with water from their wells to cool themselves off. Just before we reached the bungalows, the road came to an abrupt end at a wide lagoon, which ran from the jungle to the sea. We heaved our bikes onto our shoulders and waded through the shallowest part of the lagoon. Supan, the young Thai who owned the bungalows, was waiting for us at his tiny restaurant on the beach. His pet monkey chattered excitedly when he spotted us approaching.

We made friends our first day with the local fishermen, who got together in the late afternoons at a huge beach hut not far from the bungalows. They invited us to join them in their afternoon ritual of investing countless bottles of Mekong whiskey and mounds of coconut pastries. Afterward, we would body-surf, then walk home along the beach. At sunset, Supan would bound up the hill to our bungalow with a feast as exotic as the view from our porch—fish cooked in a pineapple, tomato, and cucumber sauce, fried rice with egg and vegetables, and two Mai Tais in hollowed-out pineapples. I was beginning to wonder if we'd died and gone to heaven.

When darkness set in, the fishermen lined the lagoon and fished by the light of the bonfires they built along its banks. The firelight illuminated the nets tossed into the air, glimmering sprays of delicate white mesh across the black of the night. We stayed on the porch until nearly midnight and watched the fires and listened to the sea and the jungle.

In the morning, when the shadows receded from the beach, the lagoon and the sand turned white, the water began to sparkle, and the palms on the tiny island moved gently in the breeze, the fishermen pushed their handcarved wooden sailing canoes off the beach and into the sea. And the young Thai boy who worked at the restaurant below us waded across the lagoon, past the herons and water buffalo, to pick up first the enormous block of ice, and then, on his next trip, the box of supplies left at the end of the dirt road by the early morning delivery truck.

Four days passed before we were able to pry ourselves away from Supan's bungalows and return to the low-rent district at the other end of Karon beach. But life at the other end, though not as perfect as at Supan's, was paradise too, and we settled into more days and evenings of snorkeling, body surfing, reading, resting, and feasting on fish and coconut milkshakes. We also discovered Kata beach, just below Karon. Except for its one cold-drink hut, Kata was almost always deserted during the day, and its coral and sunsets were even more spectacular than Karon's.

When it came time for us to start pedaling south in order to reach Kuala Lumpur by the twenty-first, we were in no mood to leave. But we didn't want to lose the plane ticket refunds, so we hit on a compromise. We would stay in Karon for another week, until just before the twenty-first, then catch the bus from Phuket to the train station in Hat Yai, southeast of Phuket near the Malaysian border, and from there, the train to Kuala Lumpur. After we'd taken care of the tickets, we would pedal through the jungles of central Malaysia back to southern Thailand, then south along Malaysia's quiet east coast, to Singapore. That way we could avoid the congested, industrial west coast of Malaysia.

It was during our second week in Karon that we discovered that all was not well in paradise. First, Larry noticed an armed guard roaming around the bungalows at night. We were informed that he'd been hired to keep away any thieves. A few nights later, two robbers tried to enter one of the bungalows. The woman inside screamed bloody murder, the guard unloaded a barrage of bullets everywhere, and the thieves fled. After that episode, the Thais cut loose with all sorts of stories about bandits robbing people on the beaches in broad daylight, and about bandits killing two foreigners on the beach near the bungalows. Like the rest of Thailand, Karon had its two sides, although in Karon the good far outweighed the bad. When our second week came to an end, we wanted to cling to our paradise of sorts, and yet we felt a sense of relief knowing that very soon we would no longer need to worry about Thai bandits. But first came the bus ride to Hat Yai.

The bus left from downtown Phuket. We pedaled into town early in the morning and loaded our bikes on the roof along with an assortment of boxes and crates. There were only two other foreigners on the bus, an Australian woman and an Englishman. And the Englishman had some words of advice for the rest of us.

"All right now, I'm givin' you folks some advice, since I've been ridin' these buses all over Thailand, and I've learned a thing or two in the process, I 'ave. First of all, always sit in the back o' the bus so you can keep an eye on that door to the luggage compartment where they'll put our gear. 'Cause if you don't keep an eye on your gear, some bloke'll bloody well take off with your things at one of the stops, and you'll never see 'em again, you won't. You've got to keep your eyes on everything that's yours on these buses, and don't trust anyone, not *anyone*. I was settin' next to the relief driver on the ride down 'ere from Bangkok, and the bloody bastard lifted me watch right off me wrist, 'e did. Oh, 'e was smooth, 'e was. I never felt a thing, not a thing, mind you.

"I don't fancy this ride to 'At Yai. Just as soon as give it a miss if I could. But I'm on me way to Malaysia, and so I've got to go through southern Thailand. No way around it. But I've 'eard this route takes us right through these mountainous areas packed with Communist insurgents. The insurgents normally stick to pickin' off the military, but I've 'eard tell too they'll rob a bus when they need money. I'm keepin' me money well hid on this ride, I am, and I'd advise you three to do the same."

The Englishman and the Aussie sat in the last row of seats at the back of the bus, while Larry and I took the next row up. Ten minutes after we climbed onto the bus, our Thai driver, dressed in jeans and a black T-shirt, jumped into his seat and drove his foot into the gas pedal. We blasted out of the bus station at full speed. When we barreled into the first curve in the highway, the driver didn't slow down. I realized our chances of surviving the eight-hour ride to Hat Yai were close to nil. The man drove like a maniac. He put the bus into a forty-five-degree tilt at every curve, and each time I swore we'd never pull out in time. The farther we tilted, the deeper into the arm rests I dug my fingers. My stomach knotted up, and my throat refused to swallow. But each time, just when I'd given up all hope, the bus would miraculously bounce back onto all fours.

"Not to worry!" yelled the Englishman over the bus's deafening motor. "They all drive like this. If you think this is bad, you should 'ave been on that ride with me from Bangkok. It was nighttime, and we pulled out in front of the oncomin' traffic all the time to pass the cars and buses and lorries in front of us. Don't know why we never 'it anyone 'ead on. Every time we pulled out into some lorry's blindin' 'eadlights, I swore we'd never make it. But we did; so I reckon these blokes must know what they're doin', all right."

The Englishman's words did little to reassure me, and I continued to cringe in horror at each curve. Larry, on the other hand, was worried about being robbed. The fact that we'd stashed all our money, travelers' checks, passports, and credit cards into our handlebar bags at our feet made him uneasy. And too, there were the military roadblocks to worry about. Each was enclosed by rolls of barbed wire and contained one or more machine-gun nests and often a tank and grenade launchers. In the regions where the insurgents were especially thick, tanks patrolled the highway. At the roadblocks, soldiers armed with submachine guns and grenades boarded our bus and searched for suspected insurgents and smuggled guns. And often they asked to see people's identification.

"Look Barb," said Larry at our third or fourth checkpoint. "It's only a matter of time before we get ambushed by the insurgents in one of the mountain jungle areas between the roadblocks. We're nothing but sitting ducks. The bandits and the insurgents all know when this bus is coming through, and if they want to rob us, who's to stop them? I think we should split up our valuables. We'll leave some money and the camera in our packs so there'll be something there for them to take and they won't get too suspicious. But I'm hiding the rest of the stuff."

"Do what you want," I shrugged. "You know me. Good ol' Barb's over here worrying about dying as usual. You can take care of worrying about the bandits 'cause I'm all tied up praying us through the curves."

What Larry did next, however, managed to draw my attention. I couldn't believe what I was seeing. First, he pulled out our trusty roll of silver duct tape, which by now we'd used to hold together everything from fenders, brake levers, and panniers, to shoes. Next, he taped our credit cards to the inside of the top part of his legs underneath his shorts. Then he opened the book he was reading and taped our duplicate credit cards to one of the middle pages. After that, he placed our travelers' checks and passports into a plastic bag and dropped the bag in with the banana peels in the trash bag we'd hung from the back of the seat in front of us. All this took only a matter of minutes, and although Larry tried to be very secretive about what he was doing, I was sure that the Thais sitting across the aisle had witnessed everything and were wondering what in the world would possess a man to tape small pieces of white plastic near his private parts.

A few hours after Larry had completed his task and informed me that he thought everything, except for the small amount of cash he'd left in his front handlebar pack, was safely hidden from any insurgents or bandits who might hold up the bus, the young boy who took care of loading and unloading the luggage at each stop noticed that our trash bag was full and decided he'd get rid of it for us. Just as the boy was preparing to heave the bag through an open window, Larry leaped to his feet and snatched at it. But his hand scratched a hole in the bottom of the bag and out tumbled everything. The boy and everyone seated in the rear section of the bus stared in total bewilderment at the collection of travelers' checks and American passports that plopped onto the floor, along with wadded cracker wrappers, banana peels, and used kleenex. They stared at it all for a while, then they turned their curious eyes on Larry.

As fate would have it, when Larry jumped up to save the bag, his shorts caught on the duct tape, pulling one end loose. So there he stooped, picking through the mess on the floor, trying to gather up our valuables as quickly and inconspicuously as possible, our credit cards dangling from his crotch. I was laughing so hard I could barely force myself to watch.

A few hours later, the bus dropped us off at Hat Yai, alive and with all our possessions, and the next day we hopped the train to the Malaysian border.

From the border, we caught the overnight train to Kuala Lumpur, a congested city that was very modern in parts. We stayed there just long enough to pick up the money Dad had wired to the Bank of America, which would last us through the rest of the journey, and to settle our refund and buy our plane tickets back to America.

The swank airlines office was housed in a deluxe hotel next door to the Hilton and the Bank of America. One of the airline clerks ushered us into a back room, and there the three of us spent nearly two hours haggling over the price of the Singapore to New Zealand to Tahiti to Los Angeles flight. The clerk began the bargaining by asking seven hundred and fifty dollars (fifteen hundred Malaysian dollars), and we countered with a six-hundred-dollar offer. By the end of the session, Larry and I had pared the price tag down to six hundred and sixty-eight dollars. We were given reservations on the February 7 night flight from Singapore to Auckland.

Malaysia was even hotter than Thailand and equally humid, so we took it slow and easy pedaling through its central jungles and along the eastern coastline. The parts we put on our bikes back in London now had some four thousand miles on them, a lot of them over dirt and rock roads, and they were worn and tired. Our supply of spare parts was dwindling. Just north of Kuala Lumpur, when his rear derailleur cracked in two and fell into the spokes (breaking a few in the process), Larry slapped on our last spare derailleur. Our chains had stretched out and no longer mated properly with the gear teeth, which themselves were badly worn, making shifting difficult. Two of the teeth on the smallest gear of Larry's rear cluster had broken off, and we were getting low on brake and shifter cables. The supply of spokes we'd bought in Athens was still holding up, but unfortunately the bike shop had sold us the wrong nipples, and every time we changed a spoke we had to remove the old nipples from the old spokes to use them on the new ones. When it came to spokes though, I was batting a thousand. After over eighteen thousand miles, I still hadn't broken a single one.

From Kuala Lumpur, we pedaled north through the hilly jungles and rubber-tree plantations to Kuala Lipis, where the road ended, and we caught the train through the more remote jungles to Kuala Kerai, in northern Malaysia. From there we pedaled northeast to the coast of the South China Sea. Between Kuala Lumpur and Kuala Lipis, and Kuala Kerai and the coast, the jungles were crammed with chattering monkeys, which often sat at the side of the road with their hands on their knees watching the traffic go by. Communist insurgents hid in these jungles, and tanks and military roadblocks were everywhere. But everyone assured us that in Malaysia the insurgents never bothered the common people, only the military. A lot of the jungle roads were embedded with alligators and giant snakes run over by passing motor vehicles; and enormous spiders, much larger than the ones in the bungalows at Karon beach, hung from the power lines. Fortunately, the sight of snakes and spiders no longer made my skin crawl—I'd finally become accustomed to it.

As in the rest of Malaysia, Malays, Chinese, and Indians lived in the jungle towns and villages. The Malays looked like dark-skinned Polynesians and dressed in sarongs or western-style clothing. They were primarily Muslims, and they loved their hot, spicy foods. They were laid-back people, so it was the Chinese that ran most of the businesses in Malaysia.

Along the east coast, the pace was slow and easygoing. We pedaled through sleepy fishing villages and deserted tropical beaches and never worried about bandits. But the east coast people were standoffish, and we had a tough time finding food and drink in the sparsely populated areas between the major towns. What little food there was at the occasional food stands we came across, usually rice, tiny fried fish, and a spicy cabbage and pineapple mixture, ran us two to three times the price of a meal in Thailand.

And then came Singapore, the ultramodern shopping center of Southeast Asia, where a McDonald's had sold more Big Macs on its opening day than any other McDonald's in the world—or so the rumor went. Out of the Malaysian jungles and beaches, with their primitive, raised wooden and thatched houses, we pedaled into bustling, rich, spic-and-span Singapore, and did something which we hadn't been able to do in well over a year. We walked into an A&W rootbeer stand. It was a spotless place, sitting in the grassy island of a wide, tree-lined boulevard. Sweating fiercely from the morning's sizzling ride onto the island, we sat down to two of the coldest, most divine-tasting rootbeer floats ever to be had. The Chinese man sitting next to us looked at the expressions of sheer ecstasy on our faces and then at our tired, battered, and filthy bicycles and packs leaning against the side of the building.

"Where you come from?" he asked, turning his eyes back to our faces.

"Malaysia."

"I mean where you from?" he corrected himself.

"America."

"Ah! You bicycle around world from there to here?" he smiled broadly.

"Except for the Middle East," I answered.

"Oh yes, very bad there. You fly home now?" he asked.

"No, we're headed to New Zealand and Tahiti first."

"And South America?"

"That we're saving for another trip," said Larry. "That and maybe central and southern Africa. But right now we're running out of money, and we've been on the road for almost two years. We're ready to go back home and stay put for a while. Then maybe we'll set out again if the itch hits us."

The man translated our conversation for his two children and then turned back to us.

"Congratulations, both of you. You come long, long way."

I smiled and nodded to the man. It had been a long, long way. I put the frosted glass mug up to my mouth, tilted my head back, and watched the last of the ice cream come sliding down.

WORLD'S FRIENDLIEST FOLKS

◆ CHAPTER EIGHTEEN ◆

It was well after midnight when we landed in Auckland. At the suggestion of the information-desk people, who sold us maps of North and South Islands, we spent the night on some nicely padded couches in the lounge on the second floor of the airport. We leaned our bikes against the couches, pulled out our down jackets for pillows, and passed out until seven in the morning, when the early morning passengers marched in.

The cold felt strange when I stepped out of the terminal. It was a sensation I hadn't experienced in nearly two months, not since Kathmandu, and I hurried to pull on my sweatshirt and wool socks. Yet if the cold made us feel out of place, what met Larry and me after we'd pedaled across the airport parking lot only added to our disorientation. We had expected to find a freeway connecting the airport with the city of Auckland, but there was nothing at the end of the lot but a two-lane country road along which rambled a few old British-made cars. Auckland was nowhere in sight. In fact, for as far as the eye could see, there was nothing but green rolling pastures. It seemed incredible, but the evidence spread out for miles. Auckland's international airport was sitting smack-dab in the middle of cow and sheep pastures. We'd made it to New Zealand, the land of three million people and sixty million sheep.

For the next two months, we wove our way side by side along the tranquil two-lane roads of North and South Islands. There was a startling absence of litter, noise, and crowds. And because only seventeen percent of its citizens lived outside of the cities, there wasn't much traffic in the countryside. We rarely had to cycle single file.

We were cruising. We'd returned to "civilized" bicycle touring.

Everyone spoke our language, and we were no longer forced to communicate with people in some awkward mixture of grunts, hand motions, and a few foreign words. There was no need to hassle with purifying water or to worry about getting sick on it or the food we ate. We camped out anywhere we pleased without a thought about cobras, bandits, crowds of staring faces, or government regulations forbidding free camping. The campgrounds in New Zealand, which we rolled into now and then when the idea of a hot shower struck our fancy, provided washers and dryers; kitchens with stoves, ovens, toasters, and sinks; and rest rooms filled with sit toilets and hot showers.

The scenery that greeted us ran a broad spectrum. Punctuating the twenty-two million acres of rolling, emerald pastureland were tropical coastlines with rocky or sandy beaches, volcanoes, and geysers; snow-covered mountain ranges, glaciers, crystal clear rivers; streams and lakes that boasted some of the best trout fishing in the world; fjords and pine forests. The only drawbacks we encountered in this spotless, unspoiled outdoors were high winds, cold rainy weather that set in without notice, and, especially along South Island's west coast, bloodsucking sand flies.

In New Zealand, it seemed we encountered more than a bicycler's fair share of stiff head winds and side winds. Our worse day came as we pedaled south out of the city of Christchurch, in South Island, and into a gale-force windstorm, which ripped across the Canterbury Plain and pounded us from the side. For twenty miles we fought the wind, until a thundering blast of air blew my bike completely out from under me and sent Larry and his bike skidding across the road into an oncoming car. I bounced into the shoulder of the road; the right side of my body dug a long, deep trough through the gravel while my bike stayed tangled in my legs. The fall did an extremely painful job of removing all the skin from my right thigh.

Larry pulled through his collision without an injury, and after we finished the touchy task of digging gravel out of my body, we walked our bikes in hopes that the wind would die down soon. Since we couldn't keep our footing in the gravel, we walked on the edge of the pavement. I turned my back to the wind and leaned into it to avoid being tossed over on top of my bike and back across the shoulder. I held onto my handlebars with my right hand and with my left I clasped my saddle. Moving forward without falling over was a real struggle. At times the force of the gusts was strong enough to flick my seventy-pound bike into the air as if it were nothing more than a cardboard box. There it flew, lying on its side in midair, parallel to the ground, tugging at my grip. Straining to maintain my balance, I'd give the bike a yank and bring its wheels back down onto the ground, and then I'd stumble on down the road until the next blast of wind sent my bike and gear skyward again.

We walked for a half hour, but the winds never died. Eventually we mustered enough nerve to climb back onto our bikes. Weaving back and forth across both lanes of traffic, we struggled forward until we came to a sheltered river basin, and there we spent the night, praying that the gales wouldn't demolish our tent.

The winds, the steep climbs, the rocky roads that ate up our tires, and, during rainstorms, the landslides that buried whole sections of the road beneath a mattress of mud and boulders, all made for some physically tough cycling in New Zealand. Yet it was something else all together that oftentimes prevented us from pedaling at all, something that some days made the simple act of cycling from point A to point B impossible, and that something was the Kiwi hospitality.

The New Zealanders, especially those who lived in the countryside, were rugged individuals, and without a doubt the friendliest and most kindhearted people we'd ever come across. In Thailand foreign travelers talked about the bandits, the beaches, the cheap food, and the massage parlors. In Nepal, talked centered around trekking, drugs, and getting sick on the food and water. In Egypt, it was the pyramids, Luxor, and the dirt; while museums, cathedrals, and old quaint villages filled travelers' conversations in Europe. But in New Zealand, it was the people that travelers talked about. Every tourist we met, unless confined to a structured tour group, had his or her own Kiwi hospitality story to tell. And the two Israeli students who stopped to talk with us while we sat munching granola and Granny Smith apples outside a grocery store on North Island were especially anxious to recount theirs.

"We were hitchhiking into Wellington this one afternoon," explained one of the two women, "and this middle-aged couple picks us up, and right away they invite us to have tea—that's what they call supper here—and spend the night at their home in the city. Well, of course we accepted the offer. And in the morning when we were getting ready to leave, the husband sits us down, and you won't believe what he says to us. He says, 'Me and my wife talked it over last night, and we've decided that a person can't see all too much of the country by hitchhiking. The prettiest scenery in New Zealand is back in some of the most unpopulated areas, up deserted roads where not too many people go. There wouldn't be enough traffic on those roads for you two to hitchhike in and out without running the risk of being stranded in the middle of nowhere for a day or two waiting for a car to come by. So here's what we'll do. I'll mark on your maps the places I think you should see on both islands, and then you can take one of our cars and drive it around everywhere for the rest of the time you're in New Zealand. Keep it for as long as you want, a month, whatever. Then when you're finished, just drop it back by here.'

"I'm serious! I'm telling you the truth. That's exactly what the man said to us, and that's exactly what he did. He loaned two total strangers, two foreigners no less, his car for a month and a half, and that's it parked right over there. Now you tell me just where else in this whole wide world you're going to find people like that! These Kiwis are remarkable! We met this Canadian couple at the campground by the volcanoes over at Chateau Tongariro. They had hitchhiked in, and the Kiwis who gave them the ride in drove back to their house in Turangi, thirty miles away, hitched up their trailer, towed it back up to the campground, and left it there for the Canadian couple to stay in! I could go on and on. This place is hospitality heaven!"

If Larry and I grumbled through the head winds and the cold and the rain and the bugs in New Zealand, we were also served up some pretty generous portions of Kiwi hospitality, which more than made up for the weather and the insects. From the Auckland airport we had expected to reach Geoff's house in Gisborne, southeast of Auckland, in just four days. When we finally showed up a week later, Geoff wanted to know what took us so long.

"What took us so long?" bellowed Larry. "Man you're lucky we got here at all! I thought for a while there we'd have to take up bicycling at night to get here before our hair turned gray and our teeth fell out! Every time we stopped to eat a snack along the way, someone'd come waltzing over and either spend the next hour or so talking with us or invite us home for the rest of the day, for tea, and for the night! The first few times it happened, we happily took the folks up on their offers, and we sure had some great times visiting with them, seeing how they lived, hearing about New Zealand's sixty million 'shit-hot little woolies' and their one hundred percent plus lambing rate, and learning about the native Maoris and their culture.

"But pretty soon it became real apparent that if we accepted everyone's invitations, we'd never get here to see you. So then we started turning down people's offers right and left. But hell, sometimes they'd even pull up alongside us while we were pedaling down the road and offer us a lift to their houses so we could spend a few days with them! And if we asked permission to pitch our tent in someone's pasture for the night, we'd always get invited in for tea and an all-night talk session. When we pulled up to the little grocery stores, sometimes the owners would go running into the back room and quick fix us a pot of tea and some biscuits!

"You know, it was raining this morning when we came down out of the mountains into Gisborne, and three different drivers waved us over to offer us a ride or a place to say. I'm telling you, Geoff, this here country of yours has one enormous collection of the friendliest, kindest, and most caring souls imaginable!"

"Yeah?" Geoff grinned. "Well then, welcome to New Zealand, troopers!"

Larry and I stayed with Geoff and his family at their home in Gisborne and at their lakeside cabin near Rotorua for a week. We did some sightseeing; feasted on roast legs of lamb, potatoes, vegetables, salads, and gallons of creamy New Zealand ice cream; went swimming and water-skiing; and reminisced with Geoff about our travels together. We visited the family's kiwi orchards, and spent some time at Geoff's twin brothers' farm. The twins farmed with Clydesdales; and they tended bee hives and packaged and sold the honey.

The day we left Gisborne, Geoff promised he'd come and visit us in America. That someday the three of us would get together again was something we all considered supremely important. Ours was a valued friendship, cemented by our having gone through so much together.

"Someday years from now we'll get together and we'll lie back and kick our feet up, and we'll have a beer, and we'll talk about Jingus, and the lug nuts goin' by Larry's 'ead, and the Thai that pulled the knife on us over a lousy four *baht*, and we'll laugh about that memorable mornin' when little Barb shat in the shower, and we'll feel just like we're doing it all over again. You wait and see, my friends; maybe when I'm forty and you two are pushin' fifty, I'll ring you up on the phone and yell, 'Hey mates! Let's pack it up and do it again!' And off we'll go! And who knows, maybe by then I'll 'ave meself a wife and a few kids to bring along with us!"

From Gisborne we headed down to South Island. The population was sparser than on North Island, and the towns were often few and far between. The people on South Island, though always friendly, kept more to themselves, and they rarely invited us into their homes.

We pedaled along the quiet roads and camped on the beaches, next to glaciers, and in the mountains beside deserted lakes and streams. And if we happened to come into a town around lunchtime, we'd prop our bikes against the local pub, stroll inside with our apples, bread, and peanut butter, and order an ice-cold pitcher of hearty New Zealand beer for just over a dollar. Afterward, we'd hit the local grocery store for a gigantic ten-cent scoop of vanilla ice cream.

Because it boasted more natural beauty than North Island, and because there was so little traffic on its roads, the hundreds of foreigners bicycling around New Zealand during December through March, the summer months in the southern hemisphere, spent most of their time on South Island. It seemed strange to see other touring bicyclers on the road. Except for Geoff and the Dutch fellow in Nepal, we hadn't encountered another bicycler with panniers in Egypt, India, Nepal, or Southeast Asia. For the last four months, from Cairo to Singapore, our appearance and mode of travel caused nearly everyone we passed to drop whatever he or she was doing and stare or shout in amazed disbelief. But now we were nothing more than one of the scores of American bicyclers pedaling around South Island in the summertime of 1980.

Besides the foreign cyclers, there were quite a few New Zealanders touring on bicycles. Now that the price of gasoline had shot skyward, the Kiwis were taking up bicycling in a big way. In the cities and towns, people of all ages used their bikes, equipped with wire baskets, to do their shopping and run errands. It was refreshing to see a whole country turn toward the bicycle as an alternative means of transportation. The New Zealanders had found that they could slash their car expenses and gas consumption, help reduce air pollution, and keep fit all at the same time by simply relying a bit more on their bikes.

With the blossoming interest in cycling, the demand for bicycles in New Zealand far surpassed the supply on hand, and the government's stiff tariffs on imported goods made the price of a shiny new Raleigh, Nishiki or Centurion extremely steep. This situation caused many Kiwis to look forward to the stream of American cyclers. After the Americans had finished their tour, the New Zealanders would buy their bicycles for a price much lower than they would pay in a shop in New Zealand—but much higher than the Americans had paid for the bikes. By selling his bike in New Zealand, an American could make enough profit to buy another one when he returned home and pay off part of his air fare for the trip as well. Some Americans put up FOR SALE notices in the bike shops in Auckland or Christchurch when they flew in, and by the time they completed their tour through the country and returned to the shop, a list of prospective buyers was waiting for them.

While Larry and I made our way around South Island, we talked and pedaled with many of our fellow cyclers. Like any group, the bicycle-touring population had its own collection of some rather choice characters. There was Jim, the seventy-year-old American gent. He was diligently covering all of New Zealand on his trusty three-speed, to which he'd strapped three plastic trash containers: two large ones on either side of his rear wheel and a small one to his handlebars. The three containers were bright orange with green lids and held a jumbled mixture of clothes, food, tools, books, trash, soap, spare parts, and whatever else Jim had decided to toss in.

"Basically, I'm a confirmed slob," he explained to us, and everyone else he talked with. "So these here trash cans are perfect for me. Wouldn't know what to do with them fancy packs like you got there, with all them complicated pockets and compartments. Lord knows, I never organize or pack my stuff. Just throw it all together however, and when I need something I paw through it all 'til I find it. Suits me fine and dandy."

As we parted company after our lunch together, Jim turned to Larry and whispered something.

"What was that?" Larry asked. "I didn't hear you."

"I said to keep your eyes out for Debbie," Jim said aloud.

"Who's Debbie?"

"Debbie? Why Debbie's..." Jim's voice trailed off, and I could tell by the look in his eyes that we'd lost him. After a few moments, he shook his head. "Oh, you'll see when you meet her," he grinned mysteriously.

Then there was Roger, the British chap we met sitting outside a grocery store in a small town south of Christchurch. Roger was quick to inform us that whenever he got tired of pedaling, he'd remove his front wheel and stand at the side of the road holding it in the air.

"Works every time," he said. "The drivers stop straight away. They think I'm some poor sap that's 'ad 'is bike break on 'im, and they give me a ride to wherever I fancy to go. At first I tried plain 'itchhikin', but it didn't work out. No one picks up an 'itchhiker with a bike and panniers. But they'll always 'elp a bloke they reckon's stranded with a bum bike, they will."

Roger looked to be in his midtwenties, and while he talked, he was eyeing us curiously.

"Say," he said after a moment's pause, "aren't you the two cyclers that were stayin' at the Golden Hotel back in—Let's think now. When was I in Cairo? Must 'ave been November. No, make that October. In October; that's it, October. Were you the two with the bikes? I couldn't believe anyone'd be game enough to bicycle in *that* country. Not me, anyway. Was it you two?"

Larry and I stared back at Roger, too amazed by the coincidence to respond.

"All right, it *was* you two. Thought so. Small world, you know. Well, I best be on me way. 'Appy pedalin'!"

Before we could say anything more than good-bye, Roger was off down the road. He hadn't gone very far though when he slammed on his brakes and yelled back to us. "Say, you haven't seen Debbie lately have you?" he wanted to know.

We shook our heads and he shrugged and pedaled away.

The following day, we spotted Debbie standing with her bike at the edge of a park in Ashburton. No one had to tell us it was her. Debbie, as a great number of hardy, red-blooded American male travelers would comment to us in the weeks ahead, was one of the very best reasons to be a male bicycling through New Zealand in the summer of 1980. She topped the list of sights to behold on South Island. Milford Sound and Mount Cook never stood a chance.

A combination of quite a few factors made Debbie what she was. First and foremost, she was a tall, ageless, voluptuous blond. That fact could have been lost beneath the long, unflattering cycle shorts, heelless cycling shoes, and sloppy sweatshirt that most bicyclers wore, but Debbie did not wear any of these things. She somehow managed to contain her more than ample body in a skintight, short-sleeved knit sweater with a plunging neckline, which revealed an abundance of flesh and bulge, and a pair of ultra-short culottes, which afforded, to any cycler riding behind her, a view that left little to the imagination while providing many a male with a whole lot to remember. The curves in Debbie's long, fully exposed legs were accentuated by the high-heeled shoes she pedaled in.

According to rumors we'd heard, Debbie had yet to hitch up with any of the scores of admirers who were after her. She did, one witness informed us, meet in a pub somewhere on North Island an American fellow toward whom she displayed an obvious and immediate attraction, much to the dismay of the man's girlfriend who was traveling with him. The witness claimed that when Debbie zeroed in on the fellow with her boundless and overpowering sensuality, everyone in the pub tingled at the electricity in the air. When she'd finished with the man, a rough and rugged lumberjack sort, for two days afterward he could do nothing more than heave long, moaning sighs and stare off into the distance with a faraway look in his eyes. Thereafter, the fellow's girlfriend kept an ear out for rumors of Debbie's whereabouts and made sure to steer her boyfriend clear of any further encounters with the woman.

Larry and I pulled into the park in Ashburton to meet Debbie, who turned out to be a fellow Californian. When she found out about our indirect route from California to New Zealand, she was anxious to cycle with us for a few days and hear more about our journey. In the three days we were together we discovered that Debbie was a kind and generous soul and a tough cycler to boot. She talked mostly about the past year spent in Australia painting houses and about her desire to return soon to northern California. After she finished her vacation bicycling around New Zealand, she would fly back to Australia, paint for a few months, then head back to the States. At times she mentioned a boyfriend in Australia, but on that point she divulged little. When we split up, we exchanged addresses, and Debbie invited us to visit her in California to go river rafting together.

The fact that he had spent three days with *the* Debbie and knew where she planned on cycling during the remainder of her tour through New Zealand made Larry a very important person among the male cycling population on South Island. One fellow went so far as to offer him "all the beer you can drink, the last of my granola, and my two spare tires, if you can someway find it in your heart to hand over that woman's address." Debbie was enough to make many a man lose all direction in life.

By the time we had meandered through most of the bottom half of South Island and were cycling north along the west coast toward Westport, we'd pushed our pedals over some twenty-two thousand five hundred miles and through more rainstorms than we could remember since the start of our journey. One might think that by now, after twenty-two months on the road, we would be immune to all the discomforts rainstorms afford the bicycler. But that is an entirely false assumption. Bicycling in an icy rain was the one experience we dreaded more than anything else, even more than pedaling into a head wind. And so, when a projected three-day rainstorm caught us near Westport, and we discovered by the end of the first day of the deluge that our tired rain jackets had lost all their ability to stop the free flow of ice water over our bodies, Larry suggested that we check into a motel and stay there through the rest of the storm. This was the first and only time on our trip that, instead of plowing through the whole downpour and cursing the cold and the wet and the misery of it all, we took refuge in a warm, dry motel room.

While the rain crashed down outside for two days straight, we stayed inside our room. Like all motel rooms in New Zealand, it had a separate kitchen and bedroom. We took full advantage of the fully equipped kitchen and prepared some of the food we'd spent evenings dreaming about while we steamed our vegetables and rice over our tiny camping stove. We cooked up feasts of baked potatoes heaped with sour cream and chives, roast lamb, and chocolate cake. On our first night in the motel, Larry stretched out on the long couch in the living room, listened to the rain patter against the roof, and dropped huge chunks of cake into his mouth. It felt wonderful to be out of the freezing rain, in a heated room with floors and a roof that didn't leak.

"We're gettin' soft, Barb," Larry sighed. "But you know, sometimes it feels awfully nice to be soft."

Before we left South Island, we decided to hike the Abel Tasman trail along Tasman Bay at the north end of the island. The owners of the campground at the start of the trail, at Sandy Bay, offered to store our bikes and gear for us while we hiked, and a fellow from Wellington, who was camping there, loaned us his day pack, in a typical gesture of Kiwi hospitality and trust in one's fellowman—and woman.

"I'll be gone by the time you finish the hike," he explained. "So here's my work address in Wellington. It's right near where you'll get off the ferry from South Island; so you can drop the pack off to me when you come through the city."

The Tasman trail snaked through dense tropical vegetation and along coastal cliffs and deserted sandy coves. We hiked for three days. The two nights, we slept in one of the hikers' huts spaced a day's walk apart along the trail. On the second night, it started to rain just before we reached the hut. We raced inside, and there before us stood Robbie and Janie Guillermo, friends of ours from Santa Barbara. Robbie and Janie had decided on the spur of the moment to visit friends in Wellington and do some backpacking on both islands. The four of us screamed and hugged one another, and Larry and I fired off questions about life and friends back in Santa Barbara. As I listened to Janie talk about beach volleyball, the harbor, Mexican food, and skiing in the Sierras, the old gnawing homesickness began to swell. The way Robbie and Janie looked and acted, the way they talked, and what they talked about was all so familiar. Suddenly, I felt as if I'd been traveling in some alien, faraway land for longer than I could remember. I wanted to go home. I missed my old familiar surroundings, and I'd had enough of traveling.

But the ride from Wellington up to Auckland helped me forget my homesickness. After we crossed back onto North Island, once again there were people at nearly every turn in the road inviting us to stay with them. Allen Robinson, a sheepherder in the mountains north of Wunganui, spotted us resting part way up the long, steep grade on the way to the volcanoes halfway between Wellington and Auckland. He extended one of those irresistible Kiwi invitations.

"Well now, you've got yourselves a good fifteen to twenty miles o' 'ard, steep climbin' up ahead before you reach Raetihi. It's four o'clock right now, and you've got your choice. You can either spend the rest o' daylight grindin' up these mountains in the drizzle, or you can quit for the day and come on up to the 'ouse, and I'll show you a thing or two about my sheep dogs and livin' on a sheep station. Me and my wife Robyn'll fix us all a good 'ome-cooked meal, and you can 'ave yourselves a nice 'ot shower and sleep on a nice firm mattress out o' the cold and wet. It's up to you, though. What do you say?"

Allen was a typically rugged New Zealander with light hair and a ruddy complexion. And like most of his countrymen, he wore shorts even in the cold and the rain. As soon as we moved our gear into the ranch house, he took us around to meet his dogs and demonstrate how they responded to his commands of calls and whistles. In the evening, he and Robyn told us about life on a sheep station and invited us to stay on for as long as we pleased, to see for ourselves.

We would like to have stayed, but there were two other families we'd promised to visit before we left New Zealand on April 4, which was less than two weeks away. We'd met both of them on South Island, where they were vacationing, and they had invited us to stop by at their homes on North Island. The Slatterys, a middle-aged couple, owned a small dairy farm in Turangaomoana, a dot on the map near Matamata, north of Rotorua. The Foxes, a retired couple, lived in Auckland. Lord, I thought to myself as I thanked Robyn and Allen for their invitation, it seemed as if we could spend the rest of our lives in New Zealand visiting with all the folks who invited us into their homes.

Larry and I reached Turangaomoana, one hundred miles south of Auckland, on March 31, just two days before we were to pick up our reservations at the airline office in Auckland. We expected to spend only one day with the Slatterys, then pedal on to Auckland the next, but Ray and June had other plans.

"Look," Ray insisted, "you folks stay 'ere until the second, the day you pick up the tickets, and we'll drive you and your bikes and gear up to Auckland that morning. That'll give June and me more time to show you life in Turangaomoana."

"I give up!" Larry chuckled. "It's damned-near impossible to bicycle around New Zealand! The people here are too friendly! And you know, that's just fine with me."

"All right then," Ray grinned, nudging Larry, "it's settled. Now let's you and me 'ead on down to the local men's club for a drink or two and a game o' pool."

When they returned an hour and a half later, Larry looked a bit tipsy. They had lost the pool game mainly because, after downing three liters of beer, Larry had managed to sink only three balls. That evening, June sat us all down to a dinner of roast mutton complete with fresh mint, creamed cauliflower, sweet potatoes, and peaches and ice cream for dessert.

Ray was up at five-thirty the next morning, milking the cows. Afterward, while June went to a golf meeting in town, he took us to visit a ranch owned by his friend Monty.

"Monty's raisin' a special type o' steer that only you Americans buy," he said with his wide Irish grin. "You mix in this type o' steer meat with your regular beef, and that gives your hamburger meat its red color. No one else in the world cares what color their hamburger is, but in America it's gotta be real red!

"Anyway, Monty's had a bit o' bad luck lately. The price on the steer 'it an all-time 'igh last week, but Monty's broker advised 'im not to sell. 'E told 'im to wait and sell at the auction comin' up, because the price was supposed to go up even 'igher in the next couple o' weeks. Well, it's been doin' nothin' but drop, and now Monty's already lost one hundred dollars per 'ead!"

Monty's ranch spread across the steep green hills and the rolling pastureland just east of Turangaomoana. When we found Monty, he was getting ready to take his dogs up into the hills to round up the hundred and fifty head of steer there and herd them into a lower pasture. Whereas Ray was a short stocky fellow with a curly head of hair and bushy eyebrows, Monty was a tall, lean, and weathered man. He walked with a slight limp and wore a green and blue beret.

Ray stayed with Monty's jeep and inhaled the entire supply of Granny Smiths resting on the dashboard, while Larry and I went into the hills with Monty and the dogs. Responding to Monty's shouts and whistles, his dogs took only a half hour to chase the steers down into the pasture. Then Monty had them weed out a group of younger steers, which they herded down the road to another pasture. We followed behind in the jeep. The few cars that passed the dogs and steers were especially careful to pull way over to the side of the road as they eased by.

"People 'ere are real cautious 'bout drivin' past the dogs," explained Monty. "In this country, if a driver 'its a sheep dog, 'e gets sued. And you know what?" he asked with a twinkle in his eye. "If someone 'its one o' your dogs, you always put down the claim that it was your *best* dog. You get the most money that way."

Once the steers had been taken care of, we drove to the farmhouse. Coleen, Monty's tall vivacious wife, had lunch waiting. While we ate, Ray and Monty cracked jokes. It wasn't long before they started in on their stories about duck season, which was coming up again soon.

"There's a big group o' us men that get together 'ere at Monty's the night before openin' day, and we stay up all night drinkin' beer and playin' poker," began Ray. "And the next morning, when we're all 'ung over, we make a feeble attempt at 'untin' ducks. But 'eck, you know some o' us are so bloody bad off we can 'ardly stumble right! Somehow, though, we all manage to get on out to this place we always go to not far from 'ere, that we've always 'ad to ourselves, and 'ave a go at 'untin'.

"Well you know, last year, just when we got out there—there we were all sittin' together tryin' to get ourselves 'alfway organized and alert—I'll be damned if that new game warden didn't come sneakin' up behind us. Now none o' us ever bothers about a license, you see, and all of a sudden out o' nowhere 'ere's this warden askin' to see licenses. So we all just go along pretendin' like the chap's not there. We keep on talkin' amongst ourselves, and no one answers the warden's questions or says anything to 'im or even looks at 'im.

"Now 'round 'ere, most wardens are pretty easygoin', and straight away they would reckon from seein' the shape we're in that botherin' with us would be a waste o' time. I'm sayin' that *anyone* could tell by a quick glance at us that the duck population in the area wasn't in a whole lot o' trouble. But not this warden. No sir. 'E keeps right on standin' there and askin' to see our licenses, and we keep right on ignorin' 'im. And then 'e starts to get upset. And that's when I reckon 'e needs to be cooled down."

At this point, Ray paused. A mischievous grin slid across his face, and he looked over at Monty, who by now was already laughing.

"So there we all are," broke in Monty with a gleam in his eyes, "and still no one's said a word to the chap. We're not even lookin' at 'im. And then all of a sudden, Ray 'ere reaches into the jeep and picks up one o' those big liter bottles o' Coca Cola. Now the warden's not really lookin' at Ray. 'E's busy chewin' me out, 'cause I'm the closest to 'im. So before 'e can see what's coming, Ray's already jammed the opened bottle of Coke upside down into 'is left boot!"

Here, Ray and Monty fell into hysterics and started slapping each other on the back.

"And you know what 'appened then?" roared Monty. "'Bout the time the bottle emptied itself into 'is boot, that ol' warden comes to 'is senses and departs our company! Simple as that!"

The next morning I helped June prepare a picnic lunch, Ray loaded our bikes and gear into Monty and Coleen's station wagon, and the six of us—Ray and June, Monty and Coleen, and Larry and I—took off for Auckland. We had planned on eating lunch at a rest stop along the way, but it started to rain, so we drove on into the city. We picnicked in an underground parking lot, spreading out our food on the rear door of the station wagon.

"That's us country folks for you," Ray snickered as he dove into the sandwiches and hot coffee. "We can 'ave ourselves a good time anywhere, even in a parking lot!"

It was a fitting end to our stay with the folks in Turangaomoana.

After we picked up our reservations at the airline office and a packet of mail at the American Express office, Stan and Kath Fox welcomed us into their home on Auckland's North Shore.

"Oh you finally made it!" Kath exclaimed as she rushed to meet us at the front door. "We received your card saying you'd be here today. Oh my goodness, ever since we met you down on South Island, we've been so very excited about you coming to visit with us! We're dying to hear all about your trip! We've already fixed a room up for you."

Kath and Stan had come to New Zealand from England in 1952. In England, Stan had raced bicycles, and for a while he'd built frames. He and Kath had ridden their tandem all over Britain. And according to Kath, Stan had always kept a pace that "was so fast I didn't even have time to blow my nose."

They lived alone now in their homey apartment on the North Shore, but their four grown children all had homes around Auckland and visited often. Ten minutes after we arrived, the Foxes had succeeded in making Larry and me feel right at home. The Kiwis were like that. They took the time to take an interest in other people, to invite a stranger into their homes, and to show him or her what friendliness and caring were all about.

That evening, after Stan and Kath had gone to bed, Larry and I sat in the bedroom they'd fixed up especially for us, two strangers they'd spoken with for only fifteen minutes along an isolated road on South Island. We opened our mail packet from home. It was crammed full of Christmas letters from around the world. Some of the letters came from our friends in California, but most were from the people we'd stayed with during our journey—people like Stan and Kath who, for a night, a few days, or weeks, had cared for us and shared their lives with us. These were the people we'd thought about almost every day while we pedaled. We wrote to them as often as possible, and so they'd made the journey along with us. Even more than our desire to experience adventures and see the world, it was the people who had kept us going, giving us a home and a family away from home.

Larry and I sat on the bed and read every card over and over to each other and cried, because we felt so lucky to have met so many kind people. The Bulls had written, and so had Bruno and Maria—in Italian—and Lee and Sheila, and Bonnie Wagner, and the Eltzroths in Michigan, and the folks at Deep Lagoon, and Pat Rigo, a Yorkshire woman. When we stopped at Pat's house to ask for drinking water, she insisted that we spend the night in her home. We slept in her bed, she slept in a bed in her children's room, and her son slept on the floor.

Ned and Cathy Houst had written, too. They found us out on the road after dark in the Catskills near their house, took us in for the night, and fed us a gigantic baked-ham dinner. And there was a card from Mrs.

Smith, a spunky widow in her seventies, who lived in Belmont, Ontario. As we rolled into Belmont, she was standing out on her front lawn talking with a neighbor. When we asked her if there was a campground nearby, she immediately opened her home to us.

The pile of letters seemed endless, and we stayed up most of the night savoring it.

Two days after we arrived at the Foxes, Larry and I were standing at the north shore landing near their home waiting to catch the ferry back across the harbor to Auckland. We were headed to the airport for our midnight flight to Tahiti. In just two weeks we would be stepping onto American soil.

Stan and Kath, their daughter Helen, and granddaughter Amanda had come with us to the wharf to see us off. It was an emotional good-bye. In the two days we'd spent with the Foxes, we had all become close friends. Before the ferry pulled up, everyone hugged and kissed each other and tears rolled down our cheeks. As the ferry pulled away, our four friends stood at the landing and waved and waved, and we waved back until we could no longer see them. A bittersweet sensation overcame me while I watched the four figures grow small and disappear. I felt as if I were leaving home and yet heading home at the same time.

When Larry and I finally stopped waving, a young American tourist walked over to talk with us. He'd arrived in New Zealand only that day and had yet to head out into the countryside to meet the people.

"Waving good-bye to your relatives, huh?" he said. "You all sure looked sad to say good-bye to each other."

I smiled at Larry. "No," I replied, "they're not our relatives, just New Zealanders."

TAHITI

CHAPTER NINETEEN

We were both a bit nervous when we landed in Papeete. During the flight, we'd listened to people talk about Tahiti's sky-high food prices and laws against free camping. Larry and I had enough money to see us through two weeks in the islands only if we camped on the beaches every night. If the police forced us to stay at a resort hotel, we'd go broke in a few days.

But by the end of our first day on the island, we discovered there was nothing to worry about. From the airport, we cycled into Papeete and bought a two-days' supply of food for under ten dollars, then pedaled to the far side of the island near Taravao, where there were no hotels or tourists, and pitched our tent on a secluded and deserted section of beach. No one asked us to leave, and we stayed for a week.

Our camping spot had all the elements of an island paradise. There was the clear, turquoise Pacific. And only a few hundred feet from the beach was a jungle thick with vines, banana, breadfruit, and palm trees, and a huge variety of flowering bushes. In the jungle we found twin water-falls shooting from the top of a black wall of lava edged by bright, sweet-smelling yellow and red flowers. Some days we played under the waterfalls; other days we hiked to the top of the lava, where the water cascaded along five oblong pools. We spent hours bathing in the pools beneath the flowers and breadfruit trees. Occasionally, a few Tahitian children came in-to the jungle to rinse off under the waterfalls, but no one ever climbed up to the pools. They were our own special place.

The day after we set up camp, the five children from the thatched house two hundred yards up the beach from us came swimming into our tiny cove. Larry invited them to have a look inside our tent, and gave each one a handful of the cookies we'd bought in Taravao, five miles down the road. From then on, they came by to visit us at least once a day. Sometimes they swam in. Other times they walked in from the road carrying flowers, which they decorated our tent with, and loaves of coconut bread their mother baked for us every afternoon. The three girls wore bright, printed *pareus* (wraparound skirts) and in their long black hair they pinned bunches of white and yellow flowers. The two boys lived in their swimming trunks.

In the evenings Larry and I sat on our beach and listened to the birds and the ocean. Coconuts thumped to the ground somewhere back in the jungle. As the long green coastline grew dark, our neighbor's fire pit shot spears of light past the coconut trees and over the ocean.

After a week in this heaven we packed up and headed back around the island to Papeete, to catch the boat to Moorea. During one of our daily trips to Taravao for food, an American woman told us about the magnificent coral in Moorea and gave us directions to the house of her American friends on whose coconut plantation we could pitch our tent.

A battered, aging barge carried us to Moorea. We tossed our bikes and ourselves in with the lumber and the crates and sacks of food, and one of the friendly Tahitians on board shared his stash of beer with us the whole way over. At the end of the bumpy, two-hour ride, the barge grumbled into Moorea's awesomely beautiful Cook's Bay.

Donna and Bill lived around one end of the bay, and just as the woman in Taravao had assured us, they were happy to have us stay the week. An hour after we arrived at their plantation, our tent was pitched in the shade of the mango tree near the outdoor shower, and Donna had outfitted us with snorkels, masks, and fins, and sent us off the end of their wooden pier into the most incredible beds of coral we had ever set eyes on. Gigantic mounds of coral in every imaginable hue erupted from the white sandy ocean floor. Through them darted schools of brilliantly colored fish.

Larry and I spent the rest of the afternoon and each of the next seven days swimming through coral, chasing fish, and popping our heads out of the water every few minutes to look at the towering mountains and green jungle valleys behind us. It was easy to see why, after sailing to Tahiti from Los Angeles a few years back on their way to Australia, Donna and Bill had decided to sail no further. They had no intention of ever forsaking their patch of paradise on Moorea.

Besides directing us to all the choice snorkeling spots around Moorea, Donna also supplied us with a handy bit of advice on keeping our food expenses down.

"Up the road about ten miles is the Club Med," she commented, after Larry and I had finished our first afternoon of snorkeling and were lying on the pier watching the sunset. "And every day, from noon to one, they serve up this enormous all-you-can-eat buffet to all the folks at the Club. And you know, I was thinking that if you two went in there you could probably inhale enough food at one sittin' to last you a whole day. But there's this one catch, you see. There's a big wall around the compound, and there's a guard at the only entrance. So you've got to figure out some way to sneak in there.

"Now, I've given it some thought, and this is what I figure you could do. You take your snorkeling gear and pedal out to the Les Tipaniers Hotel, which is just before the Club. OK, now you leave your bikes at Les Tipaniers and swim out to the two tiny islands just off the Club. Then, from the islands, you swim on into the beach at the Club, and everybody'll figure you're just one of them, 'cause they're always swimming back and forth to the islands anyway.

"OK, now that you're in, you just kind of hang around the beach until noon rolls around, and then all you've got to do is follow the crowd on into the buffet. At lunchtime, everybody wears their swimming suits to the restaurant anyway, and no one ever checks to make sure the people in line are all members.

"Now to back up a minute. Once you get into the place, there's one thing you've got to remember, and that's that you'll be all right as long as you don't order a drink at any of the bars. That's because everybody pays for their drinks with these beads that I guess they buy at the main desk or someplace—I really don't know where exactly. But anyway, if you go and order a drink, and you don't have the beads, they'll know you sneaked in and you'll get tossed out. Just stay away from the bars, and you're all set. You got all that?"

"Sure, no sweat," chuckled Larry. "We'll give it a try."

The following morning, Larry and I pedaled out to Les Tipaniers and began our swim to the Club. Larry, who'd been a member of his high school's swim team, was a strong swimmer, while I classified as well below average. I managed well enough until, part way between the islands and the Club, we crossed a deep, turbulent channel separating the shallow waters of the islands and the beach. As soon as I hit the channel, which looked to be some three hundred feet wide, I could feel the current tug me toward the open ocean.

I struggled against it for the first fifty yards or so, but the waves kept forcing water down into my snorkel. Every time I pulled out my mouthpiece and surfaced to gasp for air, a swell slapped me in the face and drove more water into my nose and mouth. At first I could cough up the water and continue swimming, but after a while, my battle against the current took away my wind, and I choked. I quit swimming altogether, then, and fought desperately to keep breathing. But the more I worked to catch my breath, the more I choked. And in the back of my mind, I was lamenting the irony of the whole situation—after all I'd gone through the last two years, here I was, less than six days from the end of our journey, on the verge of drowning!

My arms lashed out at the water. I wrestled to force my head above the waves, but I was losing the battle. I was choking so badly that almost no air at all could enter my lungs. Suddenly I felt my mask and snorkel being ripped off my head. Larry had grabbed me around the shoulders and was lifting my head above the waves. It seemed like an eternity before I finally stopped choking.

"I'll carry your snorkel and mask. Try and swim to the boats," he yelled when he lowered me back into the water.

There was a string of sailboats anchored in the channel, and I took off for the nearest one. Without the snorkel to choke on, I had no problem breathing. I swam from boat to boat, and at each one I held onto the anchor rope and rested for a few minutes before pushing on to the next. When my feet touched sand at last, it felt great to be alive.

We floated into the beach just before noon, and after I'd collapsed on the sand for a half hour, we followed the Club members to the restaurant. We ended up sitting at a table with a Canadian fellow, who confided in us that he too had sneaked in.

"It's easy," he said. "I come here a lot. All you've got to do is walk in along the beach. Too bad you two went to all that trouble of swimming in."

When we left the Club, Larry and I walked along the beach to the end of the Club's property. The Canadian was right; there was no fence separating the Club's beach from the next. We kept right on walking until we reached Les Tipanier. That proved to be our only excursion to the Club Med.

For the rest of our stay in Moorea, we spent our time fishing off Bill's outrigger, snorkeling in the shallow waters, hiking into the mountains, and pedaling to different parts of the island to explore the beaches. In the evenings we sometimes hiked up the narrow valley behind the plantation to visit with Jean, the English artist. She lived in a thatched Tahitian bungalow on a deserted ridge with a magnificent view of Cook's Bay, the mountains, and the Pacific. As soon as we arrived, Jean would mix up a batch of her famous gin and tonics, and the three of us would sit on the wooden porch with our feet dangling over the edge and watch the sun go down, the sky turn crimson, and the shadows creep in. Other evenings, we picnicked on the pier or visited with Donna and Bill. And every night, just after we climbed into our tent, a couple of young Tahitian men would show up with their bottles of cheap, imported wine—commonly referred to in Tahiti as Algerian barrel rot—and call us out to share a few rounds with them before they headed on over to the bar in Pao Pao.

Once, one of the Tahitians came stumbling back from Pao Pao in the middle of the night in an especially plastered condition, and decided to call on Jean. According to Jean, who hurried down to tell us all about it first thing the next morning, the man was just about to step through one of her windows when she blasted him with a shot of mace. By late that afternoon the word was out among the young male Tahitians on Moorea to give the painter lady up the ridge a wide berth.

On April 18, the day before our flight home, Larry and I reluctantly said good-bye to Donna and Bill, Jean, the Tahitians, and Moorea, and caught the barge back to Papeete. We pedaled to a beach four miles south of the Papeete airport in the late afternoon, and there we set up camp for the last time on our journey. It was a perfect camping spot. A wide stream, lined with breadfruit and coconut trees and flowering vines, flowed nearby. We bathed in the fresh water, then cooked our fish on the beach and watched the sun turn the sky and the Pacific a brilliant orange. The silhouette of Moorea's tall, dark cliffs loomed in the distance.

We sat on the beach that night until long after dark and talked about going home. In some ways, we were anxious to return home. We looked forward to seeing our parents and friends and to settling down for a while; to not moving from place to place every day or every week. The prospect of settling into a home that would shelter us from the elements and the bugs, that would provide a real bed, a toilet and shower, and a fully equipped kitchen, all under one roof, sounded awfully nice.

But we were apprehensive, too. For the last two years, constant exercise, adventure, and living in the outdoors had been our way of life. And there was a lot about that life we would miss: falling asleep in our tent to the sound of streams, birds, and the wind dancing through the trees; the scents of flowers or pine sap or crisp clean air, and the elation we experienced each time we pedaled through seemingly endless miles of freezing rain, sweltering heat, walls of mosquitoes, and seas of people to finally reach those places we'd so often dreamed about back home. Then too, the idea of abandoning our Tahitian paradise to fly into Los Angeles, with its ugly face of smog, freeways, asphalt, and cement, kindled even more second thoughts.

But if I harbored mixed feelings about ending our journey, there was one thing that I was soundly sure of, and that was of the future of our relationship. That night I felt closer to Larry than at any other time during the nine and a half years I'd known him. After two solid years of constantly being with one another, of sharing and working together, of weathering the disasters and savoring the triumphs, we were now more a part of each other than I had ever before dreamed possible. Our journey had helped us to come to know each other almost completely, and out of that knowledge had blossomed a special love and respect.

It was nearly midnight on April 18, 1980, when Larry and I crawled into our tent and fell asleep thinking about the things that had happened to us during the last two years and wondering what it was going to feel like to be back home. Twenty hours later, we were pushing our battered, trusty bikes through customs at LAX. We rolled out into the reception area and threw our arms around my parents and a group of our friends. Our journey had ended.

In Remembrance

As this book was going to press, author Barbara Savage died from head injuries suffered in a cycling accident near her home in Santa Barbara, California. Her husband, Larry, along with her family, friends, and colleagues would like this book to stand as a memorial to her high-spirited journey through life.

With the generous cooperation of Larry Savage, The Mountaineers has established **The Barbara Savage/**Miles from Nowhere **Memorial Award.** Presented for the first time in 1990, this prize will be given for an outstanding unpublished nonfiction manuscript that presents a compelling account of a personal journey of discovery undertaken in an outdoor arena. The Award is intended to commemorate Barbara Savage's life and spirit, and to foster both the kind of adventuring and adventure-travel writing that she so enjoyed. An award-winning manuscript will exemplify the comedy of the human condition and the dignity of the human quest — the fact that we are all, like it or not, unwitting adventurers in a strange landscape.

Write for information about entry requirements and competition deadlines to The Barbara Savage/*Miles from Nowhere* Memorial Award, The Mountaineers Books, 1001 S.W. Klickitat Way, Suite 201, Seattle WA 98134.

Other books about bicycling from The Mountaineers include:

BICYCLING THE PACIFIC COAST: A Complete Route Guide, Canada to Mexico, 3rd Ed., by Tom Kirkendall and Vicky Spring

Classic touring guide with information on road conditions, campgrounds, and points of interest. Mileage logs, elevation profiles, maps.

BICYCLE GEARING, by Dick Marr

Complete gearing how-to and shifting strategies for all cyclists.

BICYCLING THE BACKROAD Series:

- Around Puget Sound, 4th Ed., by Erin and Bill Woods
  Trips ranging from 4- to 132-mile tours
- Of Northwest Oregon, 2nd Ed., Philip N. Jones and Jean Henderson
  45 trips from Portland to Eugene
- Of Northwest Washington, 4th Ed., by Erin and Bill Woods
  39 tours in northern King and Kitsap counties to the Canadian border and into British Columbia
- Of Southwest Washington, 3rd Ed., Erin and Bill Woods
  45 tours from Gig Harbor area to Columbia River

ENGLAND BY BIKE: 18 Tours Geared for Discovery, by Les Woodland

Day trips and longer tours to all corners of England, written by a native Briton for American cyclists.

BICYCLING THE ATLANTIC COAST: A Complete Route Guide, Florida to Maine, by Donna Aitkenhead

Only complete touring guide to the East Coast. Covers where to buy provisions, camping, and points of interest, plus daily mileage logs and maps.

CHINA BY BIKE: Taiwan, Hong Kong, China's East Coast, by Roger Grigsby

Nine extended tours through the eastern coastal and northwest regions of China, plus Taiwan and Hong Kong.

EUROPE BY BIKE: 18 Tours Geared for Discovery, 2nd Ed., by Karen and Terry Whitehill

Detailed information for bicycling in 11 countries.

LATIN AMERICA BY BIKE: A Complete Touring Guide,
by Walter Sienko

Only complete cycling manual from Central America to Patagonia. Features best cycling regions, sample tours, and information on terrain, scenery, culture, and history.

BIKING THE GREAT NORTHWEST: 20 Tours in Washington, Oregon, Idaho, and Montana, by Jean Henderson

Presents multi-day tours, many of them loops, for great Pacific Northwest cycling vacations.

NEW ZEALAND BY BIKE, 2nd Ed., by Bruce Ringer

Guide to 14 tours on North and South islands, geared for visiting pedalers.

Write for illustrated catalog of more than 300 outdoor titles.
The Mountaineers
1001 S.W. Klickitat Way, Suite 201, Seattle, WA 98134
or phone 1-800-553-4453

Other books from The Mountaineers include:

ON TOP OF THE WORLD: Five Women Explorers in Tibet, by Luree Miller

Adventures of Nina Mazuchelli, Annie Taylor, Isabella Bird Bishop, Fanny Bullock Workman and Alexandra David-Neel, each an explorer in Tibet in the late 1800s.

WALKING SWITZERLAND: The Swiss Way, 2nd Ed., by Marcia and Philip Lieberman

Routes for hikers staying in Alpine centers or traveling by public transport. Maps, photos.

100 HIKES IN THE ALPS, 2nd Ed., by Vicky Spring and Harvey Edwards

Guide to a wide range of mountain hikes in six countries. Maps, photos.

HIMALAYAN PASSAGE: Seven Months in the High Country of Tibet, Nepal, China, India, and Pakistan, by Jeremy Schmidt and Patrick Morrow

Winner of the Barbara Savage/*Miles from Nowhere* Memorial Award. The story of two young couples' adventure traveling around the Himalaya by bike, truck and foot. "…travel and adventure par excellence." — *Publishers Weekly*

JOURNEY ON THE CREST: Walking 2,600 Miles from Mexico to Canada, by Cindy Ross

A compelling narrative of a young woman's journey on the rugged Pacific Crest Trail.

TWO WHEELS & A TAXI: A Slightly Daft Adventure in the Andes, by Virginia Urrutia

The Andes by bike and taxi with an observant, lighthearted, loving 70-year-old adventuress.

THE GALAPAGOS ISLANDS: The Essential Handbook for Exploring, Enjoying and Understanding Darwin's Enchanted Islands, by Marylee Stephenson

Only complete guide to touring this archipelago off Ecuador.

SOUTH AMERICA'S NATIONAL PARKS: A Visitor's Guide,
by William Leitch

Guide to 32 parks in seven countries. Information includes recreational opportunities, climate, location and access, and trail directions.

WALKING THE ALPINE PARKS OF FRANCE & NORTHWEST ITALY,
by Marcia Lieberman

Complete details on over 100 hikes through the national and regional parks of France and NW Italy.

TREKKING IN RUSSIA & CENTRAL ASIA: A Traveler's Guide,
by Frith Maier

Complete details for 35 treks through these regions. Covers planning, safety, hiring guides, accommodations, history, and culture

COSTA RICA'S NATIONAL PARKS AND PRESERVES: A Visitor's Guide, by Joseph Franke

Complete guide to Costa Rica's 40 national parks and preserves. Includes park attractions, maps, camping information, plus information about wildlife, health and safety, and responsible eco-tourism.

MOMENTS OF DOUBT and Other Mountaineering Writings of David Roberts

Collection of 20 essays and articles on mountaineering and adventure, selected from Roberts' work of two decades. "...most perceptive American writer about mountaineering today." *New York Times*

H. W. TILMAN: The Eight Sailing/Mountain-Exploration Books

Collected in one volume, complete and unabridged, the classic sailing-adventure narratives by the legendary British explorer H.W. Tilman:
Mischief in Patagonia, Mischief Among the Penguins, Mischief in Greenland, Mostly Mischief, Mischief Goes South, In Mischief's Wake, Ice with Everything, Triumph and Tribulation

Write for illustrated catalog of more than 300 titles on the outdoors:
The Mountaineers
1001 S.W. Klickitat Way, Suite 201, Seattle, WA 98134
or phone 1-800-553-4453

THE MOUNTAINEERS, founded in 1906, is a non-profit outdoor activity and conservation club, whose mission is "to explore, study, preserve and enjoy the natural beauty of the outdoors…" Based in Seattle, Washington, the club is now the third largest such organization in the United States, with 15,000 members and five branches throughout Washington State.

The Mountaineers sponsors both classes and year-round outdoor activities in the Pacific Northwest, which include hiking, mountain climbing, ski-touring, snowshoeing, bicycling, camping, kayaking and canoeing, nature study, sailing, and adventure travel. The club's conservation division supports environmental causes through educational activities, sponsoring legislation, and presenting informational programs. All club activities are led by skilled, experienced volunteers, who are dedicated to promoting safe and responsible enjoyment and preservation of the outdoors.

The Mountaineers Books, an active, non-profit publishing program of the club, produces guidebooks, instructional texts, historical works, natural history guides, and works on environmental conservation. All books produced by The Mountaineers are aimed at fulfilling the club's mission.

If you would like to participate in these organized outdoor activities or the club's programs, consider a membership in The Mountaineers. For information and an application, write or call The Mountaineers, Club Headquarters, 300 Third Avenue West, Seattle, Washington 98119; (206) 284-6310.